T0115131

THE INDIVIDUAL PSYCHOLOGY OF
ALFRED ADLER

THE
INDIVIDUAL PSYCHOLOGY
OF ALFRED ADLER

A SYSTEMATIC PRESENTATION IN
SELECTIONS FROM HIS WRITINGS

Edited and annotated by

HEINZ L. ANSBACHER, Ph.D.
Professor of Psychology, University of Vermont

and

ROWENA R. ANSBACHER, Ph.D.

HarperPerennial
A Division of HarperCollinsPublishers

THE INDIVIDUAL PSYCHOLOGY OF ALFRED ADLER

Copyright, © 1956, by Basic Books, Inc.

Printed in the United States of America

This book was originally published in 1956 by
Basic Books, Inc., New York, and is here reprinted
by arrangement.

First HARPER TORCHBOOK edition published 1964

HarperCollins Publishers
195 Broadway
New York, NY 10007

Library of Congress Catalog Number: 55-6679

ISBN: 0-06-131154-5

FRONTISPIECE PHOTO COURTESY OF DR. ALEXANDRA ADLER

HB 03.13.2023

CONTENTS

PART II. ABNORMAL PSYCHOLOGY AND RELATED FIELDS

Chapter 9. The Neurotic Disposition   239

Chapter 10. Neurotic Safeguarding Behavior   263

PREFACE

When we hear such expressions as feelings of inferiority and insecurity, striving for self-enhancement and power, woman's revolt against her feminine role, the oversolicitous mother, the dethronement of the first-born, the need for affection; when maladjustment is spoken of as self-centeredness, psychological health as other-centeredness, psychiatry as the science of interpersonal relations, neurotic symptoms as ego-defenses and forms of aggression, to mention only a few instances—we are meeting ideas in which Alfred Adler was the pioneer from 1907, the date of his first important publication, until his death in 1937.

Yet Adler's name appears relatively infrequently in the literature of psychology and psychiatry today. How is this paradox to be explained? The explanation, in our opinion, is in large part the fact that Adler's writings are unsystematic and therefore make unsatisfactory reading. As the number of those who learned from Adler through personal contact has grown smaller, he has understandably become less well known, and others who expressed the same ideas more lucidly and more recently are referred to instead.

The purpose of the present volume is to make Adler's contributions to the theory and practice of psychology available in a systematic and at the same time authentic form. To this end we made selections from his writings and organized them with the aim of approximating the general presentation of a college textbook. Because every word in the main body of the work is Adler's, the outcome of our efforts, if we have been successful, should be the equivalent of a textbook by Adler on Individual Psychology, the name which he gave to his system.

Three reasons for the compilation of such a book might be given. As indicated at the outset, the ideas of Adler have today come into their own. Thus it would seem important to show them at their source. This was the main reason for our undertaking.

It is our thesis that Adler may be regarded as the original field theorist in a dynamic or depth psychology which has a social-science and "subjectivistic" orientation. Since his contributions represent a comprehensive and relatively simple system once all the parts are gathered together, Adler's Individual Psychology might well introduce the orientation in psychology for which he laid the groundwork. By starting with Adler, the student would obtain a good foundation for better appreciating subsequent developments. To provide this introduction for the student was a second reason for our work.

After an initial close association with Freud, Adler, in the course of his development, not only separated from him, but provided what one might call the antithesis to Freud's theory all along the line. Because of this antithetical parallelism and because Adler was the adversary whom Freud heeded most, a better knowledge of Adler will at the same time afford a better understanding of Freud, regardless of one's position toward his theories. To afford this better understanding was then a third reason for the present work.

In making the selections we were guided by the following criteria: (1) Adler's mature theory of the normal and abnormal personality should be presented completely. (2) All his diagnostic and therapeutic methods should be included. (3) All the fields into which his interest and influence extended should be presented. (4) The points in Adler which are of particular current pertinence should be brought out. (5) The concepts that Adler is known for—or misunderstood for—should be clarified. (6) Adler's development should be traced in order to explain certain apparent inconsistencies between earlier and later writings. (7) The full range of his historical controversy with Freud should be shown. (8) Little case material need be included, since such material can be found in many of Adler's publications; this would keep the present work to a convenient size.

The selections are preceded by an introduction by the editors in which we show that Adler is the original proponent of a depth psychology which is "subjectivistic," in contrast to Freud who founded depth psychology from an "objective" position. This is followed by a discussion of the similarities of various other "subjectivistic" points of view to Individual Psychology.

A running commentary accompanying the selections seeks to give explanations, emphasis, and integration to the material. It is also a continuation of the introduction to the extent that it points out contrasts to

Freud and similarities with other systems. These comments by the editors are distinguished from the selections by italics.

Nearly half of the selections were translated by the editors. Much of this material has not appeared in English heretofore, while for the rest the existing translations were considered inadequate. When existing translations were used, occasional changes were made where checking with the original indicated this to be necessary, or where the English version could be improved.

As the editors consider lack of systematization the great shortcoming of the extant writings of Adler, they consider it their most important contribution to have provided the organization of the material, including nearly all the headings and side headings. To accomplish such an organization, sequences by Adler could be left intact only in certain instances, whereas in others even what is found under a single side heading had to be brought together from material widely scattered throughout Adler's writings.

In Part I of the selections, "Personality Theory and its Development," the first two chapters deal with Adler's writings between 1907 and 1911. They are essentially historical and include a detailed account of his fundamental differences from Freud, which led to the separation from Freud. Chapter 3 deals with Adler's philosophical background and his own finalism or purposivism; it could be dated 1911–1912.

Chapters 4 to 8 present Adler's theory of personality proper. Here the historical approach has been abandoned. Instead, it was often found best to start with Adler's latest writings which present his theory most comprehensively, and to fit the earlier writings into the framework provided by the later views. Chapters 4, 5, and 6 are concerned with the general, nomothetic aspects of the theory organized around the concepts of striving for superiority, social interest, and degree of activity. Chapters 7 and 8 deal with the individual, idiographic aspects under the headings of "Style of Life" and "Psychology of Use," Adler's term for his complete functionalism. For the reader whose first interest is the actual theory of Individual Psychology it is entirely feasible to begin with Chapter 4.

In Part II, "Abnormal Psychology and Related Fields," Adler's theory of the neuroses is covered in Chapters 9 to 12. Methods of treatment and diagnosis, including dream theory, are presented in Chapters 13 and 14. The next two chapters are concerned with psychological problems of childhood, Chapter 15 with the social factors of early childhood, especially as these may influence the development toward a neurotic disposition, and Chapter 16 with the behavior disorders of childhood and their treatment in the clinic and in the classroom. The remaining Chapters 17 to 19 deal with crime and related disorders, problems of everyday living, and problems of social psychology, specifically including social prejudice, war, and religion.

Autobiographical and biographical material on Adler is found in the last part of Chapter 7 and incidentally throughout the book.

In addition to the selections from Adler and the comments by the editors the book contains three readings by other authors. The first, in Chapter 2, is from a paper by Kenneth M. Colby presenting an account of the discussion which followed Adler's critique of Freud before the Psychoanalytic Society of Vienna in 1911. The second, in Chapter 3, consists of excerpts from The Philosophy of 'As If' by Hans Vaihinger which exerted a far-reaching influence on Adler, as becomes evident throughout this volume. The third, in Chapter 5, is from the monograph on "Psychoanalysis and Ethics" by Carl Furtmüller, Adler's foremost early coworker; this paper seems to have played an important part in Adler's formulation of the concept of social interest.

This book could not have been conceived nor completed if we had not had extensive personal contact with Adler. From his public lectures, many informal seminars, and private conversations we had become well enough acquainted with Adler's ideas to continue the search of his writings until we found what we knew ought to be there somewhere. We must add, however, that in this search we also found a considerable amount of material, especially among the earlier writings, which was altogether new to us.

In a sense this book originated when the first editor was introduced to psychology through popular lectures which Adler gave under the auspices of Columbia University in 1930. From that time on he was challenged by Adler's system and the problem of its place in and relationship to the larger body of psychology. As he took up the formal study of psychology, Individual Psychology furnished him a serviceable point of departure for approaching and evaluating results and theories in many areas of psychology. The second editor, while working for her doctorate at the University of Vienna in 1928, attended for a year the informal lectures which Adler gave daily in his home at Dominikanerbastei 10, as well as the weekly meetings of the Individual Psychology Society of Vienna. Close contact by both editors with Adler continued throughout the rest of his life.

Despite our positive attitude toward Individual Psychology we are not unaware of certain limitations. A deliberate critical examination and evaluation is, however, beyond the scope of this book, which is the presentation and clarification of the work of Adler.

HEINZ L. ANSBACHER
ROWENA R. ANSBACHER

Burlington, Vermont
October, 1955

ACKNOWLEDGMENTS

We are glad to express our thanks for the help we have received in the preparation of this book. Professor A. H. Maslow gave the first and most sustained stimulation by concurring with us in the need for a comprehensive book on the psychology of Alfred Adler, by urging us to embark upon such an enterprise, and by supporting us throughout the years with his continued interest. Professor Paul F. Lazarsfeld suggested that a book of readings would best fill this existing need, and through his suggestion our plan began to take its final shape. Professors Gordon W. Allport and Gardner Murphy read our preliminary introduction and advanced our work through their understanding and their criticism. Professors David Krech and Richard S. Crutchfield helped us indirectly through their book, *Theory and Problems of Social Psychology*. This work, based on the related points of view of Wolfgang Köhler, Kurt Lewin, and Edward Chace Tolman, has helped us to see many points of Individual Psychology in a broader perspective. Certain preliminary work was aided through a summer research grant to the first editor by the University of Vermont. In the preparation of the manuscript with all its tribulations, the unfailing care and efficiency of Mrs. Madeline W. Chaplin was a great consolation.

Great support and encouragement came to us from those who are actively carrying on the Adlerian tradition. Dr. Alexandra Adler, daughter of Alfred Adler and herself a psychiatrist, has given continuous assurances of her confidence in us to present and interpret her father's work and has made available to us certain of his inaccessible yet important publications. Dr. Kurt A. Adler, the son of Alfred Adler, and also a psychiatrist, undertook the task of giving the manuscript a careful and critical reading. He gave us invaluable suggestions which could only have been made by someone in his position of long and most intimate association with the development of Individual Psychology. Through the offices of

Mrs. Danica Deutsch, the Individual Psychology Association of New York provided stimulation and a sounding board for our study of Adler by inviting the first editor to give a number of lectures before the Association. Dr. Rudolf Dreikurs, editor of the *American Journal of Individual Psychology*, furthered the course of the book by requesting several articles.

We wish to express our appreciation to the Estate of Alfred Adler for their permission to reprint his writings and to thank the following publishers and periodicals for permission to use excerpts from his writings:

Clark University Press, Worcester, Mass., publisher of *Psychologies of 1930*, 1930.

Faber & Faber, Ltd., London, publisher of *Social Interest*, 1933.

Greenberg: Publisher, New York, publisher of *The Science of Living*, 1929, and *The Education of Children*, 1930.

Kegan Paul, Trench, Truebner and Co., London, publisher of *Problems of Neurosis*, 1929.

Little, Brown & Co., Boston, publisher of *What Life Should Mean to You*, 1931.

Rinehart & Company, Inc., New York, publisher of *Pattern of Life*, 1930.

The American Journal of Sociology, University of Chicago Press, Chicago.

The British Journal of Medical Psychology, London, England.

International Journal of Individual Psychology, International Publications, Inc., Chicago.

Individual Psychology Bulletin.

Individual Psychology Pamphlets, The C. W. Daniel Company, Ltd., Ashingdon, England.

The Journal of Abnormal and Social Psychology.

Furthermore we also take pleasure in acknowledging permissions received from the following publishers and periodicals to quote excerpts from the work of their authors:

Adler, Alexandra. *Guiding Human Misfits; a Practical Application of Individual Psychology*. New York: Philosophical Library, Inc., 1948.

Asch, Solomon. *Social Psychology*. New York: Prentice-Hall, Inc., 1952.

Birnbaum, Ferdinand. Applying Individual Psychology in school. *Int. J. Indiv. Psychol.*, 1, No. 3, 109–119, 1935.

———. The Individual-psychological experimental school in Vienna. *Int. J. Indiv. Psychol.*, 1, No. 2, 118–124, 1935.

Bottome, Phyllis. *Alfred Adler; a Biography.* New York: G. P. Putnam's Sons, 1939.

Colby, Kenneth Mark. On the disagreement between Freud and Adler. *Amer. Imago.*, 8, 229–238, 1951.

Colm, Hanna. Healing as participation; comments on Paul Tillich's existential philosophy. *Psychiatry*, 16, 99–111, 1953.

Dreikurs, Rudolf. The socio-psychological dynamics of physical disability; a review of the Adlerian concept. *J. Social Issues*, 4, No. 4, 39–54, 1948.

Freud, Sigmund. *The Basic Writings of Sigmund Freud.* New York: Modern Library, Inc., 1938. As originally published in *Three Contributions to the Theory of Sex* (Mon. #7). New York: Nervous and Mental Disease Monographs.

———. *Beyond the Pleasure Principle.* New York: Liveright Publishing Corp., 1950.

———. *Civilization and Its Discontents.* London: The Hogarth Press, Ltd., 1946.

———. *Collected Papers*, Volumes I–V. London: The Hogarth Press, Ltd., 1924–1950.

———. *The Ego and the Id.* London: The Hogarth Press, Ltd., 1949.

———. *Group Psychology and the Analysis of the Ego.* New York: Liveright Publishing Corp., 1949.

———. *New Introductory Lectures on Psychoanalysis.* New York: W. W. Norton & Company, Inc., 1933.

———. *An Outline of Psychoanalysis.* New York: W. W. Norton & Company, Inc., 1949.

Goldstein, Kurt. *The Organism; a Holistic Approach to Biology Derived from Pathological Data in Man.* New York: American Book Company, 1939.

Helson, Harry, Ed. *Theoretical Foundations of Psychology.* New York: D. Van Nostrand Company, Inc., 1951.

Hitschmann, Edward. The history of the aggression-impulse. *Yearbook of Psychoanalysis.* New York: International Universities Press, Inc., Vol. IV., 1948.

Holub, Martha. Conversations with parents and children. *Int. J. Indiv. Psychol.*, 1, No. 2, 96–112, 1935.

James, William. *Pragmatism: A New Name for Some Old Ways of Thinking.* New York: Longmans, Green & Co., 1907.

Jaspers, Karl. *Allgemeine Psychopathologie*, 4th ed. Berlin and Heidelberg: Springer Verlag, 1946.

Lewin, Kurt. *A Dynamic Theory of Personality: Selected Papers*. New York: McGraw-Hill Book Company, Inc., 1935.

————. Time perspective and morale. In G. Watson, Ed. *Civilian Morale*. Boston: Houghton Mifflin Company, 1942.

Murphy, Gardner. *An Introduction to Psychology*. New York: Harper & Brothers, 1951.

————. *Personality: A Biosocial Approach to Origins and Structure*. New York: Harper & Brothers, 1947.

Rayner, Doris. Individual Psychology and the children's clinic. *Indiv. Psychol. Pamphlets*, No. 7, 20–28, 1933.

Simpson, George Gaylord. *The Meaning of Evolution*. New Haven: Yale University Press, 1949.

Symonds, Percival M. *The Ego and the Self*. New York: Appleton-Century-Crofts, Inc., 1951.

Vaihinger, Hans. *The Philosophy of 'As If': A System of the Theoretical, Practical and Religious Fictions of Mankind* (Translated by C. K. Ogden.) London: Routledge and Kegan Paul Ltd., 1924.

Wertheimer, Max. Gestalt theory. *Social Research*, 11, 78–99, 1944.

————. *Productive Thinking*. New York: Harper & Brothers, 1945.

BIBLIOGRAPHICAL NOTE

At the end of the book the reader will find two separate bibliographies, one of the works of Adler and one of a general bibliography. In the Adler bibliography the items are identified by the date of their first publication and a letter in the cases of more than one publication per year. In the general bibliography the items are identified by a number.

The source for each paragraph selected from Adler's writings is given by the following method. Each side heading is followed by a superior figure which refers to a footnote at the end of the chapter. In the footnote each paragraph under the respective side heading is represented by a bold face number. This number is followed by the title of the publication from which the paragraph has been taken, the identification of this item in the Adler bibliography (in parentheses), and page from which the selection has been taken. For the following German references, no specific pages are given: 1927c, 1929f, 1930e, 1931b, 1931c, 1932a, 1933e, 1933f, 1935b, 1936b, and 1937b.

Do not forget the most important fact that not heredity and not environment are determining factors.—Both are giving only the frame and the influences which are answered by the individual in regard to his styled creative power.—

Adler

Do not forget the most important fact that not heredity and not environment are determining factors.—Both are giving only the frame and the influences which are answered by the individual in regard to his styled creative power.—

ADLER

INDIVIDUAL PSYCHOLOGY IN ITS LARGER SETTING

By Heinz L. Ansbacher and Rowena R. Ansbacher

A. Basic Propositions of Individual Psychology

A summary of the theory of Individual Psychology might well be helpful to the reader as an initial orientation to the work of Alfred Adler. To serve this purpose we submit the following set of propositions which have suggested themselves to us.

1. There is one basic dynamic force behind all human activity, a striving from a felt minus situation towards a plus situation, from a feeling of inferiority towards superiority, perfection, totality.

2. The striving receives its specific direction from an individually unique goal or self-ideal, which though influenced by biological and environmental factors is ultimately the creation of the individual. Because it is an ideal, the goal is a fiction.

3. The goal is only "dimly envisaged" by the individual, which means that it is largely unknown to him and not understood by him. This is Adler's definition of the unconscious: the unknown part of the goal.

4. The goal becomes the final cause, the ultimate independent variable. To the extent that the goal provides the key for understanding the individual, it is a working hypothesis on the part of the psychologist.

5. All psychological processes form a self-consistent organization from the point of view of the goal, like a drama which is constructed from the beginning with the finale in view (1912a, p. 46). This self-consistent personality structure is what Adler calls the *style of life*. It becomes firmly established at an early age, from which time on behavior that is

apparently contradictory is only the adaptation of different means to the same end.

6. All apparent psychological categories, such as different drives or the contrast between conscious and unconscious, are only aspects of a unified relational system (1926b, p. 402) and do not represent discrete entities and quantities.

7. All objective determiners, such as biological factors and past history, become relative to the goal idea; they do not function as direct causes but provide probabilities only. The individual uses all objective factors in accordance with his style of life. "Their significance and effectiveness is developed only in the intermediary psychological metabolism, so to speak" (1926b, p. 402).

8. The individual's opinion of himself and the world, his "apperceptive schema," his interpretations, all as aspects of the style of life, influence every psychological process. *Omnia ex opinione suspensa sunt* was the motto for the book in which Adler presented Individual Psychology for the first time (1912a, p. 1).

9. The individual cannot be considered apart from his social situation. "Individual Psychology regards and examines the individual as socially embedded. We refuse to recognize and examine an isolated human being" (1926a, p. ix).

10. All important life problems, including certain drive satisfactions, become social problems. All values become social values.

11. The socialization of the individual is not achieved at the cost of repression, but is afforded through an innate human ability, which, however, needs to be developed. It is this ability which Adler calls *social feeling* or *social interest*. Because the individual is embedded in a social situation, social interest becomes crucial for his adjustment.

12. Maladjustment is characterized by increased inferiority feelings, underdeveloped social interest, and an exaggerated uncooperative goal of personal superiority. Accordingly, problems are solved in a self-centered "private sense" rather than a task-centered "common sense" fashion. In the neurotic this leads to the experience of failure because he still accepts the social validity of his actions as his ultimate criterion. The psychotic, on the other hand, while objectively also a failure, that is, in the eyes of common sense, does not experience failure because he does not accept the ultimate criterion of social validity.

The remainder of this introduction will present Individual Psychology in its larger context.

B. Individual Psychology as Subjective Psychology

1. FREUD AND ADLER

Adler's psychology was often called a "depth" psychology, that is, a psychology which discovers deeply buried unconscious phenomena. For Adler, however, the unconscious was, as stated above, merely that part of an individual's life style which he does not understand, and understanding is afforded by viewing all processes in their larger context. Therefore, one would better speak of Adler's psychology as "context" psychology.

Depth psychology was of course founded to all intents and purposes by Sigmund Freud, who named his theory and method *psychoanalysis*. Freud and Adler and Carl G. Jung have often been mentioned as the first triumvirate of this new field. Both Adler and Jung were at first associated with Freud but later separated from him, Adler in 1911 and Jung in 1913. Jung's form of depth psychology, known as *analytic psychology* or *complex psychology*, will not concern us because Adler gives no indication of having been stimulated by Jung. The influence of Freud, however, is reflected throughout Adler's work, which to a large extent developed as an antithesis to that of Freud.

When Adler was invited by Freud in 1902 to join the psychoanalytic circle, he was a young practicing physician, fourteen years younger than Freud (15, p. 57). Soon he became a prominent member of the group. He was highly esteemed by Freud, was eventually named his successor as president of the Vienna Psychoanalytical Society, and became coeditor of an early psychoanalytic journal, the *Zentralblatt für Psychoanalyse*. At the same time theoretical differences developed. These gradually increased to the point where both Adler and Freud regarded them as irreconcilable, and Adler resigned from his positions in the psychoanalytic movement (24; 1911d). The small group which left the Freudian circle with Adler established itself at first as the Society for Free Psychoanalytic Research. But by the next year Adler's ideas had crystallized sufficiently for him to decide on the new name of Individual Psychology. The new society became known by this name, and in 1914 Adler founded his own journal, the *Zeitschrift für Individualpsychologie*.

At the time of the separation it appeared to some that the similarities between Freud and Adler were greater than their differences (24); the two used similar methods, described and interpreted much the same phenomena, and often did so in parallel terms. Since then many have believed that the difference was primarily one of terminology, aggravated by personal antagonisms. Others, while appreciating the difference between Freud's *libido* as the basic drive and Adler's *striving for superiority*, thought nevertheless that the two theories were otherwise essentially similar, so that the difference was "merely a change of content, comparable to Heraclitus's substitution of fire for Thales's water as the basic element" (21, p. 60). But actually the difference in theory is about as fundamental and far-reaching as is possible within a given area. The change of this one "element" is in fact symptomatic of a change in the whole theory and all its parts.

2. OBJECTIVE VERSUS SUBJECTIVE PSYCHOLOGY

A difference such as that between Adler and Freud is to be found not in depth psychology alone. On the contrary, it exists to some extent in psychology as a whole and in every separate aspect of psychology. In the psychology of learning we have those who stress association, reinforcement, and conditioning, and those who stress reorganization and insight. In the field of testing there are those who stress objective tests and statistics, and those who rely primarily on the psychologist's judgment. In motivation there are those who wish to reduce all motives to basic drives, and those who speak of the functional autonomy of motives. Some formulations of these differences are listed in the following table of opposites.

Objective (objectifying) psychology	Subjective (subjectifying) psychology
Minimizing consciousness	Full appreciation of consciousness
Psychology without a soul	Psychology with a soul
The depleted self	The self as central
Peripheralism	Centralism
Emphasis on finding general laws: nomothetic laws	Emphasis on laws applying to the individual case: idiographic laws
Atomism	Holism
Molecular units of analysis	Molar units of analysis
Analysis into elements	Phenomenological description
Classification into definite categories	Field theory

Static structuralism	Functional relativism
Emphasis on learning	Emphasis on perception
Learning by association and conditioning	Learning by reorganization and insight
Behaviorism	Gestalt psychology
Stimulus-response psychology	Psychology emphasizing the variables intervening between stimulus and response.
Mechanistic conception	Organismic conception
Motivation by pushes	Motivation by pulls
Explanation through objective causes; reductionism	Understanding through empathy
Genetic, historical approach	Ahistorical approach
Determinism	Immanent teleology
"Hard" determinism from external pressures alone	"Soft" determinism from the inner nature of life
Psychology as a natural science	Psychology as a mental science (Geisteswissenschaft) or social science

The left and right sides of this list (which makes no claim to being complete) have been arranged so that a common factor for each side becomes apparent. To designate these factors, we have chosen the pair objective—subjective provided by Karl Jaspers and defined by him as follows. "Objective corresponds to the psyche as seen from without, by the observer, and subjective corresponds to the psyche seen from within, by the subject himself" (59, p. 250). While we are quite aware of the inadequacy of these terms to denote the entire syndrome of concepts in each column, we decided on them nevertheless because no other set of terms would be completely satisfactory, and these have at least the advantage of being simple to use.

3. TOUGH-MINDED VERSUS TENDER-MINDED TEMPERAMENTS

The above list bears an obvious likeness to William James's memorable distinction between the tough-minded and the tender-minded temperaments. The objective psychologist is apt to be tough-minded, the subjective psychologist tender-minded, and hence we can extend our list by adding James's description of his antithesis.

The Tough-Minded	*The Tender-Minded*
Empiricist (going by fact)	Rationalist (going by principles)
Sensationalistic	Intellectualistic
Materialistic	Idealistic
Pessimistic	Optimistic
Pluralistic (starting from parts, making of the whole a collection)	Monistic (starting from wholes, making much of the unity of things)
Irreligious	Religious
Hardheaded	Feeling
Fatalist	Free-willist
Sceptical	Dogmatical

James finds that the tough and the tender "have a low opinion of each other. . . . The tough think of the tender as sentimentalists and soft-heads. The tender feel the tough to be unrefined, callous, or brutal. . . . Their antagonism, whenever as individuals their temperaments have been intense, has formed in all ages a part of the philosophic atmosphere of the time. It forms a part of the philosophic atmosphere of today" (58, pp. 12–13). In our day in philosophy the tough are represented by logical empiricism or logical positivism and the tender by existentialism.

We only need to add that in psychology as well as in philosophy this antagonism forms a part of the atmosphere today as it always has in the past, despite the fact that "most of us have a hankering for the good things on both sides of the line" (58, p. 13). While in psychology today we are striving after unity and away from opposing schools, still the difference exists, and for clarification of thinking, especially for describing Adler's position, we consider it worthwhile to point it out rather than to minimize it.

4. FREUD—OBJECTIVE PSYCHOLOGIST

When the field of depth psychology became established through the work of Freud, with free association and dream interpretation, it obviously belonged in the general area of subjective psychology. But—and this is the point of the entire present discussion—within the field of depth psychology itself, as within any other field of psychology, the divergence between the objective, tough-minded, and the subjective, tender-minded, is still possible. Freud wanted to be a natural scientist, sought causal explanations, employed the genetic approach, minimized consciousness by assigning prime importance to the unconscious, left the self depleted by making the ego the mere battleground for the superego and the id, and thus by intent was an objective psychologist, although he worked in an area which by its nature belonged on the subjective side. Furthermore, by temperament he could be called tough-minded; he was pessimistic, irreligious, fatalistic, and hardheaded, in James's terms.

Freud belongs on the objective side not only because of his stress on biological causation but also by the criterion that he was a class theorist rather than a field theorist. This was shown best by John F. Brown (18), a student of Kurt Lewin who, using ten criteria for field versus class theory, found that Freud met only two of these. On the positive side Brown states that Freud lacked dichotomies. But here the present writers would add that, although Freud did away with the class concepts of normal versus abnormal, he retained others and introduced many of his own, such as conscious versus unconscious and life instinct versus death instinct. Lewin, the founder of modern field theory, in a later paper (69) confirmed Brown in essence and pointed out certain further differences between himself and Freud.

The position of Freud as an objective psychologist was well summarized by Donald W. MacKinnon and A. H. Maslow in the following: "Freud rested squarely on 19th century scientific theory in his reductionism, his tendency to analyze, to dissect, to dichotomize ('Aristotelianism'). Presented with a problem, Freud spontaneously and automatically split the field into two or three discrete parts, mutually exclusive, not at all alike in any way, and usually in antagonistic relation to each other, for example, the conscious vs. the unconscious, ego vs. id vs. superego, instinct vs. society, death instinct vs. life instinct. The individual's interests are for Freud intrinsically opposed to the interests of any and all other individuals. Even within the id, each impulse goes its own way, seeking only its own satisfaction, at whatever cost to other id-impulses or the whole individual" (74, pp. 642–643).

If the field theorist finds fault with Freudian theorizing, then, according to our list, the associationist should find it congenial. And indeed Clark L. Hull observed that there were "numerous equivalent concepts and behavior principles existent in the two disciplines but now hidden under differences in terminology" (55). The id appears to Hull to be the basic physiological source of drives; and the superego is a mass of habits set up at an early age through punishment or threats, habits that are not verbalized. Ten years later, John Dollard and Neal E. Miller (26) continuing the tradition of Hull presented an analysis of personality and psychotherapy in terms of learning, thinking, and culture, where they found it feasible to integrate the ideas of Freud with those of Pavlov, Thorndike, Hull, Sumner, Murdock, and Warner.

Freud has been classified with objective psychology by various observers and on various accounts. According to David Krech and Richard S. Crutchfield (63), psychoanalysis shares with behaviorism and stimulus-response psychology the genetic or historical approach to the problem of motivation. Edwin G. Boring (13) points out the similarity between Freud and Watson's behaviorism in that both minimize the importance of consciousness. Percival Symonds notes: "The ego as used in psychoanalytical literature is the objective self as it might be observed by a behaviorist. . . . Freud . . . seems quite the behaviorist as contrasted with those who profess the phenomenological point of view. . . . The *self*, on the other hand, is the subjective self as it is perceived, conceived, valued, and responded to by the individual" (107, p. vi). Leonard S. Kogan and Joe McV. Hunt (61) find that psychoanalysis is on the side of objective learning theory and frustration theory in regarding behavior as the cause and the self-concept as the effect, in contrast with phenomenological and field theory where the situation is, of course, reversed, with the self-concept the cause and behavior the effect. Francis W. Irwin likens Freud to behaviorism on the basis of his determinism. "Since Freud insisted upon a deterministic psychology, and since his stress upon the inadequacy of an individual's understanding of his own motivation amounted to a devaluation of introspective explanations of behavior, psychoanalysis is more sympathetically related to the general position of the deterministic behaviorists than might at first be expected" (56, p. 208).

5. ADLER—SUBJECTIVE PSYCHOLOGIST

Theories and systems apparently evolve, as does life in general, by following the opportunities that are presented (95, p. 51). In the perspective of the history of ideas, one might say that since Freud took up the objective position in the depth psychology he had originated, the subjective position which was thereby created was vacant. It was Adler who took up this position. Plainly it coincided with his tender-minded temperament.

Freud advanced scientific thought by showing that nervous disorders, like all psychological manifestations, including dreams and slips of the tongue, were determined by unconscious motives which can be ascertained by free association. Up to this point his psychology is "subjective," as was stated earlier. But at this point a splitting of the ways into the objective or the subjective direction becomes possible, in answer to the question, What determines the unconscious? According to Freud the unconscious is ultimately determined by physiological drives and the past of the individual or the race, in any event by something that is or was objective.

The prime example of this is the fact that he took sex quite literally, not figuratively, not as a metaphor or schema for understanding. When Adler replaced the sex drive with the masculine protest—that is, with the desire to be above, to be like a real man—and thus replaced biological, external, objective causal explanation with psychological, internal, subjective causal explanation, it was this departure which strained his relationship with Freud critically, ultimately leading to the break in 1911. The fact that Freud could never forgive Adler for the conception of the masculine protest testifies that Freud maintained to the end his intention to be the natural-science, objective psychologist.

According to Adler the unconscious as well as the conscious is determined by subjective values and interests, all of a social orientation, all without counterpart in physical reality, and in the last analysis a creation of the individual. Adler's determiners are not reducible to physiology, but rather dominate and direct the drive component of human nature. It is in this sense, then, that we see Freud as the objective natural scientist and Adler as the subjective social scientist. If we classify Adler as a subjective psychologist, this does not mean that he overlooked objective factors. Actually he took them very much into account, but limited them to the role of providing probabilities, of "soft" determiners, while the ultimate determination comes from the inner nature of the self.

In order to clarify Adler's position further we shall in the following section show his relationships to various psychological trends which are on the subjective, tender-minded side of the ledger. These trends are today achieving increased significance in American psychology and psychology elsewhere in the world as well, and mark the passing of the climax of behaviorism in its original form and of objective psychology at any price.

c. Individual Psychology and Other Subjective Psychologies

1. PERSONALISTIC PSYCHOLOGY

The psychological system with which Adler was most in sympathy, according to his biographer (15, p. 59), was that of William Stern. Stern defined his personalistic psychology as "the science of the person having experience. . . . The immediate subject-matter of psychology, experience, is therefore to be identified and interpreted in terms of its matrix, the unitary, goal-directed person" (102, p. vii).

Adler acknowledged his relationship when he said: "William Stern, in a different way, has arrived at results similar to mine" (1914f, p. 1). He made this acknowledgment in connection with the following early definition of Individual Psychology. "It attempts to gain from the separate life manifestations and forms of expression the picture of the self-consistent personality as a variant by presupposing the unity and self-consistency [both *Einheit*] of the individuality. The separate traits are then compared with one another, are reduced to their common denominator, and are combined in an individualizing manner into a total portrait" (1914f, p. 1). Adler felt indebted to Stern "primarily for his great contribution of a philosophical foundation for finalism," that is, the interpretation of life processes in terms of their goals (1931b, p. 1).

The emphasis in the above definition of Individual Psychology lies on the "individualizing manner," which led Adler later to the concept of the style of life. By this token Adler's psychology was from the start an idiographic science. According to the classification of Wilhelm Windelband (117) the term idiographic pertains to laws which are particular to the individual case, while nomothetic formulations are laws of general validity. To be sure, Adler's psychology, like any science, developed nomothetic principles as well—compensation, the striving for superiority, social interest; but the emphasis always rested on the idiographic aspect—the style of life, the opinion of the self, the individual goal. In fact the very first paper in Adler's journal, one by Alexander Neuer, proclaimed Individual Psychology "the idiographic science *par excellence*" (86). By contrast, most Freudian concepts are nomothetic (4, p. 561)—Oedipus complex, sex drive, death wish, penis envy, and the like.

Among present-day psychologists Gordon W. Allport is particularly closely related to Stern, and although Allport hesitates to be labeled a personalistic psychologist (3, p. 183) he called his work on personality "a contribution to the same line of thought" (4, p. 19). Accordingly we are not surprised to find considerable similarity between Allport and Adler (8; 73).

Gardner Murphy is a second contemporary psychologist whose viewpoint, according to his own statement, "shows obvious affinities to those of William Stern and Gordon W. Allport, and could be called by Stern's term 'personalistic'" (83, p. xvi). Consistent with his closeness to Stern, Murphy has expressed strong appreciation for Adler. "The mass of data relative to the problems of the ego that has come to us from Adler and his school is tremendously rich; we shall remain forever indebted for the ruthlessness and simplicity with which such problems were described in an era when Adler was generally ridiculed by the analysts and ignored by 'hard-headed' medical men. Adler did as much as any individual to make clear that ego problems are as central as sex or any other problems —indeed, that for most civilized men they are the most burning problems of all" (84, p. 593).

2. GESTALT PSYCHOLOGY

The obvious similarity between Individual Psychology and Gestalt psychology lies in the emphasis on the whole rather than on elements, and on the interaction between the whole and its parts. As Adler once said: "The same tones tell a different tale in Richard Wagner and in Liszt" (1926b, p. 403). It was just such demonstrations that Max Wertheimer, one of the founders of the Gestalt school, enjoyed conducting in his classes. Both Adler and Wertheimer were very musical.

Their general similarity in viewpoint led to further specific similarities, including in particular the realization of the importance of man's social context. Wertheimer stated in 1925: "Man is not only part of a field, but a part and member of his group. When people are together . . . then the most unnatural behavior . . . would be to behave as separate Egos. If for any outward or inner reasons a harmonious balance is not attainable between a person and the people with whom he lives, then definite disturbances of the equilibrium must appear. . . . A wide range of mental disease . . . might be the consequence of such fundamental processes" (115, pp. 91–92).

A recent development in Gestalt psychology is the use of the term *social interest* itself, some thirty years after Adler had introduced it. Under the heading of social interest Solomon E. Asch describes the striving for society as a primary, natural tendency, and makes a sharp distinction between this and the conception of socialization by Freud and others (10).

3. FIELD THEORY

A special aspect of Gestalt psychology is the field theory of Lewin. The parallels between Lewin and Adler are particularly marked. Lewin is said to have once characterized the position of Gestalt psychology "as having confirmed experimentally the correctness of the Adlerian views" (87), and in fact his studies on level of aspiration are an example of such a confirmation.

In the present connection we shall limit ourselves to the brief discussion of two fundamental similarities of theory. The first is the rejection of fixed class concepts. In his first book, published in 1912, Adler took a stand against Aristotelian class concepts and against all dichotomies as doing violence to the facts. He showed that categorical and dichotomized thinking is characteristic of the primitive mind and of the neurotic in his prejudiced mode of apperception and greater need for security. It was in accordance with this denial of specific categories that Adler also denied the existence of specific mental diseases as such, and stressed the unity of the neuroses (1912a). This rejection of categories was later worked out in much greater detail by Lewin in his important paper on Aristotelian and Galilean modes of thought, in which he described the process of progressive homogenization, that is, the doing away with rigid classes and antitheses, which has been found to accompany the advance of scientific theorizing (67).

Adler believed that different parts of life are made entities artificially by giving them more or less adequate man-made names (1937a). He had a profound distrust of incisive terminology and therefore kept his technical terminology to a minimum. This is quite in contrast to the way of a categorizing mind like that of Freud, who built up a rich terminology to express a highly ramified theory. Categories and terms are familiarly the delight of the pedant, and the class theorist has the advantage over the field theorist in that he appears to give more, and more definite, information.

Secondly, and related to the first point, Lewin and Adler both consider dynamic forces not as fixed and absolute quantities of energy, but as forces which can be expressed only in relational terms. Thus we find Adler recurrently speaking of "movement," a term which has much the same significance as Lewin's "vector," namely the expression of a force directed from one point to another. In accordance with the nature and properties of movement, Adler was more interested in describing its direction than in giving it a definite name. As a result he was fluid and elastic in his terms referring to dynamics. For example, he referred to his basic dynamic force variously as the striving for superiority, for overcoming, for completion, for totality, from below to above, for self-enhancement, of which terms none was to be taken literally. Wherever he uses a dynamic name it is safe to say that it is to be taken as a tentative proposal for describing a vector.

On the basis of such theoretical accord and certain similar developments therefrom, some of which are mentioned below (see pp. 245 and 344), we believe that the understanding of Adler is greatly facilitated if he is regarded as the original field theorist in the area of modern dynamic psychology.

4. UNDERSTANDING PSYCHOLOGY

Individual Psychology in important aspects is an "understanding" psychology. It is probably not a mere coincidence that Adler's first book addressed to the general reader was translated under the title *Understanding Human Nature*.

What is meant by "understanding" psychology in contrast to "explanatory" psychology? The first to make the distinction between the two psychologies was Wilhelm Dilthey, who called understanding psychology also descriptive psychology. Eduard Spranger, a student of Dilthey, distinguished between natural-science and mental-science psychology. Karl Jaspers, who has become probably the foremost proponent of this differentiation, defines explanatory psychology as the attempt to explain psychological processes by externally observable causal relationships. This is objective psychology, which corresponds to the psyche seen from without as was mentioned earlier. Understanding psychology aims at understanding how a psychological process follows from a preceding psychological process. Thus it, too, looks for a causal explanation, with the important difference that the cause is presumed to lie within the individual. This is subjective psychology (59, p. 250).

Jaspers points out that the internal relationships observed by understanding do not constitute genuine causality as revealed by objective psychology, but rather a figurative causality, with an unbridgeable gap between the two (59, p. 250). The complete understanding of an individual results in a "schema." It would be altogether wrong to take this schema for reality or for the theory of some objective foundation; but it has truth in the sense of a methodological auxiliary construct (59, p. 468).

This bears a striking similarity to Hans Vaihinger's theory of fictions (111) as it was embodied by Adler in his understanding psychology; Adler's concept of the individual's unconscious goal of superiority is in part an auxiliary construct, a working hypothesis, a useful fiction, and corresponds to Jaspers' "schema." To understand is "to recognize the relationship between things" (1929a, p. 9). Furthermore Adler denied the possibility of explaining a personality on the basis of objective causation. "Objective determiners are probabilities only, not direct causes" (1933c, p. 74). Explanation of the individual case is possible only from the individual's own inner nature.

The inner relationships are discovered by the method of phenomenology, which Jaspers uses in Edmund Husserl's sense as the descriptive psychology of the phenomena of consciousness. The understanding of these descriptions is based on empathy (59, p. 253). Phenomenology is an empirical method based exclusively on communication on the part of the subject, and in principle does not differ from the method of objective description (59, p. 47). But in practice a good phenomenological description is particularly difficult. "Just as children at first draw what they know rather than what they see, so the psychopathologist goes through a stage where he somehow reasons out the psychological content of the patient before he reaches an unprejudiced immediate comprehension of the psychological content as it is. The phenomenological attitude represents an ever new effort and a property which must be ever newly acquired through the overcoming of prejudices" (59, p. 48).

Although Adler did not use the term phenomenology, he consistently used the method in that he emphasized the unprejudiced approach to the patient, and based his understanding on empathy. This he defined simply in the demand, "We must be able to see with his eyes and listen with his ears" (1931a, p. 72).

As soon as Jaspers' work began to appear in 1912–1913, his similarity to Adler was observed (50; 86) and continued to be observed (93).

5. PHENOMENOLOGICAL PSYCHOLOGY AND CLIENT-CENTERED THEORY OF PERSONALITY

In recent years the importance of the phenomenological approach and, along with it, the concept of empathy have attracted growing attention (75; 63). Donald Snygg and Arthur W. Combs have presented a textbook from the phenomenological point of view. They consider their book "but one more step in what we have come to feel is an inevitable trend in psychology" (96, p. viii), and their system is closely connected with the understanding psychologies of Dilthey, Spranger, and Jaspers, although the authors do not mention these names (75, p. 225). In accordance with this systematic similarity, Snygg and Combs arrive at many formulations similar to those presented by Adler a generation earlier. Adler's concept of striving from below to above and for completion, as the basic dynamic force, finds its counterpart in Snygg and Combs' definition of the basic human need as "the preservation and enhancement of the phenomenal self"; Adler's concept of the constancy of the style of life finds its counterpart in their "stability of the phenomenal self"; and his individually unique schema or mode of apperception becomes their "phenomenal field."

The mention of Snygg and Combs and phenomenology brings us to another recent development, the personality theory of Carl Rogers (90), based on clinical and research evidence obtained with his method of client-centered therapy. The fascinating aspect in Rogers is that at first he approached the patient or client without any theory at all, following him empathically without any attempt at explanation, not even on the basis of internal causes. Methodologically he thus represents the unprejudiced phenomenological approach in its purest form, applied to psychotherapy.

Eventually Rogers developed a theory on the basis of careful observation of the entire therapeutic process and a synthesis of some fifteen authors whom we would for the most part classify as subjective. The outcome is a series of propositions which could be matched to a considerable extent with the propositions derived from Adler and presented above. Just to give a few examples, Rogers refers to: one basic tendency and striving to actualize, maintain, and enhance the experiencing organism; behavior as goal-directed; the individual as an organized whole; the consistency of the self; the individually perceived world; and better interpersonal relations as the outcome of therapy.

6. PSYCHOLOGICAL EXISTENTIALISM

Through Adler's relationship to Jaspers, Individual Psychology has also much in common with psychological existentialism, a new development of which Jaspers was one of the original leaders. The great similarity is the thought that man in order to overcome his very definite limitations (*anguish over the inevitability of death* in existentialism, and *the feeling of inferiority* in Individual Psychology) must transcend himself. According to Martin Heidegger man transcends himself by active participation in his world, by direct intercourse with others, and by a time-transcendence through his preoccupation with the future (108, p. 581–582). The counterpart in Adler to this transcendence is the concept of social interest, which results in social relatedness but is not limited to any concrete present society and includes, or may be replaced by, an interest in an ideal future society.

Thus existentialist psychotherapy has come to practically the same conclusion regarding the nature of neurosis as Adler had. According to Hanna Colm "The existentialist analyst . . . felt that man could not become himself merely through an inner integration with himself, but must experience an inner integration between the self and the other. . . . Buber says, 'Man wants to be accepted in his being by man and wants to mean something to the being of the other person.' . . . Neurosis is the outcome of the refusal of a self-centered self to meet another self" (25, p. 103).

D. Neo-Freudian or Neo-Adlerian?

In addition to various early deviators from Freud subsequent to Adler's separation, a large number of more recent deviators have developed, and these are often referred to by the term "neo-Freudian." As representative neo-Freudians we might mention Franz Alexander, Thomas M. French, Erich Fromm, Frieda Fromm-Reichmann, Karen Horney, Abram Kardiner, Patrick Mullahy, Harry Stack Sullivan, and Clara Thompson, to name just a few. Their position may be briefly described as stressing social relations rather than biological factors, the self rather than the id and the superego, the striving for self-actualization rather than the sex instinct, and the present situation rather than early experiences. Thus they belong on the subjective, tender-minded side of our original schema, and if the basic difference between Freud and Adler is that between objective and subjective, they should come very close to Adler. Such a similarity has indeed been noted in the literature in various instances, a few of which we shall cite.

When Sullivan stated in 1931 that "the process of therapy consists of deepening and widening the interest for interpersonal relations" (104), the similarity to Adler was immediately recognized (14). Regarding the work of Franz Alexander, Thomas M. French, and others (2) Keith Sward stated: "As for their dynamics of personality, or their theories of the structure of neurosis . . . the Chicago group would seem to be Adlerian through and through" (106). Regarding Karen Horney (54) Sward observed again: "It [is] difficult to think of a single basic 'Horney' tenet, the kernel of which cannot be found in books or papers which Adler published thirty or thirty-five years ago" (105). The similarities of Horney and Erich Fromm (43) to Adler have been pointed out in detail in a paper by Walter T. James: "Adler must be considered as one of the two most important intellectual antecedents of Horney and Fromm. . . . Most of all Horney and Fromm are indebted to Adler for his keen awareness of the reality of the influence of the total environment upon personality. Freud's persistent adherence to a biological etiology made any real 'social' psychology an impossibility except on the grounds of sexual symbolism. . . . Certain of Adler's conclusions are indispensable parts of the social psychologies of Horney and Fromm" (57, pp. 115–116).

In view of such frequently noted similarity with Adler, the question arises whether the so-called neo-Freudians would not more aptly be named neo-Adlerians, a term proposed for them by Fritz Wittels (118). And indeed a large number of classical Freudian psychoanalysts seem to agree with this proposition (9).

Parallel to the treatment of the other trends in psychology we may conclude the present part by stating that the understanding of Adler is aided if we regard him as the forerunner and prototype of such developments as have been discussed here.

E. A Restatement of Adler's Position

It has been the aim of this chapter to outline the position of Adler. We did this to a large extent by stressing the similarities between Individual Psychology and various other subjective psychologies. We are quite aware that in doing so we have disregarded the finer differences so dear to the heart of the painstaking theoretician. Our justification is that we wanted to provide an uncomplicated introductory background.

A second expedient was to call Adler a subjective psychologist, without qualifying the designation sufficiently. To begin with, as we have already pointed out, the term stands for a whole syndrome which is certainly not completely homogeneous. Secondly, we must stress again that Adler's particular subjectivity refers to dynamics: he was not a reductionist attempting to trace dynamic forces to a physiological origin, but saw in ideas, which in the last analysis are the creation of the individual, the ultimate determiners. Yet while his view of causality was subjectivistic, he combined in his method of observing the phenomenological with the objective behavioristic approach: "If we want to understand a person [that is, understand the hidden meaning of his introspections] we have to close our ears. We have only to look. In this way we can see as in a pantomime" (1931d, p. 25). Adler's favorite way of expressing this principle was through Martin Luther's aphorism, "not to watch a person's mouth but his fists" (1913f, p. 154n.). This combination of postulating subjective causality with employing objective methods of observation corresponds to Adler's philosophic position as an idealistic positivist. Idealistic positivism is the philosophy of Vaihinger, by whom Adler was so greatly influenced (see Chapter 3).

If today so many theoretical trends in psychology seem to take the direction which Adler originally took, this has, in our opinion, not come about fortuitously, but because their formulations fitted better the more carefully observed subjective and objective data and the practices which proved most effective. Inasmuch as Adler stands at the beginning of this trend, his work can serve as a synthesis in retrospect, while it is indeed in the nature of a remarkable original creation and anticipation.

PART I

PERSONALITY THEORY AND ITS DEVELOPMENT

CHAPTER ONE

COMPENSATION AND CONFLUENCE

COMMENT   Chapters 1 and 2 present Adler's early views as expressed
primarily in a series of papers published largely between
1907 and 1911, when he was still associated with Freud, and collected
in Heilen und Bilden (1914a). We have made selections from these papers for their intrinsic present-day significance, which we shall point out
specifically for the various topics below, and for two additional reasons:

1. These selections show steps in Adler's development. An appreciation
of this development, which went from drive psychology to phenomenological psychology, is felt to be necessary for a proper understanding of all
his contributions. As in any development, the earlier stages partly blend
with the later stages and are partly superceded by them.

2. These early papers show to what extent Adler anticipated Freud;
they contain a number of ideas which later were taken over by Freud. Of
these the following are included in the present chapter: the confluence of
drives, the transformation of a drive into its opposite, the direction of a
drive to one's own person, the aggression drive, and the relationship of
aggression to anxiety. These concepts were retained by Freud once he had
adopted them, but not by Adler, at least not in their original form.

Additional ideas taken over by Freud, presented in the next chapter,
are: the safeguarding tendencies, which he later called defense mechanisms; the idea that repression is not the indispensable generic factor in
neurosis, but must be subsumed under the safeguarding tendencies; and
the idea that libido and ego instincts are an untenable antithesis. Freud's
eventual acceptance of the last two points is all the more remarkable because he had originally rejected them, and they had been points of
difference partially responsible for bringing about the break with Adler.
The term and concept of ego-ideal were used by Freud shortly after Adler
had introduced the term personality-ideal or self-ideal (see pp. 94–95).

And finally, the main features of Freud's super-ego were anticipated in Adler's counter-fiction (see pp. 143–145).

These instances of Adler's influence on Freud contradict the frequent statement that Adler's relation to Freud was merely that of a student and disciple who later parted from the master to go his own way. This error has been corrected before (15, p. 57). It has persisted, however, probably because it seems very plausible in view of the fact that Adler was fourteen years younger than Freud and joined his circle, and because the counter-evidence remained obscure in Adler's early writings. These are difficult to understand and have not been translated into English heretofore. His style was extremely terse, so that a number of important ideas may occasionally be found in a single sentence. He generally introduced his concepts only in bare outline, one might say almost as hints. Especially in the beginning, Adler presents the picture of a man in a hurry. And indeed he created the foundation of his system within a relatively few years after 1908.

In building on Freud, Adler went in a direction which partly anticipated Freud's own development, and to a greater extent anticipated the many later deviators from Freud now often called neo-Freudians.

In a discussion of the Adler-Freud interaction, one important point must be stressed. Since Freud remained dualistic, atomistic, mechanistic, and biologically oriented throughout his life, the Adlerian concepts were treated and utilized differently in the Freudian frame of reference, just as Freudian ideas assumed different meaning in the Adlerian setting.

A. Organ Inferiority and Compensation (1907)

COMMENT   *The following selections on organ inferiority establish Adler as a field theorist from the very beginning of his work. Written by a physician who until a few years earlier had been a general practitioner, they are a contribution to the theory of disease, according to which diseases can no longer be understood as separate entities. A disease afflicts only the inferior organs. But what constitutes an inferior organ? Inferiority is a relative concept, relative to the environmental demands, to the total situation. In this way, outcomes previously understood as due to independent agents are now seen as the result of the interaction of forces. The various aspects of such interaction refer to: the organism and the physical environment, the organism and the social en-*

vironment, the separate organs with one another, and body and mind. From the point of view of the psychologist, then, the significance of these selections is, firstly, that they represent an exposition of field theory, albeit in terms of medical material.

The significance of these selections is, secondly, that they present the first formulation of Adler's theory of compensation. If in the organ-environment interaction, the balance threatens to turn against the organism, it responds through attempts at compensation. Through the superstructure of the central nervous system the mind, as part of the entire organism, will play its part in the process of compensation or maintenance of equilibrium. Thus Adler arrived at the concept of psychological compensation. The theory of compensation is similar to that of homeostasis which Walter B. Cannon presented twenty-five years later, and when Cannon's The Wisdom of the Mind appeared, Adler wrote an enthusiastic review of it (1933d). This relationship between compensation and homeostasis was recognized in a paper by John M. Fletcher entitled "The Wisdom of the Mind," where he states: "I am not sure but that in Adler's mechanism of compensation we have a phenomenon which may be subsumed under what is described by Cannon as homeostasis" (30, p. 14). In another paper Fletcher explains: "Compensation . . . becomes at once much more intelligible when conceived as homeostatic defense reaction" (29, p. 86). Since compensation, like homeostasis, aims at maintenance of equilibrium, it would as the dominating dynamic principle belong to a relatively static, closed system. Adler's theory, however, developed into a completely open system of dynamics in which the dominating force was a ceaseless upward striving (see Chapter 4, pp. 101–108) and in which compensation then assumed a secondary role.

Thirdly Adler's writings on organ inferiority are of significance in that they are an early discussion of the problem of psychosomatic disorders. In the foreword to a reprint edition of the Study of Organ Inferiority, Nolan D. C. Lewis concludes: "This little book has not only an important historical value but it presents a number of foci for future research. A thorough investigation of organ inferiority concepts should be undertaken and included as a part of the present day trends in psychosomatic medicine" (72, p. ix).

The selections below cover the theoretical essence of the material contained in the Study of Organ Inferiority (1907a), Adler's first major contribution, but are for the most part taken from a summary presented by him in a lecture held the same year. This lecture contains all the theoretical points while omitting the detailed medical material which represents the greater part of the original study.

In conclusion of this introduction we should like to point out that the term inferiority feeling, an integral part of Adler's psychology, is not to be found in the Study of Organ Inferiority or its summary. The concept of inferiority feeling did not appear until three years later (1910a: see pp. 44–45). The understandable mistake has frequently been made of assuming that the Study includes the discussion of inferiority feelings. Yet at this time Adler still confined himself to objective terms and was not concerned with anything so subjective as feelings.

As a general remark, we should add that the selections here and throughout this chapter, aside from the aspects which became integrated in Adler's system, tend to be expressed in terms of outdated physiology and deal with drive psychology which Adler subsequently attacked severely. Despite tendencies pointing toward unity of the personality, the self is still absent from the discussion.

1. ORGAN INFERIORITY AND ITS OUTCOMES[1]

The inferiority to which I refer applies to an organ which is developmentally retarded, which has been inhibited in its growth or altered, in whole or in part. These inferior organs may include the sense organs, the digestive apparatus, the respiratory tracts, the genito-urinary apparatus, the circulatory organs, and the nervous system. Such inferiority can usually be proved only at birth or often only at the embryonic stage. The innate anomalies of organs range from malformation to slow maturation of otherwise normal organs. Since there is a strong relationship between inferiority and disease, we may expect that an inherited inferiority corresponds to an inherited disease.

The fate of the inferior organs is extremely varied. Development and the external stimuli of life press toward overcoming the expressions of such inferiority. Thus we may find approximately the following outcomes with innumerable intermediate stages: inability to survive, anomaly of form, anomaly of function, lack of resistance and disposition to disease, compensation within the organ, compensation through a second organ, compensation through the psychological superstructure, and organic or psychological overcompensation. We find pure, compensated, and overcompensated inferiorities.

2. THE RELATIVITY OF ORGAN INFERIORITY TO EXTERNAL DEMANDS[2]

One way by which organ inferiority manifests itself is through localization of a disease in that specific organ. This occurs when the inferior organ reacts to pathogenic stimuli from the environment. We wish to replace the obscure concept of "pathological disposition" by the following proposition: Disease is the resultant of organ inferiority and external demands. The latter are limited in duration and to a particular cultural environment. Changes in external demands represent cultural progress, changes of the mode of living, or social improvements. They are the work of the human mind and, in the long run, tend to curb excessive straining of the organs. The external demands are related to the developmental potentialities of the organs and their nervous superstructure, and they condition the relative inferiority of an organ when their requirements exceed a certain measure.

Within these observations chance, as the correcting factor in development, seems to be precluded. A clear example would be Professor Habermann's observation that members of occupations such as blacksmiths and artillery gunners, who are exposed to loud noises, are prone to diseases of the ear. It can easily be seen that not every auditory apparatus is suited for such occupations. But it is also clear that such injuries regularly give cause for technical changes in industrial procedure, that continuous employment in certain occupations changes the affected organs, and that health hazards exist on the path to parity (Vollwertigkeit).

In summary, we may say that hygiene and preventive medicine are subject to the conditions of compensation. All therapeutic methods are likewise aimed at the compensation of organ inferiority which has become visible.

3. FORMS OF COMPENSATION[3]

As soon as the equilibrium, which must be assumed to govern the economy of the individual organ or the whole organism, appears to be disturbed due to inadequacy of form or function, a certain biological process is initiated in the inferior organs. The unsatisfied demands increase until the deficit is made up through growth of the inferior organ, of the paired organ, or of some other organ which can serve as a substitute, completely or in part. This compensating for the defect through increase in growth and function, may, under favorable circumstances, achieve overcompensation; it will usually also include the central nervous system in its increased development.

If reflex anomalies of the mucous membranes have been definitely shown to be related to the psyche, then this holds even more for childhood disorders, such as retarded speech development, stammering, blinking, thumb sucking, and eating difficulties. These are the visible expressions of an altered functioning of inferior organs and represent striking disturbances in the process of compensation.

Usually, however, the normal growth of the superordinated nerve tracts, that is, simple compensation through growth, seems to be sufficient to bring about normal functioning. In this event the organ anomaly remains the same, and upon closer examination we very often find that unextinguishable remnants last throughout life. In other cases the defect may have been overcome for all normal conditions only. It reappears as soon as psychological tension arises but remains hidden at times of rest. Frequent examples of this are: blinking in bright light, squinting during close work, stammering during excitement, and vomiting during emotion. This confirms our guess that compensation is due to overperformance and increased growth of the brain. This strengthening of the psychological superstructure is shown by the successful outcome; its relation to steady exercise is easily guessed. Thus also in the central nervous system the same relationships of inferiority and compensation prevail.

In favorable cases of compensation, the inferior organ has the better developed and psychologically more potent superstructure. The psychological manifestations of such an organ may be more plentiful and better developed as far as drive, sensitivity, attention, memory, apperception, empathy, and consciousness are concerned. In the favorable case, an inferior nutritive apparatus may muster the greater phychological potency in all relations to nourishment. But it may also be superior in everything related to the gaining of food, since its superstructure will dominate and draw the other psychological complexes into its orbit. The food drive will dominate to such an extent that it may find expression in all personal and social relations, as in gourmandism, acquisitiveness, parsimony, and avarice. The same holds true for other inferior organs. This may lead to a more extended sensory life and a more careful and correct appraisal of the world as far as it is accessible to the organ in question.

Through this process psychological axes develop according to which the individual is oriented. This always takes place in dependency on one or more inferior organs. The striving to gain pleasure for these organs becomes noticeable also in dreams and fantasy, as well as in play and occupational preference and choice, because in the case of an inferior organ, primitive activity of the organ (drive) is always associated with pleasure. Certain childhood disorders point to this pleasure with such clearness that they are mistaken for sexual activity. If we carry this thought further, we ultimately arrive at the supposition that the psychological superstructure of the organ largely functions as a substitute for the deficiencies of the organ in order to gain its pleasure in relation to the environment.

4. COMPENSATION AND THE SOCIAL ENVIRONMENT[4]

Since the inferiority of the deviating organs comes from the external environment, changes of the environment, organ inferiority, and corresponding ameliorating brain compensation all take place under mutual influence. This point of view of mutual interaction seems applicable also to the origin of highly cultivated psychomotor achievements, to the origin and development of language and art, to the nature of genius, and to the birth of philosophical systems and world philosophies. I trust that it will prove its worth also in respect to the invention and solution of new problems. This point of view forces us much more clearly than any other to avoid the pitfalls of abstraction and to observe the phenomena in their context and in flux. I have pursued it in the field of medical science; perhaps my modest suggestion will meet with approval elsewhere as well.

But the picture of the world which is founded in brain compensation cannot develop unlimitedly, for it cannot give free reign either to its drives or to its unconscious component. Rather its expressions are limited by the social environment and by the culture, which, through the drive for self-preservation, permit the expressions of the psyche to unfold only when they can fit themselves into the frame of the culture. Nonetheless the strengthened superstructure of the inferior organ often assumes new and valuable modes of operation. To be sure, these ways may also be pathological ways, as in the neuroses.

5. OUTCOMES OF OVERCOMPENSATION[5]

When overcompensation attempts to assert itself in a cultural manner and in this effort enters into new, although difficult and often inhibited, paths, the very great expressions of the psyche arise which we must attribute to genius. Lombroso in his theory of genius dealt only with the mixed cases and thus arrived at a false conception of the pathological genius. The inferior organ is not a pathological formation, although it represents the basic condition for pathology. Under favorable conditions the impulse toward brain compensation can end in an overcompensation which shows no trace of pathology.

The outcome of overcompensation depends on several conditions; in other words, it is overdetermined. As one of these conditions we have met the limitations of culture. Another determiner is the chaining of the dominant superstructure to other psychological fields. For example, the visual superstructure may be chained to the auditory organs and to the superstructure of the language organs. Only these multiple compensations, their confluences and mutual inhibitions give us an adequate picture of the psyche. The outcome of an overcompensation depends, thirdly, on its stamina. Nature very often fails in the correction of the inferior organ, in these cases creating transitory compensations which easily succumb to attacks. Inability, neurosis, psychological disease, in short, pathological forms may appear in this event. A small sample from the analysis of paranoia may serve as illustration. The overcompensation of the inferior visual apparatus plays an outstanding part, in addition to other apparatus. The drive to see, for example, has become highly developed in a great part of paranoiacs and has exhausted all visual possibilities in the world. Then an unfavorable constellation sets in and the weakness of the overcompensation expresses itself in hallucinatory fits and visual appearances. The forces constituting reason soon show a similar fallibility, the patient regarding himself as the object of the visual drive of others.

The positive counterpart may be shown in a small aspect of the psyche of the poet Schiller for which I am indebted to the Viennese writer Rank, who is familiar with my views. I should like to preface this example by stating that I must attribute especially to the dramatic poet a particular and unique overcompensation of the visual organ. In such overcompensation is founded his scenic power, the selection and elaboration of his material.

In the drama of the marksman William Tell, Schiller reveals a large number of allusions to the overcompensation of the visual organ, phrases which concern the eye and its functions. I wish furthermore to point out the blinding of Melchthal and the hymn to the light of the eyes in *William Tell*. Schiller himself had weak eyes, suffered from inflammation of the eyes, and, until adulthood, from the childhood disorder of blinking. He was much interested in hunting. Weltrich relates that the family of Schiller received its name on account of strabismus (*schielen*). This would be of interest for the study of heredity. I mention this to call attention to the relationship of the poet to the inferior organ.

Signs of an inferior visual apparatus play a large part in the development of painters (see also Reich, J., "Kunst und Auge." *Oesterreichische Rundschau*, Vienna, 1908). Guercino da Centa, 17th century, was given his name because he squinted. Piero de la Francesca, who is particularly credited with the art of perspective, became blind in old age, according to Vasaris. Among the more modern painters Lenbach had only one eye. Mateyko was extremely myopic. Manet suffered from astigmatism. Among art students, approximately seventy per cent have been found to suffer from some optical anomalies.

Among orators, actors, and singers, I have also very often found signs of organ inferiority. The Bible reports about Moses that he had a heavy tongue, whereas his brother Aaron had the talent of talking. Demosthenes, the stutterer, became the greatest orator of Greece. Camille Demoulin who usually stuttered is reported by his contemporaries to have been very fluent when he made a speech.

Musicians quite frequently suffer from ear afflictions. Beethoven and Robert Franz, both of whom became deaf, are well-known examples. Klara Schumann reports hearing and speech difficulties in childhood.

Myths have also, since time immemorial, taken hold of the phenomenon of the inferior organ and its overcompensation. The myth of the blind marksman who always hits the target is related to the William Tell saga.

The following quotation from Grimm's *German Mythology* bears witness to how closely our conception of compensation and overcompensation of the inferior organ corresponds to the popular feeling: "We find want of limbs in the heroes as well as in the Gods. Orin is one-eyed, Tyr one-handed, Loki lame, Hoeder blind, Vidar dumb, Hagano also one-eyed, Walkeri one-handed, Gunther and Wieland are lame; and there are a goodly number of blind and dumb heroes."

Far from offering these details as complete proof, the examples are intended only to direct the attention of the reader to the wide scope of the theory of organ inferiority and its relation to philosophy, psychology, and aesthetics.

B. Confluence and Transformation of Drives (1908)

COMMENT *Unity is what Adler considers the most basic aspect of his theory of personality. It was in fact dealt with already in the preceding part, for both interaction of forces and compensation imply the unity of the organism. Adler's next contribution, presented below, was more specifically concerned with unity, which he conceived in the form of a "confluence of drives." At this time, Adler was still a member of the Freudian circle and still subscribed to drive psychology and hedonism; he still had the natural-science approach, seeking to explain mental life as caused by physiological processes.*

In the same paper, he also described the "transformation of drives," an idea which came to be of the greatest importance in Freud but which in Adler merely foreshadowed his later view that all causal factors, including drives, are relative to the individual's ultimate goal and style of life.

1. CONFLUENCE OF DRIVES AND PSYCHOLOGICAL AXIS[6]

Until now every consideration of sadism and masochism has started from sexual phenomena admixed with traits of cruelty. Yet the driving force in healthy, as well as perverted and neurotic individuals, apparently stems from two drives which, originally distinct, subsequently have undergone a confluence (Verschränkung). Thus the sadistic masochistic results correspond to two drives simultaneously: the sexual drive and the drive of aggression. Similar confluences are found regularly in the drives of adults. Thus the drive to eat is connected with the drive to see and the drive to smell (see the results of Pavlov), and the drive to hear is connected with the drive to see (audition colorée, musical talent). In short, every discoverable drive is connected with one or more drives, a confluence in which the drives to urinate or to defecate often participate. Drive in this context is only an abstraction, a sum of elementary functions of the corresponding organ and its nerve tracts, the origin and development of which are derived from the coercion of the environment and its demands. The goal of the drive is determined by the satisfaction of the organic needs and by the gaining of pleasure from the environment.

COMMENT   The reader may be surprised to find a drive to see, a drive
                to smell, a drive to hear; in other words, to find the sen-
sory functions understood as having dynamic qualities. This view, however, has relatively recently been taken up by Robert S. Woodworth
in a paper on perception in which he states: "Perception is always driven
by a direct, inherent motive which might be called the will to perceive.
Whatever ulterior motives may be present from time to time, this direct
perceptual motive is always present in any use of the senses" (121, p. 123).
The recent general textbook by Gardner Murphy also takes this position.
"Every part of the body has its own tensions, its own activities, and therefore contributes directly or indirectly to the ongoing flow of bodily response which we call motivation . . . When the sense organs are stimulated and the brain is aroused, our response is frequently one of delight,
excitement, interest. The tiny child and the tiny animal are strongly
drawn toward certain sights, sounds, smells, touches, warm things, cold
things . . . Such activities might be called sensory drives, arising from
sensory tension systems" (83, p. 82).

The systematic significance of the concept of sensory drives is that they
represent an outgoing, exploratory dynamic, and by themselves cannot
be understood as merely aiming at a reinstatement of the status quo, as is
the case with Freud's conception of instincts (36, V, p. 135). The concept of sensory drives does, however, fit in with Karl Bühler's concept
of Funktionslust (22, pp. 454–455) and Goldstein's concept of self-
actualization (48).

The total physiognomy of all striking character descriptions always results from a confluence of drives in which one or several drives constitute
the psychological main axis and in which the sex drive plays a prominent
part.

COMMENT   The term "confluence of drives" was taken over by Freud,
                the following year. In a footnote to a 1909 article referring
to the present paper by Adler, Freud states: "This is the same paper from
which I have borrowed the term 'confluence of instincts'" (36, III, p.
281).

It should be pointed out that both Adler and Freud used the same
German word, Trieb, which is properly translated as drive. The translators
of Freud, however, have used instinct instead, a translation which we did

not change. A difference between Adler's "drive" as used here and Freud's "instinct" thus does not exist in the German original versions.

While Freud did not use the term "confluence of instincts" often, and limited its application, it constitutes the first instance in which Freud acknowledged that he had learned from Adler. Significantly this is along the line of unification, a conceptual direction in which Adler was eventually to go the whole way, while Freud was to remain a dualist.

Yet not only unity but also the specific structure or uniqueness of the individual are indicated in the above selection from Adler. In the process of confluence, one or several drives come to constitute "the main axis," a concept which was ultimately developed into that of the style of life. (The psychological axis was first mentioned on p. 26.)

Finally, sex is mentioned as a prominent factor, but, nota bene, only as a prominent, and not as the predominant factor. Adler always retained this evaluation of sex, all misinterpretations to the effect that he denied its importance notwithstanding.

2. TRANSFORMATION OF DRIVES[7]

Whatever part of the drives becomes conscious, be it as an idea, desire, or volition, as well as whatever part becomes manifest to the environment through words or action, may derive either directly from one or from more drives and can have undergone cultural changes, refinements, and specialization (sublimation of Nietzsche, Freud). The drive may also become inhibited in its expansion tendency through a barrier determined by culture or created by a second drive, and hence may not become manifest directly. In this event certain characteristic phenomena in consciousness correspond to drive inhibition in the unconscious, among which Psychoanalysis [later editions: Individual Psychology] reveals especially the following:

1. Transformation of the drive into its opposite. For example, the unconscious drive to eat becomes the conscious refusal to eat; almost analogously with this, unconscious avarice becomes conscious generosity.

2. Displacement of the drive to another goal. The unconscious love for the father becomes conscious love for the teacher, the physician, the cousin, and others; or the repression may go so far that the sex drive manifests itself only in a perverted direction, in homosexuality.

3. Direction of the drive to one's own person. For example, the unconscious, repressed drive to see becomes the conscious drive to be looked

at. This constitutes exhibitionism, and also, in further sequence, the root of ideas of reference, grandeur, and persecution in paranoia and dementia praecox. An important variation of the drive directed to one's own person is looking and listening within, together with recollection, intuition, introspection, premonition, illusion, hallucination, and anxiety.

4. *Displacement of the accent on a second strong drive.* This often expresses itself also in the form of point 1 above (transformation of the drive into its opposite). For example, the repression of the sex drive increases the activity of the drive to look to such an extent that either sexual symbols are seen everywhere or that the conscious seeing of sexual symbols is interfered with by nervous attacks and hysteria.

These viewpoints are of great importance for the understanding of culture, religion, consciousness, forgetting, morals, ethics, aesthetics, anxiety, and symptoms of repression in the psychoneuroses.

COMMENT *In his paper on "Instincts and their Vicissitudes (1915)"* *(36, IV, 60–83) Freud, whose psychology always remained a drive psychology, took up two of the above points, namely, the transformation of a drive into its opposite and the direction of the drive to one's own person. He listed them together with repression and sublimation under the expressions "reversal of an instinct into its opposite" (reaction formation) and "turning round of an instinct upon the subject." While he refers to Adler's present article, he does not mention the above two points specifically as coming from it. Adler, however, in his 1922 revision, takes note of Freud's inclusion of these propositions with the simple statement: "Freud in 1915 has characterized the behavior of drives in similar fashion" (1922a, p. 20). These two propositions ultimately became included among the ten ego-defense mechanisms listed by Anna Freud who, in speaking of these together with regression, says, "We should not be surprised to find that these are the very earliest defense mechanisms employed by the ego" (32, p. 56).*

Adler, on the other hand, who soon was to abandon the more mechanistic, categorizing drive psychology for a finalistic, contextual, and relativistic system, made very little further mention of these concepts. All transformations became possible and self-understood under a more general conception of behavior. To behavior, including that of drives, he ascribed an almost infinite modifiability in accordance with the style of life under which the safeguarding and defense of the self became subsumed.

c. The Aggression Drive (1908)

COMMENT   *Together with the concept of the confluence of drives, Adler postulated a superordinated dynamic force which would direct the confluence. Thus the primary drives would lose their autonomy to a higher principle of motivation. The aggression drive was this principle. Two years later the superordinated principle became the masculine protest, which subsequently was replaced by various formulations of striving, ultimately the striving for perfection.*

1. AGGRESSION AS A SUPERORDINATED DRIVE[8]

From early childhood, we can say from the first day (first cry), we find a stand of the child toward the environment which cannot be called anything but hostile. If one looks for the cause of this position, one finds it determined by the difficulty of affording satisfaction for the organ. This circumstance as well as the further relationships of the hostile, belligerent position of the individual toward the environment indicate a drive toward fighting for satisfaction which I shall call "aggression drive."

This drive is to be understood not as clinging directly to the organ and its tendency to gain pleasure, but as belonging to the total superstructure which represents a superordinated psychological field connecting the drives.

COMMENT   *It is interesting to note that in this attempt to describe a unifying dynamic principle, Adler uses the term psychological field. Although we shall refer to Adler repeatedly as a field theorist, this is to our knowledge the only time that he himself uses the term.*

The unfinished excitation enters this field when one of the primary drives is prevented from satisfaction. This is the simplest and most frequent case of affect displacement. In cases of organ inferiority where the primary drives are stronger, we normally find the stronger aggression drive also. The aggression drive means to us a sum of sensations, excitations, and their discharges (Freud's motor discharge in hysteria belongs here), the organic and functional substratum of which is innate. As with the primary drives, the excitation of the aggression drive is set off by the relation of drive strength to demands from the environment. Its goal is fixed by the satisfaction of the primary drives and by culture and adaptation.

The unstable psychological equilibrium is always re-established by the fact that the primary drive is satisfied through excitation and discharge of the aggression drive.

2. TRANSFORMATIONS OF THE AGGRESSION DRIVE[9]

Fighting, wrestling, beating, biting, and cruelties show the aggression drive in its pure form. Its refinement and specialization lead to sports, competition, duelling, war, thirst for dominance, and religious, social, national and race struggles. (Lichtenberg says approximately: "It is remarkable how rarely and reluctantly men live according to their religious commandments and how readily they like to fight for them.") When the aggression drive turns upon the subject, we find traits of humility, submission and devotion, subordination, flaggelantism, and masochism. We may point out that outstanding cultural traits are related to this reversal, such as educability and belief in authority, as well as suggestibility and hypnosis. The extreme is suicide.

The aggression drive dominates the entire motor behavior, its motor irradiations being unusually clear in childhood. Crying, fidgeting, throwing oneself on the floor, biting, and grinding one's teeth, are simple forms of this drive which are not infrequently found again later in life, particularly in hysteria.

The aggression drive also dominates consciousness (for example, in anger) as does any drive. It directs attention, interests, sensation, perception, memory, phantasy, production, and reproduction into the paths of pure or altered aggression. In doing so, it enlists the aid of the other drives, especially those of the inferior organs which are the basis of the psychological main axes, and thus it explores the entire world of aggression possibilities. All this can be regularly observed when the drive-life is reasonably strong.

The excited but contained aggression drive creates the cruel figures of art and phantasy, as well as the horrors of history and of individual life. The psyche of the painter, sculptor, and especially the tragic poet, who with his creation wants to awaken "fear and pity," reveals the confluence of originally strong primary drives to see, to hear, to touch. By the detour of the aggression drive, these become effective in highly cultivated forms and, at the same time, give us a good illustration of the transformation of drives.

The stronger aggression drive creates and chooses a large number of occupations, not to mention criminals and revolutionary heroes. The occupations of judge, police officer, teacher, minister, physician, and many others are taken up by persons with a larger aggression drive and often show continuity with analogous children's games. Some children's games, the world of the fairy tales and its favorite figures, the sagas of the various peoples, hero worship, and the many cruel stories and poems of children's books and readers are created by the aggression drive for the aggression drive. A further haven for the aggression drive is politics with its innumerable possibilities for activity and logical interpretation of any attack, Napoleon being the favorite hero. Interest in funerals and death notices, superstition, fear of sickness and infection, as well as fear of being buried alive and interest in graveyards often uncovers a secret lascivious cruelty, while the aggression drive may be otherwise repressed.

Whereas the aggression drive so often withdraws from our perception through turning against the self and through refinement and specialization, it becomes altogether a hidden-figure puzzle in the reversal into the antithesis of the aggression drive. Charity, sympathy, altruism, and sensitive interest in misery represent new satisfactions on which the drive, which originally tended toward cruelty, feeds. If this seems strange, it is nevertheless easy to recognize that a real understanding for suffering and pain can only come from an original interest in the world of torment. The greater the aggression drive, the stronger will become this cultural transformation. Thus the pessimist becomes the preventor of dangers, Cassandra becomes a warner and prophet.

All these manifestations of the aggression drive are found again in the neuroses and psychoses. We find pure expressions of the aggression drive in temper tantrums and attacks of hysteria, epilepsy, and paranoia. Phases of the turning round of the drive upon the self are hypochondria, neurasthenic and hysterical pain, the entire syndrome of complaints in neurasthenia, hysteria, accident neurosis, ideas of reference and persecution, self-mutilation, and suicide. Reversals into its opposite are the mild traits and Messianic ideas of hysterics and psychotics.

We must mention one more phenomenon, anxiety, which has the greatest significance in the structure of the neuroses. It represents a phase of the aggression turned upon the self and is to be compared with the hallucinatory phase of other drives. The various forms of anxiety come about because the aggression drive, which is at the basis of anxiety, can take hold of various systems. It may enervate motor systems (tremor, shaking, cramps, catatonic phenomena, functional paralysis as inhibition of aggression). It may also excite the vasomotor system (heart palpitations, paleness, blushing) or other tracts, so that we may find perspiration, incontinency and vomiting, or prevention of secretion as an inhibition phenomenon.

COMMENT   *It is well known that Freud recognized an aggressive instinct, but not so well known that this was not until about 1920 to 1923, whereas Adler's paper was published in 1908. After this paper had appeared, Freud commented on it in 1909 as follows:* "Alfred Adler, in a suggestive paper, has recently developed the view that anxiety arises from the suppression of what he calls the 'aggressive instinct,' and by a very sweeping synthetic process he ascribes to that instinct the chief part in human events, 'in real life and in the neuroses' . . . I am unable to assent to this view, and indeed I regard it as a misleading generalization. I cannot bring myself to assume the existence of a special aggressive instinct alongside the familiar instincts of self-preservation and of sex, and on an equal footing with them" (36, III, p. 281). *Freud immediately appreciated that Adler's aggression drive was a coordinator and initiator, depriving the primary drives of their autonomy. In accordance with his orientation, which was analytical rather than holistic, he explained his rejection by adding:* "I should prefer for the present to adhere to the usual view which leaves each instinct its own power of becoming aggressive." *Whereas Adler's aggression drive, as a superordinated drive, was intrinsically connected with bringing the self back into psychology, it was just this which Freud resisted. By retaining the independence of the drives, he kept the self depleted.*

When Freud later reversed his stand and accepted an aggression drive, he did so in a form which still did not provide for a unified self. He expressed this in a footnote attached to the above passage in 1923. "Since then I have myself been obliged to assert the existence of an 'aggressive instinct,' but it is different from Adler's. I prefer to call it the 'destructive' or 'death instinct.' [See Beyond the Pleasure Principle (1920) and Das Ich und das Es (1923).] Its opposition to the libidinal instincts finds an expression in the familiar polarity of love and hate. My disagreement with Adler's view, which results in a general characteristic of all instincts being encroached upon for the benefit of a single one of them, remains unaltered" (36, III, p. 281n).

Edward Hitschmann, a contemporary of Freud and one of the earliest psychoanalysts, continues from here, in a paper on the history of the aggres-

sion drive: "The recognition and broad description of the aggression-impulse [on the part of Freud] we do not find earlier than 1929 in Civilisation and its Discontents: 'A powerful measure of desire for aggression has to be reckoned as part of the instinctive endowment of men. Homo homini lupus . . . I can no longer understand how we could have overlooked the universality of nonerotic aggression and destruction and could have omitted to give it its due significance in our interpretation of life . . .' " (51, pp. 138–139).

According to Hitschmann, "Freud was in 1908 very impressed by this paper of Adler" (51, p. 138) and Hitschmann reflects: "It is a very interesting event in the history of science, that one man [Adler] finds a certainly all-important impulse in human mind and considers the fate of this impulse in the development of men with great intelligence, but relinquishes the problem again entirely. And that a man of Freud's genius hesitates twenty-two years to accept the aggression-impulse, but does it then in full extent, admitting his failure finally in his seventy-fourth year!" (51, pp. 139–140).

But Hitschmann is mistaken when he maintains that Adler subsequently relinquished the problem of aggression. Actually Adler retained it as the basis of his understanding of abnormal behavior, and he considered every symptom as an act of aggression aimed at a single opponent, or society at large. The crucial change in Adler's theory, however, was that aggression was no longer regarded as an independent innate drive but was subsumed under the larger concept of striving for overcoming, under which aggression was only the abnormal form which occurs when social interest is not properly developed (see pp. 267–273).

Years later Adler commented in retrospect: "In 1908 I hit upon the idea that every individual really exists in a state of permanent aggression, and I was imprudent enough to call this attitude the 'aggression drive.' But I soon realized that I was not dealing with a drive, but with a partly conscious, partly irrational attitude towards the tasks which life imposes; and I gradually arrived at an understanding of the social element in personality, the extent of which is always determined by the individual's opinion of the facts and the difficulties of life" (1931e, p. 4).

In this connection, Bottome quotes Adler as saying to his friends with a grim smile, "I enriched psychoanalysis by the aggressive drive. I gladly make them a present of it" (15, p. 64).

We may summarize this history of the aggression concept and restate it in the light of the subsequent development of psychological theory as follows. Adler postulated the aggression drive, but eventually subordinated it to the general striving for "overcoming," making it the pathological form of this striving. Today most psychologists would agree with Adler that aggression is a reactive form of behavior, not one based on an innate tendency irrespective of the experience and interpretation of the individual. Freud on the other hand, first rejected Adler's concept of aggression, then elevated it to an independent, innate impulse, formulated in the death instinct. This understanding of aggression is today probably the most contested of all of Freud's views, not only among psychologists in general but also among psychoanalysts.

D. The Need for Affection (1908)

COMMENT In 1908, Adler not only published his important concept of the aggression drive which ultimately became the general striving for superiority or perfection, but also presented the forerunner of the concept of social interest or social feeling, the need for affection. The expression "social feelings" is actually used several times in this paper.

1. A CONFLUENCE OF DRIVES FOR CONTACT[10]

Among the externally observable psychological phenomena in children, the need for affection (Zärtlichkeitsbedürfnis) shows itself relatively early. This need must not be understood as a circumscribed psychological formation which might possibly be located in the psychomotor sphere of the brain. We rather perceive in it the reflection of several tendencies, of open and unconscious wishes, and of the expressions of instincts which in part are strong enough to become conscious. Separated components of the drives to touch, to look, and to listen [see above, p. 31] furnish the driving force in a unique confluence. The goal lies in the satisfaction of these tendencies which are struggling for their object. Our first conclusion may be put in these words: A strong need for affection in the child leads one to assume, other things being equal, the existence of a strong drive life (Triebleben).

The strength of the affectional tendencies, the psychological apparatus which the child can bring into play to achieve satisfaction, and the way in which he bears lack of satisfaction represent an essential part of the child's character. The original expressions of the need for affection are sufficiently striking and well known. Children want to be fondled, loved, and praised. They have a tendency to cuddle up, always to remain close to loved persons, and to want to be taken into the bed with them. Later this desire aims at loving relationships from which originate love of relatives, friendship, social feelings (Gemeinschaftsgefühle), and love.

COMMENT   *This earliest formulation of the social component by Adler differs characteristically from those which Freud subsequently presented. In the case of Adler, satisfaction of the need for affection depends on other people, and therefore the need for social relationships is present from the start. By contrast, Freud's libido, the closest counterpart to the need for affection, is originally directed toward one's own person; it is originally auto-erotic or narcissistic. This finding of Freud seems to be contradicted by his own statement that "a child's first erotic object is the mother's breast that feeds him." But he saves the situation for narcissim when he continues: "To start with, the child certainly makes no distinction between the breast and his own body; when the breast has to be separated from his body and shifted to the 'outside,' because he so often finds it absent, it carries with it, now that it is an 'object,' part of the original narcissistic cathexis" (42, pp. 89–90). "Others of the component instincts also start by being auto-erotic and are not until later diverted on to an external object" (36, V, p. 133).*

This directional difference was pointed out by Adler when he said: "One can always observe that the child directs his effort for affection towards others, not towards himself, as Freud believes" (1927a, p. 32). Adler holds, to the contrary, that it is only after satisfaction has been denied to the out-going seeking for affection that the child turns upon himself in self-love, as stated below.

2. MANAGEMENT OF THE NEED FOR AFFECTION[11]

As a rule, and with good reason, a satisfaction of the need for affection cannot be had for nothing (that is, without giving something in return). Thus the need for affection becomes the lever of education. A hug, a kiss, a friendly look, a loving word can only be obtained when the child subordinates himself to the educator (Erzieher) via the detour of culture. Just as the child desires this satisfaction from the parents, so he also comes to desire it from the teacher and later from society. The need for affection thus becomes an essential part of the social feelings.

A large part of the child's development depends on the proper guidance of this drive complex. A partial satisfaction of the drive life is an indispensable factor of culture, while the remaining unsatisfied drive complex furnishes the eternal immanent impulse for the progress of culture. The erroneous directions which the need for affection may take can easily be understood.

Before attaining satisfaction, the impulse should be forced to detour in order to furnish the drive for the cultural behavior of the child. Thus the way and goal of the need for affection are raised to a higher level. The derived purified social feelings awake in the soul of the child as soon as the goal permits substitute formations and the place of the father can be taken by the teacher, the friend, or the brother-in-arms. The perseverance of the drive impulse must be strongly connected with this. The lack of satisfaction must not destroy the psychological equilibrium. It is meant only to awaken energy and to produce the position of cultural aggression (*kulturelle Aggressionsstellung*). If the child is spared the detour via culture, if he attains only satisfactions of a primitive kind without delay, his wishes will remain directed toward immediate, sensual pleasure.

COMMENT *These remarks on the management of the need for affection come very close to a description of the process of sublimation to which Adler has already made a reference in connection with the transformation of drives (see p. 32). In his late years, Adler had the following to say in respect to sublimation: "The possibility of sublimating a socially reprehensible, according to Freud pleasurable, drive component means, in our sense, utilizing it for the benefit of society. This can be carried out honestly only when social interest grows. If someone should succeed in honestly carrying out a sublimation, as Fourier and Nietzsche have thought and as also Freud proposes, and at the same time contradict the individual psychological formulation of the necessary increase of social interest, let alone act contrary to it—then I should say that this is an impossibility. It may be a case where the chick was smarter than the hen; the patient increased his social interest contrary to the will and the intention of the therapist" (1933c, p. 75).*

The contrast is furnished by an education which withdraws from the need for affection even the cultural satisfaction, leaving the child alone with his yearning for love. When the child is cut off from all objects of affection, he has only his own person as the goal of his desire. The social feelings remain rudimentary, and those tendencies toward satisfaction which have the various forms of self-love for their content gain control.

The child may arrive at a position of aggression. Every unsatisfied drive ultimately orients the organism toward aggression against the environment. The rough characters and the unbridled, incorrigible children can instruct us in the way the continuously unsatisfied drive for affection stimulates the paths of aggression. We believe that an understanding of the delinquent is considerably facilitated by this consideration.

A great many educational applications follow from this. May every educator test these out and continue to work on them, but may he beware of unknowingly carrying his own wishes and feelings onto his argumentation, as often happens when we work with a subject matter with which we are connected by memory traces of our own. One should also keep in mind that nature is not narrow-minded. It would be a pity if each error of education had its consequences. As a general rule one can maintain, however, that the child's need for affection should not be satisfied as a game (zum Spiel) alone, but primarily for culturally useful results. Furthermore the child should not be blocked in the satisfaction of his affection, as long as he can achieve this along cultural paths.

COMMENT *In this last paragraph, we find a warning to the educator, which must be understood to hold also for the psychotherapist, not to project his own feelings onto the subject. We also find a foreshadowing of Adler's view of the individual's creativity, with its consequent encroachment upon determinism, when he voices the reminder that an error in education does not have inevitable consequences.*

FOOTNOTES TO CHAPTER ONE

1. **1 and 2:** "Die Theorie der Organminderwertigkeit und ihre Bedeutung für Philosophie und Psychologie" (1907b), pp. 11–13 and 11.
2. **1, 2, 3:** "Organminderwertigkeit" (1907b), pp. 12, 12–13, and 13.
3. **1 to 5:** "Organminderwertigkeit" (1907b), pp. 12, 14–15, 15–16, 16, and 16–17.
4. **1 and 2:** "Organminderwertigkeit" (1907b), pp. 17 and 17–18.
5. **1 to 8, 10:** "Organminderwertigkeit" (1907b), pp. 19, 19–20, 20, 20–21, 21, 21, 21–22, 21, and 22; **9:** *Study of Organ Inferiority and its Psychical Compensation* (1907a), p. 66.
6. **1 and 2:** "Der Aggressionstrieb im Leben und in der Neurose" (1908a), pp. 23 and 24.

7. 1 and 2: "Aggressionstrieb" (1908a), pp. 24–25.
8. 1, 2, 3: "Aggressionstrieb" (1908a), p. 28.
9. 1 to 8: "Aggressionstrieb" (1908a), pp. 29, 29 and 32, 29, 30, 30, 30–31, 31, and 31.
10. 1 and 2: "Das Zärtlichkeitsbedürfnis des Kindes" (1908b), pp. 50 and 51.
11. 1 to 6: "Zärtlichkeitsbedürfnis" (1908b), pp. 50–51, 51, 51, 52, 52, and 52–53.

CHAPTER TWO

MASCULINE PROTEST AND CRITIQUE OF FREUD

COMMENT   *Adler's first contributions from the years 1907 to 1908 were toward establishing the unity of the organism on the basis of organic interaction and organization. He described the modifiability of the expression of the drives and their organization into higher orders. Although he mentioned the psyche and psychological compensation, he dealt with organs, nervous superstructures, and drives, and thus remained within the terms and confines of a biologically oriented psychology. Feelings of inferiority had not even been mentioned. It was "the unsuccessful but indulged organ which keeps the psyche in a state of continual irritation" (1907a, p. 41). "Ordinarily the central nervous system will play the largest part in this compensation" (1907a, p. 57). Although Adler deviated from Freud in emphasizing the whole and organization, there was still a meeting ground in the form of the biological basis which both still shared.*

In the following papers from 1910 to 1911, Adler took the important step from biologically oriented "objective" drive psychology toward a psychologically oriented, subjectivistic psychology by the recognition of the "subjective feeling of inferiority." Objective conditions were thus gradually replaced in their dominant importance by subjective attitudes; that is, organ inferiorities became psychologically effective not through the nervous superstructure, but through the intervention of feelings of inferiority.

What differentiates this view from Adler's ultimate theory is that objective causality is still accepted. It is "objective phenomena" which give rise to the "subjective feeling of inferiority." Later, when fictional finalism (see Chapter 3) had replaced objective causality, Adler wrote on this point: "More important than innate disposition, objective experience, and environment is the subjective evaluation of these. Furthermore, this evaluation stands in a certain, often strange, relation to reality" (see p. 93).

The shift in emphasis from biological conditions and drives to subjective feelings was no longer reconcilable with the Freudian position. It led to a detailed critique of Freudian concepts and ultimately to the complete parting of ways.

A. Inferiority Feeling and Masculine Protest (1910)

COMMENT   The present paper introduced a concept which was, of necessity, unacceptable to Freud. Whereas for Freud sexual libido was the main dynamic force, Adler now called the main dynamic principle the "masculine protest" and conceived it as the striving to be strong and powerful in compensation for feeling unmanly, for a feeling of inferiority. The masculine protest shares most of the characteristics of the earlier aggression drive, which, however, was not based on a subjective feeling, but on a confluence of drives.

The sexual terms which Adler uses here, in contradistinction to Freud's usage, are not to be taken literally. Feeling unmanly is the analogy for the feeling of inferiority; masculine and feminine are metaphors for strength and weakness. Psychological hermaphroditism, another term introduced here, merely means that an individual usually has submissive ("feminine") as well as aggressive ("masculine") traits.

Two explanations may be offered for this choice of sexual analogies. The first is that Adler was still a member of the Freudian circle, and the change from understanding sex literally to seeing it symbolically could still take place within that frame of reference, at least in terminology. The second reason is that the social situation in Europe at that time may well have corresponded to the sexual analogy of masculine superiority and feminine inferiority.

Whatever the reasons, the choice of the metaphor was not a particularly happy one, for it naturally led to a good deal of confusion. It was therefore a considerable advance in clarity when Adler, a few years later, formulated the basic dynamics as the striving for superiority and overcoming, and reserved the term masculine protest for a new, restricted meaning (see below, p. 49).

1. HOMOSEXUALITY AND HERMAPHRODITISM[1]

Almost every author who has investigated the problem of human hermaphroditism [the union of the two sexes in the same individual], has mentioned the fact that, in addition to the physical characteristics of the opposite sex, there are often or even regularly to be found psychological attributes and traits of the opposite sex. Krafft-Ebing, Dessoir, Halban, Fliess, Freud, Hirschfeld, and others are examples. Among these men, Freud in particular has studied the phenomena of inversion, that is, homosexuality, in neurosis and found that homosexual traits are present in every case of neurosis. Since then, this observation has been amply confirmed. The relationship between prostitution and homosexuality has been shown (1908c). Before this, Fliess was of the opinion that the male neurotic suffered from suppression of his feminine traits, the female neurotic, from repression of her masculine traits. Sadger held similar ideas.

A careful study of the neuroses in reference to traits of hermaphroditism yields the following results. Physical signs of the opposite sex are indeed found with striking frequency. Thus we find feminine habitus in male neurotics and masculine habitus in female neurotics, as a rule together with inferiority of other organs. Whether these bodily phenomena right from the start bear any kind of genetic relationship to the psyche of the opposite sex, as Fliess assumes and as Krafft-Ebing specified, at present cannot be proven.

2. FEELING UNMANLY AS INFERIORITY FEELING[2]

It can be shown, however, that in children with inferior organs and glandular systems, motor and general bodily development often deviate from the norm, that their growth and functioning show deficiencies, and that sickness and weakness are prominent especially at the beginning of their development, although these may later on often give way to robust health and strength.

These objective phenomena frequently give rise to a subjective feeling of inferiority and thus hinder the independence of the child, increase his need for support and affection, and often characterize an individual thoroughout life. Weakness, clumsiness, awkwardness, sickness, childhood disorders such as enuresis, stuttering, deficiencies in the visual and auditory apparatus, innate or early acquired blemishes, and extreme ugliness, are all able to give a deep foundation for the feeling of inferiority in relation to stronger persons and to fixate it for life. This is especially true of the feeling toward the father. Significant traits of obedience, submission, and devoted love toward the father are characteristic of many children, especially those disposed toward neurosis.

Such children are thus often placed in a role which appears to them as unmanly. All neurotics have a childhood behind them in which they were moved by doubt regarding the achievement of full masculinity. The renunciation of masculinity, however, appears to the child as synonymous with femininity, an opinion which holds not only for the child, but also for the greater part of our culture. Thus a wide area of originally childish value judgments is given. Accordingly, any form of uninhibited aggression, activity, potency, power, and the traits of being brave, free, rich, aggressive, or sadistic can be considered as masculine. All inhibitions and deficiencies, as well as cowardliness, obedience, poverty, and similar traits, can be considered as feminine.

3. PSYCHOLOGICAL HERMAPHRODITISM[3]

One can now easily see that the child plays a double role for a while. He shows tendencies of submission to the parents and educators on the one hand, and wishes, fantasies, and actions which express his striving for independence, a will of his own, and significance on the other hand. This inner disunion in the child is the prototype and foundation of the most important psychological phenomena, especially neurosis, the splitting of consciousness, and indecision, and may result in a variety of outcomes in later life. As a rule, individuals tend sometimes in the feminine and sometimes in the masculine direction. Along with this they will make efforts toward self-consistency. This usually initiates a compromise: feminine behavior in men (for example, shyness and submissiveness, masochism, homosexuality) and masculine roles in women (emancipation, polyandry, compulsion neurosis as disturbance of the feminine role), or an apparently random co-existence of masculine and feminine character traits.

4. THE MASCULINE PROTEST AS OVERCOMPENSATION[4]

The starting point for the feminine tendencies of the neurotic is the child's feeling of weakness in the face of adults. From this arises a need for support, a demand for affection, a physiological and psychological dependency and submission. In cases of early and subjectively felt organ inferiority, these traits are intensified. Increased dependency and the intensified feeling of our own littleness and weakness lead to inhibition of aggression and thereby to the phenomenon of anxiety. Uncertainty regarding our own ability arouses doubt and inaugurates vacillation between the feminine tendencies of anxiety and related phenomena and the masculine tendencies of aggression and compulsion phenomena.

The structure of the neuroses (neurasthenia, hysteria, phobia, paranoia, and especially compulsion neurosis) shows the often ramified feminine traits carefully hidden by hypertrophied masculine wishes and efforts. This is the masculine protest. It follows necessarily as overcompensation, because the feminine tendency is evaluated negatively and is retained only in sublimated form for external advantages (love, freedom from punishment, praise for obedience and submission).

Every form of inner compulsion in normal and neurotic individuals may be derived from this attempt at a masculine protest. Where it succeeds, it naturally strengthens the masculine tendencies enormously, posits for itself the highest and often unattainable goals, develops a craving for satisfaction and triumph, intensifies all abilities and egotistical drives, increases envy, avarice, and ambition, and brings about an inner restlessness which makes any external compulsion, lack of satisfaction, disparagement, and injury unbearable. Defiance, vengeance, and resentment are its steady accompaniments. Through a boundless increase in sensitivity, it leads to continuous conflicts. Normal and pathological phantasies of grandeur and daydreams are forced by such overly strong masculine protests and are experienced as surrogates of drive satisfaction. Dream life also comes entirely under the dominance of the masculine protest. Every dream, when analyzed, shows the tendency to move away from the feminine line toward the masculine line.

One can easily understand that the child uses the traits of the mother for the representation of his feminine lines and those of the father for his masculine lines. The masculine protest intensifies the desires of the child, who then seeks to surpass the father in every respect and comes into conflicts with him. Thus those secondary traits arise which correspond to desires aimed at the mother (Oedipus allegory).

5. THE MASCULINE PROTEST IN WOMEN[5]

All this applies, of course, to women as well as to men. The masculine protest in women is usually covered up and transformed, seeking its triumph with feminine means. Very frequently one finds during analysis the wish to become transformed into a man. Vaginism, sexual anesthesia, and many well-known neurotic manifestations originate from this tendency.

COMMENT *When the striving for superiority and overcoming replaced the masculine protest, the term became limited to the more restricted meaning of the preceding paragraph. It referred to manifestations in women protesting against their feminine role. In girls "fighting and scuffling, climbing and chasing, exaggerated achievements in sports, as well as dreams of such activities, as Smith and Stanley Hall also have stressed, point to dissatisfaction with the feminine role and to the 'masculine protest' " (1930c, p. 28).*

When the masculine protest is increased, it produces such symptoms as "dysmennorrhea, vaginism, frigidity, few children; sometimes a late marriage, a weak husband; and nervous disorders which are often related to the menses, pregnancy, childbirth, and the menopause" (1930c, p. 11).

But the masculine protest may also result in positive adjustment. "The girl, under the influence of our present-day cultural pressures, develops a pronounced feeling of inferiority and pushes on vigorously. She thus dis-closes a more thorough training which often gives her marked traits of greater energy. This is the prelude to the masculine protest, which in the development of girls can produce a vast number of both good and bad consequences; these comprise all sorts of human excellencies and short-comings, possibly leading to the rejection of love or homosexuality" (1933a, p. 153).

6. THE MASCULINE PROTEST AND NEUROSIS[6]

COMMENT *The discussion of the masculine protest so far presents a parallel to the description of the neurotic disposition in Chapter 9. The masculine protest has been described as a cluster of certain overcompensatory character traits which make an individual neurotically disposed. The neurosis breaks out, that is, the disabling symptoms appear, when this disposition leads to complete failure in the face of a new situation. From here on the masculine protest is described in its manifestations after the individual has been cut off from all personal success. This section is parallel to the discussion of the onset of neurosis in Chapter 11.*

If the patient finds himself cut off from all personal success, if the satisfaction of his usually overreaching masculine protest has failed in the main line, which also consists [but only in part] of the sex drive, then the neurosis, towards which steps have long since been taken, finally breaks out. He then tries to satisfy his masculine ambition through displacement onto other persons and goals. The inhibition and blocking also may be more intense in their effect, and such transformations of the aggression drive result as described in the article on "The Aggression Drive" [1908a].

The neurosis breaks out when the masculine protest has failed in a main line. The feminine traits then apparently predominate, but only under continuous increase of the masculine protest and pathological attempts to break through along masculine side lines. The fate of such attempts differs. Either they succeed without bringing real satisfaction and harmony, or they fail, as often in neurosis, and force the patient further into the feminine role, apathy, anxiety, and mental, physical, and sexual insufficiency.

It is the concern of education and psychotherapy to uncover these dynamics and to make them conscious. Overgrowth of masculine and feminine traits then disappears, and the childlike evaluation makes room for a more mature philosophy of life. Oversensitivity disappears, and the patient learns to bear the tensions from the environment without losing his equanimity. He who was before "a toy of dark and unconscious impulses becomes the conscious master or sufferer of his feelings."

COMMENT   *Freud took an immediate interest in Adler's use of the term masculine protest, "but in a sense different from his" (36, III, p. 426), and he continued the argumentation against Adler's original definition to his last years, by which time Adler had long since given the term a much more restricted meaning and a subordinate position in his system.*

In his paper "On Narcissism," in 1914, Freud stated that Adler had exalted the conception of the masculine protest "almost to the position of the sole motive power concerned in the formation of neurosis and also of character," and that he had conceived it "as having its origin, not in a narcissistic, and therefore still libidinal, trend, but in a social valuation. Psychoanalytic research has, from the very beginning, recognized the existence and significance of the 'masculine protest,' but has always regarded it, in opposition to Adler, as narcissistic in nature and derived from the castration complex. It appertains to the formation of character, into the genesis of which it enters along with many other factors, and it is completely inadequate to explain the problems of the neuroses, in which Adler will take account of nothing but the manner in which they serve the interests of the ego" (36, IV, pp. 49–50). This is, of course, exactly what Adler was aiming at, namely to understand the neuroses, like all other psychological manifestations, as serving the interests of the ego, or rather the self in its relations to society, although he had not yet expressed this so clearly.

Freud's masculine protest, by contrast, is the equivalent of the castration complex, which he defined as "in the boy, anxiety concerning the penis; in the girl, envy of the penis" (36, IV, p. 49). Whereas for Adler the biological factors of sex were subsumed under the masculine protest, for Freud the order remained reversed. How literally Freud took his biological interpretation is well illustrated in the following passage: "We can indicate the ultimate outcome of the infantile penis-wish in those persons in whom the conditions for a neurosis in later life are absent: it changes into the wish for a man, accepting the man as an appendage, as it were, of the penis" (36, II, p. 167). Thus even the whole man is reduced to that biological aspect which has the most immediate and distinguishing biological significance.

Despite the fact that Freud later became more cognizant of the ego and social relationships, he strongly maintained to the end his original position in the above regard. He wrote in 1937: "At no point in one's analytic work does one suffer more from the oppressive feeling that all one's efforts have been in vain and from the suspicion that one is 'talking to the winds' than when one is trying to persuade a female patient to abandon her wish for a penis on the ground of its being unrealizable, or to convince a male patient that a passive attitude towards another man does not always signify castration and that in many relations in life it is indispensable . . . We often feel that, when we have reached the wish for a penis and the masculine protest, we have penetrated all the psychological strata and reached 'bedrock' and that our task is accomplished. And this is probably correct, for in the psychical field the biological factor is really the rock-bottom. The repudiation of femininity must surely be a biological fact, part of the great riddle of sex. We must not be misled by the term 'masculine protest' into supposing that what the man repudiates is the attitude of passivity, or, as we may say, the social aspect of femininity. Such a notion is speedily contradicted by the observation that the attitude such men display towards women is often masochistic or actually slavish. What they reject is not passivity in general but passivity in relation to men. That is to say, the 'masculine protest' is in fact nothing other than fear of castration" (36, V, p. 357).

This view of Freud was criticized by Clara Thompson, a psychoanalyst, writing more than forty years after Adler's paper. In showing that Freud failed to recognize the importance of social factors, she says: "Much which is known today to be culturally determined behavior in man was believed by him to be the expression of unalterable biological trends" (110, pp. 135–136). Where he did include cultural influences, "he assumed that the cultural attitude was determined by the biological situation" (110, p. 133). She criticizes Freud's literal concept of the penis envy, stating that lack of penis may become a symbol for a felt inferiority in a member of the underprivileged sex just as a dark skin may become a symbol and a justification for discrimination (109).

B. Inferiority Feeling and Defiance and Obedience (1910)

COMMENT   In the preceding part, we found that the masculine protest as overcompensation for the inferiority feeling could find expression through both masculine and feminine means. In the present part, which is taken from a paper addressed to educators, this thought is expressed in the parallel terms of defiance and obedience.

The significance of this paper for Adler's development is that it contains the first use of the term attitude, thereby marking a further step in the direction toward a subjective psychology, and that it describes the inferiority feeling as an attitude. Although the concommitant use of the term drive indicates that Adler had not yet reached consistency, he must have been aware of the importance of introducing the term attitude. In a procedure unusual for him, he made a footnote regarding the origin of the term: "It is von Kries who was the first to point out the 'attitude mechanism' (Einstellungsmechanismus)" (1910b, p. 91). And indeed this is confirmed by Woodworth (120, p. 794), who cites von Kries (64) as giving the first comprehensive discussion of set or Einstellung.

From this first mention of the term, Adler's psychology grew rapidly into one in which attitudes and opinions became the very core. Two years later when his The Neurotic Character appeared it carried as motto: Omnia ex opinione suspensa sunt.

1. INFERIORITY FEELING AND COMPENSATORY ATTITUDES[7]

Children who have an organ inferiority, who are weak, clumsy, sickly, retarded in growth, ugly or deformed, or who have retained infantile forms of behavior are very prone to acquire through their relations to the environment a feeling of inferiority [later revision: increased feeling of inferiority]. This feeling rests heavily upon them, and they aim to overcome it by all means.

The character traits which are grouped around this inferiority feeling, and those usually more clearly grouped around the resulting increased aggression against the environment, may be called abnormal attitudes. Such traits as timidity, indecision, insecurity, shyness, cowardliness, increased need for support, submissive obedience [which Adler calls "dishonest obedience" below], as well as phantasies and even wishes, which one can summarize as ideas of 'smallness' or masochistic tendencies, correspond to the inferiority feeling. Above this network of personality traits there appear, with defensive and compensatory intent, impudence, courage, impertinence, inclination toward rebellion, stubbornness, and defiance, accompanied by phantasies and wishes of the role of a hero, warrior, robber, in short, ideas of grandeur and sadistic impulses.

The inferiority feeling finally culminates in a never-ceasing, always exaggerated feeling of being slighted, so that the Cinderella fantasy becomes complete with its longing expectation of redemption and triumph. The frequent fantasies of children regarding their princely origin and temporary banishment from their "real" home are of this kind.

But reality defies the harmlessness of the fairy tale. The entire drive life of the child is intensified and gains the upper hand. At the slightest injury, thoughts of revenge and death become expressed against the self and the environment, childhood disorders and bad habits are defiantly retained, and sexual precocity and desire burst forth in order to be like the grown-ups, those who really count. The father is the one who is big, knows everything, and has everything, or it is his substitute, the mother, older brother, or the teacher. He becomes the opponent who must be fought. The child becomes blind and deaf to his guidance, misunderstands all good intentions, becomes suspicious and extremely keen to all injuries coming from him. In short, the child has an attitude of defiance, but precisely on account of it has rendered himself completely dependent upon the opinion or attitude of others.

In other cases the child may lose his aggression tendency through his disposition and his experiences and, learning from the latter, may seek to gain drive satisfaction and his final triumph through passive behavior, submission, and honest and dishonest obedience. Hate breaks out at times, although often only in dreams and neurotic symptoms. These are signs, however, to those who understand, that the ground has been undermined and is suited for neurosis and prohibited behavior, unless the child proves himself capable of triumphant achievements or complete indifference. If the attitude of obedience and submission predominates, the next of kin frequently congratulate themselves on their model child without suspecting that in unfavorable cases life, love, or vocation may easily bring about decay and submersion into neurosis.

Thus in both main groups of character traits we see the effect of erroneous attitudes, the compensatory significance of which consists in the annihilation of the inferiority feeling through a compensatory protest and through phantasies of greatness. For the most part, we find mixed cases in which traits of obedience and defiance run parallel.

2. THE SEXUAL ROLE AND DEFIANCE[8]

We have found a second reinforcing condition for the attitude of defiance in the child's subjective uncertainty regarding his sexual role. This condition does not in any way exist in isolation but is closely connected with the first. The search for the sexual role usually begins in the fourth year of life and increases the child's general curiosity. In this connection, a lack of sexual enlightenment makes itself particularly felt. Not knowing the significance of his sexual tools, the child seeks the differences between the sexes in dress, hair, bodily and mental traits, and, in doing so, often makes mistakes. Even when the child has recognized the difference in the sex organs in their significance for the sexual role, there is often a remnant of uncertainty in that thoughts of a change of the sex organs come into mind suddenly, or are brought on by threats from the parents.

To this is added the arch evil of our culture, the excessive pre-eminence of manliness. All children who have been in doubt as to their sexual role exaggerate the traits which they consider masculine, above all defiance.

3. PRACTICAL IMPLICATIONS[9]

Here, as elsewhere, love can be an ameliorating factor. Hate or punishment certainly cannot be. Such children, in their everlasting greed for triumph, may at times even become the material from which, under favorable conditions, the great personages, the artists and poets develop. For the many others, however, for those children who are harmed by their erroneous attitude, only Psychoanalysis [in later editions: Individual Psychology] can bring about a change. The starting point, the erroneous attitude, and the final goal of the masculine protest are withdrawn from consciousness, and the whole sequence of effects necessarily takes place in the unconscious.

I have tried to show in bare outlines that the character traits of defiance and obedience are based on unconscious and erroneous attitudes of the child, and I may now well add that educational measures at home and at school cannot cope with these traits as long as such measures are unable to improve the erroneous attitude. Education must remove the possibility of an [increased] feeling of inferiority arising in the child. Sick and weakly children should be treated and strengthened as soon as possible. Where this is precluded, the educational plan must aim particularly at bringing the child to self-reliance of judgment, at making him more independent of the opinion of others, and at setting up substitute goals. One should not educate for obedience if one wants to avoid the attitude of defiance. Even if in doing so a large part of the belief in authority is left out, this is not to be regretted. The defiant child is only defying authority. We are approaching a time where everyone will take his place as an equal, self-reliantly and freely, no longer in the service of a person, but in the service of a common idea, the idea of physical and mental progress.

c. Critique of Freud's Concept of Sexuality (1911)

COMMENT   *In the autumn of 1902 Freud, according to Ernest Jones,*[1] *addressed a postcard to Adler, Max Kahane, Rudolf Reitler, and Wilhelm Stekel, suggesting that they meet at his apartment for discussions of the psychology of the neuroses. This was the beginning of the Vienna Psychoanalytic Society. Kahane and Reitler had attended Freud's university lectures, while Stekel had been a patient of Freud. In explanation of Adler's invitation his biographers have reported that he had written a letter to a newspaper in in defense of Freud's The Interpretation of Dreams. We have not been able to verify this, but neither have we found any other explanation why Adler was invited.*

On the other hand, Jones[2] *and Carl Furtmüller (44) agree that there was never a close personal relationship between Adler and Freud. Still, Adler was one of the most valued members of the Vienna Psychoanalytic Society, eventually its president, and co-editor with Freud and Stekel of the Zentralblatt für Psychoanalyse, as mentioned initially (p. 3). Thus when Adler now become Freud's critic, he was well qualified. His understanding of psychoanalysis was probably second only to Freud's.*

When the difference in theory between Adler and Freud had become acute, the Vienna Psychoanalytic Society, of which Adler was then president, decided to hear a comprehensive presentation of his theories, which the members could discuss at length. Adler read three papers in the course of these meetings, the last on February 1, 1911 (24, pp. 230–231). Selections from these papers, as found in Heilen und Bilden, are presented in this and in the next two sections. This series of addresses represented the culmination of a development which led to Adler's resignation from his psychoanalytic offices and his complete separation from Freud.

1. LIMITATION OF THE SEX DRIVE[10]

It is idle to ask whether a neurosis is possible without inclusion of the sex drive. After all, it has a similarly great significance in the life of everyone. The real question is whether the beginning and the end and all the symptom formations of the neurosis are to be found in the fate of the

---

[1] Jones, E. *The Life and Work of Sigmund Freud.* Vol. 2. New York: Basic Books, 1955, pp. 7 and 8.

[2] *Ibid.*, p. 131.

sex drive. I must answer this question with a brief description, not of the isolated sex drive, but of its development in the ensemble of the drives.

Biologically speaking it would not be possible to maintain that every drive has a sexual component, including the drive to eat, the drive to see, and the drive to touch. One must assume rather that organic evolution has led to developments which we must regard as the differentiation of originally present potentialities of the cell. Thus a nutritive organ has followed the will and need of assimilation; touch, auditory, and visual organs have followed the will and necessity to feel, hear, and see; a procreative organ followed the will and necessity for progeny.

The protection of all these organs became so necessary that it was approached from two sides: through the sensations of pain and of pleasure. But this was not enough, and thus a third safeguard developed in the form of the organ of prudence, the organ of thinking, the brain. In the laboratory of nature, all three safeguards can be found. While peripheral defects or accentuated pain and pleasure sensations may arise in the inferior organ, the most variable part, the central nervous system, takes over the final compensation.

COMMENT *What Adler does here in fact is to state his position as a centralistic rather than a peripheralistic psychologist. It is the central nervous system which inaugurates the compensation, thus making all peripheral functions, including sex, subordinate to one central function. Later the safeguarding tendency virtually replaced compensation.*

2. RELATIVITY OF LIBIDO[11]

It is a double wrong to confuse the concept of the inferior organ with the "erogenous zone" of Havelock Ellis. First, only a small part of the inferior organs shows an increased pleasure feeling or feels a tickle in its peripheral part. Should one, as Sadger attempts, count the inferior urinary passage, gall bladder, pancreas, adenoids, and lymph glands among the erogenous zones? Second, the concept of the erogenous zone is unjustly prejudiced. We do not want to deny that conscious and unconscious perverse fantasies may be associated with the inferior organ. But this occurs only later in life, with the aid of false notions about sex or under the pressure of certain safeguarding tendencies. In order to become erogenous, such zones need a secondary confluence of drives under the pressure of mistaken sexual theories or conflicting superfluous safeguarding tendencies.

The statement that the child is a polymorphous pervert, is a hysteron proteron [reverses the order of things], is a poetic license. The "sexual constitution" can be cultivated at will through experiences and education, especially on the basis of organ inferiorities. Even prematurity can be kept down or advanced. Sadistic and masochistic impulses are simply a development from the more harmless relationships of the regularly present need for support and the impulse toward independence once the masculine protest is involved with its intensification of rage, anger, and defiance.

COMMENT   *The term polymorphous pervert had been used by Freud in the following connections. "I have described in my Drei Abhandlungen zur Sexualtheorie how the constitutional disposition of the child is by far more variegated than we might have expected, how it deserves to be called 'polymorphously perverse,' and how what is called the normal sexual function develops from this disposition through certain components of it becoming repressed . . . I was able to designate neurosis as the 'negative' of perversion" (36, I, p. 280). "In this respect, the child perhaps does not behave differently from the average uncultured woman in whom the same polymorphous-perverse disposition exists . . . The same polymorphous or infantile disposition fits the prostitute for her professional activity. Still it is absolutely impossible not to recognize in the uniform disposition of all perversions a universal and primitive human tendency, as shown by an enormous number of prostitutes and by many women who do not necessarily follow this calling" (33, pp. 592–593).*

Only the sexual organ, and it alone, develops the sexual factor in real life and in the neurosis. If sexuality enters relations with the total drive life and its causes, the same is true of any other drive. Before the sex drive has reached a degree worth mentioning, approximately at the end of the first year, the psychological life of the child is already richly developed. Freud mentions the view of old authors, who were joined by Czerny, that children who are stubborn on the toilet often become nervous. In contrast to other authors, he traces this defiance to the fact that they have sexual pleasure-feelings during retention of feces. Although I have seen no incontestable case of this sort, I do not wish to deny that children who have such sensations when they retain feces will prefer precisely this kind of resistance when they become defiant. But here, nevertheless, it is the defiance which is decisive, while the organ inferiority determines the localization and selection of the symptoms. I have much more frequently observed that such defiant children produce the feces before or after they have been brought to the toilet or right next to the toilet; the same is true of the urination of such children. It is the same with eating and drinking; we need only to curb the drinking of certain children, and their libido increases into infinity; we need only to tell them that eating regularly is important, and their libido drops to zero. Can we take such "libido quantities" seriously, let alone energetically, and use them for comparisons? I have seen a thirteen-month-old boy who had barely learned to stand and to walk. If we sat him down, he got up; if we told him, "Sit down," he remained standing and looked mischievous. His six-year-old sister said on one such occasion, "Keep standing," and the child sat down. These are the beginnings of the masculine protest. The sexuality which is meanwhile budding is continuously exposed to its impacts and urges.

I have pointed out in several papers that especially children who have a noticeable organ inferiority, who suffer from defects, who are insecure, and who fear humiliation and punishment the most develop the craving and haste which ultimately dispose to neurosis. At an early age they will avoid tests of their worth or evade injuries to their sensitivity. They are bashful, blush easily, evade any test of their ability, and lose at an early age their spontaneity. This uncomfortable condition strongly urges toward safeguards. They want to be petted or want to do everything alone, are afraid of any kind of work, or read incessantly. As a rule they are precocious. Their thirst for knowledge is a compensatory product of their insecurity and reaches at an early age toward questions about birth and sex differences. This strained and continuous fantasy activity must be understood as a stimulus for the sex drive as soon as the primitive knowledge of sex processes has been achieved. Here, as well, their goal is to prove their masculinity.

3. SEX AND THE MASCULINE PROTEST[12]

Again we ask if that which the neurotic shows as libido is to be taken at face value. We would say no. His sexual prematurity is forced. His compulsion to masturbate serves his defiance and as a safeguard against the demon woman, and his love-passion only aims at victory. His love-bondage is a game which aims at not submitting to the "right" partner, and his perverted fantasies, even his active perversions, serve him only to keep him away from actual love. They of course serve him as a substitute, but only because he wants to play his hero role and because he is afraid of getting caught under the wheels if he goes the normal way. The so-called core problem of the neurosis, the incest fantasy, usually nourishes the belief in one's own overpowering libido and therefore avoids as much as possible any "real" danger.

How, then, does sexuality come into the neurosis and what part does it play there? It is awakened early and stimulated when existing inferiority and a strong masculine protest are present; it is regarded and felt in gigantic proportions so that the patient may safeguard himself in good time; or it is devaluated and eliminated as a factor if this serves the tendency of the patient. In general it is impossible to take the sexual impulses of the neurotic or of civilized man as genuine and to count on them, let alone to continue to represent them, no matter how they are viewed, as the fundamental factor of the healthy or diseased mental life. They are never causes, but always worked-over material and means of personal striving.

D. Critique of Other Freudian Concepts (1911)

1. REPRESSION[13]

I may presuppose in this circle a knowledge of repression as this has been outlined and described by Freud. The causes of the repression, however, and the path which leads from the repression to the neurosis are by no means as clear as one generally assumes in the Freudian school. The number of auxiliary constructs which appear in attempts of explanation are exceedingly great, and they often turn out to be unproven, even unprovable. Constructs which, in the most obvious manner, take recourse to an analogy from physics or chemistry by speaking of damming up, increased pressure, fixation, flowing back into infantile paths, projections, and regression must also be mentioned.

COMMENT   It is, of course, no accident that Freud chose analogies from physics or chemistry. Rather, these are an expression of his ontological position as a reductionistic natural scientist. As such, he hoped that ultimately psychology could be reduced to physiology and chemistry. Thus we find the following significant statement by Freud in a discussion of processes related to the life and death instincts: "The deficiencies in our *description would probably vanish if we were already in a position to re-place the psychological terms by physiological or chemical ones" (34, p. 83).*

In the papers of this school, the causes of the repression are conceived too summarily and as dogmatically used stereotypes. Yet these expositions contain elements of intuition, the basis of which is always worth determining. If we trace repression back to the "sexual constitution," the problem of successful and unsuccessful repression becomes all the more mysterious. If we go no further than the simple statement of repression, we show a lack of psychological insight. The causes of sublimation and substitute formations are likewise not explained by repeating the same idea in different words. Organic repression appears, then, as nothing but an emergency exit, showing that changes in the modes of operation are possible. It has hardly any bearing on the theory of the neuroses. Repressed drives and drive components, repressed complexes, repressed fantasies, repressed events from life, and repressed wishes are considered under organic repression.

The real question is this: Is the driving factor in the neurosis the repression, or is it, as I should like to state it in neutral terms for the time being, the deviating, irritated psyche, in the examination of which repression can also be found?

COMMENT   *Adler's definitely affirmative answer to this question appears in the next section under the side-heading, Safeguarding tendencies in place of repression. Freud, years later, modified his views in the direction of the Adlerian answer when he subsumed repression under the ego-defense-mechanisms (see p. 264). He then, indeed, recognized that repression was exerted by the ego, the equivalent of Adler's "irritated psyche" here.*

And now I beg you to consider the Freudian position: Repression takes place under the pressure of culture, under the pressure of the ego drives. In giving this explanation, the thoughts of an abnormal sexual constitution, of sexual prematurity are resorted to. Question: Where does our culture come from? Answer: From the repression.

COMMENT   *In this question, Adler tersely accuses Freud of circular reasoning. The accusation did not go unanswered, although Freud took it as one of "playing with words" rather than circular reason-*

ing. His reply was: "What it means is simply that civilization is based upon the repressions effected by former generations, and that each fresh generation is required to maintain this civilization by effectuating the same repressions. I once heard of a child that thought people were laughing at it, and began to cry, because when it asked 'Where do eggs come from?' they told it 'From hens', and then when it went on to enquire where hens came from, they said 'From eggs.' But they were not playing with words; on the contrary, they were telling it the truth" (36, I, p. 346). The difference between Adler's "culture" and Freud's "civilization" is one of translation only; the original German word for both is Kultur.

At first the chicken-and-the-egg argument would seem irrefutable, but significantly, the child's crying furnishes the clue that there is something wrong here. Obviously the child did not find the answer to his question satisfactory. And why not? Because though they were telling him the truth, they remained on a level of superficial, one might say symptomatic, description, making no attempt to show the underlying genetic relationship. Similarly Freud's reply merely restates the original proposition which Adler criticized, without adding anything, or going any deeper.

Adler broke up this circularity by supplying the underlying explanatory principle in the form of the "psyche" or the self, subsequently formulated more dynamically as the individual's unique style of life. According to Adler, both repression and the culture are products of the self, the latter the common product of many selves.

The Adler-Freud controversy thus was one of the psychology with a soul against a psychology, where the soul or the self was eclipsed. In this connection, Allport is "inclined to believe history will declare that psychoanalysis marked an inter-regnum in psychology between the time when it lost its soul, shortly after the Franco-Prussian War, and the time when it found it again, shortly after World War II" (3, p. 116). If this is true, then Adler was one of the voices in the wilderness of pre-World War I days crying that the self or the soul must remain the focal point if psychology is to provide satisfactory explanations.

2. THE EGO-LIBIDO ANTITHESIS[14]

What about the "ego drives," a concept as redundant and empty of meaning as few others? Do they not have the same "libidinal" character as the sex drives?

COMMENT *In spite of its brevity, this question contains perhaps the greatest indication of Adler's astuteness as a theoretician. Accepting for a moment, for the sake of argument, Freud's point of view, Adler here predicts the development which Freud took nine years later. In his important 1920 monograph, Freud actually saw the necessity of attributing to the ego instincts the same libidinal character as attributed to the sex instincts. Freud summarized the development of his new instinct theory as follows: "To begin with . . . we opposed the ego instincts to the sexual instincts of which the libido is the manifestation. Subsequently we came to closer grips with the analysis of the ego and recognized that a portion of the 'ego instincts' is also of a libidinal character and has taken the subject's own ego as its object. These narcissistic self-preservative instincts had thenceforward to be counted among the libidinal sexual instincts" (34, p. 84n).*

But Freud replaced the ego vs. libido dualism by a new one. "Our views have from the very first been dualistic, and today they are even more definitely dualistic than before" (34, p. 72). "A fresh opposition appeared between the libidinal (ego and object) instincts and others, which must be presumed to be present in the ego and which may perhaps actually be observed in the destructive instincts. Our speculations have transformed this opposition into one between the life instincts (Eros) and the death instincts" (34, p. 84n).

3. PLEASURE PRINCIPLE AND BACKWARD ORIENTATION[15]

Above all this, there hovers, as *deus ex machina*, one magic formula, namely, that of pleasure. Of this Nietzsche says so well, "because all pleasure wants eternity, wants deep, deep eternity." And Freud says: "Man cannot forego any pleasure he has ever experienced." According to this proposition, those drastic forms arise which every work of a disciple of Freud must show: the boy who is compelled to suckle at his mother's breast; the neurotic who seeks again and again the enjoyment of being bathed in wine or amniotic fluid; on up to the purer sphere where the man who is seeking the right girl will never find her because he is seeking the irreplaceable mother. Although this method created an important step forward, it tended to reify and freeze the psyche which, in reality, is constantly at work contemplating future events. The fastening upon the concept of the complex was a further step in giving priority to the topological view over the dynamic view. Naturally this was not carried so far that the principle of energetics, the *panta rhei* [constant flux], could not have been brought in as an afterthought.

COMMENT   *When Freud revised his hedonic theory in 1920, he retained his backward orientation. The revision actually represented a further strengthening of the backward view through the new concept of "a compulsion to repeat, which overrides the pleasure principle" (34, p. 25). "But how is the predicate of being 'instinctual' related to the compulsion to repeat? . . . An instinct is a compulsion inherent in organic life to restore an earlier state of things which the living entity has been obliged to abandon under the pressure of external disturbing forces; that is, it is a kind of organic elasticity, or, to put it another way, the expression of the inertia in organic life" (34, pp. 46–47).*

As Adler did not fail to point out, the principle of energetics, by which he meant the forward movement, is actually brought in at this point by Freud, when he says in regard to the tendency of children to repeat unpleasurable experiences in their play: "Each fresh repetition seems to strengthen the mastery they are in search of" (34, p. 45). But it is indeed brought in as a subordinate thought and dismissed again toward the end of the same monograph.

E. Social Values Instead of Drives (1911)

1. THE RELATIVITY OF DRIVES[16]

The ego drives must be understood, not as something rigidified and separate, but as the tension and attitudes toward the environment, as a striving toward power, toward dominance, toward being above. In accordance with this view, two possibilities must be considered, from the theoretical as well as from the practical standpoint: Wanting to be significant may inhibit, repress, or modify certain drives, and wanting to be significant will effect primarily the enhancement of other drives.

For our consideration, the constant factor is the culture, the society, and its institutions. Our drives, the satisfaction of which has been considered the end, act merely as the direction-giving means to initiate the satisfactions in the distant future. The eye, the ear, and also the skin have acquired the peculiar ability to extend our radius of effectiveness beyond the bodily-spatial sphere. By means of pre-sensitivity, our psyche steps beyond the present, that is, temporally beyond the limits of primitive drive-satisfaction. Here increased tensions are as urgent as repressions. In these relations [to the culture] rests the necessity for an extensive system of safeguards, one small part of which we must recognize in the neurosis.

These tensions begin on the first day of infancy and change all bodily and psychological tendencies to such an extent that, for example, what we see never represents something original or primary, something that has not been influenced, or something that has become changed only at a later time. Instead, the adaptation of the child directs and modifies the drives until he has adjusted himself in some way to the environment. In this first stage of life, one cannot speak of a permanent model nor of identification when the child orients himself by a model. For this is often the only way for immediate drive satisfaction.

If we consider the varied manner and tempo in which the satisfaction of drives has asserted itself everywhere and at all times, and how much it has depended on social institutions and economic conditions, we arrive at a conclusion which is analogous to the above, namely, that drive-satisfaction, and consequently the quality and strength of the drive, are at all times variable and therefore not measurable [with regard to their original condition]. In the talk on "Sexuality and Neurosis," I likewise came to the conclusion, based on observations regarding the sex drive of neurotics, that the apparently libidinous and sexual tendencies in the neurotic, as in the normal individual, in no way permit any conclusion regarding the strength or composition of his sex drive.

2. VALUES IN PLACE OF PLEASURE[17]

How then does the adaptation of a child to a given family environment take place? Let us recall how diversely the expressions of the child's organism shape themselves, even during the first months when it is still most possible to attain an over-all view. Some children can never get enough to eat, others are quite moderate; some refuse changes in diet, others want to eat everything. The same is true with regard to seeing, hearing, excretion, bathing, and relations to other persons of the environment. Yet already during the first days the child feels reassured if we take him into our arms. Educational influences which smooth the way for the child are of far-reaching significance here.

Already these first adaptations contain affective values in relation to the persons of the environment. The child is reassured, feels secure, loves, and obeys, or he becomes insecure, timid, defiant, and disobedient. If one intervenes early with intelligent tactics, a condition results which might be described as one of carefree cheerfulness, and the child will hardly feel the coercion which is contained in every education. Mistakes in education, on the other hand, especially when the organs are insufficiently developed, lead to such frequent disadvantages and feelings of displeasure that the child seeks safeguards. By and large, two chief trends remain from this situation: over-submissiveness or rebellion and tendency toward independence. Obedience or defiance—the human psyche is capable of operating in either of these directions.

Both these direction-giving tendencies modify, change, inhibit, or excite every drive-impulse to such an extent that anything that manifests itself as an innate drive can be understood only from this point of view. "Fair is foul, and foul is fair," as the witches chant in *Macbeth*. Grief becomes joy, pain changes into pleasure, life is thrown away, death appears desirable—as soon as defiance interferes strongly. What the opponent loves will be hated, and what others discard will be highly valued. What culture prohibits, what parents and educators disadvise, precisely that will be chosen as the most ardently desired goal. An object or a person will attain value only if others will suffer in consequence. Defiant individuals will always persecute others, yet will always consider themselves persecuted. Thus a certain greed or hasty desire arises which has one analogy only, namely, the murderous struggle of all against all, the kindling of envy, avarice, vanity, and ambition in our modern society. The tension from person to person is too great in the neurotic; his drive desire is so intensified that in restless expectation he continuously chases after his triumph. The clinging to old childhood disorders, such as thumb sucking, enuresis, nail biting, and stuttering, is to be explained in this way. In cases where these tendencies, which are only apparently libidinous, have been permanently retained we can confidently speak of defiance.

The same holds for so-called early masturbation, sexual precocity, and premature sexual intercourse. I knew a seventeen-year-old girl from a good family who had frequent sexual intercourse from her fourteenth year on. At that she was frigid. Whenever she quarreled with her mother, which happened regularly at brief intervals, she always knew how to secure sexual intercourse for herself. Another girl wet the bed after each depreciation on the part of her mother, and soiled it as well. Poor progress in school, forgetfulness, lack of occupational satisfaction, and compulsion to sleep likewise reveal themselves as phenomena of protest in the neurotic. In the struggle with the opponent they are retained as valuable, I do not say as pleasurable.

3. THE BASIS OF THE NEUROTIC VALUE SYSTEM[18]

Where do this craving for significance, this joy in the perverse, this defiant clinging to disorders, these safeguarding measures take their origin? As you know, I have made two foci of psychological development responsible for this, which will be mentioned here only briefly. The one rests in the emergence of an increased inferiority feeling which I was always able to observe in connection with inferior organs. The other is a more or less distinct hint of an earlier fear of playing a feminine role. Both support the need of rebellion and the attitude of defiance to such an extent that neurotic traits will always develop, whether the individual concerned is considered well, is being treated for neurosis, or makes a name for himself as a genius or as a criminal.

4. SAFEGUARDING TENDENCIES IN PLACE OF REPRESSION[19]

But now to the main question: Through what does the neurotic become ill? When does his neurosis become manifest? Freud has paid less attention to this point. But we know that he assumes the cause to lie in an incident through which the repression is strengthened and the old psychological conflict is renewed. It cannot be denied that this lacks clarity. Perhaps the present discussion will help to solve the problem.

According to my experience with the neurotically disposed individual, who in fact suffers continually, it is any feeling of disparagement or even any expectation of it to which he responds with an acute or chronic attack. The latter gives us the time from which we date the onset of the neurosis. If new drive-repressions appear, these are only incidental phenomena which form under the accentuated pressure of the masculine protest and of the striving for significance and the safeguarding tendencies.

5. DEPRECIATION TENDENCY[20]

Incidentally, the "olfactory component" to which Freud repeatedly has attributed special significance as a libidinous component appears more and more as a neurotic fraud. A neurotic actress in talking about love affairs said: "I am not at all afraid of such affairs. I am actually completely amoral. There is only one thing: I have found that all men smell bad, and that violates my esthetic sense." We will understand that with such an attitude one can well afford to be amoral without incurring any danger. Europeans and Chinese, Americans and Negroes, Jews and Arians mutually reproach one another for their smell. A four-year-old boy says each time he passes by the kitchen, "It stinks." The cook is his enemy. We wish to call this phenomenon the depreciation tendency, a tendency which finds an analogy in the fable of the fox and the sour grapes. [See pp. 267–269.]

COMMENT *Regarding olfaction, Freud had made the following state-*
ment in a discussion of a case of obsessional neurosis: "I
have come to recognize that a tendency to osphresiolagnia [erotic stimula-
tion produced by odors], which has become extinct since childhood, may
play a part in the genesis of neurosis, for instance, in certain forms of
fetishism. And here I should like to raise the general question whether
the atrophy of the sense of smell (which was an inevitable result of man's
assumption of an erect posture) and the consequent organic repression
of his osphresiolagnia may not have had a considerable share in the origin
of his [man's] susceptibility to nervous diseases. This would afford us
some explanation of why, with the advance of civilization, it is precisely
the sexual life that must fall victim to repression. For we have long known
the intimate connection in the animal organization between the sexual
instinct and the function of the olfactory organ." (36, III, p. 382)

From what does the depreciation tendency originate? It originates from the fear of an injury to one's own sensitivity. It is likewise a safeguarding tendency, initiated by the urge toward significance, and is psychologically of the same rank as the wish to be above, to celebrate sexual triumphs, to fly, or to stand on a ladder, staircase, or the gable of a house. One quite regularly finds in the neurotic that the tendencies to depreciate a woman and to have intercourse with her go closely together. (I have never yet met a neurotic who was not, at least secretly, beset by the fear that a woman might be superior to him.) The feelings of the neurotic express plainly: "I wish to depreciate the woman by sexual intercourse." Afterwards he is likely to leave her and to turn to others. I have called this the Don Juan characteristic of the neurotic. It corresponds to Freud's "love series" (*Liebesreihe*) which he interprets in a fantastic manner. Whether and how much libido is involved here is completely immaterial. The neurotic's masculine protest may also turn to masturbation and pollution, not without associating these with safe-guarding tendencies against the demon woman.

6. THE OEDIPUS COMPLEX[21]

What does such a patient "repress"—his sex drive, his libido? Of this he is so conscious that he thinks continuously of how to protect himself from it. A fantasy? His fantasy is in brief that woman is above him, that woman is the stronger. Much preparation is necessary to show the connection between this and similar fantasies and the neurosis. But then it turns out that this fantasy itself is only a warning, erected by the patient himself to obtain significance even by secret paths. Do such patients repress libidinal urges toward the mother; that is, do they suffer from the Oedipus complex? I have seen many patients who have come to know their Oedipus complex very well, without feeling any improvement. Once one appreciates the masculine protest in the Oedipus complex, one is no longer justified in speaking of a complex of fantasies and wishes. One will then learn to understand that the apparent Oedipus complex is only a small part of the overpowering neurotic dynamic, a stage of the masculine protest, a stage which in itself is insignificant although instructive in its context. It is a situation which must be taken symbolically and which yields important insights into the characterology of the neurotic, as other situations do.

F. Discussion of Adler's Ideas by Freud and Others
By Kenneth Mark Colby [22]

Since these particular meetings of the Psychoanalytic Society, held in January, 1911, [during which the preceding three selections were read] were of such crucial significance, a more factual account of what occurred should be of historical worth. Fortunately the verbatim statements of the discussants were recorded by the Society secretary. Copies of these minutes are now in the possession of Dr. Siegfried Bernfeld, who was good enough to make them available for study and who helped me in translating them from German into English. As accurate documents they are subject to the flaws of short-hand recording, perhaps missing emotional under- and overtones, but providing valuable additions and corrections to the inadequate reports available heretofore (16, 101, 119).

Henceforth the quotation marks will designate translated fragments of the secretary's minutes.

COMMENT   An abstract, of over one page, of Adler's paper is given at this point by Colby. It is a faithful presentation of the preceding two sections, attesting to the accuracy of the secretary's minutes on which Colby's paper is based.

A discussion of Adler's ideas then began and extended throughout the next three meetings of the Society. I shall quote most of Freud's and Adler's remarks verbatim and summarize the comments of the other discussants.

Freud opened by saying: "First of all, Adler's works are difficult to understand because of his abstract manner . . . Personally I take it ill of the author that he speaks of the same things without designating them by the same names which they already have and without trying to bring his new terms into relation with the old. Thus one has the impression that repression exists in the masculine protest; either the latter coincides with the former or it is the same phenomenon under different viewpoints. I have touched on these viewpoints in my own writings. For example, the concepts of flight into illness and of the secondary gains of illness coincide in fact with much of what Adler has brought out. But one looks in vain for a discussion of these thoughts in his works. Even our old idea of bisexuality is called psychic hermaphroditism by him as if it were something else . . .

"Two traits are evident in Adler's works: (1) an anti-sexual trend (in an unpublished paper he already speaks of an asexual infantile history) and (2) a trend against the value of the details of the phenomenology of neuroses. Adler has advocated the unity of neuroses, which is trivial, since according to psychoanalysis neuroses have basically the same etiology and the same mechanism. Rather what he asserts is actually the sameness of all neuroses. This trend is methodologically deplorable and condemns his whole work to sterility . . .

"I do not consider these Adlerian doctrines insignificant and would like to predict that they will make a great impression, at first damaging psychoanalysis very much. The great impression has two sources: (1) it is obvious that a remarkable intellect with a great talent for writing is working on these matters, (2) the whole doctrine has a reactionary and retrograde character which thereby offers a larger number of pleasure premiums. For the most part it deals with biology instead of psychology and instead of the psychology of the unconscious it concerns surface phenomena, that is, ego psychology. Finally, it deals with general psychology rather than the psychology of libido—sexuality. Thus to attain superiority the doctrine will capitalize on the still existing latent resistances in every psychoanalyst. At first it will harm the development of psychoanalysis while remaining sterile as far as psychoanalytic results are concerned . . .

"The entire presentation of neurosis is seen from the standpoint of the ego and considered from the ego just as the neurosis itself appears to the ego. It is ego psychology deepened by knowledge of the psychology of the unconscious. Therein lies the strength and weakness of Adler's presentation. Adler continuously mixes up primary and secondary things. But insofar as they offer a keenly perceived ego-psychology, his works contain real worth . . . It is characteristic that Adler never discovers new things—such as we psychoanalysts discover—but merely reinterprets them . . . When he accuses Freudian pupils of always finding only the same things, he himself provides even more stereotypes. Again and again we hear only of wishes for superiority, of security and of protection . . .

"Of course the ego must come into consideration in every neurotic manifestation. The ego plays exactly the same role in the genesis of neurosis as in the genesis of the dream, where the individual wishes to sleep. In a similar manner there must be an ego wish in every neurosis. However, as little as this wish to sleep explains to us the detail of the dream, so little will the ego-motive of masculine protest clarify for us the origin and variety of neurosis. If Adler incessantly gives us the ego-motivations for neuroses, then other motivations, interesting to us cannot be substituted . . . The core of a neurosis is the anxiety of the ego confronted by libido and Adler's presentation has only reinforced this interpretation . . .

"Finally, I would like to mention one more point in this detailed critique. One becomes absolutely muddled from Adler's concepts whether a neurosis is a defense of the ego (a gain from illness) or whether it represents a failure of this defense. Today it was said that the neurosis is evoked as a defense while at other times Adler states a neurosis originates from the failure of the masculine protest. This shows that a coherent interpretation of neurosis on the basis of Adler's doctrine is simply impossible. It is character theory but it repeats only the usual misconceptions of the ego. It is the denial of the unconscious—of which the ego itself is guilty and which here is reformulated as a theory."

COMMENT   *Without going into the details of Freud's criticism, we only*
wish to point out his misunderstanding of Adler when he
accuses him of dealing "for the most part . . . with biology instead of
psychology." The existing reverse relationship, namely that Adler is more
psychologically oriented and Freud more biologically oriented, is a good
part of the burden of our comments.

Adler replied to Freud's comments: "The sexual references described
by Freud are [indeed] found in neuroses. But my findings show that
whatever one sees as sexual, behind it are much more important connections, namely the masculine protest disguised under sexuality. Concerning the objection that the masculine protest coincides with repression, I have tried to show today that repression is only a small segment
of the effects of masculine protest."

In the next meeting of the Society, on February 8, the discussion
continued with Rosenstein criticizing Adler's extreme generalizations in
ascribing all world literature and cultural history to the masculine protest. Hitschmann felt that Adler denied the strength of sexual factors in
neuroses while other discussants defended Adler's views by stating that
the masculine protest did not deny sexuality but served only to guide
sexual forces in a certain direction.

The final meeting, on February 22, in which Adler's views were considered, included further remarks by Freud. He referred to Adler's criticism
of the theory of repression and culture. "Adler has alleged the theory of
repression asserts that repression comes from culture and, in turn, culture
comes from repression. Now that is not playing with words but exactly
the point and if the sentences are specified as they originally were, there
is no contradiction in them. Repression takes place in the individual
and is necessitated by the demands of the culture. Now, what is culture?
It is a precipitate of the work of repression of all previous generations.
The task demanded of the individual is to carry out all repressions which
were already effected before him. One who emphasizes so much that
no one alter his words and who reproaches others that they milk his
words, should especially beware of lapsing into these errors . . .

"Adler has requested the omission of praise and recognition which several speakers have added to their critiques. He has thereby done them
an injustice because he has no right to assume that these positive remarks were insincere. I feel the Adlerian teachings are incorrect and
dangerous for the development of psychoanalysis. They are scientific

errors due to false methods, still they are honorable errors. Though one rejects the content of Adler's views, one can recognize their consistency and meaning."

Stekel commented that he felt Adler's views to be great improvements in the theory of neurosis which cannot be completely understood as yet. "Adler's concepts are a deepening and extension of facts already discovered by us and they are in no contradiction with them. They are simply further constructions on the Freudian foundation." Freud disagreed with Stekel by saying: "When Stekel maintains he finds no contradiction between these ideas and Freudian theory, I want to point to the fact that two of the participants do find a contradiction, namely Adler and Freud."

Steiner pointed out that there was considerable emotion being stirred up in the discussion, that Adler's adherents conducted arguments in a strikingly weak fashion, and also that Freud has postponed his feelings too long. "Adler has tried to bring us, who gathered together to investigate the vicissitudes of libido, nearer to surface psychology to such a degree that we might have to rename our society into whose program and framework Adler's ideas do not fit at all." This is the statement which Stekel in his autobiography claims sounded like a motion.

Adler closed by "shrugging off Steiner's general objections but not without remarking that if he were in Steiner's place he would not have had the courage to talk like that." He repeated that masturbation serves only as a protective tendency, that a neurotic wishes only in the direction of the masculine protest, and that the mechanism of displacement from below to above is an expression of masculine protest.

In the immediately following committee meeting Adler resigned his position as president of the Society "because of the incompatibility of my scientific position with my post in the Society." Stekel also resigned as vice president. Adler was not voted out of the Society as maintained by Bottome (in fact, as many spoke for as against his theories), nor invited to leave as reported by Wittels. He simply resigned his office and withdrew.

The minutes of the board of directors of the Society tell of Freud's election to the presidency. Also it was proposed in reference to Adler's statement regarding incompatibility that the Society clearly indicate that it was not of this opinion, thank the recent president for his activities, and regret his departure. Freud commented that they could spare Adler the remark on incompatibility, but the majority present voted for the motion. Adler never returned to the Society meetings and from then on the break between the two men remained complete.

COMMENT Nine others of the psychoanalytic group, which consisted of some thirty-five members, withdrew with Adler, according to Wittels as quoted by Murphy (82, p. 337).

The controversy between Freud and Adler continued throughout their lives. Yet, despite the fact that Adler never tired of pointing out his differences from Freud, he did, in several instances, give him credit for basic observations. "A renaissance was experienced in psychology with the advent of psychoanalysis" (1933a, p. 22). This tribute was paid by Adler when he pointed out that psychoanalysis, in contrast to the usual academic psychology, provided an overall organizing principle of behavior, although the content of this principle was sexual libido, with which Adler, of course, thoroughly disagreed. The emphasis Freud placed on unconscious factors in behavior was acknowledged by Adler as "the significant attempt to read between the lines of consciousness" (1933a, p. 22). Altogether, one may say that, while he disagreed with the interpretations, Adler recognized most of Freud's observations. Freud "seems to have known much more than he understood" (1933a, p. 166). Going beyond the literal interpretations which Freud gave to many of his observations, Adler considered them as symbolic forms of expression. For example, he did not consider the boy's desire for his mother literally in the sense of a sexual longing, but symbolically, as an expression of an insatiable desire to possess everything, to be on top. The death wish and masochism were not taken as manifestations of the desire to do away with one's self, but as escapes from defeat and symbols of prevailing. Fear of castration was not the fear of losing one's penis, but an expression of the fear of being unmanly, of becoming worthless. In this sense then, Adler could finally say: "The important pioneering work of Freud has not lost any of its value. Our criticism is only that what he found in the unconscious is not a mainspring, but a misguided striving for power, assimilated by the erroneous underlying style of life" (1929f).

An early credit is the following: "Possibly the forceful accent which Freud placed on child life and the uncovery of the tragic conflicts which spring from the anomalies of the child's experiences were necessary to make the great importance of a science of education clear to us" (1904, p. 3).

The most outspoken praise for Freud was expressed by Adler in reference to dream interpretation. "One cannot overemphasize that only through Freud's work on dream content, dream thoughts, and day residue has dream analysis of any kind been made possible" (1910c, p. 98). "Freud was the first to have undertaken the attempt of developing a scientific dream theory. This, as well as certain observations which he described as belonging to the 'unconscious,' are a lasting contribution which no one can lessen" (1933a, p. 166). Dream theory elicited this recognition of Freud from Adler in his later years, the same work which, it will be remembered, had originally roused him to Freud's defense and brought the two together thirty years earlier.

FOOTNOTES TO CHAPTER TWO

1. 1 and 2: "Der psychische Hermaphroditismus im Leben und in der Neurose" (1910a), pp. 74 and 74-75.
2. 1, 2, 3: "Hermaphroditismus" (1910a), p. 75.
3. 1: "Hermaphroditismus" (1910a), p. 76.
4. 1 to 4: "Hermaphroditismus" (1910a), pp. 77, 77, 77-78, and 83.
5. 1: "Hermaphroditismus" (1910a), p. 78n.
6. 1, 2, 3: "Hermaphroditismus" (1910a), pp. 78, 79, and 83.
7. 1 to 6: "Trotz und Gehorsam" (1910b), pp. 86, 86, 87, 87, 87, and 87-88.
8. 1 and 2: "Trotz" (1910b), p. 88.
9. 1 and 2: "Trotz" (1910b), pp. 89 and 91-93.
10. 1, 2, 3: "Die Rolle der Sexualität in der Neurose" (1911a), p. 94.
11. 1 to 4: "Die Rolle" (1911a), pp. 94, 95, 95-96, and 96-97.
12. 1 and 2: "Die Rolle" (1911a), pp. 97-98 and 102.
13. 1 to 4: " 'Verdrängung' und 'Männlicher Protest'; ihre Rolle und Bedeutung für die neurotische Dynamik" (1911b), pp. 103, 103-104, 104, and 104.
14 and 15. 1: " 'Verdrängung' " (1911b), p. 104.
16. 1 to 4: " 'Verdrängung' " (1911b), pp. 104-105, 105, 105, and 105.
17. 1 to 4: " 'Verdrängung' " (1911b), pp. 106, 106, 106-107, and 107.
18. 1: " 'Verdrängung' " (1911b), pp. 107-108.
19. 1 and 2: " 'Verdrängung' " (1911b), p. 110.
20. 1 and 2: " 'Verdrängung' " (1911b), pp. 112-113, and 113.
21. 1: " 'Verdrängung' " (1911b), p. 114.
22. Kenneth Mark Colby. "On the disagreement between Freud and Adler" (24), excerpts: pp. 229-233; verbatim: pp. 233-238.

CHAPTER THREE

FICTIONALISM AND FINALISM

COMMENT When Adler separated from Freud, he had developed away
from a biologically oriented, elementaristic, objective drive
psychology and toward a socially oriented, subjectivistic, holistic psychology of attitudes. The present chapter will show the part which Hans
Vaihinger's fictionalism, "idealistic positivism," played in Adler's further
development in this direction.

Vaihinger's work appeared in 1911, the same year in the beginning of
which Adler withdrew from the psychoanalytic circle. When Adler
presented in the following year, 1912, his "Comparative Individual Psychology" in The Neurotic Character, his most important book, this was
replete with evidence of Vaihinger's influence and contained several sin-
cere acknowledgments of this, such as: "It was good fortune which made
me acquainted with Vaihinger's ingenious Philosophy of 'As If' (Berlin,
1911), a work in which I found the thoughts familiar to me from the
neurosis presented as valid for scientific thinking in general" (1912a, p.
22).

In our experience, it is impossible to gain a complete understanding
of Adler's theory, especially with respect to his important concept of
the "fictional goal," without a knowledge of Vaihinger's fictionalism.
Accordingly, the present chapter will deal firstly, with a brief presentation
of Vaihinger through selections from his book, and secondly, with Adler's own fictional finalism.

A. Fictionalism
By Hans Vaihinger

COMMENT *Fictions, according to Vaihinger, are ideas, including unconscious notions, which have no counterpart in reality, yet serve the useful function of enabling us to deal with it better than we could otherwise. The statement "All men are created equal" would be an example of a fiction. The statement is in contradiction to reality; yet, as an ideal, it is of great practical value in everyday life. This sort of fiction comes close to a working hypothesis which is adopted as a basis for action because it works in practice, although its truth is dubious. Such fiction can better be understood by comparing it to hypothesis; while the hypothesis submits its reality to the test and demands verification, the fiction is a mere auxiliary construct, a scaffolding to be demolished if no longer needed. As distinguished from both fiction and hypothesis, dogma refers to an idea which is considered definitely established. Another aspect of the fiction, helpful in understanding the concept, is its subjective character. According to Vaihinger the subjective is fictional.*

The main influence of Vaihinger on Adler was to provide him with a philosophic foundation for his developing subjective finalism, as will be shown in the selections from Adler in the second part of this chapter. Beyond this, however, Adler adapted a number of concepts from Vaihinger to his theory of personality and abnormal psychology; this will be shown in the comments after some of the selections from Vaihinger which follow.

1. THE MEANING OF FICTIONS[1]

The mind is not merely appropriative, it is also assimilative and constructive. In the course of its growth, it creates *its* organs of its own accord in virtue of its adaptable constitution, but only when stimulated from without, and adapts them to external circumstances. Such organs are, for example, forms of perception and thought, and certain concepts and other logical constructs.

Our subject is the fictive activity of the logical functions; the products of this activity—fictions. The fictive activity of the mind is an expression of the fundamental psychical forces; fictions are mental structures. The psyche weaves this aid to thought out of itself; for the mind is inventive.

Fictio means, in the first place, an activity of *fingere*, that is to say, of constructing, forming, giving shape, elaborating, presenting, artistically fashioning, conceiving, thinking, imagining, assuming, planning, devising, inventing. Secondly, it refers to the *product* of these activities, the fictional assumption, fabrication, creation, the imagined case. Its most conspicuous character is that of unhampered and free expression.

The organic function of thought is carried on for the most part unconsciously. Should the product finally enter consciousness also, this light only penetrates to the shallows, and the actual fundamental processes are carried on in the darkness of the unconscious.

Nominalism naturally declared all general ideas to be *ficta*, *fictiones*, without, however, attaching to fiction the positive meaning which it has for us. The *negative sense* of the fiction we call the assumption, for instance, that general ideas are expressions for something unreal, that is, definitely invented and fabricated; whereas by its *positive sense* we mean the realization that these fictions have nevertheless great practical value, that they serve as the means for acquiring knowledge.

For us the essential element in a fiction is not the fact of its being a conscious deviation from reality, a mere piece of imagination—but we stress the useful nature of this deviation. If we simply say, "The whole world is our idea and all forms are subjective," we get an untenable subjectivism. But if we say: "Conceptual forms and fictions are expedient psychical constructs," then these are closely related to "cosmic agencies and constituents" (Lass), for it is they that call these expedient forms into existence in the organic being.

The "as if" world, which is formed in this manner, the world of the "unreal" is just as important as the world of the so-called real or actual (in the ordinary sense of the word); indeed it is far more important for ethics and aesthetics. This aesthetic and ethical world of "as if," the world of the unreal, becomes finally for us a world of values which, particularly in the form of religion, must be sharply distinguished in our mind from the world of becoming.

It is senseless to question the meaning of the universe, and this is the idea expressed in Schiller's words: "Know this, a mind sublime puts greatness into life, yet seeks it not therein" (*Huldigung der Künste*, 1805). This is positivist idealism.

2. TYPES OF FICTIONS[2]

a. Abstractive (Neglective). Among these a celebrated statistical fiction is the *homme moyen* of Quetelet, the fiction of a normal, average man. This fiction is not of value for statistics alone, for in medicine we meet with the concept of an absolutely healthy individual, of an average man in whom all abnormal deviations have disappeared. Here we may also include all the arbitrary determinations found in science, such as, for example, the meridian of Ferro, the determination of the zero point, the selection of water as the measure of specific gravity, of the movements of the stars as an index of time. In all these cases, certain points of reference are taken and lines similar to co-ordinates drawn in different directions for the determination and classification of phenomena.

We might also remark here that the whole conceptual classificatory system and, in general, the differentiation of concepts is based upon abstractions of the most one-sided nature, as Lotze has clearly demonstrated in his *Logic* (see Pfleiderer, *Der Moderne Pessimismus*, p. 81): "Light and darkness, black and white, life and death are merely the artificial products of rationalistic abstraction; they may be necessary, with all their inaccuracy, for purposes of reference, but when applied to reality they must always be used with caution."

COMMENT *Adler refers repeatedly to fixed points and lines of orientation which are created and used in order to find one's way in the chaos of life, and he even likens these psychological devices to meridians and parallels (see p. 96). In the neurotic, due to his greater need for security-giving points of orientation, Adler finds "exaggerated abstraction" characterized by an "antithetical schema of apperception" which according to the analogy of "below" and "above" artificially divides the world into "something like the debit and credit sides in bookkeeping" (see p. 248).*

b. Symbolic (Analogical). All cognition is the apperception of one thing through another. In understanding, we are always dealing with an analogy and we cannot imagine how otherwise existence can be understood. Anyone acquainted with the mechanism of thought knows that all conception and cognition are based upon analogical apperceptions. The only ideational constructs by means of which existing things can be apperceived are either the corresponding general conceptions or other concrete objects.

[An example of a symbolic or analogical fiction is] the popular modern analogy whereby the state or a society is compared with an organism, and the similar analogy of the world with an organism or a work of art. Even where such analogies are purely fictional, they are often of service in arriving at true theoretical laws.

COMMENT   In The Neurotic Character, Adler often used the term analogical thinking to describe a device for the simplification of a problem to master it better. Later he used the concept without the term. For example, the second-born, whose childhood situation provided him with a pace-maker, often dreams of running after trains and riding in races (see p. 379). "In the neurotic . . . 'analogical thinking', i.e., his attempted solution of problems according to the analogy of former experiences, is more strongly and distinctly expressed than is the case in normal individuals" (see p. 248).

c. Heuristic. Another type of fiction to be examined is the heuristic [serving and facilitating discovery]. It is true that a number of those fictions already considered also have heuristic value, but the fictions which we specifically group together under this term serve heuristic purposes to a particularly marked degree. For the explanation of a complex of real events the assumption of unreal causes is first made and when this has been systematically worked out, not only is order brought into the phenomena, but the ground is also prepared for the correct solution of the problem. For this very reason the method has heuristic value. Such assumptions are not directly created for the purpose but arise wherever the hypotheses hitherto employed prove insufficient and erroneous. Such discarded hypotheses frequently still continue to perform good practical and heuristic service. The Ptolemaic cosmic system was already regarded by the Arabs of the Middle Ages as a fiction and not an hypothesis. All these discarded hypotheses are useful as fictions, including the teleological hypothesis, which from a theoretical standpoint is without value, at least in its earlier form.

d. Practical (Ethical). We encounter at the very threshold of these fictions one of the most important concepts ever formed by man, the idea of freedom; human actions are regarded as free and therefore as "responsible" and contrasted with the "necessary" course of natural events. It not only contradicts observation which shows that everything obeys unalterable laws, but is also self-contradictory, for an absolutely free, chance act, resulting from nothing, is ethically just as valueless as an absolutely necessary one. In spite of all these contradictions, however, we not only make use of this concept in ordinary life in judging moral actions, but it is also the foundation of criminal law. In the course of their development, men have formed this important construct from immanent necessity, because only on this basis is a high degree of culture and morality possible.

In the category of practical fictions a number of other moral concepts and postulates are also to be enumerated, such as the concept of duty and of immortality. Here belong all the so-called "ideals" of ordinary life. The ideal is a practical fiction.

e. *Aesthetic.* Having introduced a certain order into the differences between the various fictions themselves, we must now indicate the boundaries which separate scientific fiction [to which the above four types belong] from what is also often designated by the same term. I would suggest that in the future we call scientific fictions fictions, and the others, the mythological and aesthetic *figments.* For instance, Pegasus is a figment, atom, a fiction. The opponents of the fiction misrepresent it in so far as they regard it as a mere figment.

The aesthetic fictions not only include all similes, metaphors, and comparisons, but also those ideational forms that deal even more freely with reality. Here we must group not only all personifications, but also allegories and all idealizing forms of thought. The aesthetic fiction and its theoretical explanation are, in part, closely related to the scientific fiction. This is quite natural when we remember that the same elementary psychical processes contributed to the construction of both. Aesthetic fictions serve the purpose of awakening within us certain uplifting or otherwise important feelings. Like the scientific, they are not an end in themselves but a means for the attainment of higher ends.

The degree in which the imaginative faculty may deviate from nature is an old dispute. As in science so in poetry, of which we are here speaking in particular, fictions have been greatly abused, and this has frequently led to reactions, based on exactly the same grounds as those resulting from the misuse of scientific fictions. The real criterion as to how far such fictions are to be admitted into either field, and one which has always been adopted by good taste and logical tact alike, is simply the practical value of such fictions.

COMMENT *From the above, it would seem that the aesthetic fiction or figment could also be called autistic fiction, while the scientific fiction could be called the more purposive fiction or working hypothesis. A typical example of Adler's use of the aesthetic fiction in* the sense of awakening certain important feelings is found in his interpretation of dreams. "The dream strives to pave the way towards solving a problem by a metaphorical expression of it, by a comparison, an 'as if'. . . . In dreams we produce those pictures which will arouse the feelings and emotions which we need for our purposes, that is, for solving the problems confronting us at the time of the dream, in accordance with the particular style of life which is ours" (see pp. 360–361).

3. ASPECTS OF FICTIONS[3]

a. *Fiction and Hypothesis*. An hypothesis is directed towards reality, that is, the ideational construct contained in it claims, or hopes, to coincide with the perception in the future. It submits its reality to the test and demands *verification*, that is it wants to be proved true, real, and an expression of a reality.

The fiction, however, is a mere auxiliary construct, a circuitous approach, a scaffolding afterwards to be demolished, while the hypothesis looks forward to being definitely established. What is untenable as an hypothesis can often render excellent service as a fiction.

To the verification of the hypothesis corresponds the *justification* of the fiction. If a fictional construct is formed, its excuse and justification must be that it is of service to discursive thought. This justification is always a matter of special proof, like verification. Fictions that do not justify themselves, that is, which cannot be proved to be useful and necessary, must be eliminated no less than hypotheses that cannot be verified. The principle of the rules of hypothetical method is the *probability of the conceptual constructs*, that of fictional method is their *expediency*.

b. *Linguistic Analysis of "As If."* We must now also examine the way in which fictions are expressed in language. Let us concentrate our attention upon the strange combination of particles, *as if*, and compare the form it takes in different languages: Latin, *quasi*, also *sicut*; French, *comme si, que si*; German, *als ob, wie wenn*; Greek, ὡς εἰ [ὡσεί], ὡς εἴ τε.

Our assertion that in the last analysis all fictions derive from comparative apperception, is supported by their linguistic form. This is quite manifest, for *als, wie* are particles of comparison. But this comparison is then modified by the *wenn* and the *ob*. What, then, is contained in the *as if*? What, then, does it mean if we say that matter must be treated *as if* it consisted of atoms? It can only mean that empirically given matter must be treated as it would be treated *if* it consisted of infinitesimals. This formula, then, states that reality as given, the particular, is compared with something whose impossibility and unreality is at the same time admitted.

We can now also understand the linguistic similarity of the fiction to error and to hypothesis. As is well known, the grammatical formula for error is exactly the same. That is why the fiction is so frequently confused with error. We say, for instance, that Descartes regarded the idea of God and the absolute *as if* they were innate, but that is an error. Here the error is marked by the same formula, and psychologically it has the same formation as the fiction. Fiction is, after all, merely a more conscious, more practical and more fruitful error.

c. *Fiction, Error and Truth*. What we generally call "truth," namely a conceptual world coinciding with the external world, *is merely the most expedient error*. The conceptual world, is, as we both assumed and found to be the case, subjective in its forms: Only the observed and the unchangeable are real. The whole framework in which we place what is perceived is only subjective; subjective is fictional; fictional is false; falsehood is error. It is the ambition of science to make of the world of ideas an ever more useful instrument for dealing with things and for action. The world of ideas which results from this ambition and which we generally call truth, is consequently only the most expedient error, that is, that system of ideas which enables us to act and to deal with things most rapidly, neatly, and safely, and with the minimum of irrational elements. The limits between truth and error are therefore just as movable as all such limits, for example, those between cold and warm. Cold is a degree of temperature that is unsuitable for us, warm that which is most suitable. The difference between them objectively is merely one of degree. Subjectively the differences can be shifted according to circumstances and the nature of the object concerned. In the same manner, truth is merely the most expedient degree of error, and error the least expedient degree of ideation, of fiction. We call our conceptual world true when it permits us best to gauge objectivity and to act therein. So-called agreement with reality must finally be abandoned as a criterion.

COMMENT   *The idea of truth as merely the most expedient error became an essential part of Adler's subjective psychology. In the following where Adler speaks of "meaning," this is equivalent to belief or opinion. "There are as many meanings given to life as there are human beings, and . . . perhaps each meaning involves more or less of an error. . . . Any meaning which is at all serviceable cannot be called* absolutely wrong. . . . However, we can distinguish some which answer better and some which answer worse; some where the error is small and some where it is large" (1931a, p. 4). "In the world of the psyche there is no principle of individual orientation beyond our own beliefs. Very great are the consequences of our real beliefs. Big errors can produce neuroses but little errors, a nearly normal person" (1929b, p. 62).

4. THE LAW OF IDEATIONAL SHIFTS[4]

Formulated in general, the law of ideational shifts is to the effect that a number of ideas pass through various stages of development, namely those of fiction, hypothesis, and dogma, and conversely dogma, hypothesis, and fiction.

If we compare the dogma with the hypothesis, we notice that the latter involves a condition of tension which must be exceedingly disagreeable to the mind. The mind has a tendency to bring all ideational contents into equilibrium and to establish an unbroken connection between them. An hypothesis is inimical to this tendency in so far as it involves the idea that it is not to be placed on an equality with the other objective ideas. It has been only provisionally accepted by the psyche and thus interferes with the general tendency to adjustment.

The only way to transform an unstable into a stable equilibrium is to support the body in question. In the psyche this takes the form of making the hypothesis more stable through repeated confirmation. This, the only legitimate way, may, in the case of certain ideas, not merely involve centuries of labor, but in many cases be quite impossible. So the psyche circumvents it by simply transforming the hypothesis into a dogma by illegitimate methods.

We may now turn to the shift from fiction to hypothesis. If fiction and hypothesis are compared, the condition of tension developing in the psyche due to the fiction is far more important than that resulting from the hypothesis. Indeed a fiction is a positive hindrance and definitely interferes with the tendency toward an equilibration of ideational constructs. The hypothesis only hampers this adjustment negatively and indirectly. The simplest way of preventing this unpleasant condition of tension is to recognize the whole idea as a dogma. The fiction becomes simply a dogma, and the as if a because and a so that. The other method, which is just as frequent, passes through the stage of the hypothesis; the ideational form receives the smaller tension-coefficient of the hypothesis; and the *as if* becomes *if*.

It is different when experience and reflection have gradually made dogmas doubtful. The psyche still tries to adhere to them in obedience to the law of inertia, and does actually adhere to them; when this is no longer possible with a stable equilibrium, when the position has been too much shaken, then it contents itself with the unstable equilibrium of the hypothesis. The dogma becomes an hypothesis and the idea is reduced in value by one degree.

New doubts, new shocks follow; and here again the psyche has but two paths available. Either the idea is simply eliminated and falls to the ground—science having completed its destructive work, the false ideational constructs are discarded; or the other way may be taken. The idea may possess such a theoretical and practical value that the psyche will not readily reject it; it cannot do without it forever, or even indefinitely. The conceptual construct is then transformed from an hypothesis into a fiction.

Examples can be found in the mythology and legendary history of every people and in the philosophy of religion. Myths, similes, even the conscious fictions of the founders of religions either become dogmas to the founders themselves or to their adherents among the people and rarely pass through the stage of hypothesis. On the other hand, during the decline and break-up of a religion all three stages stand out very clearly.

COMMENT   *The law of ideational shifts was used by Adler to describe the rigidity and lack of adaptability of the abnormal psyche* (see pp. 246–247).

5. FICTION IN KANT[5]

The overwhelming number of passages from Kant which we have quoted and discussed sufficiently prove that the as-if view plays an extraordinarily important part in Kant. This side of Kant has hitherto been almost entirely neglected.

The only writer to recognize and expound Kant's true doctrine in this respect was Friedrich Carl Forberg [1770–1848]. He clearly grasped and presented, at least in its basic principles, Kant's as-if doctrine, particularly in relation to the philosophy of religion.

[According to Forberg:] "It is not the (theoretical) belief that the kingdom of God is coming, which constitutes religion; but the endeavour to make it come, even if we believe that it never will come. This and this alone is religion."* In this sense religion is a practical belief in the "kingdom of God," it is to act as *if* by our action it could be brought into being. Here we have the religion of as-if in its most clearly defined and purest form. Forberg definitely denies the existence of a moral world order, for the high dignity and sublimity of this form of the religion of 'as if' lies precisely in the fact that a good man does good although theoretically he does not believe in a moral world-order; he acts as if he did believe in it.

The Kantian justification of religious ideas is a purely fictive, or better perhaps, a fictionalistic one. They are for him practical, expedient fictions, whereas the pre- and post-Kantian justification of religious concepts and judgments is a rationalistic one. They are rationally grounded hypotheses. The real and genuine Kantian criticism draws no theoretical inferences whatever, but says: You must act as you would *if* a God existed. Therein lies Kant's critical pragmatism.

6. FICTION IN NIETZSCHE[6]

That life and science are not possible without imaginary or false conceptions was also recognized by Friedrich Nietzsche. Nietzsche early observed that such invented and therefore erroneous conceptions are unconsciously employed by men to the advantage of life and science. He was here following Schopenhauer and probably Richard Wagner and his doctrine of "hallucination." But that such false ideas must be employed both in science and in life by intellectually mature people with the full realization of their falsity is a fact which Nietzsche came to perceive more and more clearly.

There is a great deal of Kant in Nietzsche; not, it is true, of Kant in the form in which he is found in the textbooks (and in which he will probably remain for all eternity), but of the spirit of Kant, of the real Kant who understood the nature of appearance through and through, but who, in spite of having seen through it, also consciously saw and recognized its usefulness and necessity.

[According to Nietzsche:] "The erroneousness of a concept does not for me constitute an objection to it; the question is—to what extent is it

* In the development of the concept of religion, *Philosophisches Journal*, Part I, 1798.

advantageous to life? Indeed I am convinced that *the most erroneous assumptions are precisely the most indispensable for us*, that without granting the validity of the logical fiction, without measuring reality by the invented world of the unconditioned, the self-identical, man could not live."

COMMENT   One quarter of Vaihinger's book is devoted to showing how Kant, and also Nietzsche, used the fictional method of the "as if." Knowledge of Vaihinger in this way clarifies Adler's relationship to Kant and Nietzsche, to whom Adler refers frequently, especially in his earlier writings, and more often to Nietzsche.

Through the link of Vaihinger, we are also enabled to appreciate the relationship of Adler to William James and John Dewey, to whom Adler also refers in his later writings. According to Frank Thilly and Ledger Wood, Vaihinger's fictionalism is similar to James' pragmatism and John Dewey's instrumentalism in that it interprets thought as an activity which fulfills the biological function of assisting the organism to adapt itself to its environment. But, whereas "the typical pragmatist ascribes 'truth' to his conceptual schemes—a truth which is attested by their practical consequences, Vaihinger's fictional constructs, although they are in contradiction to reality, have a predictive function: by their help we are enabled 'to calculate events that occur;' in themselves fictitious, they lead to 'correct' predictions regarding the future appearance of sensations" (108, p. 588). Vaihinger's contribution is that he elevates fictions as such to rank and dignity.

Whereas idealism regards ideas as the ultimate reality, and positivism recognizes only observable facts, Vaihinger's system regards ideational constructs, even when in contradiction to reality, of great practical value and indispensable for human life. This is what Vaihinger means when he calls his philosophy "Idealistic Positivism" or "Positivist Idealism."

B. The Fictional Final Goal

COMMENT   Freud's biologically oriented system tacitly accepted a mechanistic, reductionistic positivism; it looked for ultimate causes in the past and in objective events. As we have seen, Freud held that "in the psychological field the biological factor is really the rock-bottom" (see pp. 51–52), and he anticipated that we may reach "a position to replace the psychological terms by physiological or chemical ones" (see pp. 60–61).

Adler's subjectivism, where values, goals and secondary motives had replaced drives and primary motives in importance, was not a physiological reductionism. If mental events cannot be reduced to physiological events, systematization is possible only by establishing a hierarchy of these mental events, that is, a hierarchy of values and goals. This leads to the philosophical position of teleology and finalism, the determination by final causes. But in this position there lay the danger of parting from the scientific basis and approaching theology. It was in Vaihinger's idealistic positivism that Adler now found for his subjectivistic and finalistic psychology a philosophical foundation which was acceptable, encouraging, and stimulating.

The influence of Vaihinger on Adler finds its most obvious expression in his use of the term fictional. Three attributes of Vaihinger's term are important for the understanding of Adler's use of it.

1. From the psychological, not logical point of view, Vaihinger's concept of fiction comes very close to what one would today call the subjective or the personal frame of reference or the phenomenal field. Vaihinger says that the fictional includes the subjective, "subjective is fictional" (see p. 83).

2. Fictions are not reducible to objective causes. According to Vaihinger "fictions are mental structures. The psyche weaves this aid to thought out of itself; for the mind is inventive" (see pp. 77–78). Fictional structures are thus creations of the individual.

3. Thought processes, including the fictional activity, are fundamentally "carried on in the darkness of the unconscious" (see p. 78).

When Adler combined the concept of the fiction with that of the goal, as in the fictional goal or the fictional final goal or the guiding fiction, he implied that his view of causality was subjectivistic, that it was deterministic only in a restricted sense, and that it took unconscious processes into account. These three points may be expanded as follows.

1. Adler had already taken the observable forward orientation of the individual and his concern with the future as the center of his dynamic psychology. By now describing goals and the future as fictional, he expressed in effect that this future was not the objective future but a subjective future as experienced in the present. Thus he avoided the teleological dilemma of the determination of present events by something which remains in the future. This solution is, of course, the one generally ac-

cepted today in one form or another. Wolfgang Köhler stated it most succinctly from the point of view of Gestalt psychology when he said: "It is not the actual future, the future as such, toward which we are directed in our planning, and in which we perceive our goals; it is that part of an actually present phenomenal field which we call the 'future'" (62, p. 380). Adler's fictional or subjective finalism or teleology does not violate Kurt Lewin's principle of the contemporaneity of motivation (68, p. 34). Adler's fictional (subjective) goal is a present one; it derives its great importance from the postulate that it is an ever-present goal (1930a, p. 5), although it is not necessarily present in consciousness. "We can comprehend every single life phenomenon, as if the past, the present, and the future together with a superordinated, guiding idea were present in it in traces" (1912a, p. iii). If we translate "as if" into "subjective," we find that this sentence refers to the subjective past, present, and future as being present in the phenomenological field in traces.

2. The term fictional goal also expressed Adler's conviction that the origin of the goal is, in the last analysis, not reducible to objective determiners. Although the objective factors of heredity and environment, organ inferiorities, and past experiences are utilized by the individual in the process of forming his final goal, the latter is still a fiction, a fabrication, the individual's own creation. Such causality corresponds to "soft" determinism, that is, "determinism from the inner nature of life," as contrasted to "hard" determinism "from external pressures alone" (William James, according to Murphy, 84, pp. 644–645).

Adler was not aware of the term "soft" determinism, nor of Jaspers' distinction between external, objective causation and internal, subjective causation (see pp. 13–14). When Adler rejects causality without qualification, he is in fact rejecting "hard" determinism or external causation. Thus each time the word cause or any of its derivatives is found below, the reader should understand it to signify external, objective causation, the old causa efficiens. It is only this which Adler rejected and not internal causation or the old causa finalis.

3. Finally the fictitiousness of the goal also implies its unconscious nature. Adler's goal concept is characterized particularly by the fact that the individual is largely unaware of his goal, that it is a hidden or unconscious goal, a goal which the individual does not understand. It is the true nature of the individual's hidden goal which constitutes, according to Adler, the essential content of the unconscious.

As the five sections within this part will show: (1) the fictional final goal became for Adler the principle of internal, subjective causation of psychological events, similar to Jaspers' concept of the schema (see p. 14); (2) the goal represented a creation of the individual and was largely unconscious; (3) it also became the principle of unity and self-consistency of the personality structure; from the point of view of the subject, the fictional goal was taken (4) as the basis for orientation in the world; and (5) as one aspect of compensation for felt inferiorities.

One more characteristic of fictional which played a part in Adler's use of the word should be mentioned. This characteristic, which belongs to the logical, not to the psychological, properties, is that a fiction can also be a working hypothesis, as in the case of the "heuristic fiction" (see p. 80). Accordingly, the fictional goal was at first used by Adler also as a heuristic concept in that he regarded the individual "as if" he were striving toward a final goal. Several years later, Adler dropped this last, logical connotation from his use of the word fictional. "Our experience and our impressions strengthen in us the conviction that this heuristic method represents more than an auxiliary method of research, and that it fundamentally coincides to the largest extent with real events of psychological development, which are partly consciously experienced and partly deducible from the unconscious. The goal-striving of the psyche is consequently not only our view but also a basic fact" (1927a, pp. 56–57).

Eventually Adler relinquished the term fictional altogether when speaking of the goal. However, the three psychological meanings of the term fictional, as subjective, created, and unconscious, remained the most essential components of Adler's goal concept.

1. PRINCIPLE OF INTERNAL CAUSATION[7]

Life, especially daily life without scientific prejudice, is so fascinated by the "whither?" of a phenomenon that it must be said that, in spite of all scientific views to the contrary, no one has ever formed a judgment about a psychological event without having reached for a line which seems to connect all the psychological phenomena of a person with his fictional goal.

When we know the goal of a person, we know approximately what will follow. In an association test [for example], we should never expect a man suffering from some great disappointment to associate "tree" with "rope." The moment we knew his objective, however, namely suicide, then we might very well expect that particular sequence of thoughts, expect it with such certainty that we would remove knives, poison, and weapons from his immediate vicinity.

The most important question of the healthy and the diseased mental life is not whence? but, whither? Only when we know the effective direction-giving goal of a person may we try to understand his movements, which for us have the value of individual preparations. In this whither? the cause is contained.

This view to some extent limits the importance of the principle of causality for the understanding of what takes place in the mind. That is to say, we do indeed assume the validity of that principle, but we recognize that it is inadequate to solve a mental problem and even to enable us to predict the adoption of a particular attitude of mind.

Causality, removed from all philosophy, was a hurdle to Individual Psychology, and one which was taken. We regard man as if nothing in his life were causally determined and as if every phenomenon could have been different.

All thinking, feeling, and acting is based on an [interpretation, a greater or lesser] error which we can influence by discovering it. This view is not new. We find it in Kant, in pragmatism, in Vaihinger's *Philosophy of "As If."* But, although our entire practical action is founded in it, it has never been taken into practical consideration. We could not remove a [psychological] disease which is causally determined. We can, however, remove an erroneous attitude. To nature errors cannot be ascribed because events are causally determined; but in psychology we cannot speak of causality or determinism.

We do not think of a conservation of psychological energy because we know that the causality which we seem to meet was actually placed into the situation by the given individual himself. Man makes one thing the cause and another thing the effect, and then joins the two. Much appears as causally determined although causality was only attributed to it. This goes so far that even organ inferiorities are effective only to the extent that we wish. Man can raise these inferiorities to rank and dignity; he can make them a cause. A large number of people cannot resist the tendency to do so. A child born with serious shortcomings is likely to take a timid, hostile attitude toward life, but this is not causally determined, for we know that the attitude can pass if we make things easier for him.

For example, a child was pampered and takes over the corresponding forms of expression with all their disadvantages. As the child grows up, he may become aware of the misfortune toward which he is headed. If such a child would ask what is the cause for this, everyone would say the mother. We ourselves would be tempted to agree, and also to blame the mother. But this argument collapses when the child changes his behavior, either on his own or through outside help and no longer makes these same errors. The mother is the cause only as long as the child makes these errors. When the child no longer makes these errors, is then the mother suddenly no longer the cause? In cases like this one cannot speak of causality.

Every semblance of causality in the psychological life is due to the tendency of many psychologists to present their dogmas disguised in mechanistic or physical similes. At one time they use as a comparison a pump handle moving up and down, at another a magnet with polar termini, at another a sadly harassed animal struggling for the satisfaction of its elementary needs. From such a view, to be sure, little can be seen of the fundamental differences which human psychological life manifests.

Individual Psychology insists absolutely on the indispensability of finalism for the understanding of all psychological phenomena. Causes, powers, instincts, impulses, and the like cannot serve as explanatory principles. The final goal alone can. Experiences, traumata, sexual development mechanisms cannot yield an explanation, but the perspective in which these are regarded, the individual way of seeing them, which subordinates all life to the final goal, can do so.

The science of Individual Psychology developed out of the effort to understand that mysterious creative power of life which expresses itself in the desire to develop, to strive, to achieve, and even to compensate for defeats in one direction by striving for success in another. This power is teleological, it expresses itself in the striving after a goal, and, in this striving, every bodily and psychological movement is made to cooperate. It is thus absurd to study bodily movements and mental conditions abstractly without relation to an individual whole. It is absurd, for instance, that in criminal psychology we should pay so much more attention to the crime than to the criminal. The same outward act may be criminal in one case and not criminal in another. The important thing is to understand the individual context, the goal of an individual's life, which marks the line of direction for all his acts and movements. This goal enables us to understand the hidden meaning behind the various separate acts and to see them as parts of a whole. Vice versa when we study the parts, provided we study them as parts of a whole, we get a better sense of the whole.

2. UNCONSCIOUS CREATION[8]

The healthy individual as well as the neurotic would have to forego orientation in the world if he did not organize the picture of the world and his experiences according to fictions. In hours of insecurity, these fictions become more prominent. They become imperatives of belief, of the ideal, of free will, but beyond this they are effective in secret, in the unconscious, like all psychological mechanisms.

The final goal emerges for everyone, consciously or unconsciously, but its significance is never understood [by the individual himself]. From individual evaluation, which usually causes a permanent mood of inferiority feeling, there develops a fictional goal. This is in accord with the unconscious technique of our thinking apparatus and is to be understood as an ideational, ultimate compensation. The fictional goal is blurred and pliable; it cannot be measured; it has been constructed with inadequate and definitely ungifted powers. It has no real existence and therefore cannot be completely comprehended causally. But it can well be understood as a teleological device of the soul which seeks orientation. This teleology is self-imposed. It arises in the psychological organ and must be understood as a device and as the individual's own construction.

Let me point out the following in support, and as mitigation, of these heretical propositions. More important than disposition, objective experience and environment is the subjective evaluation of these. Furthermore, this evaluation stands in a certain, often strange, relation to reality.

Every individual acts and suffers in accordance with his peculiar teleology, which has all the inevitability of fate, so long as he does not understand it [that is, so long as it remains unconscious]. Its springs may be traced to his earliest childhood, and nearly always we find that they have been diverted into false channels by the pressure of the earliest situations in the child's life.

3. THE UNITY OF THE PERSONALITY[9]

Our mental life is not a matter of simple existence but is subject to certain impulsions. It is through this urge towards processes directed to a given end that the whole mental life receives an impetus in a forward direction, and in this stream of processes all the categories and forces belonging to our minds receive their mold, their direction, and their characteristic form. The development of the mental life of man is accomplished with the help of a fictional teleology through the proposing of a certain end under the pressure of a teleological apperception. Thus it finally becomes evident that in every mental phenomenon we discover anew the characteristic of pursuit of a goal, and all our powers, faculties, experiences, wishes and fears, defects and capacities fall into line with this characteristic.

The goal of the mental life of man becomes its governing principle, its *causa finalis*. Here we have the root of the unity of the personality, the individuality. It does not matter what the source of its energies may have been. Not their origin but their end, their ultimate goal, constitutes their individual character.

While all psychological movements derive their direction from a predetermined goal, all the preliminary separate goals after a short existence in the psychological development of the child come under the dominance of the fictional final goal, of the finale which is thought or felt as fixed. In other words, the psychological life of a person is oriented towards the final act, like that of a character created by a good dramatist.

The fictional, abstract ideal is the point of origin for the formation and differentiation of the given psychological resources into preparatory attitudes, readinesses, and character traits. The individual then wears the character traits demanded by his fictional goal, just as the character mask (*persona*) of the ancient actor had to fit the finale of the tragedy.

In every case, the point of the self-ideal (*Persönlichkeitsideal*) posited beyond reality remains effective. This is evidenced by the direction of the attention, of the interests, and of the tendencies, all of which select according to points of view given in advance. It is the setting of a purpose in our psychological behavior and the readiness created by it which determine that actions are initiated and broken off at a certain distance; that, as Ziehen emphasizes, voluntary as well as involuntary impulses are always aimed only at the attainment of a certain effect; and that we must assume a generally intelligent function of the organs, as follows also from Pavlov's presentations. All these phenomena are so compellingly impressive that what is [actually] a calculated attempt at orientation, according to a point assumed to be fixed, has always been understood by philosophers and psychologists as a principle of teleology.

The self-ideal has been created as guiding point by the safeguarding tendency and fictionally carries within itself all abilities and gifts of which the so-disposed child considers himself deprived.

COMMENT   Adler introduced the term "guiding self-ideal" in 1912 in The Neurotic Character where, to all appearances, he used it interchangeably with the fictional final goal. In 1914 Freud formulated his "ideal ego" (36, IV, p. 50), which later became the super-ego (37, pp. 43–44). Adler acknowledged this by inserting the following statement in a revision of The Neurotic Character: "A replacement [of self-ideal] by 'ego ideal' as Freud attempts would have to be rejected on several grounds" (1912a, p. 41).

There are indeed several noteworthy differences between these two ideals. Adler's ideal was the goal of a forward movement; Freud's was the substitution for the "lost narcissism of childhood" (36, IV, p. 51). For Adler, the self-ideal was a genuine creation of the individual, but for Freud, the ideal ego was a reaction to parental criticism (36, IV, p. 53). Adler's ideal is posited for everyone, is actually the sine qua non of the personality, whereas Freud's is set up by some individuals and not by others (36, IV, p. 50). The most important difference is that for Adler the self-ideal or fictional goal was the unifying principle of personality and, as such, of central importance, an integral part of the self-consistent individual; whereas the super-ego, the successor to the ideal ego, was only one of "the three realms, regions or provinces into which we divide the mental apparatus" (41, p. 102), one of the "three harsh masters" which "the poor ego" has to serve, in addition to the id and the outside reality (41, p. 108).

This final goal, abstract in its purpose of assuring superiority, fictional in its task of conquering all the difficulties of life, must appear in concrete form in order to meet its task in actuality. Deity in its widest sense, it is apperceived by the childish imagination and under the exigencies of hard reality, as victory over men, over difficult enterprises, over social or natural limitations. It appears in one's attitude toward others, toward one's vocation, toward the opposite sex. Thus we find concrete single purposes, such as the purpose to operate as a member of the community or to dominate it, to attain security and triumph in one's chosen career, to approach the other sex or to avoid it. We may always trace in these special purposes what sort of meaning the individual has found in his existence and how he proposes to realize that meaning.

4. POINT OF ORIENTATION[10]

A person would not know what to do with himself were he not oriented toward some goal. We cannot think, feel, will, or act without the perception of some goal. All the causalities in the world do not enable the living organism to conquer the chaos of the future and the planlessness of which we should be the victims. All activity would persist in the stage of an indiscriminate groping, and the economy in our psychological life would remain unattained. Without any self-consistency, physiognomy, and personal note we would rank with the amoeba. Inanimate nature obeys a perceptible causality, but life is [subjectively] a demand.

The human mind shows an urge to capture into fixed forms through unreal assumptions, that is, fictions, that which is chaotic, always in flux, and incomprehensible. Serving this urge, the child quite generally uses a schema in order to act and to find his way. We proceed much the same when we divide the earth by meridians and parallels, for only thus do we obtain fixed points which we can bring into a relationship with one another. In all similar attempts with which the human psyche is filled, it is always a matter of entering an unreal, abstract schema into real life. I consider it the main task of this work [*The Neurotic Character*] to advance this knowledge which I have gained from the psychological consideration of the neurosis and psychosis and which is found, according to the evidence of Vaihinger, in all scientific views. No matter at which point one investigates the psychological development of the healthy or the neurotic person, one always finds him enmeshed in his schema, the neurotic believing in his fiction and not finding his way back to reality, the healthy person using it to attain a goal in reality.

This artifice of thinking would have the stamp of paranoia and of dementia praecox—which conditions create for themselves hostile forces out of life's difficulties for the purpose of safeguarding their self-esteem —were not the child able at all times to free himself from the bonds of his fiction, to eliminate his projections (Kant) from his calculations, and to use only the impetus which springs from this guiding line. His insecurity is great enough to make him set up a fantastic goal for the purpose of orientation in the world, but not so great as to devalue reality and to dogmatize the guiding image, as occurs in the psychoses. One must point out, however, that insecurity and the artifice of the fiction have a similar significance in normal persons, neurotics, and the insane.

It is the fiction which teaches us to differentiate, which gives us support and security, which shapes and guides our doings and actions, and which forces our mind to foresee and to perfect itself. Along with this there is the dark side. It brings a hostile, belligerent tendency into our life, robs us of the simplicity of our sensations, and continuously attempts to alienate us from reality by tempting us to violate it. Furthermore, anyone who formulates this goal of godlikeness as real and personal, who takes it literally, is soon forced to flee from real life—since it is a compromise—and to seek a life apart from real life, at best in art, but usually in pietism, neurosis, or crime.

COMMENT *When Freud criticized Adler for introducing the term "fiction" into his writings, it became evident that it was the useful nature of the fiction in coping with reality which Freud did not recognize, and that he thought of fiction as merely another word for fantasy. Freud wrote: "A host of familiar features come to light in Adler's propositions when one restores the original 'phantasized' and 'phantasy' in place of 'manufactured (fingiert), fictive, and fiction.' This identity would be emphasized by psychoanalysts, even if the author had not for many years taken part in our common work" (36, I, pp. 342–343). The difference here is that Freud had defined fantasy as a "mode of thought-activity . . . free from reality-testing and . . . subordinated to the pleasure-principle alone" (36, IV, pp. 16–17), whereas for Adler fiction, far from being a mere subjective fancy, was an indispensable device for problem-solving in real life.*

5. COMPENSATION[11]

COMMENT *The fictional goal is, in many ways, a device of the individual to pull himself up by his bootstraps, as it were. In addition to serving the useful purpose of orienting the individual in the* world, it serves two compensatory functions. (1) It initiates compensation, and (2) it creates positive feelings in the present which mitigate the feelings of inferiority.

a. A Device for Achieving Compensation. The guiding fiction is originally the means or device by which the child seeks to free himself from his inferiority feeling. It initiates the compensation and stands in the service of the safeguarding tendency. The greater the inferiority feeling, the more urgent and stronger will be the need for a safeguarding guiding line, and the more distinctly will it emerge. As in organic compensation, the effectiveness of psychological compensation is linked with increased activity and brings about striking, often superior and novel psychological phenomena.

The real deprivation, as for instance, the restriction of food in childhood, is felt as an abstract "nothing," as want, in contrast to which the child now demands everything, abundance, until he brings this goal conceptually nearer in the person of the father, a fabulous rich person, or a mighty emperor. The more intensely the want has been felt, the stronger and higher the fictional ideal is posited.

It is the child's helplessness, clumsiness, and insecurity which necessitate the exploration of possibilities, the gathering of experiences, and the creation of memory for the purpose of constructing a bridge into the future where reside greatness, power, and satisfactions of all sorts. The construction of this bridge is the most important achievement of the child, because otherwise he would find himself without composure, counsel, guidance, or comfort in the midst of inpouring impressions. One can scarcely delimit or express in words this first stage of the awakening subjective world, of the formation of the self. Nevertheless, we can say that the guiding image of the child must be constructed 'as if' it were able, by influencing the direction of his will, to bring him greater security and orientation.

Our consideration has led us to understand how, from the absolute inferiority of the child, especially of the one who is constitutionally burdened, a self-evaluation develops which produces the feeling of inferiority. Analogous to the δός που στῶ ["Give me where I can stand," the opening words of Archimedes' "Give me a fixed point and I shall move the earth"], the child seeks to gain a standpoint from which to appraise the distances to life's problems. From this standpoint of a low self-evaluation which is assumed as the fixed pole in the ever-changing appearances, the child's psyche spins threads of thought to the goals of his longing. These goals are comprehended by the abstracting form of apprehension of the human mind also as fixed points and are interpreted rather concretely. The goal to be big and strong, to be a man, to be above is symbolized in the person of the father, the mother, the teacher, the driver, and the locomotive engineer. The entire bearing, the identifying gestures, the play of children and their wishes, their day-dreams and favorite fairy tales, thoughts about their future occupational choice, all indicate that the compensation tendency is at work making preparations for the future role.

In the soul of the child, a guiding line forms which urges toward the enhancement of the self-esteem in order to escape insecurity. Myths, the common people, poets, philosophers, and founders of religions have all taken from their time the material for transforming the guiding lines, so that now bodily and intellectual strength, immortality, virtue, piety, wealth, knowledge, the morality of the master, social sense, or self-righteousness are available as final goals and are taken up by the individual in his craving for adequacy (Vollwertigkeit) depending on his receptive peculiarity.

b. *The Goal Itself as Compensation.* The fiction is, so to speak, the marshall's staff in the knapsack of the little soldier and thus a down payment demanded by the primitive feeling of insecurity. (For psychologists of keen sensitivity, I note here that I have accumulated so many examples from military life quite intentionally. In military training the starting point and the fictional purpose are brought into closer relation and thus can be more readily seen together. Through training, every movement of the soldier becomes a readiness which has for its purpose the transformation of a primary feeling of weakness into a feeling of superiority.) In the fiction, disquieting inferiorities and inhibiting realities are set aside, as always happens when the psyche in its plight seeks a solution and security. The painful insecurity is reduced to its lowest possible, albeit apparently causal amount, and this is transformed into its very antithesis which in the form of the fictional goal is made the guiding point of all wishes, phantasies, and tendencies. Next this goal must be made concrete to become clearer.

In each mind there is the conception of a [fictional] goal or ideal to get beyond the present state and to overcome the present deficiencies and difficulties by postulating a concrete goal for the future. By means of this concrete goal, the individual can think and feel himself superior to the difficulties of the present because he has in mind his success of the future.

The consideration of the unity of the personality led us to the conviction that early in life, in the first four or five years, a goal is set for the need and drive of psychical development, a goal toward which all its currents flow. Such a goal not only determines a direction which promises security, power, and perfection, but also awakens the corresponding feelings and emotions through that which it promises. Thus the individual mitigates his sense of weakness in the anticipation of his redemption.

FOOTNOTES TO CHAPTER THREE

1. **1 to 8:** Hans Vaihinger. *The Philosophy of 'As If'* (111), pp. 2, 12, 81, 7, 145, 99, xlvii, and xlvii.
2. **1 to 10:** *'As If'* (111), pp. 23, 24, 29, 31–32, 39–40, 43, 48, 81, 82, and 82–83.
3. **1 to 7:** *'As If'* (111), pp. 85, 88, 89, 91, 91–93, 94, and 108.
4. **1 to 7:** *'As If'* (111), pp. 124, 125, 125, 126, 127, 127, and 128–129.
5. **1 to 4:** *'As If'* (111), pp. 319, 321, 326, and 305.
6. **1, 2, 3:** *'As If'* (111), pp. 341, 342, and 354.
7. **1 and 2:** "Die Individualpsychologie, ihre Voraussetzungen und Ergebnisse" (1914f), p. 2; **3:** "Lebenslüge und Verantwortlichkeit in der Neurose und Psychose; ein Beitrag zur Melancholiefrage" (1914c), p. 183; **4:** "Progress in Individual Psychology" (1923a), p. 23; **5 to 8:** "Psychische Kausalität" (1923c), p. 38; **9:** *Der Sinn des Lebens* (1933a), p. 8; **10:** "Individual Psychology" (1930f), p. 400; **11:** *The Science of Living* (1929c), pp. 32–33.
8. **1:** *Über den nervösen Charakter* (1912a), p. 15; **2 and 3:** "IP Voraussetzungen" (1914f), p. 4; **4:** "Progress in IP" (1923a), pp. 22–23.
9. **1 and 2:** "Progress in IP" (1923a), pp. 22 and 23; **3:** "IP Voraussetzungen" (1914f), p. 3; **4, 5, 6:** *Nervöser Charakter* (1912a), pp. 46, 40–41, and 43; **7:** "IP" (1930f), p. 400.
10. **1 and 4:** "IP Voraussetzungen" (1914f), pp. 2 and 6; **2 and 3:** *Nervöser Charakter* (1912a), pp. 25–26 and 34.
11. **1 to 6:** *Nervöser Charakter* (1912a), pp. 35, 46, 33, 25, 31, and 46; **7:** *Science of Living* (1929c), p. 34; **8:** "IP" (1930f), p. 399.

CHAPTER FOUR

STRIVING FOR SUPERIORITY

COMMENT   We have seen that Adler tended from the beginning toward a theory of the unity and self-consistency of the personality. Such a theory would need a prepotent dynamic force. This was at first described as the aggression drive, the outcome of a confluence of drives (see p. 34). After Adler had abandoned drive psychology, it became the "wanting to be a real man" of the masculine protest (see p. 250). With Adler's full commitment to fictional finalism in 1912, the fictional goal became the principle of unity of the personality (see pp. 94–96) and the striving toward this goal the prepotent dynamic force.

While in the preceding chapter our selections were concentrated on the theoretical significance of the goal, its origin, and its functions for the subject, and we omitted as much as possible discussion of the content of the goal and the goal striving itself, still it became evident that the goal is one of superiority, that consequently the striving is toward superiority, and finally that the striving is compensatory, originating in a feeling of inferiority.

From then on and throughout the years of Adler's writings the general description of the governing dynamic force as one of striving from inferiority to superiority, from "below" to "above" remained the same. But the meaning of superiority, or above, that is, the specific goal point, underwent an important change.

At first, above meant being a real man, power, self-esteem, security; all these goal points were expressed in terms of the individual. But in these early days, Adler as a psychiatrist, wrote in terms of the neurotic patient; it was the neurotic whom Adler showed as striving for enhancement of his self-esteem or for the safeguarding of it. When he generalized from the neurotic, he described the normal individual as behaving in the same way, only less clearly so and to a lesser degree. The neurotic was the frame of reference, the standard of comparison so to speak.

Later, above came to mean perfection, completion, or overcoming, goal points which are no longer fully expressed in terms of the self but which can be applied to outside objects also. While overcoming may refer to internal obstacles, it usually refers to external ones; completion usually refers to a task; and perfection to an achievement or a product. When Adler wrote in these terms, the frame of reference was no longer the neurotic, but man in general, the mentally healthy individual. When he now generalized, it was from the normal to the abnormal; the abnormal also strives for perfection, although it may hardly be recognizable as such.

What brought about this change in frame of reference from the abnormal to the normal? Originally Adler had drawn his inferences from his patients; regarding normal individuals, he only knew that they must be similarly motivated. The difference between the two was one of degree, the normal showing a less accentuated, less dogmatized, goal of superiority and less urgency in reaching it than the abnormal. The greater motivation of the neurotic came from his greater inferiority feeling. But Adler had not answered the question: In what respect, if any, is the normal more motivated than the neurotic? This question would certainly need to be answered since the normal would seem to strive as much as the abnormal, certainly at least in many instances.

The change and the answer were made possible by the fact that Adler developed a criterion for normality, during the period roughly from 1920–1930. Once he had such a criterion, he could rewrite his motivational theory in terms of the normal. Adler's ultimate concept of social interest, which will be presented in the next chapter, became this criterion. The ideally normal individual has an ideal amount of social interest. Thus, while the neurotic is more concerned with his self-esteem, and has a personal goal of superiority, the normal individual, due to his greater social interest, is more concerned with gaining satisfaction by overcoming difficulties which are appreciated as such by others as well. He has a goal of superiority which includes the welfare of others. The difference in motivation between the normal and the abnormal then became primarily one of kind instead of degree. While the abnormal is more motivated in the direction of a private intelligence and is more self-centered in his striving, the normal is more motivated in the direction of common sense; that is, he is more task-centered in his striving.

When Adler replaced the earlier formulations of the meaning of superiority by striving for perfection, he did not leave the earlier out of account; they were given a subordinate position in his system, just as he had given the drives and heredity and environment a subordinate place. Our reason for beginning the presentation of the selections on the striving for superiority with Adler's late writings is that thereby we can best present the entire picture, with all the parts organized according to their relative significance.

Accordingly, the first part of the present chapter will deal with the striving for superiority in terms of perfection, and the second part in terms of self-enhancement. This will be followed by the discussion of the inferiority feeling, the origin of all the striving, according to Adler, while the last section will deal with his further views on the position of drives in human dynamics.

A. The Striving for Perfection

1. THE CEASELESSNESS OF STRIVING[1]

I began to see clearly in every psychological phenomenon the striving for superiority. It runs parallel to physical growth and is an intrinsic neeessity of life itself. It lies at the root of all solutions of life's problems and is manifested in the way in which we meet these problems. All our functions follow its direction. They strive for conquest, security, increase, either in the right or in the wrong direction. The impetus from minus to plus never ends. The urge from below to above never ceases. Whatever premises all our philosophers and psychologists dream of—self-preservation, pleasure principle, equalization—all these are but vague representations, attempts to express the great upward drive.

The history of the human race points in the same direction. Willing, thinking, talking, seeking after rest and pleasure, learning, understanding, working and loving, all betoken the essence of this eternal melody. From this network, which in the last analysis is simply given with the man-cosmos relationship, no one may hope to escape. Even if anyone wanted to escape, even if he could escape, he would still find himself in the general system, striving upward from below. This not only states a fundamental category of thought, a thought construct, but, what is more, represents the fundamental fact of our life.

The origin of humanity and the ever-repeated beginning of infant life impresses with every psychological act: "Achieve! Arise! Conquer!" This feeling, this longing for the abrogations of every imperfection, is never absent. In the search for relief, in Faustian wrestling against the forces of nature, rings always the basic chord: "I relinquish thee not, thou bless me withal." The unreluctant search for truth, the ever-unsatisfied seeking for solution of the problems of life, belongs to this longing for perfection of some sort.

2. THE UNIVERSALITY OF STRIVING[2]

We all wish to overcome difficulties. We all strive to reach a goal by the attainment of which we shall feel strong, superior, and complete. John Dewey refers, very rightly, to this tendency as the striving for security. Others call it the striving for self-preservation. But whatever name we give it, we shall always find in human beings this great line of activity —this struggle to rise from an inferior to a superior position, from defeat to victory, from below to above. It begins in earliest childhood and continues to the end of our lives.

As for the striving for perfection, for superiority, or for power, some have always known about it, but not thoroughly enough to spread this knowledge to a larger mass or to illuminate the fundamental significance of this striving for the structure of the entire personality. Only Individual Psychology has pointed out that this striving for perfection is found in every individual and fills every individual [the prepotent dynamic principle]. It is not necessary to inoculate man with the desire to develop into superman, as the daring attempt of Nietzsche has shown.

I should like to emphasize first of all that striving for perfection is innate. This is not meant in a concrete way, as if there were a drive which would later in life be capable of bringing everything to completion and which only needed to develop itself. The striving for perfection is innate in the sense that it is a part of life, a striving, an urge, a something without which life would be unthinkable.

COMMENT   Here again Adler presents the antithesis to Freud. According to Freud: "It may be difficult, for many of us, to abandon the belief that there is an instinct towards perfection at work in human beings, which has brought them to their present high level of intellectual achievement and ethical sublimation and which may be expected to watch over their development into supermen. I have no faith, however, in the existence of any such internal instinct and I cannot see how this benevolent illusion is to be preserved. The present development of human beings requires, as it seems to me, no different explanation from that of animals. What appears in a minority of human individuals as an untiring impulsion towards further perfection can easily be understood as a result of the instinctual repression upon which is based all that is most precious in human civilization . . . The backward path that leads to complete satisfaction is as a rule obstructed by the resistances which maintain the repressions. So there is no alternative but to advance in the direction in which growth is still free—though with no prospect of bringing the process to a conclusion or of being able to reach the goal" (34, pp. 55–56). This backward orientation leads Freud to say a year later: "He (the father, chief, or leader of the primal horde), at the very beginning of the history of mankind, was the Superman whom Nietzsche only expected from the future" (39, p. 93). Freud shows himself here clearly as the objective reductionist, explaining the observable phenomenon of man's forward push as nothing but the outcome of an obstructed backward desire, while Adler, the subjectivistic phenomenologist, considers the observed phenomenon as irreducible.

In contrast, the general affinity of Gestalt psychology to Individual Psychology finds expression also in this respect. According to Kurt Koffka, "Our Ego, that is, the opinion we have of ourselves . . . is always under a force which propels it 'upwards' " (60, p. 671).

The views of Kurt Goldstein, closely related to Gestalt psychology, show a striking similarity to those of Adler, in this as well as in other points treated in this chapter. On the basis of his work with brain-injured patients, Goldstein arrived at the conclusion that there is only one basic drive, namely, the need for self-actualization, which he described as follows: "We can say, an organism is governed by the tendency to actualize, as much as possible, its individual capacities, its 'nature,' in the world" (48, p. 196). A special form of self-actualization is the tendency towards completion and perfection: "In the innumerable repetitions of children, we are not dealing with the manifestation of a senseless drive for repetition, but with the tendency to completion and perfection . . . The nearer we are to perfection, the stronger is the need to perform. This is valid for children as well as for adults . . . After the child has perfected the performance of walking, he uses this instrument in order to reach a special point which attracts his attention, i.e., to complete another performance, and so on" (48, pp. 204–205).

In Adler, the concept of perfection is carried further in that it comprises subjective, and partially unconscious, notions of perfection, including in the final fictional goal the perfection of mankind. This is only vaguely conceived by the individual, but in accordance with a projected societal evolution, as shown in the following.

3. STRIVING AS ULTIMATE ADAPTATION[3]

Individual Psychology stands firmly on the ground of evolution and, in the light of it, regards all human striving as a striving for perfection. Bodily and psychologically, the urge to life is tied unalterably to this striving.

COMMENT   To the extent that it is pertinent to psychology, Adler uses the term evolution in the sense of societal evolution, as described by George G. Simpson, in distinction from organic evolution. Societal evolution "operates directly by the inheritance of acquired characters, of knowledge and learned activities," including value judgment and ethical decisions, and is subject to conscious control (95, pp. 138–142). "Man's essential nature is defined by qualities found nowhere else . . . It is part of this unique status that in man a new form of evolution begins . . . Plan, purpose, goal, all absent in evolution to this point, enter with the coming of man and are inherent in the new evolution, which is confined to him. With them comes the need for criteria of choice. Good and evil, right and wrong, concepts largely irrelevant in nature except from the human viewpoint, become real and pressing features of the whole cosmos as viewed by man . . ." (95, p. 179).

We must connect our thought with a continuous active adaptation to the demands of the outer world if we are to understand the direction and movement of life. We must think that this is a question of something primordial, of something that was inherent in primeval life. It has always been a matter of overcoming, of the existence of the individual and the human race, always a matter of establishing a favorable relationship between the individual and the outer world. This coercion to carry out a better adaptation can never end. In speaking of active adaptation I am referring to adaptation sub specie aeternitatis [under the aspect of eternity, Spinoza], for only that bodily and psychological development is "right" which can be deemed right for the future. Furthermore, the concept of active adaptation implies that body and mind and the whole organization of living must strive toward this ultimate adaptation, toward the conquest of all the advantages and disadvantages set by the cosmos.

An adaptation to immediate reality would be nothing other than an exploitation of the accomplishments of the striving of others, as the picture of the world of the pampered child demands. The continuous striving for security urges toward the overcoming of the present reality in favor of a better one. This goal of perfection must bear within it the goal of an ideal community, because all that we value in life, all that endures and continues to endure, is eternally the product of social interest.

No one knows which is the only correct way. Mankind has frequently made attempts to imagine this final goal of human development. The best conception which one has gained so far of this ideal elevation of mankind is the concept of God. There is no question that the concept of God actually includes this movement as a goal and that it best serves the purpose of a concrete goal of perfection for the obscure desire of man to reach perfection.

Man as an everstriving being cannot be like God. God who is eternally complete, who directs the stars, who is the master of fates, who elevates man from his lowliness to Himself, who speaks from the cosmos to every single human soul, is the most brilliant manifestation of the goal of perfection to date. In God's nature, religious mankind perceives the way to height. In His call it hears again the innate voice of life which must have its direction towards the goal of perfection, towards overcoming the feeling of lowliness and transitoriness of the existence here below. The human soul, as a part of the movement of life, is endowed with the ability to participate in the uplift, elevation, perfection, and completion.

4. PERFECTION IN THE ABNORMAL[4]

Whether one thinks or acts more wisely or less, one always moves along the lines of the upward tendency. In our right and wrong conceptions of life and its problems, in the successful or the unsuccessful solution of any question, this striving for perfection is uninterruptedly at work. And even where foolishness, imbecility, and inexperience seem to belie the striving to conquer some defect or tend to depreciate it, the will to conquer is nevertheless operative.

Of course there are countless attempts to envisage this goal of perfection. Individual Psychologists, especially those of us who are physicians and have to deal with failures, with persons who suffer from a neurosis or psychosis, with delinquents, and alcoholics, see this goal of superiority in them also, but it tends in a direction which is opposed to reason to the extent that we cannot recognize in it a proper goal of perfection. When, for example, a person seeks to concretize his goal by wanting to domineer over others, such a goal of perfection seems unfitted to guide the individual or the mass of men. No one could posit such a goal for himself without being forced to come into conflict with the coercion of evolution, to violate reality, and to protect himself fearfully against the truth and those who stand up to it. A goal of perfection of leaning on others also appears to contradict reason. A goal which leaves the tasks of life unsolved, in order not to suffer sure defeats, also appears altogether unsuited, although many find it acceptable.

By having established that the norm for perfection is social interest, we are in a position to understand approximately the direction towards ideal perfection.

B. Striving for Self-Enhancement

COMMENT *The previous part described the striving for superiority in terms of the well-adjusted individual, and the selections all dated from 1930 on. In the present part, where we are dealing with the neurotic striving for superiority, the selections are almost entirely from The Neurotic Character (1912a). We should like to remind the reader once more that when Adler speaks here of the normal, it is an extrapolation from the neurotic.*

1. ENHANCEMENT OF THE SELF-ESTEEM[5]

The neurotic purpose is the enhancement of the self-esteem, for which the simplest formula can be recognized in the exaggerated "masculine protest." This formula, "I want to be a real man," is the guiding fiction, the "fundamental apperception" (Jerusalem) in every neurosis, where it demands realization to a higher degree than in the normal psyche. The libido, the sex drive, and the inclination toward perversion, irrespective of their origins, become subordinated to this guiding thought.

Form and content of the neurotic guiding line originate from the impressions of the child who feels humiliated. These impressions, which emerge by necessity from an original feeling of inferiority, evoke an attitude of aggression, the purpose of which is the overcoming of a great insecurity. In this attitude of aggression are found all attempts of the child which promise an enhancement of the self-esteem. All neurotic phenomena originate from these preparatory means which strive toward the final purpose of superiority. They are psychological readinesses for initiating the struggle for self-esteem.

On account of his [greater] feeling of insecurity, the gaze of the neurotic is directed much further into the future. All present life appears to him only a preparation. His realm is not of this world and he cannot free himself from the deity which he has created for himself, the enhancement of the self-esteem.

The pathological fear, which we find in patients, is always the fear of loss of the goal of superiority, the fear of loss of self-esteem. Although the structure of the fear is individually different in each case, it can always be traced to an oversized longing to be pampered and to a lack in ability to cooperate, which expresses itself in wanting to take and not in wanting to give.

The nature of a psychogenic disease will remain unclear as long as the guiding characteristic of striving toward above has not been brought out. Valuable as the insights of the psychotherapists have become, so long as the secondary guiding lines such as gaining pleasure, self-preservation, affectivity (Bleuler), and those others which grow from organ inferiority (Adler) are not brought into relationship with the self-ideal, our insight remains incomplete, the psychological coherence is missing. (*Fehlt leider nur das geistige Band.*)

A preliminary, certainly incomplete schema which is still lacking the corrections of social interest and which does more justice to the psyche of the neurotic than to the structure of the healthy psyche is shown in Figure 1 [on the next page].

2. SAFEGUARDING THE SELF-ESTEEM[6]

I have repeatedly described "safeguarding tendencies" as the essential character trait of the neurosis. They are evoked by the oversensitivity of the neurotic and his fear of disparagement and disgrace.

The safeguarding tendency which originates in the feeling of insecurity forces us all, especially the child and the neurotic, to leave the more obvious ways of induction and deduction and to use such devices as the schematic fiction. Through the safeguarding tendency the individual aims at getting rid of the feeling of inferiority in order to raise himself to the full height of the self-esteem, toward complete manliness, toward the idea of being above.

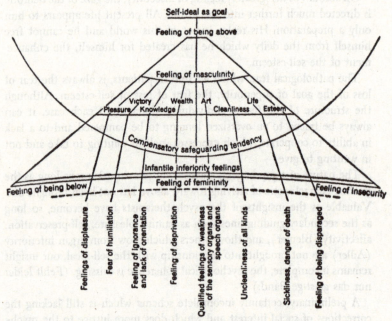

FIG. 1. The inferiority-superiority dynamics.

The answer to the problem of life, actually the way in which life is to be taken, is identical with the attempt to make an end to the uncertainty of life and the chaos of the perceptions and sensations, and to take the necessary steps to overcome the difficulties. Even reflection, observation, thinking and thinking ahead, admiration, memory, attention, judgment, and valuation are brought out by the safeguarding tendency. Since the sense of one's own inferiority yields an abstract measure for the inequality among men, the greater and the stronger men and their size are made into the fictional final goal in order that the self may be protected in this way from insecurity and trembling.

3. STRIVING FOR POWER[7]

Much of our view of the enhancement of the self-esteem as the guiding fiction is included in Nietzsche's "will to power" and "will to seem." Our view touches in many points also on those of Féré and older authors, according to whom the feeling of pleasure is founded in a feeling of power, that of displeasure in a feeling of powerlessness.

So far we have considered the guiding force and final purpose of the neurosis to be a desire for enhancement of the self-esteem which always asserts itself with special strength. This is merely the expression of a striving which is deeply founded in human nature in general. The expression and the deepening of this guiding thought, which could also be described as will to power, teaches us that a particular compensatory force is involved which attempts to put an end to the general human inner insecurity.

Every neurotic character trait reveals through its direction that it is permeated by the striving for power which tries to make the trait an infallible means for excluding permanent humiliation from the patient's experiences.

The constitutional inferiority and similarly effective childhood situations give rise to a feeling of inferiority which demands a compensation in the sense of an enhancement of the self-esteem. Here the fictional, final purpose of the striving for power gains enormous influence and draws all psychological forces into its direction. This fictional final purpose, itself originating in the safeguarding tendency, organizes psychological readinesses for the purpose of [further] safeguarding. Among these the neurotic character and the functional neurosis stand out as prominent devices.

We wish to point out the absolute primacy of the will to power, a guiding fiction which asserts itself the more forcibly and is developed the earlier, often precipitously, the stronger the inferiority feeling of the organically inferior child comes to the foreground.

In the functioning of constitutionally inferior organs, the impression of insecurity increases due to the greater tension towards the demands of the external environment, and the low self-estimation of the child brings about a permanent inferiority feeling. Already in early childhood mastery of the situation according to a model, and usually beyond this model, is taken as the guiding motif. A permanent volitional impulse is fixed and automatized to ascribe the permanent leadership to a guiding idea, the will to power. This is also the goal setting in the neurotic psyche which consciously or unconsciously corresponds to the formula: "I must act so that in the end I will be master of the situation."

With great avidity, directly or by detours, consciously or unconsciously, through appropriate thinking and action or through the arrangement of symptoms, the neurotic strives for increased possession, power, and influence, and for the disparagement and cheating of other persons.

4. SELF-ENHANCEMENT AND THE NORMAL STRIVING[8]

COMMENT   *In the following selections, Adler attempts to integrate his early statements regarding human dynamics with the later development of his theory, the striving for perfection. From these selections it becomes quite clear that, while self-enhancement with its "self-boundedness" and its emphasis on self-centered striving is the prepotent dynamic force in the neurotic, it is not the prepotent force in the healthy individual. He automatically safeguards himself by striving for a goal beyond himself, "a goal based on interest in reality, interest in others, and interest in cooperation."*

Self-boundedness (Ichgebundenheit) is the central point of attack of Individual Psychology. The self-bound individual always forgets that his self would be safeguarded better and automatically the more he prepares himself for the welfare of mankind, and that in this respect no limits are set for him. The numerous quotations from the Bible are confirmations to be grateful for. They are the deep insight of sublime leaders into the foundations of human welfare and express in an imposing way much of what Individual Psychology attempts to make available to thought through modest scientific work.

Only a child who desires to contribute to the whole, whose interest is not centered in himself, can train successfully to compensate for defects. If children desire only to rid themselves of difficulties, they will continue backward. They can keep up their courage only if they have a purpose in view for their efforts and if the achievement of this purpose is more important to them than the obstacles which stand in the way. It is a question of where their interest and attention is directed. If they are striving towards an object external to themselves, they will quite naturally train and equip themselves to achieve it. Difficulties will represent no more than positions which are to be conquered on their way to success. If, on the other hand, their interest lies in stressing their own drawbacks or in fighting these drawbacks with no purpose except to be free from them, they will be able to make no real progress. A clumsy right hand cannot be trained into a skillful right hand by taking thought, by wishing that it were less clumsy, or even by avoiding clumsiness. It can become skillful only by exercise in practical achievements, and the incentive to the achievement must be more deeply felt than the discouragement at the hitherto existent clumsiness. If a child is to draw together his powers and overcome his difficulties, there must be a goal for his movements outside of himself, a goal based on interest in reality, interest in others, and interest in cooperation.

Are there not some of us who should learn, first of all, to guard our own interests or to strengthen our own personalities? I believe this view raises a false problem and is a great mistake. If an individual, in the meaning he gives to life, wishes to make a contribution, and if his emotions are all directed to this goal, he will naturally be bound to bring himself into the best shape. He will begin to equip himself to solve the three problems of life [behavior toward others, occupation, and love] and to develop his abilities. If we are working to ease and enrich our partner's life, we shall make of ourselves the best that we can. If we think that we must develop personality *in vacuo*, without a goal of contribution, we shall merely make ourselves domineering and unpleasant.

Regarding the striving for power, we find the misunderstanding that Individual Psychology not only regards psychological life as the striving for power, but propagates this idea. This striving for power is not our madness, it is what we find in others.

COMMENT *The misunderstanding to which Adler refers here does in fact have some justification in that he at one stage treated the striving for power as the usual manifestation of the basic striving. This stage came at a time after he had observed the will to power as characteristic of the neurotic, but while he still conceived the dynamic of social interest as a sort of counterinfluence. The formulations on the striving for power are to be found for the most part in Menschenkenntnis, which, though first appearing in 1927, is a compilation of lectures antedating publication by many years. Throughout this book Adler refers to the child's goal of power (Machtziel). Regarding individuals generally he states: "Behavior is determined by a goal, one which shows itself as nothing other than a goal of superiority, of power, of overpowering others" (1927a, p. 128). Elsewhere he writes: "The desire to make oneself felt,* a desire whose goal is superiority over others, is the guiding force which directs all human activities, and is not a more or less negligible factor" (1923a, p. 25). "All psychological phenomena are united in an inseparable relationship; on the one hand they come under the law of society and on the other hand under the striving of the individual for power and superiority" (1927a, p. 232). Adler's later statements, which appear below, show how he modified these views.

The striving of each actively moving individual is towards overcoming, not towards power. Striving for power, for personal power, represents only one of a thousand types, all of which seek perfection, a security-giving plus situation.

The psychological archetype (Urform) of the line of human movement is the striving for perfection, which is supported by the weakness of the child, his ever-present inferiority feeling. It is the striving for the solution of the life problems in the sense of the evolution of the individual as well as mankind. There are millions of variations of the striving for perfection, a large part of which can be regarded as the striving for personal power. This movement-form more or less lacks the proper degree of social interest, must therefore be designated as erroneous, and carries in itself the sign of later inadequacy in the event of an emerging social problem.

The neurotic strives toward personal superiority and, in doing so, expects a contribution from the group in which he lives, while the normal individual strives toward the perfection which benefits all.

The views of Individual Psychology demand the unconditional reduction of striving for power and the development of social interest. The watchword of Individual Psychology is the fellow man and the fellow-man attitude to the immanent demands of human society.

c. Inferiority Feeling

COMMENT On the opening page of The Neurotic Character (1912a), Adler gives special credit to Pierre Janet by saying: "His emphasis on the sentiment d'incomplètude of the neurotic agrees so much with my findings that I may see in my work an extension of this most important fundamental fact of the mental life of the neurotic" (1912a, p. 1). Adler adds, however, that Janet did not see a compensatory interaction between the feeling of incompleteness and striving toward a goal. Furthermore, Janet was interested in a general, classificatory description of the sentiment d'incomplètude, whereas Adler assumed a feeling of inferiority for everyone, and sought to find the way in which this general phenomenon worked itself out in the individual case. In 1914, Robert Freschl (31) wrote a paper pointing out the similarities between Janet and Individual Psychology in the attempt to call the work of Adler to the attention of Janet. Yet as late as 1930, according to Oliver Brachfeld, Janet still "spoke of an 'inferiority complex imported from America' but without knowing the name of Adler" (17, p. 76).

1. THE NORMAL INFERIORITY FEELING[9]

COMMENT Regarding the normal inferiority feeling, Adler's earlier writings were primarily concerned with tracing it to the child's smallness and dependence in a world of adults. In his later writings, problems and pressures of the present were more clearly seen as belonging within the framework of the inferiority feeling. Included within it was also the goal of perfection as inducing an inferiority feeling, which in turn "presses towards its own conquest." In this sense then the inferiority feeling came close in meaning to what Lewin called a quasineed, that is, a tension system, effected by a purpose (67, p. 242).

a. Genetic Considerations. We pointed out long ago that to be human means to feel inferior. Perhaps not everyone can recall having such a feeling. Possibly some may feel repelled by this expression and would rather choose another term. I have nothing against such a substitution, especially since I see that various authors have already made use of it. To put us in the wrong, certain overly clever people have figured that in order to arrive at a feeling of inferiority the child must originally have had a sense of high personal value.

If we consider that every child is actually inferior in the face of life and could not exist at all without a considerable measure of social interest on the part of those close to him, if we focus on the smallness and helplessness of the child which continues so long and which brings about the impression that we are hardly equal to life, then we must assume that at the beginning of every psychological life there is a more or less deep inferiority feeling. Because he is exposed to the environment of adults, each child is tempted to regard himself as small and weak and to appraise himself as inadequate and inferior. This is the driving force, the point from which originate and develop all the child's efforts to posit a goal for himself from which he expects all comfort and safeguarding of his life for the future, and which causes him to enter a course which appears suitable for the achievement of this goal.

COMMENT   When Adler, with his emphasis on forward orientation, engaged in genetic considerations, it was consistent for him to assume a less satisfactory original condition in the infant and an urge to advance toward a more satisfactory condition. For Freud, in contrast, with his emphasis on backward orientation and his understanding of instincts as urges to reinstate the past (34, p. 47), it was consistent to assume that the past corresponds to a golden age, so to speak, the state of "absolute, primary narcissism" (42, p. 23), to which one wants to return.

The degree of the feeling of insecurity and inferiority depends primarily on the interpretation of the child. Certainly the degree of objective inferiority is significant and will make itself felt. But we must not expect that the child will make correct appraisals in this connection, any more than will the adult. One child will grow up in such complicated circumstances that an error regarding the degree of his inferiority and insecurity is almost certain, while another child will be able to appraise his situation more correctly. By and large, however, it is always the feeling of the child which must be considered. At first this fluctuates daily until eventually it becomes somehow consolidated and expresses itself as a self-appraisal.

b. Dynamic Considerations. In the struggle for perfection, man is always in a state of psychical agitation and feels unsettled before the goal of perfection. It is only when he feels that he has reached a satisfying stage in his upward struggle that he has the feeling of rest, of value, and of happiness. In the next moment his goal draws him farther on. Thus it becomes clear that to be a human being means to possess a feeling of inferiority which constantly presses towards its own conquest. The paths to victory are as different in a thousand ways as the chosen goals of perfection. The greater the feeling of inferiority that has been experienced, the more powerful is the urge to conquest and the more violent the emotional agitation.

The inferiority feeling dominates the psychological life and can easily be understood from the feeling of imperfection and of incompletion and from the incessant striving of man and mankind.

Difficult questions in life, dangers, emergencies, disappointments, worries, losses, especially those of loved persons, social pressures of all kinds, may always be seen as included within the framework of the inferiority feeling, mostly in the form of the universally recognizable emotions and states of mind which we know as anxiety, sorrow, despair, shame, shyness, embarrassment, and disgust.

Inferiority feelings are not in themselves abnormal. They are the cause of all improvements in the position of mankind. Science itself, for example, can arise only when people feel their ignorance and their need to foresee the future; it is the result of the strivings of human beings to improve their whole situation, to know more of the universe, and to be able to control it better. Indeed, it seems that all our human culture is based upon feelings of inferiority.

Man would necessarily have succumbed before the assault of the powers of nature if he had not employed them to his advantage. He lacks everything that could have made the more powerful animals his conquerors. Climatic conditions compel him to protect himself from the cold by clothes, which he takes from animals better protected than he is. His organism requires artificial housing and artificial preparation of food. His life is only assured by means of division of labor and by sufficient propagation. His organs and his mind toil continually for conquest and security. To all this have to be added his greater knowledge of life's dangers and his awareness of death. Who can seriously doubt that the human individual treated by nature in such a stepmother fashion has been provided with the blessing of a strong feeling of inferiority that urges him towards a plus situation, towards security and conquest? This tremendous, enforced rebellion against a tenacious feeling of inferiority as the foundation of human development is awakened afresh and repeated in every infant and little child.

In comparison with unattainable ideal perfection, the individual is continuously filled by an inferiority feeling and motivated (angetrieben) by it.

COMMENT *Here again we find Goldstein expressing himself very similarly to Adler. Speaking of the tendency to completion and perfection in normal individuals, Goldstein states: "The driving force* is given in the experience of imperfection—be it thirst, hunger, or experience of being unable to fulfill any performance which seems to be within our capacities—the goal is the fulfillment of the task" (48, pp. 204-205). Goldstein's "experience of imperfection" would certainly seem to correspond to Adler's "feeling of inferiority," in the present connection.

2. THE ABNORMAL INFERIORITY FEELING[10]

Children born with inferior organs experience their bodies and its pains and weaknesses as a burden. They, much more than normal children, develop inferiority feelings, strive to compensate these lacks and to arrive at a goal in which they foresee and presume a feeling of superiority. In this movement from below to above, from a felt minus to a presupposed plus, they are attacked much more by the difficulties of life and feel and live as though they were in an enemy country. Fighting, hesitating, stopping, escaping, much more occupied with their own persons than with others, they are therefore selfish, inconsiderate, lacking in social interest, courage, and self-confidence because they fear defeat more than they desire success.

This same burden and pessimistic view originates also when the environment is unfavorable. Therefore we find this great feeling of inferiority also among pampered children. Living in a kind of symbiosis, like parasites, always connected with their mother, their goal of superiority is to make this relationship permanent. Each change terrifies them. But changes are unavoidable. Thus the normal feeling of inferiority becomes increased. Their social interest is lacking in a high degree and only developed towards the mother. They consider other people enemies. Later in life they are not adapted for occupation, love, and marriage, because they consider only their own welfare and are not looking for the interests of others. Sometimes they turn towards crime, and they are, in childhood, the majority of the problem children.

Nearly the same symptoms appear in hated children, that is, illegitimate or unwanted children. They feel curtailed and behave like enemies. They use their strength only if they are stronger, sometimes in a cruel manner against weaker persons or animals. Their goal of superiority is to suppress the other person. Their increased feeling of inferiority makes them suspicious and sly. It is difficult to win them and to develop social interest and courage to do useful work.

It is such children who become the criminals, problem children, neurotics, and suicides. They are lacking in social interest and therefore in courage and self-confidence. Their treatment and cure, as in the case of adult neurotics, would be for the psychotherapist to take on the double function of the mother [which she had not properly fulfilled]: (1) to join with the child and to give him the experience of a trustworthy fellow man, and (2) to increase and spread the social interest and thus to strengthen independence and courage. [See p. 341.]

The neurotic individual comes from a sphere of insecurity and in his childhood was under the pressure of his constitutional inferiority. In most cases this may be easily proven. In other cases the patient merely behaves as if he were inferior [the inferiority is merely subjective]. In all cases, however, his willing and thinking are built upon the foundation of a feeling of inferiority. This feeling must always be understood as relative, for it has grown from the individual's relationship to his environment or to his goals. It was always preceded by a matching, a comparing of himself with others, at first with the father, the strongest in the family, at times with the mother, the brothers and sisters, later with every person whom the patient meets. Upon closer observation one finds that every child, but especially the one less favored by nature, has made a keen appraisal of himself.

Since the feeling of inferiority is generally regarded as a sign of weakness and as something shameful, there is naturally a strong tendency to conceal it. Indeed, the effort of concealment may be so great that the person himself ceases to be aware of his inferiority as such, being wholly preoccupied with the consequences of the feeling and with all the objective details that subserve its concealment. So efficiently may an individual train his whole mentality for this task that the entire current of his psychic life flowing ceaselessly from below to above, that is, from the feeling of inferiority to that of superiority, occurs automatically and escapes his own notice. It is not surprising, therefore, that we often receive a negative reply when we ask a person whether he has a feeling of inferiority. It is better not to press the point, but to observe his psychological movements, in which the attitude and individual goal can always be discerned.

D. Drive Satisfaction

1. SUBORDINATION OF DRIVES[11]

Regarding drive psychology in general, one must ask oneself from where the drives receive their direction. As we understand it, the drive has no direction; it is the drive psychologist who anthropomorphizes it into a ready demon which possesses intelligence, selectivity, direction, a life of its own. In short, he represents a complete self, equipped with cunning and tricks. The displacement of the self into the drive is carried to a fantastic degree. The drive, in as far as we can disregard its abstract nature, like the character, thinking, feeling, volition, doubt, emotion, or action, is a part of the self-consistent personality, and as such depends on the law of movement of the individual. The drive receives its direction from the totality and can be changed only simultaneously with the self-consistent personality.

The purely physiological form of drive satisfaction will endure only until the proper way has been found [by the individual] to become stabilized and rendered secure against the greatest attacks. By the time the child carries out independent, purposeful actions which are not merely directed toward drive satisfaction, when he takes his place in the family and begins to adapt himself to his environment toward the end of infancy, he already possesses readinesses, psychological gestures, and attitudes [which supercede the primacy of drive satisfaction]. Furthermore his actions have become unified, and one sees him on the road toward conquering a place in the world.

COMMENT   Goldstein considers separate drives an artifact of observation. "Under various conditions, various actions . . . give the impression of independently existing drives. In reality, however, these various actions occur . . . in accordance with those instrumental processes which are then necessary prerequisites of the self-actualization of the organism. The concept of different, separate drives is based especially upon . . . observations on young children, and on animals under experimental conditions" (48, pp. 197–198).

2. SUBORDINATION OF PLEASURE AND SELF-PRESERVATION[12]

It is easier to trace the manifestations of the guiding fiction than to name the fictive final purpose itself. Previous psychological research has named several such final purposes. For our considerations it will suffice to discuss critically just two of these. Most authors have favored the view that all human behavior, all volition is dominated by feelings of pleasure and displeasure. On superficial consideration, these authors seem to be right because the human mind does actually tend to seek pleasure and avoid pain. But the foundation of this theory is shaky. There is no standard for sensations of pleasure, indeed no standard for sensations at all. Furthermore, there is no perception or action which may not cause pleasure to one and pain to another, depending on place and time. Even the primitive sensations of organ satisfaction turn out to be a matter of degree depending on the degree of satiation and on cultural guiding lines.

Only great deprivations are capable of making organ satisfaction the goal. Once such satisfaction has actually been attained, does the psyche then really lose its directing line? The need of the psyche to gain orientation and security requires for proper development and achievement a firmer basis than the unstable principle of experiencing pleasure and a more strongly fixated point of orientation than the goal of attaining pleasure. The impossibility of orienting oneself and one's actions according to such a goal forces even the child to abandon efforts in this direction. Finally it is an abuse of an abstraction to single out from among the various complex psychological movements and to emphasize by means of circular reasoning the seeking of pleasure as the guiding motive, when every impulse has already been explained as pleasure seeking, libidinous.

The disproval of the principle of self-preservation appears more difficult, especially since this principle is fitted out with teleological auxiliary constructs on the one hand, and with the impact of Darwin's biological theory of selection on the other. But we can see every minute that we act in violation of this and of the principle of the preservation of the species. Furthermore, a certain arbitrariness permits us to raise or lower our valuations regarding self-preservation, as in the case of pleasure, and we often also forego self-preservation wholly or in part, up to the point of the death wish, when pleasure or pain become involved. On the other hand, we often give up the attainment of pleasure when injury threatens the self and the self-esteem.

COMMENT   *Here again Goldstein comes to a similar conclusion from his own approach. Only in cases of pathology does he find evidence for the dominance of the principle of self-preservation. "Frequently, the law of maintaining the existent state—the self-preservation —is considered as the basic law of life. I believe such a concept could arise only because one had assumed, as a starting point, the experiences in abnormal conditions or experimental situations. The tendency to maintain the existent state is characteristic for sick people and is a sign of anomalous life, of decay of life. The tendency of normal life is toward activity and progress" (48, p. 197).*

In what manner do these two admittedly effective incentives [pleasure and self-preservation] subordinate themselves to the main guiding line which drives toward enhancement of the self-esteem [even where they seem to dominate]? [Apparent dominance of pleasure or self-preservation] corresponds to two types of persons, among other types. One is least able to forego the contribution of pleasure to his self-esteem, whereas the other demands primarily the thought of life and of immortality. Modified modes of apperception originate from these views which determine an antithetical thinking in the sense of pleasure—displeasure, or of life —death. The one is unable to devalue pleasure, the other to devalue life. In neurotics the one type has developed by trying to compensate for feelings of displeasure based on his organ inferiority, while the other type has grown up in the fear of death, of early dying. The view of the world of both types furnishes them with fragments only. It is as if their souls were partially colorblind.

3. INFERIORITY FEELING AS DISPLEASURE[13]

COMMENT   *While Adler does not recognize pleasure and displeasure derived from the satisfaction or lack of satisfaction of the drives as important factors in human dynamics, except in so far as the attainment of physical pleasure may have become a condition for self-esteem and a part of one's value system, the inferiority feeling is understood as inherently displeasurable. In this sense displeasure and dissatisfaction become important in human motivation, as shown in the following passages.*

The feeling of insufficiency is a positive pain and, at the very least, lasts as long as a task has not been accomplished, a need relieved, or a tension released. Plainly it is a feeling given and made possible by nature, comparable to a painful tension that seeks relief. This relief need not necessarily be pleasurable, as Freud assumes, but it may be accompanied by feelings of pleasure, a conception that is in accordance with Nietzsche's position. In certain circumstances, the relief of this tension can also be accompanied by permanent or temporary suffering, somewhat like parting from a faithless friend or like a painful operation.

The feeling of one's own inferiority and unfitness, the sense of weakness, of being little, of insecurity, through its inherent feelings of displeasure and dissatisfaction, becomes a suitable basis for goal striving in that it permits the inner impulses to come closer to a fictional final goal.

Human beings are in a permanent mood of inferiority feeling, which constantly spurs them on to attain greater security. The pleasure or displeasure which accompany this striving are only aids and rewards received on this path.

Tensions come to light which go far beyond the measure of what we would expect from the most effortful bodily performance of the drives and from the strongest desire for organic pleasure. Among others, Goethe also points out that while perception is connected with the practical satisfaction of needs, man leads a life beyond this, a life of feelings and imagination. Thereby the coercion toward enhancement of the self-esteem has been excellently comprehended. This also becomes clear from one of Goethe's letters to Lavater where he remarks: "This passionate desire to drive the pyramid of my existence, the base of which is given to me, as high as possible outweighs everything else and barely admits momentary forgetting."

COMMENT   *If we regard this chapter as a whole, we gain the impression of a hierarchy of dynamic forces descending from the striving for perfection to the striving for self-enhancement and to the physiological drives. The concept of a hierarchy was suggested to us by the writings of A. H. Maslow (78, pp. 80–92). He groups the basic needs into a hierarchy of five levels which he terms, in order of ascendancy, the physiological needs, safety needs, belongingness and love needs, esteem needs, and need for self-actualization. For the term self-actualization, Maslow gives credit to Goldstein, and, as we have seen, Goldstein includes the striving for completion and perfection under self-actualization.*

The essence of Maslow's theory is that: "When a need is fairly well satisfied, the next prepotent ('higher') need emerges in turn to dominate the conscious life and to serve as the center of organization of behavior, since gratified needs are not active motivators" (80, p. 395). Under conditions of unsatisfied lower needs the individual may lose the higher needs. Finally the lower needs are also the more "selfish" ones (79, p. 404).

While rudiments of Maslow can be found in Adler, Maslow's theory is helpful for a fuller appreciation of Adler, which is the reason for our present discussion.

Adler makes it quite clear that normally the relationship of drives to the strivings is one of subordination. Furthermore, he adds that under certain abnormal conditions this may not be the case, and the drives may become prepotent. "Only great deprivations are capable of making organ satisfaction the goal" (see p. 121). The important consideration here is that extreme dissatisfaction of the lower dynamic forces is what makes them prepotent. This then is in full accordance with Maslow's theory.

With regard to striving for self-enhancement and the striving for perfection, Adler does not make it clear whether the relationship is one of subordination or not, and whether prepotency of the second depends upon prior essential satisfaction of the first. But the following considerations seem to permit the conclusion that this is indeed the case: (1) Maladjustment consists essentially of the more "selfish" striving for a goal of personal power and self-enhancement rather than of a more selfless striving for perfection. The most general precondition for neurosis and other forms of maladjustment are the three overburdening childhood situations mentioned in the selections above. These represent an early extreme lack of satisfaction of the striving for security and self-esteem. With regard to this, Adler states: "Nothing stands more in the way of the development of social interest than an increased inferiority feeling" (1926b, p. 404). Thus it is indeed dissatisfaction of the striving for self-esteem which renders this striving prepotent. On the other hand, "as long as the feeling of inferiority is not too great, a child will strive . . . on the useful side of life" (see p. 155). (2) The two steps of psychotherapy (see p. 119) permit the conclusion that the striving for self-enhancement must be satisfied before the striving for perfection can become prepotent. Everything which Adler has written about the first requirements of the psychotherapeutic relationship implies that it aims at making up for the lack of self-esteem in the patient (see pp. 340–342). "The important thing is to decrease the patient's feeling of inferiority" (1929c, p. 111). Once the great deprivation of the self-esteem has been sufficiently made up, the prepotency of the higher striving is restored. This is what Adler then calls "awakening the social interst." This is followed by the second step which is aimed at increasing and spreading this newly awakened social interest.

Adler had left open the question of the extent to which his later dynamic formulations superceded the earlier ones or the extent to which they could be integrated with them. We believe we have shown by the above considerations that through the application of Maslow's theory an integration of Adler's earlier and later formulations is indeed possible.

FOOTNOTES TO CHAPTER FOUR

1. **1, 2, 3:** "Individual Psychology" (1930f), pp. 398, 398–399, and 399.
2. **1:** What Life Should Mean to You (1931a), pp. 197–198; **2 and 3:** "Über den Ursprung des Strebens nach Überlegenheit und des Gemeinschaftsgefühles" (1933e), pp. 257–263.
3. **1 to 4:** Der Sinn des Lebens (1933a), pp. 23, 179–180, 64–65, and 180; **5:** "Religion und Individualpsychologie" (1933c), p. 59.
4. **1:** "IP" (1930f), pp. 398–399; **2 and 3:** Sinn des Lebens (1933a), pp. 181 and 182.
5. **1, 2, 3, 5, 6 and Figure 1:** Über den nervösen Charakter (1912a), pp. 3, 16, 17, 43, 43, and 44; **4:** "Religion" (1933c), p. 86.
6. **1:** "Zur Erziehung der Eltern" (1912b), p. 119n; **2 and 3:** Nervöser Charakter (1912a), pp. 26 and 31.
7. **1 to 7:** Nervöser Charakter (1912a), pp. 3, 19, 7, 24–25, 43, 53, and 68.
8. **1, 5, 6:** "Religion" (1933c), pp. 84, 58, and 83–84; **2 and 3:** What Life Should Mean to You (1931a), pp. 36–37 and 10; **4:** "Persönlichkeit als geschlossene Einheit" (1932a), pp. 81–88; **7:** "Der nervöse Charakter" (1931b), pp. 1–14; **8:** Nervöser Charakter (1912a), p. vi.
9. **1, 4, 5, 6, 8, 9:** Sinn des Lebens (1933a), pp. 63, 48, 67, 71, 65, and 23; **2 and 3:** Menschenkenntnis (1927a), pp. 53–54 and 58; **7:** What Life Should Mean to You (1931a), p. 55.
10. **1 to 4:** "Individual Psychology" (1927e), pp. 117, 117–118, 118, and 119; **5:** Nervöser Charakter (1912a), p. 13; **6:** Problems of Neurosis (1929b), p. 2.
11. **1:** "Religion" (1933c), p. 87; **2:** Nervöser Charakter (1912a), p. 33.
12. **1 to 4:** Nervöser Charakter (1912a), pp. 41, 41–42, 42, and 42–43.
13. **1 and 3:** Sinn des Lebens (1933a), pp. 63 and 64; **2 and 4:** Nervöser Charakter (1912a), pp. 25 and 26.

CHAPTER FIVE

SOCIAL INTEREST

COMMENT   *"Adler's was the first psychological system in the history of psychology that was developed in what we should today call a social-science direction," according to a statement by Gardner Murphy in his Historical Introduction to Modern Psychology (82, p. 341). Next to the striving for overcoming and perfection, the social aspect is indeed the most important factor in Adler's Individual Psychology.*

The general approach of Adler was, in fact, one of field theory, before this term had been coined. This was seen from the start in his first contribution on organ inferiority where the very definition of inferiority became relative to the social situation (see p. 25). Concomitant with this, the second basic characteristic of Adler's psychology was its holistic rather than elementaristic approach. These two aspects together meant that the various psychological processes of an individual must be understood within the framework of his individuality. This subject will be discussed in Chapter 8. Going consistently further in this direction, Adler saw that the whole individual must be understood within the larger whole which is formed by the groups to which he belongs, ranging from the face-to-face groups to the whole of mankind ultimately. Adler formulated this position, as already cited on page 2: "Individual Psychology accepts the viewpoint of the complete unity and self-consistency of the individual whom it regards and examines as socially embedded. We refuse to recognize and examine an isolated human being." Thus Adler could call Individual Psychology "probably the most consistent theory of the position of the individual towards the questions of social living, and in the same sense therefore, social psychology" (1929a, p. 108). The realization of human interrelatedness and its theoretical implications is the subject matter of the present chapter.

The first part is concerned with the fact that the individual must be seen and must see himself as embedded in a larger whole, the social situation, a fact which was continuously stressed by Adler. It is what Adler called the "iron logic of communal life," from which there is no escaping. This represents the sociological considerations of Individual Psychology.

The next three parts of this chapter deal with the individual's means for responding to the social situation, his social coping aptitude, which Adler calls social interest. Here the first part represents Adler's fully developed views; the second gives earlier formulations; while the third is concerned with an important contribution by one of Adler's earliest co-workers, Carl Furtmüller.

The last two parts take up problems of interaction between the individual and his social setting, the first in reference to intellectual functioning, the second with regard to adjustment in general. The interaction will be successful or unsuccessful, from the point of view of the individual as well as the group, depending upon the amount of social interest present in the process.

A. Social Embeddedness

1. COMMUNAL LIFE AS THE ABSOLUTE TRUTH[1]

In addition to regarding an individual's life as a unity, we must also take it together with its context of social relations. Thus children when first born are weak, and their weakness makes it necessary for other persons to care for them. The style or the pattern of a child's life cannot be understood without reference to the persons who look after him and who make up for his inferiority. The child has interlocking relations with the mother and family which could never be understood if we confined our analysis to the periphery of the child's physical being in space. The individuality of the child cuts across his physical individuality, it involves a whole context of social relations.

In order to understand what goes on in an individual, it is necessary to consider his attitude toward his fellow men. The relationships of people to one another in part exist naturally and as such are subject to change. In part they take the form of institutionalized relationships which arise from the natural ones. These institutionalized relationships can be observed especially in the political life of nations, in the formation of states, and in community affairs. Human psychological life cannot be understood without the simultaneous consideration of these coherences.

Human psychological life is not capable of doing just as it likes but is constantly confronted with tasks which have arrived from somewhere. All these tasks are inseparably tied up with the logic of man's communal life. This is one of those main conditions which continuously act upon the individual and which yield to his influence only up to a certain degree. When we consider that not even the conditions of human relations can be fully comprehended because they are too numerous and further that these demands are subject to change, then it becomes clear that we are scarcely in a position to gain complete insight into the darknesses of a given psychological life. This difficulty of understanding others becomes all the greater the further we depart from our own circumstances.

One of the basic facts for the advancement of our understanding of human nature is that we must regard the inherent rules of the game of a group as these emerge within the limited organization of the human body and its achievements, as if they were an absolute truth. We are able to approach this truth only slowly and usually only after mistakes and errors have been overcome.

The demands made on man by communal life are really just as self-evident as the demands of climate, the demands of protection against cold, and of building houses. We recognize religion as an expression of this coercion toward communal life, although not yet in a form understood as such. In religion, the sanctification of social forms takes the place of insight into their true significance and serves as a bond between members of the community. If the conditions of life are determined in the first instance by cosmic influences, they are in the second instance determined socially. They are determined by the fact that men live together and by the rules and regularities which spontaneously arise in consequence of this. The demands of society have regulated human relations which had already existed from the beginning as self-understood, as an absolute truth. For before the individual life of man there was the community. In the history of human culture, there is not a single form of life which was not conducted as social. Never has man appeared otherwise than in society.

COMMENT *When Adler calls the fact of the social embeddedness of the individual the absolute truth, this is not to be taken in the literal sense of the term absolute. Adler was a positivistic idealist,* rather than a transcendental idealist. Thus by the absolute truth he meant something like the following: Since we do not have any absolute answers and since nevertheless we have a need for certainty to guide our conduct, the most useful fiction or working hypothesis is to consider the iron logic of the communal life of man as if it were the absolute truth. Adler's justification for this fiction was his clinical observation that all problem cases, from neuroses and psychoses to criminality, have in common their failure to abide by this "absolute truth."

2. THE NECESSITY FOR COMMUNAL LIFE[2]

Darwin already pointed out that one never finds weak animals living alone. Man must be included among these, particularly because he is not strong enough to live alone. He has only little resistance against nature, he needs a larger amount of aids to live and preserve himself. Consider the situation of a man in a jungle, alone and without aids provided by culture. He would appear incomparably more threatened than any other creature. He has not the teeth of the carnivore, the sense of hearing, nor the sharp eyes to prevail in such a struggle.

Now we can understand that man could maintain himself only when he placed himself under particularly favorable conditions. These, however, were afforded to him only by group life. Group life proved to be a necessity because it alone enabled man, through a division of labor, to solve problems in which the individual as such would have been condemned to failure. Division of labor alone was capable of providing man with weapons of offense and defense, as well as with all goods which he needed to maintain himself and which we today include under the concept of culture.

From the point of view of nature, man is an inferior being. But this inferiority with which he is afflicted, and of which he becomes aware through a feeling of deprivation and insecurity, acts as a continuous stimulus to find a way of adjusting, of providing, of creating situations in which the disadvantages of his position seem compensated. Since society played an essential part in this striving for adaptation, the psychological organ had from the beginning to reckon with the conditions of society. All its abilities are developed on a basis which embodies the component of a social life. Every human thought had to be so constituted that it could do justice to a community.

3. LANGUAGE, LOGIC, AND RULES OF THE GAME[3]

If one considers how progress continued, one arrives at the origins of logic which embodies the demand for general validity. Only that is logical which is generally valid. Language is a further clear result of social life, a miracle which distinguishes man from all other creatures. A phenomenon such as language cannot be thought of without the concept of general validity, which fact indicates that language has its origin in the social life of man. Language is quite unnecessary for a creature living by itself. Language reckons with the social life of man, is its product and, at the same time, its cement. A strong proof for this connection is that individuals who grow up under conditions under which contact with others is made difficult or is prevented, or who themselves refuse such contact, almost always suffer a deficiency in language and language ability. It is as if this bond could be formed and preserved only when the contact with mankind is secure.

Language has an extremely deep significance for the development of the human psychological life. Logical thought is possible only under the supposition of language. By making concept-formation possible, language enables us to make distinctions and to create concepts which are not private but common property. Our thinking and feeling are also understandable only when one presupposes general validity. Our enjoyment of beauty is founded on the understanding that appreciation and recognition of the beautiful and the good must be common property. Thus we arrive at the conclusion that the concepts of reason, logic, ethics, and aesthetics can have taken their origin only in the communal life of man and that they are at the same time the cement which protects culture from disintegration.

We understand now that all the rules of the game—such as education, superstition, totem and tabu, and law—which were necessary to secure the existence of the human race, had first of all to do justice to the idea of a community. What we call justice, considering it the bright side of the human character, is essentially nothing other than the fulfillment of demands which have arisen from man's communal life. It is these demands which have shaped the psychological organ. Dependability, loyalty, frankness, and truthfulness are actually demands posited and maintained by a generally valid principle of the community. What we call a good or a bad character can be judged only from the viewpoint of the community. Character, like any scientific, political, or artistic achievement, will prove its greatness and value only by being valuable to men in general.

An ideal image by which we appraise the individual is created only by considering its value and its usefulness for man in general. We compare the individual with the ideal image of a fellow man who meets his problems in a fashion which has general validity, whose social interest is developed to such an extent that "he follows the rules of the game of human society," as Furtmüller expressed it.

4. THE THREE GENERAL SOCIAL TIES[4]

COMMENT One of Adler's favorite devices for teaching and preaching the "absolute truth" of social embeddedness and the resulting necessity of a well-developed social interest was to point out that all the main problems in life are problems of human cooperation. Although Adler does not say so, he implies that in present society the satisfaction of almost all conceivable needs depends on the solution of these problems of cooperation. These problems represent the ties of the individual to social life and are somewhat loosely classified into problems of occupation, social relations in general, and love and marriage.

At this point Individual Psychology comes into contact with sociology. For a long time now I have been convinced that all the questions of life can be subordinated to the three major problems—the problems of communal life, of work, and of love. These three arise from the inseparable bond that of necessity links men together for association, for the provision of livelihood, and for the care of offspring.

The three ties in which human beings are bound set the three problems of life, but none of these problems can be solved separately. Each of them demands a successful approach to the other two.

a. Occupation. The first tie sets the problem of occupation. We are living on the surface of this planet, with only the resources of this planet, with the fertility of its soil, with its mineral wealth, and with its climate and atmosphere. It has always been the task of mankind to find the right answer to the problem these conditions set us, and even today we cannot think that we have found a sufficient answer. In every age, mankind has arrived at a certain level of solution, but it has always been necessary to strive for improvement and further accomplishments.

When somebody makes shoes, he makes himself useful to someone else, and he has the right to a sufficient livelihood, to all the advantages of hygiene, and to a good education of his children. The fact that he receives payment for this is the recognition of his usefulness in an age of developed trade. In this way, he arrives at a feeling of his worth to society, the only possible means of mitigating the universal human feeling of inferiority. The person who performs useful work lives in the midst of the developing human society and helps to advance it.

b. *Society*. The second tie by which men are bound is their membership in the human race and their association with others of their kind. The attitude and behavior of a human being would be altogether different if he were the only one of his kind alive on earth. We have always to reckon with others, to adapt ourselves to others, and to interest ourselves in them. This problem is best solved by friendship, social feeling, and cooperation. With the solution of this problem, we have made an incalculable advance towards the solution of the first. It was only because men learned to cooperate that the great discovery of the division of labor was made, a discovery which is the chief security for the welfare of mankind. Through the division of labor we can use the results of many different kinds of training and organize many different abilities, so that all of them contribute to the common welfare and guarantee relief from insecurity and increased opportunity for all the members of society.

Some people attempt to evade the problem of occupation, to do no work, or to occupy themselves outside of common human interests. We shall always find, however, that if they dodge this problem, they will in fact be claiming support from their fellows. In one way or another, they will be living on the labor of others without making a contribution of their own.

c. *Love*. The third tie of a human being is that he is a member of one of the two sexes and not of the other. On his approach to the other sex and on the fulfillment of his sexual role depends his part in the continuance of mankind. This relationship between the two sexes also sets a problem. It, too, is a problem which cannot be solved apart from the other two problems. For a successful solution of the problem of love and marriage, an occupation contributing to the division of labor is necessary, as well as a good and friendly contact with other human beings. In our own day, the highest solution for this problem, the solution most coherent with the demands of society and of the division of labor, is monogamy. In the way in which an individual answers this problem the degree of his cooperation can always be seen.

These three problems are never found apart, for they all throw crosslights on one another. A solution of one helps towards the solution of the others, and indeed we can say that they are all aspects of the same situation and the same problem—the necessity for a human being to preserve life and to further life in the environment in which he finds himself.

COMMENT To emphasize the importance of human relations, Adler made such deliberate overstatements as equating reality with society: "Reality, that is society, the community" (1914b, p. 73). Freud, by contrast, stressed external factors other than the social in his concept of reality. The following might be considered his definition: "A perception which is made to disappear by motor activity is recognized as external, as reality" (36, IV, p. 148). Only in his last formulation, in 1938, did Freud finally define the external world, or reality, as including society. But significantly he gave this part of the definition in parentheses. Speaking with reference to the neurotic ego, he said that it "is no longer able to fulfill the task set to it by the external world (including human society)" (42, p. 76). Freud's ego is confronted by the id, the super-ego (which will be mentioned in the next section), and a reality in which human society is only one of many factors. If one wishes to maintain that Freud did not overlook the social factor, one will at any rate have to admit that he did not assign to it the central overshadowing importance which Adler did.

B. Social Interest

COMMENT The term social interest denotes the innate aptitude through which the individual becomes responsive to reality, which is primarily the social situation. In Adler's mature theory, social interest is not a second dynamic force counterbalancing a striving for superiority. Like other psychological processes or traits, it is a part of the individual's equipment, although the most important part. It is used by him in his striving for superiority or perfection, which in itself is socially neutral. In one of his last papers, Adler speaks of "the brick which we call 'inherited possibility of social interest'" (see p. 156), meaning by brick the raw material by which the striving for superiority is implemented, or the style of life is constructed, by the individual.

The fact that social interest at times appears to have dynamic properties, or is linked to the earlier need for affection, does not alter Adler's intention to describe the individual's total dynamic situation as unitary and self-consistent, modified only in its direction by the degree of social interest as this becomes effective in the striving. Just as intelligence affects the mode of the striving but does not conflict with it, so social interest becomes an integral part of the striving. A positive social adjustment is thus a primary form of behavior where a developed capacity of social interest is utilized, and is not the outcome of the conquest of selfish forces by social forces.

Adler's term for the social factor, Gemeinschaftsgefühl, presented no mean difficulty to the translators. The following terms have been used as English equivalents: social feeling, community feeling, fellow feeling, sense of solidarity, communal intuition, community interest, social sense, and social interest. The last seems most adequate generally, and it is also the one which Adler came to prefer. For consistency, social interest has been substituted for other translations, except where social feeling seems the more appropriate word.

1. INNATE POTENTIALITY[5]

The high degree of cooperation and social culture which man needs for his very existence demands spontaneous social effort, and the dominant purpose of education is to evoke it. Social interest is not inborn [as a full-fledged entity], but it is an innate potentiality which has to be consciously developed. We are unable to trust any so-called social instinct, for its expression depends upon the child's conception or vision of the environment.

Social interest is innate, just as the striving for overcoming is innate, with the important difference, however, that social interest must be developed, and that it can be developed only when the child is already in the midst of life. At the present stage of man's psychological and possibly also physical development, we must consider the innate substratum of the social interest as too small, as not strong enough, to become effective or to develop without the benefit of social understanding. This is in contrast to abilities and functions which succeed almost all on their own, such as breathing.

Like the character traits which depend on it, social interest can come to life only in the social context. By social context, of course, is meant the child's subjective understanding of the same. The decision [as to how he will interpret the essentially ambiguous social context] rests in the creative power of the child, guided by the environment, and educational measures, influenced by the experience of his body, and his evaluation of it.

The development of the innate potentiality for cooperation occurs first in the relationship of the child and mother. The mother is the first other person whom the child experiences. Here is the first opportunity for the cultivation of the innate social potentiality. But even here, at the very beginning, many mistakes can be made. For instance, the mother is often satisfied with a restricted social development for the child, and does not concern herself with the fact that he must go from her care into a much wider circle of human contacts. In such a case the mother concentrates the child's social potentialities upon herself. She does not help the child to extend his interest to others besides herself. Even the father may be excluded if he does not make a special effort to enter this "closed circle." Other children and strangers are, of course, excluded also.

COMMENT   *To develop the potentiality and to spread the social interest to wider circles is the function of the mother. When she does not fulfill it, the individual remains unprepared to meet the problems presented by social living. Psychotherapy belatedly takes over the function of the mother.*

2. A VALUE EXPRESSED THROUGH EMPATHY[6]

By social interest or social feeling, we understand something different from that which other authors understand. When we say it is a feeling, we are certainly justified in doing so. But it is more than a feeling; it is an evaluative attitude toward life (Lebensform). It is an attitude quite different from what we find in a person whom we call anti-social. This evaluative attitude must not be understood as an external form only, as if it were the expression only of an acquired way of life. It is much more than that. We are not in a position to define it quite unequivocally, but we have found in an English author a phrase which clearly expresses what we could contribute to an explanation: "To see with the eyes of another, to hear with the ears of another, to feel with the heart of another." For the time being, this seems to me an admissible definition of what we call social feeling.

COMMENT   *Adler's use of the term Lebensform has certain systematic implications. It was introduced by Eduard Spranger in his important book on value types (1st German edition 1914) which was* translated as Types of Men (100). A complete definition of Lebensform is: "An ideationally designed structure of individual consciousness which results when a value is posited as dominating life" (92). Adler's meaning of the term would, of course, include unconsciousness as well. His choice of this particular term may well be taken as an expression of the affinity which existed between him and the understanding psychology of Spranger. The six value types of Spranger include a social type along with the theoretical, economic, aesthetic, political, and religious types, but Adler's social interest is a far broader and less concrete concept than Spranger's social value.

We see immediately that this ability coincides in part with what we call identification or empathy. Herder, Novalis, and Jean Paul were acquainted with the process of empathy, described it, and considered it important. Later Wundt, Volkelt, and especially Lipps stressed empathy as a fundamental fact of our experience. The latter, Dilthey, Müller-Freienfels, and others described the relationship of empathy and understanding. Individual Psychology may claim as its contribution to have pointed out that empathy and understanding are facts of social feeling, of harmony with the universe. This kind of identification or empathy always depends on the degree of our social interest; it is one aspect of social interest and is absolutely essential to the achievement of social living (Gemeinschaftsleben). Sympathy is a partial expression of identification.

The ability to identify must be trained, and it can be trained only if one grows up in relation to others and feels a part of the whole. One must sense that not only the comforts of life belong to one, but also the discomforts. One must feel at home on this earth with all its advantages and disadvantages.

Life presents only such problems as require ability to cooperate for their solution. To hear, see, or speak "correctly," means to lose one's self completely in another or in a situation, to become identified with him or with it. The capacity for identification, which alone makes us capable of friendship, love of mankind, sympathy, occupation, and love, is the basis of social interest and can be practiced and exercised only in conjunction with others. In this intended assimilation to another person or to a situation lies the whole meaning of comprehension.

The concept of identification has different usages. We speak of identification if a child aims to become like his father, to see with the eyes of the father, to "understand" him, and so has a useful goal before himself. Freud, unawares, takes identification as meaning to seize the role of another in order to gain a personal advantage. Identification in our sense would be illustrated by the following examples. We identify with a picture by regarding it. But we also identify with other inanimate objects. For example, in playing billiards or in bowling the player follows the ball with his eyes and makes the very movement which he hopes that the ball will make. At a play everyone participates in the feeling and the acting. Such identification does not mean to usurp the role of the father, to become the billiard ball, or to act. In dreams and in group psychology empathy also plays an enormous part.

COMMENT *The reference to inanimate objects in connection with empathy and identification emphasizes an outgoing transcendence of the limits of the self and of the physical individuality as the essence of social interest. The absence of self-centeredness is the common denominator between moving with the billiard ball and other forms of empathy discussed above, and forms of more actively participating, cooperative, other-directed behavior, discussed below.*

3. OTHER-DIRECTEDNESS[7]

The child and mother are dependent on each other; this relationship not only arises out of nature, but is favored by it. When other schools of psychology maintain that the child comes into the world a complete egoist with a "drive for destruction" and no other intention than to foster himself cannibalistically on his mother, this is an erroneous inference based on incomplete observation. These schools overlook in the relationship the role of the mother who requires the cooperation of the child. The mother with her milk-filled breasts and all the other altered functions of her body (not to mention the new emotional development of the love for her child) needs the child just as the child needs her. They are dependent on each other by nature. The possibilities for social interest first take on life and become tangible in the relationship between mother and child.

COMMENT *Here Adler alludes to Freud's description of this first human relationship as based on the "oral or cannibalistic stage" of libido development (36, IV, p. 160), "during which the original attachment of sexual excitation to the nutritional instinct still dominates the scene . . . In this phase the sexual aim could only be cannibalism —eating . . . Permanent marks have been left by this oral phase of sexuality upon the usages of language. People commonly speak, for instance, of an 'appetizing' love-object . . ." (36, III, pp. 587–588).*

The development of the child is increasingly permeated by the relationships of society to him. In time, the first signs of the innate social interest appear, the organically determined impulses of affection blossom forth, and lead the child to seek the proximity of adults. One can always observe that the child directs impulses of affection towards others and not towards himself, as Freud believes. These impulses vary in degree and differ with respect to different persons. In children over two years one can also see these differences in their verbal expressions. The feeling of belongingness, the social interest, takes root in the psyche of the child and leaves the individual only under the severest pathological changes of his mental life.

Social interest remains throughout life. It becomes differentiated, limited, or expanded and, in favorable cases, extends not only to family members but to the larger group, to the nation, to all of mankind. It can even go further, extending itself to animals, plants, and inanimate objects and finally even to the cosmos.

The educability of the child derives from the breadth of his innate, differentiated, and growing social interest. Through it he gains the connection with the common ideal. In this way the demands of the community become personal demands, and the immanent logic of human society, with its matters of course and necessities, becomes the individual task for the child.

The indomitable progress of social interest, growing through evolution [in the sense of societal evolution, see p. 106], justifies the assumption that the very existence of mankind is inseparably tied up with being good. Whatever seems to speak against this assumption is to be regarded as a mistake of [societal] evolution and can be traced to errors.

Self-boundedness is an artifact thrust upon the child during his education and by the present state of our social structure. The creative power of the child is misled towards self-boundedness. Teachers, ministers, and physicians must be freed from their own self-boundedness and, together with all those who want to work honestly for the common welfare, must prevent these seductions of the child. Until that time it will always be the single case only which will find its way to the physician, and not before the error of the child has led to considerable damage to all.

A man is called good when he relates himself to other humans in a generally useful way, bad when he acts contrary to social interest. When the educator and especially the psychotherapist frequently come to the erroneous conclusion that man is evil by nature, this is because it is more common for them to observe bad drives and destruction drives than to take note of man's other side.

COMMENT   While Adler recognizes the necessity for developing social interest, the greater import for his theory lies in the assertion that this development applies to an innate disposition for other-directedness. Social concern becomes in this way a primary rather than a secondary phenomenon. In this respect, Gestalt psychology with its nativistic orientation has recently advanced along similar lines through the work of Solomon E. Asch. Actually using the term social interest, he describes the striving for society as a primary, natural tendency, although his explanation of social interest differs somewhat from Adler's. Asch takes issue with those views, especially with that of Freud, which postulate a "private profit" (10, p. 326) or an "ego-centered basis of social relations" (10, p. 332), and summarizes his position on social interest as follows: "One fundamental source of the need for society is the active and insightful relation of men to their surroundings. Our intellectual and emotional capacities urge us into the surroundings . . . To recognize the nature of a situation is to be responsive to its requirements . . . This trend comes to clearest expression in the social relation. Our grasp of the properties of a person, . . . awakens the need to understand, act, and care. In this sense the striving for society is 'natural'" (10, p. 346).

4. UNIVERSALITY[8]

[While social interest must be developed in the child,] there is [on the other hand] no human being who is capable of seriously denying for himself all social interest. There are no words by which one could free oneself from the obligations to our fellow men. Social interest constantly brings itself to mind with its warning voice. This does not mean that we always proceed in accordance with social interest. We do maintain, however, that a certain effort is required to throttle it or to push it aside. In view of the general validity of social interest, no one can carry out an action without justifying himself somehow with regard to this feeling. From this is derived the human trait of producing reasons, or at least excuses, for everything one thinks and does. Herein originates the peculiar technique of life, of thinking, and of acting according to which we always wish to remain connected with social interest, to believe that we are, or at least to create the pretense that we are.

We can never find anyone who could say truly, "I am not interested in others." He may act this way—he may act as if he were not interested in the world—but he cannot justify himself. Rather does he claim to be interested in others, in order to hide his lack of social adjustment. This is mute testimony to the universality of the social feeling.

Criminals, for instance, always make excuses or accuse others. They mention unprofitable conditions of labor. They speak of the cruelty of society in not supporting them, or they say the stomach commands and cannot be ruled. When sentenced, they always find such excuses as that of the child-murderer Hickman, who said, "It was done by a command from above." Another murderer, upon being sentenced, said, "What is the use of such a boy as I have killed? There are a million other boys." Then there is the "philosopher," who claims that it is not bad to kill an old woman with a lot of money, when so many worthwhile people are starving. The logic of such arguments strikes us as quite frail, and it is frail. The whole outlook is conditioned by a socially useless goal, just as the selection of that goal is conditioned by a lack of courage. Such people have to justify themselves, whereas a goal on the useful side of life needs no excuses.

There is such a thing as a pretense of social interest which, like a veil, covers other tendencies. These tendencies must be uncovered in order to arrive at a correct evaluation of an individual. The fact that such deception may occur increases the difficulty of appraising the degree of [actual] social interest.

Today everyone speaks of community and social interest. We are not the very first, but we are the first to have strongly emphasized the basic nature of social interest. The concept of community and social interest can also be abused [as for example, a demagogue appealing to the social interest of others]. He who has properly understood this concept knows that in its nature rests an evolutionary factor which prevails over every opposition. He will be able to avoid both the abuse of the concept and being abused by others in its name.

5. THE BROADER SENSE[9]

COMMENT   Adler's stress on the necessity for developing the innate potentiality for social interest might be misunderstood to mean that everybody should become a good mixer, a back-slapping, hand-shaking "extrovert." This impression is in error on two counts. Firstly, although "the renovating winds of social contact" (1929c, p. 73) are needed for one's development and true social interest must take the form of some kind of contribution, it does not always manifest itself in concrete participation. Secondly, the society to which the individual contributes is not limited to any specific present-day group, but is indicated in a broader sense as the abstract concept of some future, ideal society.

We have already spoken of the great distance to the problems of life, of coming to a halt, and of detachment [in the neurotic]. There can be no question, however, that occasionally such a procedure is correct and in accordance with social interest. Individual Psychology is particularly concerned with cases where this position is justified. This is because we always feel obliged to attribute conditional applicability only to rules and formulas and always to supply new proofs for their confirmation. In the present connection, the exceptions are cases where an individual foregoes the solution of certain aspects of life for the purpose of making a greater contribution to the advancement of society, as the artist and genius do.

A philosopher must from time to time exile himself from society to think and write his books. But the mistake involved will never be great if a high degree of social interest is bound up with the goal of superiority. Our cooperation has need for many different excellences.

Solitary occupation in children as well as adults need not come off badly. Indeed it should even be encouraged, provided it permits a prospect of later enrichment of society. It is merely due to the technique of certain accomplishments that they can be practiced and carried out only at a distance from other persons. This in no way prevents them from actually being social in character.

Regarding social interest, certain fluctuations in the literature of Individual Psychology may have been noted. We do not wish to deal with the usual and thoughtless case, where what we call society is understood as the private circle of our time, or even a larger circle which one should join. Social interest means much more. It means particularly the interest in, or the feeling with, the community sub specie aeternitatis [Webster definition: Under the aspect of eternity; in its essential or universal form or nature. Spinoza]. It means the striving for a community which must be thought of as everlasting, as we could think of it if mankind had reached the goal of perfection. It is never [only] a present-day community or society, a specific political or religious formation. It is rather the goal which is best suited for perfection, a goal which would have to signify the ideal community of all mankind, the ultimate fulfillment of [societal] evolution.

Of course, it will be asked how do I know this. Certainly not from immediate experience. I must admit that those who find a piece of metaphysics in Individual Psychology are right. Some praise this, others criticize it. Unfortunately, there are many who have an erroneous view of metaphysics, who would like to see everything eliminated from the life of mankind which they cannot comprehend immediately. But by doing so, we would interfere with the possibilities of development, with every new thought. Every new idea lies beyond immediate experience. Vice versa, immediate experience never yields anything new. It is only the synthesizing idea which connects the data of immediate experience. Whether you call it speculation or transcendentalism, there is no science which does not have to enter the realm of metaphysics. I see no reason to be afraid of metaphysics; it has had a very great influence on human life and development. We are not blessed with the possession of the absolute truth, and on that account we are compelled to form theories for ourselves about our future and about the results of our actions.

COMMENT   Here Adler declares, although not in so many words, his metaphysical position to be that of an idealistic positivist (Vaihinger). We must give him credit for his courage in admitting the dependence of his theory on an underlying philosophy, for the psychologist today is prone "to deny the dependence, or to refuse to articulate as best he can his own thinking about human nature with that brand of philosophy with which it is most closely allied," as Allport observes. Yet, he continues, it is short-sighted to do so because: "Whether he knows it or not every psychologist gravitates toward an ontological position. Like a satellite he slips into the orbit of positivism, naturalism, idealism, personalism" (6, p. 347).

c. Antecedents of the Concept of Social Interest

COMMENT *In his efforts to express the social factor of the personality, that is, man's means of coping with the phenomenon of social embeddedness, Adler arrived at several formulations in turn. While he was still thinking of the aggression drive as the basic dynamic principle, he represented the social factor correspondingly in terms of a drive, the need for affection. When the basic striving had become the "fiction of overcoming others," Adler thought of the social factor as opposing this striving in the form of the counter-fiction. In meaning, as well as in name, the counter-fiction was an antithetical concept and thus foreign to Adler's ultimate emphasis on unity and self-consistency of the individual. Thus it was only a passing phase in his development and was only dealt with briefly. To our knowledge, it was not mentioned again after The Neurotic Character, when Adler's formulations took the neurotic as their starting point. This explains why in his description human nature took on the hostile aspect so apparent in the passage below. We are presenting the essence of the counter-fiction below in accordance with our purpose of giving a rounded picture of Adler's development and a basis of comparison with other theories.*

When Adler gave up the term counter-fiction and replaced it with social interest, the latter was at first also treated very much as a counter-force. Two brief selections showing this trend are given as the second section of this part.

1. THE COUNTER-FICTION[10]

There is nothing in the life and development of a person which proceeds with such secrecy as the setting-up of the personality ideal. If we seek the cause for this secrecy, the most important reason seems to lie in the belligerent, not to say inimical character of this fiction. It arose out of constant gauging and balancing of the advantages of others and must accordingly—in conformity with its basic principle of opposites—aim at the disadvantage of others. Psychological analysis of the neurotic always brings to light the presence of the depreciation tendency, which is directed summarily towards all. The belligerent tendencies come to the fore regularly in avarice, envy, and in the longing for superiority. But the fiction of overcoming others can only be used or become a factor if it does not disturb the establishment of social relations. So it must be made unrecognizable, must be masked at an early stage or it would undo itself.

This veiling takes place through the positing of a counter-fiction which primarily guides overt action and under whose weight the approximation to reality and recognition of its effective forces take place. This counter-fiction consists of ever-present corrective factors and brings about the change of form of the guiding fiction. The counter-fiction forces considerations upon the guiding fiction, takes social and ethical demands of the future in account with their real weight, and, in doing so, insures reasonableness. It is a safety coefficient of the guiding line towards power. The harmony of these two fictions, their mutual compatibility, is the sign of mental health.

In the counter-fiction the experiences and teachings, the social and cultural formulas, and the traditions of society are effective. In times of elevation, of security, of the normal, of peace, the counter-fiction is the form-giving force which effects a blocking of the readinesses for combat and emotion and an adaptation of the character traits to the social environment. When insecurity rises and the feeling of inferiority emerges, then along with increasing abstraction from reality, this counter-fiction becomes devalued, the readinesses [for combat] are mobilized, the neurotic uncompromising character comes to the fore, and with it the exaggerated, raised self-ideal.

It is among the triumphs of the human wit in adaptation to the counter-fiction that it enables the guiding idea to prevail: to shine through modesty, to conquer with humility and submission, to humiliate others with one's own virtue, to attack others with one's own passivity, to hurt others with one's own suffering, to pursue a masculine goal with feminine means, to make oneself small in order to appear big. Of such nature, however, are the devices of the neurotic.

2. EARLY FORMULATION[11]

Individual Psychology is a psychology on three interlocking planes: From the child's feeling of inferiority there emerges an overstimulated striving for power which either finds its limits in the demands of society and in the admonitions of social interest, which is physiologically and socially founded, or goes astray [1919].

Individual Psychology has brought evidence to show that the line of movement of human striving originates in the blending of social interest with the striving for personal superiority. Both basic factors appear to be social formations: the first is innate and strengthens human society; the second, the product of education, is an obvious general temptation which constantly endeavors to exploit society for one's own prestige [1920].

COMMENT Adler's treatment of the social factor at this stage for several years, beginning with 1912, is somewhat similar to accounts which Freud gave of it subsequently. Adler's counter-fiction is the antithetical restraining force in the face of cultural demands which, when it succeeds in providing a balance against the guiding fiction, is the condition for mental health. Freud described the ego-ideal as having a "social side" (36, III, p. 59) in 1914 and in 1923 published his monograph on the superego (37), the new term for ego-ideal. The chief function of the super-ego remained "the limitation of satisfactions" (42, p. 19). Whatever the similarities between Adler's counter-fiction and Freud's subsequent concept of super-ego were, Adler had already dropped both the counter-fiction and social interest as a counteractive force in favor of social interest as an innate disposition for spontaneous social effort, at a time when the super-ego was still a new concept in psychoanalysis.

D. The Innate Social Disposition
By Carl Furtmüller

COMMENT An antecedent of social interest which took the social factor out of the category of an antithetical force and made it an innate disposition for a positive relationship to the social environment is contained in the following selections from a monograph by Carl Furtmüller, which is of considerable importance in the literature of Individual Psychology.

Furtmüller was Adler's most prominent early co-worker. This monograph, entitled Psychoanalysis and Ethics, was the first in a series which Adler edited after his separation from Freud and appeared in 1912, the same year as The Neurotic Character, which contained the counter-fiction. At that time Adler's group was called Society for Free Psychoanalytic Research, and the name Individual Psychology had not yet been introduced, which explains Furtmüller's use of the term Psychoanalysis.

Adler often referred to this paper and gradually adopted its views. These are in essence that social adaptation and, consequently, ethical behavior are not a mere restriction of human nature or its modification through outside pressure or one outcome of an intrinsic conflict between internal opposing forces, but are a form of expression which is in harmony with a natural predisposition. Unethical behavior can be traced to an interference with the original disposition.

1. THE RELATIVE EASE OF SOCIALIZATION[12]

The psychoanalyst who turns to ethical problems will be concerned primarily with the question: Whence do the ethical imperatives derive their determining power? This question has of course been asked since time immemorial, but it has not been the center of consideration.

One must assume an underlying disposition, phylogenetically acquired, in order to understand the relative rapidity with which the infant enters relations with his environment, and the relative ease with which the normal child can be reared. The fact that reverses do occur is no counter-argument to this assumption. In training a dog we also will observe reverses; yet this will not prevent us from ascribing to the dog a disposition of domesticability which distinguishes him from the wolf.

Freud, who was more interested in the effects of ethical imperatives on the individual than in their psychological origin, regards the ethical will of the individual as a sublimation of libido or rather of certain of its components. If we want to see this assumption through, we run into considerable difficulties. We fail to arrive in this way at the root of ethics proper because sublimation could only strengthen existing tendencies but not create them. We would not know how Freud's libido, a force so vague in content, could create from within itself the concrete phenomena of an ethical life. Even more does repression, which leads to sublimation, usually presuppose the effectiveness of ethical factors.

We find more points of orientation in the papers of Alfred Adler. This is no accident, Adler's position in the development of psychoanalysis being in brief, and therefore not quite accurately, that he traced the forces behind repression after Freud had discovered its effects. Thus we can hope to find support in the discussion of ethical problems when we apply the Adlerian guiding principles to our topic.

2. ETHICS AND OVERCOMING INFERIORITY FEELINGS[13]

According to Adler, the lever of psychological development is to be found in the feeling of inferiority. This has its natural origin in the relationship of the child to his environment. Inferiority feelings may occur in the most varied nuances and degrees, depending on how much the environment lets the child feel his inferiority and on how much the psychological reactions to bodily inferiorities make themselves felt. The stronger the feeling of inferiority, the more violent the ensuing reaction. This reaction will, in many cases, not only re-establish the equilibrium but tend to disturb it again in the opposite sense. Compensation becomes overcompensation. It is easily understood how the long series of ethical imperatives which the child faces must increase his feeling of inferiority.

One possibility which helps the child to overcome his inferiority feeling, and which is the subjective origin of ethics, is the following: The individual can make the foreign demands his own. When this is done, the imperatives of compulsion have been replaced by the imperatives of freedom, which in content are equal to the former. Thus the individual will not come into conflict with his environment and will formally maintain himself as independently willing. Outwardly nothing has changed as against the stage of passive obedience, but the psychological situation is fundamentally different. A painful pressure has been removed from the individual, he has overcome the inferiority feeling and is no longer a servant but has become a master of himself.

COMMENT   *As mentioned at the outset, an innate disposition is postulated to explain the relative rapidity and ease of interiorization of outside demands, an assumption that became basic for Individual Psychology. As shown now, such interiorization is in the service of the striving for mastery and freedom. This thought was taken up by Adler with respect to a specific situation (see pp. 458-459).*

3. MENTAL HEALTH AND ETHICS[14]

While according to Freud, the neurosis is independent of the character of the patient which at the most suffers secondary changes after the outbreak of the illness, according to Adler a peculiar structure of the character virtually forms the nucleus of the neurosis. The individual filled with a particularly increased inferiority feeling reacts violently against this feeling. The more vehement this reaction the greater the certainty that he will come into conflict with the real conditions of life and that he will fail in his compensatory tendencies. Such a person will be oversensitive, unable to bear a real or an assumed slight, unable to renounce. He will remain in continuous combat readiness and want to force other persons under his dominance. The outcome is twofold. The more pronounced these traits are, the less suited will he be for an adjustment into the social context and, secondly, the less ethical will he be in essence, although he may be very ethical on the surface. The impossibility of asserting himself to the extent that he wishes will cause him to pursue his original goal by detours which may be very obscure and hard to understand. The most complicated of these detours is represented by the neurosis.

According to this view, ethics and mental hygiene arrive at a particularly close relationship. It is not as if ethics could be a means toward mental health. On the contrary, mental health appears rather to be a prerequisite for genuine ethics. Everything designed to reduce the intrapsychic tensions described above will also mitigate antisocial and unethical tendencies. This opens up important socio-ethical vistas. It is clear that our present social and economic order, with its extreme competitiveness and its enormous differences of levels, contributes materially to an increase of this tension. A change of this social order in the sense of an equalization of the contrasts should be expected to bring about an advancement of mankind in respect to mental health, as well as to establish a higher ethical level. Thus psychoanalysis seems to urge the positing of social goals.

E. Social Interest and Intelligence

COMMENT   This and the next part are concerned with the question of how the individual relates himself to a situation. In the present part Adler postulates that social interest is an important aspect of his intellectual functioning in a given situation. The degree of social interest of an individual determines whether his intellectual solution of a problem will have general validity, that is, will be reasonable, or not. Social interest thus takes on the function of an important "non-intellective" factor in intelligence, to use the term which David Wechsler has made so well known (113, 114).

1. REASON[15]

To be sure, we can disagree on terminology and we can introduce other names, but what I should like to emphasize is a fundamental difference between two abilities, namely between reason and intelligence. The question has, of course, been approached from various sides before, but our point of view may possibly provide a deeper insight.

By reason we understand, with Kant, a process which has general validity. Hence, by reasonable we understand common sense. We may define common sense as all those forms of expression and as the content of all behavior which we find beneficial to the community. This represents the kind of action and conduct which we designate as reasonable. Thus we come to a fuller understanding of Kants' conclusion, in that we now see that reason is inseparably connected with social interest.

This means at the same time that we understand by reason all actions, conduct, and forms of expression which depend on a goal of superiority in which the commonweal finds expression. Such a goal must be present to insure reasonable actions. In psychotherapy we are primarily occupied with people who have a goal of personal superiority and who, in this way, transgress the limits which, in the course of the cultural development of mankind, have come to signify the common sense.

Incidentally the common sense is not unalterable. We shall observe in it continuously new turns. For example, we do not know whether Socrates was the first to regard a torn coat no longer as a sign of humility but as a sign of vanity. But if we assume he was the first, he thereby enriched the common sense. He showed that a thing may be its own opposite and that the meaning of an expressive movement can be comprehended only from its context. The common sense is not something fixed. It is rather the sum of all psychological movements which are reasonable, generally approved, and connected with the continuance of culture.

COMMENT   *It is interesting that a close theoretical relationship between the Gestalt school and Adler exists also in the area of intelligence. According to Wertheimer in Productive Thinking, "It is an* artificial and narrow view which conceives of thinking as only an intellectual operation, and separates it entirely from questions of human attitude, feeling, and emotion . . . Even seemingly mere intellectual processes involve a human attitude—that kind of willingness to face issues, to deal with them frankly, honestly, and sincerely" (116, p. 134). The traits of frankness, honesty, and sincerity are not free from an ethical component and in this resemble Adler's social interest. But Wertheimer goes on to say: "The role of the merely subjective interests of the self is, I think, much overestimated in human action. Real thinkers forget about themselves in thinking. The main vectors in genuine thought often do not refer to the I with its personal interests; rather they represent the structural requirements of the given situation" (116, p. 135). "Self-centering is not at all the general, the natural attitude, as some influential views of our time would have us believe" (116, p. 138). The proper problem-solving attitude, according to Wertheimer, is one of centering on the problem situation, including the social situation, rather than the self. This differentiation between problem-centered and self-centered thinking comes very close to Adler's distinction between reason or common sense, on the one hand, and personal intelligence, on the other (see below).

2. INTELLIGENCE[16]

Intelligence is the broader concept, for we call reason the kind of intelligence which contains social interest and which is thus limited to the generally useful.

Let us consider intelligence as we find it in the neurotic. He acts perfectly correctly. He acts so correctly that, as in compulsion neurosis, he himself may notice the difference between his personal intelligence and the common sense. Everything he does is "intelligent."

It is essential that we make a sharp distinction between reason which has general validity, and which consequently corresponds to the commonweal, and the isolated personal intelligence of the neurotic ("everything or nothing," "wanting success at the beginning," in short the intelligence of the failures). "Intelligence" we find in both cases, the failures and the normal individuals, but we call reason only the intelligence which is connected with social interest.

The phenomenon of "personal intelligence" needs further discussion. A murderer said: "The young man had beautiful clothes and I had none.

Therefore I killed him." This is a perfectly intelligent way of thinking and acting. Since this criminal does not consider himself able to acquire clothes in the customary manner, on the generally useful side, there is actually nothing left for him but robbery. For this purpose he must kill the other person. We find in all criminals an aim to approach their goal through some kind of "intelligent" argument.

COMMENT   *The reader may object at this point that murdering for the sake of a suit of clothes does not even make private sense. Granted that this particular criminal may have had deficient personal intelligence which might be expressed in an IQ of 65, we must concede that there are others with similarly low IQ's, also in need of a suit, to whom this particular solution of their problem would not occur. A low IQ, above a certain minimum, does not preclude that a person be reasonable. As we know, the majority of morons in the psychometric sense are able to find their way in life and to keep out of courts and institutions. According to Adler, this means that they have the necessary degree of social feeling, of ability to identify. Conversely, a high IQ does not preclude unreasonableness, as is shown by the various forms of maladjustment, including crime, among the highly intelligent in the psychometric sense.*

In cases of suicide we can make similar observations. After long training such individuals forego any interest in life and are filled with the thought of attracting general attention through their suicide and of achieving thus, like a murderer, a heightened feeling of superiority. ("I have done what not everyone could do. Formerly nobody took any notice of me; but now . . .") To be master over life and death brings them close to God, as it does the murderer who disposes of the lives of others. The suicide will always find arguments which are perfectly "intelligent." Since he wants to do away with himself, nothing can interest him. These arguments are "intelligent" in reference to his goal of personal superiority on the useless side.

When we consider the alcoholic we find that he too argues intelligently, provided he is not feeble-minded. Life brings worries, but there are means of overcoming these difficulties. Thus his action is intelligent with respect to the goal of overcoming difficulties the easy way. It is not a common-sense but a personal solution. Anyone with the same goal would act as he does.

3. FEEBLE-MINDEDNESS[17]

The question of feeble-mindedness can now also be formulated more precisely. It is not a lower form of intelligence but a different form of thinking. In the feeble-minded, the above-mentioned "intelligent" arguments directed at the goal of superiority seem to be lacking, so that thought shows a certain disrespect for logic. Here we find lacking the development of a life style which is never missed in the reasonable nor in the merely intelligent. The feeble-minded individual has no style of life; his evaluative attitudes toward life are entirely removed from the comprehension of any relationship. Because the feeble-minded individual lacks planful procedure, we cannot guess what he will do when placed in a new situation, aside from mechanized movements. One cannot experience empathy with his sequence of thought and, at best, one can guess at it from without. One cannot identify with a truly feeble-minded individual.

In the feeble-minded we also miss respect for common sense, which still plays a part in private intelligence through excuses, justifications, and comparisons. Feeble-mindedness in its pure form remains cold towards the demands of reason and obeys them, at best, through compulsion. The feeble-minded individual is not subject to the laws of common sense, nor does he have the intelligence which expresses itself in a goal of personal superiority.

Pseudo-feeble-mindedness is distinguished from true feeble-mindedness by an ideal goal with which one can identify. In distinction from feeble-mindedness, we find in pseudo-feeble-mindedness, paranoia, melancholia, and catatonia a unified style of life, albeit on the useless side. A definitely intelligent but not reasonable chain of thought is found in melancholia where the patient experiences in a fiction the enhancement of his self-esteem. In catatonics, we have been able to observe that they play the role of a doll, a corpse, a hero, and similar roles.

4. GENIUS[18]

Many persons have resented the attention that I and my colleagues have drawn to the compensatory factor in the work of artists of genius or of high talent and have attempted to deny that which our experience is constantly confirming. But their objection is due to a misunderstanding of the findings of Individual Psychology. We are not so foolish as to suppose that organic imperfection is the efficient cause of genius. Many Freudians have indeed supposed that the sublimest works of human genius were directly caused by sexual repressions, but we make no such eccentric generalization.

In our view, a man of genius is primarily a man of supreme usefulness. If he is an artist he is useful to culture, giving distinction and value by his work to the recreative life of many thousands. This value, where it is genuine and not merely empty brilliance, depends upon a high degree of courage and social interest. The origin of genius lies neither in the inherited organism nor in the environmental influences, but in that third sphere of individual reaction, which includes the possibility of socially affirmative action. In the choice of its specialized expression, however, the highest talent is conditioned by the organism with which it is endowed, from the greatest defect of which it gains its particular mode of concentration.

If we apply the social measure to artists and poets, we note that they serve a social function more than anyone else. It is they who have taught us how to see, how to think, and how to feel. We owe them the greatest good of mankind. Thus we attribute to them the greatest dignity, that of being the friends and leaders of mankind.

Genius is to be defined as no more than supreme usefulness: It is only when a man's life is recognized by others as having significance for them that we call him a genius. The meaning expressed in such a life will always be, "Life means—to contribute to the whole." We are not speaking here of professed motives. We are closing our ears to professions and looking at achievements.

Mankind only calls those individuals geniuses who have contributed much to the common welfare. We cannot imagine a genius who has left no advantage to mankind behind him.

5. SUMMARY[19]

In all problem people, excluding the feeble-minded, we find that their goal of personal striving for power has miscarried but that all their partial movements are "intelligent." They strike us as "abnormal" because they contradict the reason which ties us all, or the common sense. But they will always be correctly coordinated in a frame of reference on the useless side of life. Accordingly they will lack the developed social interest and the courage which are necessary for the useful solution of the problems of life. In the structure of feeble-mindedness, neither intelligence nor reason can be found to an appreciable extent.

F. Social Interest and Adjustment

COMMENT *From a consistently field-theoretical point of view, the problem of adjustment will involve not only the individual but also the respective social situation. The extent to which Adler took both these aspects into account is reflected in the terms he used, although their deeper significance is easily overlooked because they were taken from the everyday vocabulary. In the preceding part, Adler called good intellectual functioning "common sense," meaning that it provides solutions to problems which are satisfactory and make sense, not only to the individual but also to the group. Similarly we find in the present part that adjustment is expressed in relational or vectorial terms. Good adjustment is the striving on the "commonly useful side," while poor adjustment is the striving on the "commonly useless side," as seen in the diagram below. Mental disturbances thus are understood as disturbances not only in the individual, but in the social situation as well.*

1. NORMAL ADJUSTMENT[20]

[From the sociological point of view] the normal man is an individual who lives in society and whose mode of life is so adapted that, whether he wants it or not, society derives a certain advantage from his work. From the psychological point of view, he has enough energy and courage to meet the problems and difficulties as they come along. Both of these qualities are missing in the case of abnormal persons: They are neither socially adjusted nor are they psychologically adjusted to the daily tasks of life.

Social interest is the barometer of the child's normality. The criterion which needs to be watched by the psychologist and by the parent is the degree of social interest which the child or individual manifests.

Social interest is the true and inevitable compensation for all the natural weaknesses of individual human beings. The human being, even biologically considered, is clearly a social being, needing a much longer period of dependence upon others before its maturity than any animal. The human mother also is more dependent before, during, and after giving birth.

As long as the feeling of inferiority is not too great, a child will always strive to be worthwhile and on the useful side of life. Such a child, in pursuing his end, is interested in others. Social feeling and social adjustment are the right and normal compensations.

The only salvation from the continuously driving inferiority feeling is the knowledge and the feeling of being valuable which originate from the contribution to the common welfare. In the same way, it is the individual's contribution to the welfare of mankind through his children and his work which promises him the claim on immortality, in satisfaction of the general human striving not to disappear completely from the community of men.

When social interest has been from the first instilled into the upward strivings of the psyche, it acts with automatic certainty, coloring every thought and action. Where this automatized social feeling is deficient, the individual's interest is too self-centered, and he feels that he is impotent or a nobody. All his other feelings are [then] more or less directly connected with this [social] feeling. They do not exist sui generis, nor do they control action, although they are often used to do so. Of course, they influence our secondary decisions from time to time.

It is almost impossible to exaggerate the value of an increase in social feeling. The mind improves, for intelligence is a communal function. The feeling of worth and value is heightened, giving courage and an optimistic view, and there is a sense of acquiescence in the common advantages and drawbacks of our lot. The individual feels at home in life and feels his existence to be worthwhile just so far as he is useful to others and is overcoming common, instead of private, feelings of inferiority. Not only the ethical nature, but the right attitude in aesthetics, the best understanding of the beautiful and the ugly, will always be founded upon the truest social feeling.

Feeling-at-home is an immediate part of social interest. The life on this poor earth crust of one who has social interest runs its course as though he were at home. Thus a certain evaluative attitude emerges in which we do not regard the adversities of life as a personal injustice. In this attitude we shall also find all other lines of strength which serve to overcome the adversities of life.

All the problems of life have a strong social value. The individual has to be prepared for a right, normal, worthwhile, and successful solution. This means that he must possess a sufficient degree of social interest. Therefore, the brick which we call the innate potentiality of social interest must be made living and working. Such a state of mind and attitude give him more than a feeling of social interest, for he behaves as a part of the whole of mankind, he feels at home in a conception of the world as near as possible to the real world, and he has courage and common sense, social functions which are frustrated among all failures. He is ready to accept the advantages of our social life and is a good loser whenever disadvantages cross his way. He is and wants to be the master of his fate with an effective regard for the welfare of others.

2. MALADJUSTMENT[21]

All failures—neurotics, psychotics, criminals, drunkards, problem children, suicides, perverts, and prostitutes—are failures because they are lacking in social interest. They approach the problems of occupation, friendship, and sex without the confidence that they can be solved by cooperation. The meaning they give to life is a private meaning. No one else is benefited by the achievement of their aims, and their interest stops short at their own persons. Their goal of success is a goal of personal superiority, and their triumphs have meaning only to themselves. Murderers have confessed to a feeling of power when they held a bottle of poison in their hands, but clearly they were confirming their importance only to themselves. To the rest of us, the possession of a bottle of poison cannot seem to give them superior worth. A private meaning is, in fact, no meaning at all. Meaning is only possible in communication, for a word which meant something to one person only would really be meaningless. It is the same with our aims and actions, since their only meaning is their meaning for others. Every human being strives for significance, but people always make mistakes if they do not see that their whole significance must consist in their contribution to the lives of others.

It is always the lack of social interest, whatever be the name one gives it—living in fellowship, cooperation, humanity, or even ideal-ego [Freud's original term for what he later called super-ego]—which causes an insufficient preparation for all the problems of life. In the presence of a problem, this imperfect preparation gives rise to the thousand-fold forms that express physical and mental inferiority and insecurity. In none of these cases, however, will the advantage of social interest be disputed or the distinction between good and evil obliterated. In every case there is a "yes" that emphasizes the pressure of social interest, but this is invariably followed by a "but" that possesses greater strength and prevents the necessary increase of social interest. This "but" in all cases, whether typical or particular, will have an individual nuance. The difficulty of a cure is in proportion to the strength of the "but." This finds its strongest expression in suicide and in psychosis, following on shocks, when the "yes" almost disappears.

[To understand the complete coherence of a case of failure] one must always consider an increased inferiority feeling within the first five years of childhood and, closely tied up with this, a lack of social interest and courage, the quest for strongest proofs of superiority, a new problem which is frightening, the patient's distance from the problem, the exclusion tendency of the patient, his quest for specious relief on the useless side, that is, for the semblance of superiority and not for the overcoming of difficulties. [For the complete discussion of maladjustment, its diagnosis and treatment, see Chapters 9 to 13.]

3. SUMMARY[22]

Individual Psychology is probably the most consistent theory of the position of the individual to the problems of social living and is in this sense, therefore, social psychology. The diagram (Fig. 2) presented below is meant to put the "iron network" of the Individual Psychological method of investigation at the disposal of everybody. It should be like a keyboard on which the psychological artist may compose creatively. More than twenty years of work by Individual Psychology are reflected in it.

Regarding the diagram, it should be said that the attempt to catch the psychological movement in a still picture is doomed to failure from the start. I also wish to add that the path of a neurotic or a problem child runs simultaneously on both the useful and useless sides of life, although in different degrees, which fact I am unable to express in this schema.

There is only one reason for an individual to side-step to the useless side: the fear of a defeat on the useful side. In this fear, one can see the increased inferiority feeling of the patient and, added to this, his hesitation, his halting, or his flight from the solution of one of the social problems of life (there are no others). Since all problems of life require a well-developed social interest and the patient is lacking this in his

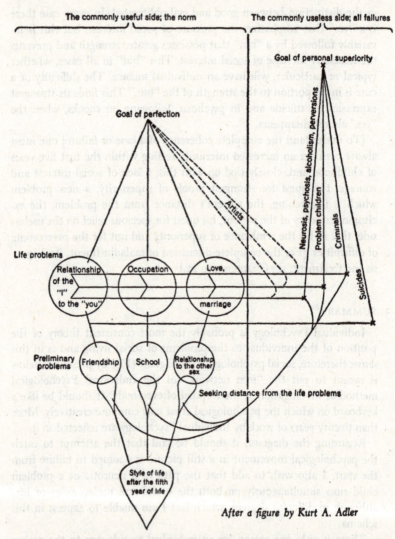

After a figure by Kurt A. Adler

FIG. 2. Individual-psychological portrayal of the norm and of failures. The circles represent situations, the lines and loops represent activities or movements of the individual. The circles schematize the situations of social embeddedness, the three social ties. Psychologically these situations are problems and as such provide tests of the individual's preparation for social living. The large circles represent *life problems* of adulthood (relationships with others, occupation, and love and marriage); the small circles represent

style of life, he is in a certain sense right to make a detour as long as he is not better prepared. Only those are able to muster the courage to advance on the useful side who consider themselves a part of the whole, who are at home on this earth and in this mankind.

COMMENT   *In concluding this chapter it seems in place to contrast Adler's view of social interest as based on a positive innate component with Freud's negative view of social behavior as a reaction-formation. According to Freud: "What appears later on in society in the shape of Gemeingeist, esprit de corps, 'group spirit,' etc., does not belie its derivation from what was originally envy . . . Social justice means that we deny ourselves many things so that others may have to do without them as well . . . This demand for equality is the root of social conscience and the sense of duty. It reveals itself unexpectedly in the syphilitic's dread of infecting other people . . . The dread exhibited by these poor wretches corresponds to their violent struggles against the unconscious wish to spread their infection on to other people; for why should they alone be infected and cut off from so much? why not other people as well?" (39, pp. 87–88).*

Freud elaborates the view that ethical demands are contrary to human nature as follows: "We might well imagine that a civilized community could consist of pairs of individuals . . . linked to all the others by work and common interests . . . But such a desirable state of things does not

---

preliminary problems met in childhood (friendship, school, and relationship to the other sex). The loops below the small circles stand for the *seeking of distance* from the problems (through hesitating, halting, and detouring). The large loop at the bottom represents the style of life formed in early childhood. Increased inferiority feeling is the essential component where the style of life is in error, and this is found most often in cases of organ inferiority, pampered children, and hated children, the three overburdening childhood situations. If through an erroneous style of life the individual is unprepared for social living, he will not continue his upward striving on the normal, or commonly useful side; instead of meeting his problems, he will try to gain distance from them. The lines leading from the left to the right side indicate detouring at various stages of life and in the face of various problems. Whereas on the left side the individual strives for a commonly acceptable individual *goal of perfection*, on the right side the striving is directed toward an exaggerated private *goal of personal superiority*, a mere semblance of genuine perfection. It corresponds to what Nietzsche called "the will to seem" and aims at false heroism and godlikeness. (Legend supplied by the editors.)

exist and never has existed . . . Restrictions upon sexual life are unavoidable if this object is to be attained . . . We may find the clue in
one of the so-called ideal standards of civilized society. It runs: 'Thou
shalt love thy neighbor as thyself'. . . . Why should we do this? What
good is it to us? Above all, how can we do such a thing? . . . If he is a
stranger to me and cannot attract me by any value he has in himself or
any significance he may have already acquired in my emotional life, it
will be hard for me to love him . . . Not merely is this stranger on the
whole not worthy of love, but, to be honest, I must confess he has more
claim to my hostility, even to my hatred. He does not seem to have the
least trace of love for me, does not show me the slightest consideration
. . . If he can merely get a little pleasure out of it, he thinks nothing of
jeering at me, insulting me, slandering me, showing his power over me;
and the more secure he feels himself, or the more helpless I am, with so
much more certainty can I expect this behavior from him towards me
. . . Civilized society is perpetually menaced with disintegration through
this primary hostility of men towards one another . . . Hence its system
of methods by which mankind is to be driven to identification and aim-
inhibited love-relationships" (35, pp. 80–87).

In the above Freud asked three interrelated questions: Why should I
love my neighbor? What good is it to me? How can I do such a thing?
Adler's answer to the third question was the assumption of an innate
potentiality for social interest. He answered the second question by pointing to the clinical findings that not to love one's neighbor is the characteristic of maladjustment. The individual whose social interest is developed finds the solution to his problems, feels at home in the world,
achieves security and courage, and even approaches nearer to true perception (1929b, p. 78).

With respect to Adler's answer to these questions we should like to
refer to Maslow once more for his essential similarity. Maslow postulates
a basis for social behavior which is "instinctoid" but weak, just as social
interest is innate but needs to be nurtured. "Human nature carries within
itself the answer to the questions, How can I be good?, How can I be
happy?, How can I be fruitful? The organism tells us what it needs (and
therefore what it values) by sickening when deprived of these values"
(78, pp. 152–153).

In fairness to Freud, it must be stated that he too recognized the asocial
character of the neurotic, although he saw it in terms of unsuccessfully
repressed sexual aims. "A neurosis should make its victim asocial and

should remove him from the usual group formations. It may be said that a neurosis has the same disintegrating effect upon a group as being in love. On the other hand, it appears that where a powerful impetus has been given to group formation, neuroses may diminish and at all events temporarily disappear. Justifiably attempts have also been made to turn this antagonism between neuroses and group formation to therapeutic account" (39, p. 124). In view of the previous quotations from Freud, it is apparent that this last-quoted thought played a subordinate role in his theorizing, although in practice this may not have been the case.

To the most general formulation of the question, "Why should I love my neighbor?", Adler is reported to have replied: "If anyone asks me why he should love his neighbor, I would not know how to answer him, and I could only ask in my turn why he should pose such a question" (112, p. 266). In the many instances where Adler quotes the question he states that it characterizes the attitude of the spoiled child, as in the following. "The most important task imposed by religion has always been, 'Love thy neighbor.' Here again in another form, we have the same striving to increase interest in our fellow men. It is interesting, too, that now from a scientific standpoint we can confirm the value of this striving. The pampered child asks us, 'Why should I love my neighbor? Does my neighbor love me?' and so reveals his lack of training in cooperation, and his interest in himself. It is the individual who is not interested in his fellow men who has the greatest difficulties in life and provides the greatest injury to others. It is from among such individuals that all human failures spring" (1931a, p. 253).

FOOTNOTES TO CHAPTER FIVE

1. 1: *The Science of Living* (1929c), pp. 59–60; 2 to 5: *Menschenkenntnis* (1927a), pp. 18, 18–19, 19, and 19–20.

2. 1, 2, 3: *Menschenkenntnis* (1927a), pp. 20, 21, and 21–22.

3. 1 to 4: *Menschenkenntnis* (1927a), pp. 22, 22–23, 23, and 23–24.

4. 1 and 4: *Der Sinn des Lebens* (1933a), pp. 27–28 and 38; 2, 3, 5 to 8: *What Life Should Mean to You* (1931a), pp. 239, 239, 239–240, 240, 241, and 241.

5. 1: *Problems of Neurosis* (1929b), p. 31; 2 and 3: "Über den Ursprung des Strebens nach Überlegenheit und des Gemeinschaftsgefühles" (1933e), pp. 257–263; 4: "The prevention of delinquency" (1935d), pp. 4–5.

6. **1, 2, 3**, and **5**: "Kurze Bemerkungen über Vernunft, Intelligenz und Schwachsinn" (1928), pp. 267, 267 and 271, 267, and 269–270; **4**: "Individual Psychology" (1930f), p. 402.

7. **1**: "Delinquency" (1935d), pp. 4–5; **2** and **3**: *Menschenkenntnis* (1927a), pp. 32 and 32–33; **4**: "Erziehungsberatungsstellen" (1922b), p. 119; **5**: *Sinn des Lebens* (1933a), p. 31; **6**: "Religion und Individualpsychologie" (1933c), p. 85; **7**: "Prevention of neurosis" (1935c), p. 8.

8. **1** and **4**: *Menschenkenntnis* (1927a), pp. 133–134 and 134; **2** and **3**: *Science of Living* (1929c), pp. 216 and 221; **5**: "Über den Ursprung" (1933e), pp. 257–263.

9. **1** and **3**: *Sinn des Lebens* (1933a), pp. 75 and 162; **2**: *What Life Should Mean to You* (1931a), p. 70; **4** and **5**: "Über den Ursprung" (1933e), pp. 257–263.

10. **1 to 4**: *Über den nervösen Charakter* (1912a), pp. 47. 47–48, 48, and 48, as corrected according to the 1912 edition pp. 42–43.

11. **1**: *Nervöser Charakter* (1912a), p. iv; **2**: *Praxis und Theorie der Individualpsychologie* (1924), p. iii.

12 to 14: Carl Furtmüller. "Psychoanalyse und Ethik" (46), pp. 1–34.

15. **1 to 4**: "Kurze Bemerkungen" (1928), pp. 267, 268, 268, and 268.

16. **1 to 6**: "Kurze Bemerkungen" (1928), pp. 270, 268, 269, 268–269, 269, and 269.

17. **1, 2, 3**: "Kurze Bemerkungen" (1928), p. 270.

18. **1** and **2**: *Problems of Neurosis* (1929b), p. 35; **3**: *Die Technik der Individualpsychologie. Tl. 2.* (1930d), p. 193; **4** and **5**: *What Life Should Mean to You* (1931a), pp. 9 and 247.

19. **1**: "Kurze Bemerkungen" (1928), p. 274.

20. **1** and **4**: *Science of Living* (1929c), pp. 103–104 and 216; **2**: *The Education of Children* (1930a), pp. 10–11; **3, 6** and **7**: *Problems of Neurosis* (1929b), pp. 31, 33, and 79; **5**: "Religion" (1933c), p. 84; **8**: "Kurze Bemerkungen" (1928), p. 267; **9**: "Psychiatric aspects regarding individual and social disorganization" (1937a), p. 777.

21. **1**: *What Life Should Mean to You* (1931a), p. 8; **2**: *Sinn des Lebens* (1933a), p. 73; **3**: "Individualpsychologie und Wissenschaft" (1927d), p. 408.

22. **1**: *Individualpsychologie in der Schule* (1929a), p. 108; **2**, **Figure 2**, and **3**: "IP und Wissenschaft" (1927d), pp. 408, 409, and 407–408.

CHAPTER SIX

DEGREE OF ACTIVITY

COMMENT *To the striving for superiority and social interest Adler later added a third primary factor of human behavior, namely, degree of activity. From the systematic point of view, he placed it on the same level as social interest, and he suggested a system of classification or typology which can be understood as based on the two variables, social interest and activity. It is for the systematic reason that degree of activity and its implications need to be presented in a separate chapter. Degree of activity is otherwise of minor importance in Adler's work, which is reflected in the small size of this chapter.*

A. Degree of Activity

1. THE NATURE OF DEGREE OF ACTIVITY[1]

I do not know more about human life than others, but I can see that it expresses itself in movement and direction toward a successful solution of outer and inner confrontations. The direction, in using all human qualities, is characterized by the subjectively expected goal of a perfect achievement and by the degree of social interest. As in physics we cannot measure any movement without relating it toward another space, so in Individual Psychology this other space is the social organization of mankind and its supposedly eternal demands. Different degrees and varieties of activity are also inherent in the structure of this striving individual life.

Individual Psychology endeavors to obtain an idea of an individual as a whole from his attitude to the problems of life, problems which are always social in nature. In doing so, it particularly emphasizes among other important facts the degree of activity with which the individual tackles his problems. Some time ago, we explained such facts as the hesitating attitude, self-blockade, detours, and restrictions in the breadth of approach, sudden spurts with subsequent sluggishness, and the jumping from one task to another as typical forms of failure when the ability to cooperate is reduced. It did not escape our attention that these erroneous gaits in their thousand-fold variations show varying degrees of activity.

Although it is probably not possible to express the degree of activity in quantitative terms, it is obvious that a child who runs away from his parents, or a boy who starts a fight in the street, must be credited with a higher degree of activity than a child who likes to sit at home and read a book.

In all cases, with their millions of variations, a uniform kind of activity can always be observed. As a rule, one will be able to perceive the degree of activity also from the extent of the sphere of activity which is different for each individual. It would be a tempting task for a psychologist to show graphically the extent and form of the individual life-space.

The degree of activity acquired in childhood becomes a constant supply which endures throughout life. This statement is not contradicted by the fact that in many cases this does not appear to be so. The degree of activity becomes apparent only conditionally, depending, for example, on whether the circumstances in which the individual lives are favorable or unfavorable.

From the least traits and expressions of childhood, we can predict with which degree of activity a child will later on meet the problems of life.

The individual degree of activity is created somewhat arbitrarily by the personality during earliest childhood.

It would be altogether a mistake to try to reduce individual differences in degree of activity or social interest to innate factors. Heredity and environmental factors play a part only in the sense of providing a certain probability. From all the impressions which the child experiences he forms, as in an inspiration, his style of life [see next chapter], and among the most important structures of this style of life are a definite degree of activity and a definite degree of social interest which gives the direction to that activity.

2. DEGREE OF ACTIVITY IN MALADJUSTMENT[2]

We should like to present that part of our findings on the constancy and identity of the degree of activity referring to failures and to their childhood. Here we must take as our point of departure the traditional conception of types of failures, although we qualify all failures as cases of insufficient social interest. We must add that each case within a type shows qualitative and quantitative differences with respect to its activity.

While the degree of cooperative ability gives the direction, it is only if taken together with the degree of activity that this will permit us to predict, when there is danger of a failure, what kind of failure it will be.

A thorough knowledge of the structure of each type of failure serves as illumination of the field of view in which we expect to find the individual case. We should like to classify the typical failures as follows: problem children, neurotics and psychotics, suicides, criminals, alcoholics and drug addicts, sexual perverts, prostitutes.

In problem children, the difference in activity is already clear and should determine the correspondingly different measures of education. Wild, unbridled, stubborn, stealing, quarrelsome children obviously have a greater degree of activity than shy, reticent, frightened children, and those who are dependent on others. Furthermore, the sphere of action of the former is greater than that of the latter. If we look for the kind of failure which will distinguish the two, it can easily be shown that the weaker degree of activity of the neurosis and psychosis will correspond to the weaker degree of activity in childhood. But it must not be overlooked that even within these disease types and symptoms, the weaker degree of activity differs qualitatively and quantitatively. It is higher, for example, in compulsion neurosis and melancholia, and lower in anxiety neurosis and schizophrenia.

Suicides and alcoholics are characterized from childhood by a somewhat higher degree of activity, which also underlies the structure of these failures. Their sphere of action is clearly larger, but their activity develops along the detour of hurting themselves. Pampered in childhood, as almost all failures have been, they feel their own person to be so valuable that an attack against themselves appears to them as an attack against their nearest and more distant environment.

Cases of sexual perversion may, from the point of view of activity, be found all the way from the lowest to the highest degree. At the low extreme we find masturbation or fetishism, at the high extreme possibly the lust murder, both characterized since childhood by a corresponding radius of action and inadequate social interest.

We find the greatest amount of activity in the criminal, but in different degrees depending on the kind of criminal tendency. At the lowest point of the activity scale is the swindler and pickpocket, at the highest point, the murderer.

3. COURAGE[3]

Activity must not be confused with courage, although there is no courage without activity. But only the activity of an individual who plays the game, cooperates, and shares in life can be designated as courage. There are many variations of courage, as well as mixed cases and cases where courage appears only conditionally, for example, in the event of extreme emergency or with the assistance of others. Anyone who has become convinced of the constancy of the degree of activity, corresponding entirely to the constancy of the individual law of movement, that is, the style of life, will observe very attentively that individual degree of activity. The appreciation of this problem opens an entirely new and valuable perspective for psychotherapy, education, and prophylaxis.

COMMENT *The significance of Adler's mention of courage and treatment in the same paragraph is that the increase of courage was one aspect of his treatment (see pp. 341–342). If courage is the resultant of social interest and activity, then the correct appraisal of these two factors would, of course, be an important aid in determining exactly how to deal with a given individual.*

B. Types

1. THE HEURISTIC NATURE OF TYPES[4]

We do not consider human beings as types, because every person has an individual style of life. If we speak of types, therefore, it is only as a conceptual device to make more understandable the similarities of individuals.

We can judge better when we postulate a conceptual classification, such as a type, and study its special peculiarities. In doing so, however, we do not commit ourselves to use the same classification at all times. We use the classification which is most useful for bringing out a particular similarity. People who take types and classification seriously do not see how, once a person is put in a pigeonhole, he can be put into any other classification.

An illustration will make our point clear. For instance when we speak of a type of individual not socially adjusted, we refer to one who leads a barren life without any social interest. This is one way of classifying individuals, and perhaps it is the most important way. But consider the individual whose interest, however limited, is centered on visual things. Such a person differs entirely from one whose interests are largely concentrated on things aural, but both of them may be socially maladjusted and find it difficult to establish contact with their fellow men. The classification by types can thus be a source of confusion if we do not realize that types are merely convenient abstractions.

Life (and all psychological expressions as part of life) moves ever toward overcoming, toward perfection, toward superiority, toward success. You cannot train or condition a living being for defeat. But what an individual thinks or feels as success (as an acceptable goal) is unique with him. In our experience we have found that each individual has a different meaning of, and attitude toward, what constitutes success. Therefore a human being cannot be typified or classified. We believe that the parsimony of language causes many scientists to come to mistaken conclusions, to believe in types, entities, and racial qualities. Individual Psychology recognizes, with other psychologies, that each individual must be studied in the light of his own peculiar development. To present the individual understandably, in words, requires an extensive reviewing of all his facets. Yet too often psychologists are tempted away from this recognition to take the easier but unfruitful roads of classification. That is a temptation to which, in practical work, we must never yield. It is for teaching purposes only, to illuminate the broad field, that we shall designate here four different types in order temporarily to classify the attitude and behavior of individuals toward outside problems.

2. SOCIAL INTEREST-ACTIVITY TYPES[5]

We find individuals whose approach to reality shows, from early childhood through their entire lives, a more or less dominant or ruling attitude which appears in all their relationships. A second type, surely the most frequent, expects everything from others and leans on others, and might be called the getting type. A third type is inclined to feel successful by avoiding the solution of problems. Instead of struggling with a problem, a person of this type merely tries to side-step it, thereby trying to avoid defeat. The fourth type struggles, in a greater or lesser degree, to solve these problems in a way useful to others.

The first three types mentioned above—the ruling type, the getting type, and the avoiding type—are not apt, and are not prepared, to solve the problems of life. These problems are always social problems, and individuals of these three types lack the ability to cooperate and to contribute. The clash between such a life style (lacking in social interest) and the outside problems (demanding social interest) results in shock. This shock leads up to the individual's failures, which we know as neurosis, psychosis, and other maladjustments. Significantly, the failure shows the same style as the individual. As we mentioned before, the life style persists.

In the fourth type (the socially useful type), prepared for cooperation and contribution, we can always find a certain amount of activity which is used for the benefit of others. This activity is in agreement with the needs of others. It is useful, normal, rightly embedded in the stream of evolution of mankind.

The first type also has activity, but not enough social interest. Therefore, if confronted strongly by a situation which he feels to be in the nature of an examination, a test of his social value, a judgment upon his social usefulness, a person of this type acts in an unsocial way. The more active of this type attack others directly. They become delinquents, tyrants, sadists. It is as if they said, with Richard III, "And therefore, since I cannot prove a lover, . . . I am determined to prove a villain." To this type also belong suicidals, drug addicts, and drunkards, whose lesser degree of activity causes them to attack others indirectly. They make attacks upon themselves for the purpose of hurting others. The second and third types show even less activity and not much social interest. This lack appears also in the expression of their shock results, which are neuroses and psychoses.

The principles which guide us when grouping individuals into these four types are the degree of their approach to social integration and the form of movement which they develop (with greater or lesser activity) to maintain that degree of approach in a manner which they regard as most likely to achieve success (in their own interpretation).

COMMENT   For the reader who would be inclined to construct a fourfold table out of the two variables of social interest and
degree of activity, we should like to point out that Adler's four types
correspond to such a table only to some extent. The socially useful type
corresponds to a high degree of social interest and a high degree of activity;
the ruling type, to a low degree of social interest combined with a high
degree of activity; the other two types, the getting and the avoiding, to
a low degree of social interest plus increasingly lower degrees of activity.
This leaves the fourth possible combination of the two variables, namely
high social interest and low degree of activity, unrepresented by a type.
Somewhat similar discussions have been presented graphically by Rudolf Dreikurs (27, pp. 72–73) and by Antonio Bruck (19, p. 85).

3. THE FOUR TEMPERAMENTS[6]

COMMENT   Several years before Adler presented the above typology
and before he had conceived of degree of activity as a primary factor, he discussed the ancient four temperaments as shown in the
following. Although he did not come back to them in later years, their
similarity to his social interest and activity types can easily be seen.

The temperaments are a very old differentiation of psychological forms
of expression. It is not easy to say what is to be understood by temperament. Is it the speed with which one thinks, speaks, or acts? Or is it the
energy or the rhythm which one puts into this? If we trace the explanations of psychologists regarding the nature of the temperaments, we must
say that since antiquity science has not advanced beyond the postulation
of four temperaments. Their classification into sanguine, choleric, melancholic, and phlegmatic originated in ancient Greece, was taken over by
Hippocrates, continued by the Romans, and today still forms a venerable
relic in psychology.

The sanguine individual is one who shows a certain joy in life, who does
not take things too seriously, who does not worry easily, who attempts
to see the most beautiful and pleasant side of everything, who on sad
occasions is sad without breaking down, and who experiences pleasure
at happy events without losing his balance. A detailed description of such
individuals shows nothing more than that they are approximately healthy
people in whom harmful tendencies are not present to any great degree.
We cannot make this assertion of the other three types.

The sanguine individual appears to be the one who, in his childhood, was least exposed to the feeling of inferiority, who showed few noticeable organ inferiorities, and who was not subjected to strong irritations, so that he could develop undisturbedly, learn to love life and to come to friendly terms with it.

The choleric individual is described in an old poetic simile as a man who furiously hurls aside a stone which lies in his way, while the sanguine individual walks over it with composure. Translated into the language of Individual Psychology, the choleric individual is one whose striving for power is so tense that he must always make large movements and wants to produce feats of energy and overrun everything in a straight-line, aggressive manner. One already finds among young children such individuals with large movements, who not only have a feeling of their strength but also want to realize and demonstrate it.

The melancholic makes quite a different impression. In the above simile, he is represented approximately as the one who, on seeing the stone, is reminded of all his sins, sinks into sad reflections, and turns back. Individual Psychology sees in this type the pronouncedly hesitating individual who does not have the confidence to overcome difficulties and to advance, but who initiates his further steps with the greatest caution and who prefers to stand still or to turn back rather than to take any risk. In other words, this is an individual in whom indecision gains the upper hand and who usually is inclined to think more of himself than of others, so that this type too has no points of contact for the great possibilities of life. He is so oppressed by his own worries that his gaze is turned backward or inward.

The phlegmatic individual appears generally to be the one who is a stranger to life and collects impressions without drawing any particular consequences, who is no longer impressed by anything, whom nothing interests particularly, who furthermore makes no particular efforts, in brief, the one who also has no contact with life and possibly is furthest removed from it.

There is no phlegmatic individual who has been phlegmatic all his life. We shall always find that this temperament is but an artificial shell, a safeguard which a very sensitive person has created for himself, which he has inserted between the environment and himself, and for which he may possibly have had an original inclination founded in his constitution. The phlegmatic temperament is a safeguarding process, a meaningful response to the problems of life. It is of course completely different from the slowness, sluggishness, and inadequacy of an individual who is entirely or partially deprived of the thyroid gland.

Even if it could be proven that only those can attain a phlegmatic temperament who show a pathological thyroid secretion, we could not overlook these important considerations. Rather we must assert that this would not be all there is to the matter. An entire sheaf of causes and goals would be involved, an entire syndrome of organ activities plus external influences, which would first create an organic inferiority feeling, from which in turn certain attempts of the individual to compensate would originate. One of these attempts can be to seek protection from annoyances and injuries to the self-esteem by a phlegmatic temperament.

COMMENT *In the light of the above it is apparent that the four temperaments can be synthesized to some extent with the four types from the preceding section. Type I, the ruling type would be the choleric; Type II, the getting, leaning type, would be the phlegmatic; Type III, the avoiding type, the melancholic; and Type IV, the socially useful, the sanguine individual.*

FOOTNOTES TO CHAPTER SIX

1. 1: "Psychiatric aspects regarding individual and social disorganization" (1937a), p. 776; 2 to 8: "Die Formen der seelischen Aktivität" (1933f), pp. 1–5.
2 and 3. "Seelische Aktivität" (1933f), pp. 1–5.
4. 1, 2, 3: *The Science of Living* (1929c), pp. 102, 102–103, and 103; 4: "The fundamental views of Individual Psychology" (1935a), p. 6.
5. 1 to 5: "Fundamental views" (1935a), pp. 6, 7, 7, 7, and 8.
6. 1 to 8: *Menschenkenntnis* (1927a), pp. 144, 144, 145–146, 144–145, 145, 145, 147, and 147–148.

CHAPTER SEVEN

THE STYLE OF LIFE

COMMENT *Up to this point, we have presented the three general, nomothetic parts of Adler's theory of personality. The basic dynamic force was the striving for a fictional goal (Chapter 3, second part), which is one of superiority (Chapter 4). Successful adaptation to life was seen to depend on the degree of social interest present in the goal-striving (Chapter 5). The striving may be more or less active and may be considered in the form of purely heuristic types (Chapter 6).*

The present chapter will deal with Adler's conception and stress of the wholeness and uniqueness of the individual, the idiographic aspects of the theory, the way the individual uniquely implements the nomothetic formulations. It deals with the nature of the individual self, the individual personality structure.

The chapter is most directly a continuation of the discussion of the fictional goal of the second part of Chapter 3, with which it overlaps. A formal difference is that the readings in Chapter 3 are mostly from Adler's early writings, especially the 1912–1914 period, while in the present chapter they are almost all from the 1930's. Regarding content, the style of life is the more general concept, comprising, in addition to the goal, the individual's opinion of himself and the world and his unique way of striving for the goal in his particular situation. Thus the style of life is also the more dynamic concept in comparison with the more static concept of the goal, reflecting Adler's development toward an ever more completely dynamic psychology. The style of life in Adler's late writings is based on the individual's "law of movement" (see pp. 195–196). The style of life is also the more field-theoretical concept in that it is closely related to the situation, as illustrated in the opening selection which otherwise uses a questionable analogy.

A. Definition[1]

If we look at a pine tree growing in a valley we will notice that it grows differently from one on top of a mountain. It is the same kind of a tree, a pine, but there are two distinct styles of life. Its style on top of the mountain is different from its style when growing in the valley. The style of life of a tree is the individuality of a tree expressing itself and molding itself in an environment. We recognize a style when we see it against a background of an environment different from what we expect, for then we realize that every tree has a life pattern and is not merely a mechanical reaction to the environment.

It is much the same way with human beings. We see the style of life under certain conditions of environment and it is our task to analyze its exact relation to the existing circumstances, inasmuch as mind changes with alteration of the environment. As long as a person is in a favorable situation, we cannot see his style of life clearly. In new situations, however, where he is confronted with difficulties, the style of life appears clearly and distinctly. A trained psychologist could perhaps understand a style of life of a human being even in a favorable situation, but it becomes apparent to everybody when the human subject is put into unfavorable or difficult situations.

How does the notion of the style of life tie up with what we have discussed in previous chapters? We have seen how human beings with weak organs, because they face difficulties and feel insecure, suffer from a feeling or complex of inferiority. But as human beings cannot endure this for long, the inferiority feeling stimulates them, as we have seen, to movement and action. This results in a person having a goal. Individual Psychology has long called the consistent movement toward the goal a plan of life. But because this name has sometimes led to mistakes among students, it is now called a style of life.

COMMENT *This definition which Adler gave in 1929 was varied considerably throughout his writings. The further definitions, as was his custom, were often merely interspersed and given in subordinate clauses. Accordingly it seems more efficient merely to cite them in this comment rather than present them in the form of readings, especially since some of these definitions and others will be found in the subsequent selections of this chapter.*

Style of life is variously equated with the self or ego (1931b, p. 4; 1935a, p. 7), a man's own personality (1931a, p. 200), the unity of the personality (1935a, p. 7), individuality (1931b, p. 4), individual form of creative activity (1935a, p. 8), the method of facing problems (1931a, p. 201), opinion about oneself and the problems of life (1933a, p. 16), the whole attitude to life (1929c, p. 135) and others.

Although in Adler's earlier writings the emphasis was on the goal, he had from the beginning used several terms foreshadowing the style of life. When he was still mechanistically and biologically oriented and attempted to express the unity of the individual through the concept of the confluence of drives, he was also aware of the uniqueness of the individual and of the need to give this idea an expression. This he did at first with the term psychological main axis. In 1912, in The Neurotic Character, the main axis became the guiding idea which provides the approach to the fictional goal through the life plan: "We may look upon every single manifestation of life as if in its past, present, and future there were contained traces of a superordinated guiding idea . . . Comparative Individual Psychology sees in every psychological process the imprint, a symbol so to speak, of the self-consistently oriented life plan" (1912a, p. iii). In 1927 we find schema of life (Lebens-Schablone) and line of movement used synonymously with style of life (1927a, p. 3). Finally, in 1933 Adler proposed the individual's law of movement as underlying the style of life (see pp. 195-196).

B. Unity and Sovereignty of the Self

1. UNITY AND SOVEREIGNTY[2]

The child is constantly confronted afresh with ever–varying problems. Since these can be solved neither by conditioned reflexes nor by innate abilities, it would be extremely hazardous to expose a child who is equipped only with conditioned reflexes or with innate abilities to the tests of a world which is continuously raising new problems. The solution of the greatest problem would always be up to the never-resting creative mind. This remains pressed into the path of the child's style of life, as does everything that has a name in the various schools of psychology, such as instincts, impulses, feeling, thinking, acting, attitude to pleasure and displeasure, and finally self-love and social interest. The style of life commands all forms of expression; the whole commands the parts.

In real life we always find a confirmation of the melody of the total self, of the personality, with its thousandfold ramifications. If we believe that the foundation, the ultimate basis of everything has been found in character traits, drives, or reflexes, the self is likely to be overlooked. Authors who emphasize a part of the whole are likely to attribute to this part all the aptitudes and observations pertaining to the self, the individual. They show "something" which is endowed with prudence, determination, volition, and creative power without knowing that they are actually describing the self, rather than drives, character traits, or reflexes.

Individual Psychology goes beyond the views of philosophers like Kant and newer psychologists and psychiatrists who have accepted the idea of the totality [wholeness] of the human being. Very early in my work, I found man to be a [self-consistent] unity. The foremost task of Individual Psychology is to prove this unity in each individual—in his thinking, feeling, acting, in his so-called conscious and unconscious, in every expression of his personality. This [self-consistent] unity we call the style of life of the individual. What is frequently labeled the ego is nothing more than the style of the individual.

The very first requisite for a science of psychology is missing from psychoanalysis, namely, a recognition of the coherence of the personality and of the unity of the individual in all his expressions.

Gestalt psychology shows a better understanding of this coherence. But we are not satisfied with the Gestalt alone or, as we prefer to say, with the whole, once all the notes are brought into reference with the melody. We are satisfied only when we have recognized in the melody the author and his attitudes as well, for example, Bach and Bach's style of life.

COMMENT *The similarity to Gestalt psychology which Adler mentions here, and which we have brought out many times, finds a further confirmation in the fact that Wertheimer formulated a concept similar to the "style of life." According to an unpublished statement, quoted by Allport, Wertheimer held that "if a personality is rightly understood, it will always be found to lie under the domination of one controlling goal, one ruling passion, possessing one radix" (4, p. 147). "The radix may never be sought on the activity level, for it lies at the root of activities. And however inconsistent activities may seem to be, they are congruent*

*so long as they spring from the same root" (4, p. 358). Adler's style of life
is to be understood in the same way.*

No matter how little one knows about the unity of the self, one cannot
get rid of it. One may dismember the self-consistent psychological life according to various, more or less worthwhile points of view. One may [as
psychoanalysis does] call on to the scene, with or against one another, two,
three, or four different topological concepts in order to comprehend the
self-consistent self. One may attempt to unfold it from the conscious,
from the unconscious, from the sexual sphere, or from the environment
—but in the end one will not be able to avoid the necessity of reinstating
it to its all-embracing effectiveness, like setting a rider once more on his
steed. Even if one believes one has dislodged the self from the unconscious, or from the id, in the end the id behaves mannerly or unmannerly
like a self. It is being more and more understood by psychoanalysis that
the so-called consciousness, or the self, is full of the "unconscious" or, as
I have shown, the not-understood, and that it always presents varying degrees of social interest. The progress which Individual Psychology has
initiated can no longer be disregarded. In the view of modern psychology,
the self has established its dignity.

COMMENT   *G. W. Allport expressed the same sentiment when he wrote
later, in 1943: "We may safely predict that ego-psychology
in the twentieth century will flourish increasingly. For only with its aid
can psychologists reconcile the human nature that they study and the
human nature that they serve" (3, p. 139). Adler, writing in German,
used the term ich which is variously translated as self or ego. We chose
self as more appropriate, especially after Symonds' distinction between
the two terms (107); in fact, however, our use of self and Allport's use of
ego are identical.*

2. CREATIVITY[8]

We concede that every child is born with potentialities different from
those of any other child. Our objection to the teachings of the heredi-
tarians and every other tendency to overstress the significance of constitutional disposition is that the important thing is not what one is born
with, but what use one makes of that equipment. We must ask ourselves: "Who uses it?" As to the influences of the environment, who
can say that the same environmental influences are apprehended, worked

over, digested, and responded to by any two individuals the same way? [See Chapter 8.] To understand this fact we find it necessary to assume the existence of still another force, the creative power of the individual. We have been impelled to attribute to the child a creative power, which casts into movement all the influences upon him and all his potentialities, a movement toward the overcoming of an obstacle. This is felt by the child as an impulse that gives his striving a certain direction.

The drive in the child is without direction as long as it has not been incorporated into the movement toward the goal which he creates in response to his environment. This response is not simply a passive re-action but a manifestation of creative activity on the part of the in-dividual. It is futile to attempt to establish psychology on the basis of drives alone, without taking into consideration the creative power of the child which directs the drive, molds it into form, and supplies it with a meaningful goal.

The finalistic point of view is an absolute necessity [for our under-standing]. In the first place, we can never regard a person other than as a self-consistent being and thus as a goal-directed and purposeful whole; in the second place, life itself and purposeful movements require of him the continuous adherence to a self-consistent goal. Thus the teleology of human psychological life arises from immanent necessities, but is in its uniqueness a creation of the individual.

Every individual represents both a unity of personality and the indi-vidual fashioning of that unity. The individual is thus both the picture and the artist. He is the artist of his own personality, but as an artist he is neither an infallible worker nor a person with a complete under-standing of mind and body; he is rather a weak, extremely fallible, and imperfect human being.

3. THE FORGOTTEN CHILD[4]

When people speak of drives, the poor self is pushed far into the back-ground, as if there had been no fertilized egg which is already complete in itself. To speak of drives which are supposed to produce the self is far-fetched. It is the self which grows into life, which we recognize later on as creative power. If anyone believes that he can attribute to the drives that which pertains to the self, such as to seek, to question, to doubt, to think, to feel, to will, and to be goal-directed this is but a sleight of hand. The most important question is: Who moves the mental life (*Seelenle-*

ben), and in which direction does he move it? The mover is always the self.

All inherited possibilities and all influences of the body, all environmental influences, including educational application, are perceived, assimilated, digested, and answered by a living and striving being, striving for a successful achievement in his view. The subjectiveness of the individual, his special style of life, and his conception of life mold and shape all influences. The individual life collects all these influences and uses them as provocative bricks in building a totality which aims toward a successful goal in relating itself to outside problems. This provocation and the child's opinion of life and opinion of himself are creations of the mostly forgotten child.

When we examine the chosen direction of individuals, we find thousands of different answers. Whatever the chosen direction, behind it is the opinion of life and the style of living. This is the creation of the forgotten child, his independent creation, forgotten so long as only the bricks are considered. Whoever considers the inside contents [the bricks themselves] as valid enough and qualified for understanding a personality, overlooks the nearly limitless possibilities of the creative power of the child and inclines toward pseudoproblems, such as ambivalence, disintegration, and so forth.

We must refute the causal significance of situation, milieu, or experiences of the child. Their significance and effectiveness develop only in the intermediary psychological metabolism, so to speak. They are assimilated by the early-derived style of life of the child. Thus it can happen that in a quite ethical family an anti-social child may grow up. The same experience has never exactly the same effect on two individuals; and we learn from experience only to the extent that the style of life permits.

COMMENT *Similar ideas have since been presented by John E. Anderson who warns against regarding the child as a passive recipient of stimuli, as "for instance some advocates of the frustration aggression hypothesis picture the child" and as does "much of the psychoanalytic teaching about children" (7, p. 409). Anderson points to recent scientific findings which show the child as a persistent personality system with a high capacity for self-repair and selectivity, "not as a storehouse or filing cabinet, but as an active system engaged in transforming input into outgo" (7, p. 410).*

The last passage uses virtually the same figure of speech as Adler does when he states above that experiences are first assimilated and digested before they become effective through the "intermediate psychological metabolism." Anderson concludes, much as does Adler: "The child, then, is not a simple passive creature molded exclusively by external forces; he is very much a creature in his own right, moving through his own experiences and creating his own world" (7, p. 416).

The implication of this part for the problem of causation, is, of course, a continuation of the position taken up in the discussion of the goal as principle of internal, subjective causation which was seen to correspond to "soft" determinism. The self, with creative power as part of its inner nature, is the important intervening variable. Murphy declared soft determinism, that is, the participation of the person as cause, "one of the most valuable working concepts available" and recognizes the necessity for adopting this principle (84, p. 645).

c. Uniqueness and Subjectivity

1. THE INDIVIDUAL AS THE VARIANT[5]

The now antiquated, older natural science with its rigid systems has been generally replaced today by views which attempt biologically, philosophically, and psychologically to comprehend life and its variants in their context (Zusammenhang). This is also true of that trend in psychology which I have called Comparative Individual Psychology. It attempts to gain, from the separate life manifestations and forms of expression the picture of the self-consistent personality as a variant, by presupposing the unity and self-consistency [both Einheit] of the individuality. The separate traits are then compared with one another, are reduced to their common denominator, and are combined in an individualizing manner into a total portrait. William Stern, in a different way, has arrived at results similar to mine.

COMMENT   This paragraph was quoted almost in full in the Introduction (see p. 10), where we have also shown that Adler established Individual Psychology as a personalistic and idiographic psychology. It is this intense concern with the uniqueness and unity of the individual which made Adler choose the name Individual Psychology for his school. It differs from what is usually known by the same name, namely the study of individual differences in specific traits. Adler takes the individual as a whole, not separate traits, as the variant. It is in line with this consideration that Furtmüller, from whom we presented a reading in Chapter 5, described Individual Psychology very early as a "centralist" rather than a "peripheralist" psychology: It is necessary "first to grasp the nucleus of the personality in order to be able at all to understand the peripheral expressions and to assess them correctly" (45, p. vi).

This way of looking upon man's psychological life appears not at all unusual or even particularly daring. It is the nature and the work especially of the artist, the painter, the sculptor, the musician, and particularly the poet, so to present all the minor traits of his characters that the observer is able to comprehend in them the basic lines of the personality and is able to build up what the artist had already hidden in them in view of the finale.

The demands of life compel the child to make his responses in a unified manner, and this unified manner of answering situations not only constitutes the child's character but also individualizes each of his acts and makes them distinct from the similar acts of other children.

It has been imputed to us that we assume and strive for the sameness of men. This is a myth. Quite on the contrary, we attempt to examine the nuances, the uniqueness of the goal, the uniqueness of the opinion of a man of himself and the tasks of life. The task of Individual Psychology is to comprehend the individual variant.

2. UNIQUENESS OF THE GOAL[6]

A goal of overcoming as an abstract formulation is unacceptable to the human mind. We need a much more concrete formulation. Thus each individual arrives at a concrete goal of overcoming through his creative power, which is identical with the self. As soon as we speak of goal striving, when we comprehend the concrete goal-concept better, an immense difficulty appears, namely that we are dealing with thousands of variations, always with a unique case, with a unique concrete setting of the goal.

The dynamic value of mental, emotional, and attitudinal movements consists of their direction toward, or determination by, a goal which has for the individual the meaning of securing for him what he regards as his position in life. Only in this way can we understand these goal-directed movements: as the individual's efforts to secure for himself what he interprets, or misinterprets, as success, or as his way of overcoming a minus-situation in order to attain a plus-situation.

The goal of superiority with each individual is personal and unique. It depends upon the meaning he gives to life. This meaning is not a matter of words. It is built up in his style of life and runs through it like a strange melody of his own creation. In his style of life, he does not express his goal so that we can formulate it for all times. He expresses it vaguely, so that we must guess at it from the indications he gives.

Even where the goal has been made concrete, there can be a thousand varieties of striving towards this goal. One man, for example, will want to be a physician, but to be a physician may mean many different things. He may not only wish to be a specialist in internal medicine or a specialist in pathology, but he will show in his activities his own peculiar degree of interest in himself and interest in others. We shall see how far he trains himself to be of help to his fellows and how far he limits his helpfulness. He has made this his aim as a compensation for a specific feeling of inferiority. We must be able to guess, from his expressions in his profession and elsewhere, the specific feeling for which he is compensating. We very frequently find, for example, that physicians in their childhood made early acquaintance with the fact of death, and death was the aspect of human insecurity which made the greatest impression on them. Perhaps a brother or a parent died, and their later training developed with the aim of finding a way, for themselves and others, to be more secure against death. Another man may make it his concrete goal to be a teacher, but we know very well how different teachers may be. If a teacher has a low degree of social feeling, his goal of superiority in being a teacher may be to rule among his inferiors. He may feel secure only with those who are weaker and less experienced than himself. A teacher with a high degree of social feeling will treat his pupils as his equals. We need not do more than mention here how different the capacities and interests of teachers may be and how significant of their goal all these expressions will be found.

3. THE SCHEMA OF APPERCEPTION[7]

a. *Opinion of Oneself and the World.* The first four to five years are enough for the child to complete his specific and arbitrary training in the face of impressions from his body and the environment. From then on the creative activity of the style of life begins its work. Experiences become assimilated and utilized according to the style of life, by the structure of which the individual is determined. To facilitate this activity personal rules and principles, character traits, and a conception of the world become elaborated. A well-determined schema of apperception (*Apperzeptionsschema*) is established, and the child's conclusions and actions are directed in full accord with the final ideal end-form to which he aspires.

The apperception connected with the law of movement [see below] is the way in which man looks at himself and the external world. In other words, it is the opinion which the child, and later, in the same direction, the adult has gained of himself and the world. Further, this opinion cannot be gathered from the words and thoughts of the person under examination. These are all far too strongly under the spell of the law of movement which aims at overcoming and therefore, even in the case of self-condemnation, still casts longing glances towards the heights.

For me there can be no doubt that everyone conducts himself in life from the very beginning of his action as if he had a definite opinion of his strength and his abilities and a clear conception of the difficulty or ease of a problem at hand. In a word, I am convinced that a person's behavior springs from his opinion. We should not be surprised at this, because our senses do not receive actual facts, but merely a subjective image of them, a reflection of the external world. *Omnia ad opinionem suspensa sunt.* This saying of Seneca's should not be forgotten in psychological investigations. It has the same effect on me whether a poisonous snake is actually approaching my foot or whether I merely believe that it is a poisonous snake. The pampered child behaves quite the same in his anxiety whether he is afraid of burglars as soon as his mother leaves him, or whether there are really burglars in the house.

A classic example of this play of subjective ideas in human action is furnished by Caesar's landing in Egypt. As he jumped ashore he stumbled and fell on the ground, and the Roman soldiers took this as an unfavorable omen. Brave as they were, they would nonetheless have turned around and gone back, had not Caesar thrown out his arms and cried out, "I embrace you, Africa!" We can see from this how little the structure of reality is causal, and how its effects can be molded and determined by the self-consistent personality.

An interesting fact in connection with the private schema of apperception, which characterizes all individuals, is that children with organic defects tend to connect all their experiences with the function of the defective organ. For instance, a child having stomach trouble is likely to show an abnormal interest in eating, while one with defective eyesight is more apt to be preoccupied with things visible. It might be suggested, therefore, that in order to find out where a child's interest lies, we need only to ascertain which organ is defective. But things do not work out quite so simply. The child does not experience the fact of organ inferiority in the way that an external observer sees it, but as modified by his own schema of apperception. Hence while the fact of organ inferiority counts as an element in the child's schema of apperception, the external observation of the inferiority does not necessarily give the cue to the child's schema of apperception.

In considering the structure of a personality, the chief difficulty is that its unity, its particular style of life and goal, is not built upon objective reality, but upon the subjective view the individual takes of the facts of life. A conception, a view of a fact, is never the fact itself, and it is for this reason that human beings, all of whom live in the same world of facts, mold themselves differently. Each one organizes himself according to his personal view of things, and some views are more sound, some less sound. We must always reckon with these individual mistakes and failures in the development of a human being. Especially must we reckon with the misinterpretations made in early childhood, for these dominate the subsequent course of our existence.

The child always behaves in the circle of his personal mistakes whenever he approaches a new and difficult situation. We know that the depth or character of the impression which the situation makes upon the child does not depend upon the objective fact or circumstance (as for example the birth of a second child), but depends rather on how this child regards the fact. This is sufficient ground for refuting the theory of causality. A necessary connection exists between objective facts and their absolute meaning, but not between mistaken views of facts.

If we wish to understand the essential difference between Freud and myself, we must ask the question, is an impression at all possible and could it have the ascribed effect without a pre-existing schema of apperception? Denying the connection between the experience and the schema of apperception is like taking single notes out of a melody to examine them for their value and meaning.

COMMENT *It is through his schema of apperception that every individual lives in a subjective world. Nobody knows the ultimately correct view of the world. All one can say is that the schema of
apperception of some individuals is obviously more in error than that of
others and that the more erroneous schemata are more in the nature of
private, personal intelligence, while the less erroneous schemata are more
in accord with common sense (see pp. 150–151 and pp. 253–254).*

*Schema of apperception is the equivalent of what Gestalt psychology
calls behavioral environment or phenomenological field, as contrasted
with geographic environment or objective situation. It is by this concept of the schema of apperception that Individual Psychology is established as a subjectivistic, phenomenological, and perceptual psychology.*

*The psychoanalytic term imago which, as the Latin origin of image,
might be mistaken for being the equivalent of schema of apperception,
has a somewhat different meaning. According to Hanns Sachs (91, pp.
65–66) who suggested the name Imago for the psychoanalytic journal
of which he was a co-founder, the term is taken from a novel in which
"the tricks and masks of the unconscious, its inroads into consciousness,
and its stimulation of the creative powers" are presented.*

*If a distinction is to be made between apperceptive schema and style
of life, it is that the former belongs to the perceptual and ideational area,
as the equivalent of the individual's opinion or view of himself and the
world, while the style of life, as the individual's consistent movement
toward his goal, is the behavioral counterpart. Frequently, however, Adler uses style of life as the generic term.*

The creative striving of the child takes place in an environment which
is individually comprehended and which posits individual difficulties.
The child starts in the direction of a final goal as he comes to find
himself, which usually takes place within the first two years of his life.
From then on, his psychological phenomena are no longer reactions but
creatively responding attitudes, corresponding to the tension in which
he experiences himself within a specific situation. What is decisive is
therefore not the absolute values of his organs and organ functions, but
their relative values, their relation to the environment. Since the environment, too, is experienced by the child individually, we must not take absolute values as foundations of the psychological structure, but impressions of a child, which, depending on a hundred influences and errors,

can never be comprehended causally. Such impressions can be understood only through empathy and comprehension of the individual style of life.

It is the individual shade of interpretation that matters in the end. When reconstructing the unity of a personality in its relationships to the outer world, Individual Psychology fundamentally undertakes to delineate the individual form of creative activity, which is the style of life.

b. *The Complex as Attitudinal Position.* Individual Psychology examines the attitudes of an individual, by which we mean his relation to the tasks of life. The attitudinal position of a person includes the development of psychological complexes for reasons of psychological economy. These complexes can be understood as active psychological instruments which characterize the individual as a schema or as a personality trait does and must always be seen in relation to the tasks presented by the environment. They are derivatives of the directive power of the final goal, simplifications, or schematizations. We must remember that schematizations may exist in thousands of variations. The perspective grown from such schematization is the essence of what one calls a complex. Perhaps this fact has so far remained unknown in the discussion of complexes. Since complex, so defined, represents a useful concept, Individual Psychology became inclined to employ it in the explanation of various attitudes.

Among the complexes of which one speaks, the inferiority complex and its sibling, the superiority complex, which Individual Psychology has used in its descriptions, are probably the best known (see pp. 256–261). All forms of failure are movement forms of an inferiority complex.

The Oedipus complex is very well known, but one cannot find the proper correspondence between its manifestations and its name. It should mean that a child has some sexual inclinations toward the parent of the other sex, but when we examine the facts they tell us only that the name Oedipus is poorly chosen; the complex characterizes a pampered child who does not want to give up his mother. According to Freud the Oedipus complex is supposed to be the foundation of the development of the mental life, but Individual Psychology has shown that it is an error of upbringing.

One of the most interesting complexes is the redeemer complex. It characterizes people who conspicuously but unknowingly take the attitude that they must save or redeem someone. There are thousands of degrees and variations, but it is always clearly the attitude of a person who finds his superiority in solving the complications of others. The redeemer complex may very well enter into medical endeavor or into the choice of the ministry. In the most extreme cases, we find the person in question acting as if he were sent by God, as if he could cure all the evils of mankind.

The proof complex can be found in many people who want to prove that they also have a right to exist or that they have no faults. They have a terrible fear of committing errors, and they feel every action tests whether they can find recognition. They are always on the defensive. The exclusion complex is found in people who want to reduce their sphere of action, who want to remove all problems. Another frequent complex is the predestination complex, which expresses itself in the attitude that nothing can happen to one. If one embarks upon complex research, if one has recognized the attitude of a person who has a schema, then one can find an infinite number of such schemas.

COMMENT   *In connection with Adler's use of the term complex, we should like to point out that originally he criticized it as being topological rather than dynamic (see p. 63). By 1925 he was seemingly forced by popular demand, as it were, into accepting it in connection with inferiority feeling (see p. 256). Finally by 1935 he had integrated the concept of complex into his theory of personality, as shown in the above selections.*

D. Development of the Style of Life

1. ORIGIN[8]

I am convinced of the free creative power of the individual in his earliest childhood and of his restricted power in later life, once the child has given himself a fixed law of movement for his life. This view leaves the child free scope for his striving for perfection, completion, superiority, or evolution.

The style of life, in our experience, is developed in earliest childhood. In this the innate state of the body has the greatest influence. In his initial movements and functions, the child experiences the validity of his bodily organs. He experiences it but is far from having words or concepts for it. Since the way in which the environment approaches the child differs in each case, what the child feels about his capacities [as such] remains permanently unknown. With great caution, on the basis of statistical probability, we may conclude that where an organ inferiority is present, the child has the experience of being overburdened at the beginning of his life. How the child attempts to cope with this overburdening can only be discovered from his movements and trials. Here every causal consideration is in vain. Here the creative power of the child becomes effective. He strives within the incalculable realm of his possibilities. From trial and error a training results for the child and a general way towards a goal of perfection which appears to offer him fulfillment.

A child, being weak, feels inferior and finds himself in a situation which he cannot bear. Hence he strives to develop, and he strives to develop along a line of direction fixed by the goal which he chooses for himself. The material used for development at this stage is less important than the goal which decides the line of direction. It is difficult to say how this goal is fixed, but it is obvious that such a goal exists and that it dominates the child's every movement.

We cannot know in advance what the child will make of all the influences and the experience of his organs. Here the child works in the realm of freedom with his own creative power. Probabilities abound. I have always endeavored to point them out and at the same time to deny that they are causally determining. It is not correct that a child born with weak endocrine organs must become a neurotic, but there is a certain probability that, in general, certain experiences will manifest themselves in an approximately similar direction, unless the proper educational influences in favor of social contact become effective. The influences of the environment are also not such that we could predict what the child will make of them. Here there are thousands of possibilities in the realm of freedom and of error. Everyone will form an error, because no one can get hold of the absolute truth.

The connection which is so often found between organ inferiorities or [negative] environmental influences and failures, shows how easily the creative power of the child can be directed the wrong way when proper educational methods do not provide a balance.

In practice we attempt to undo the great errors, to substitute smaller errors, and to reduce these further until they are no longer harmful.

The child, in his employment of the influences he has experienced from his own body and from the environment, is more or less dependent on his own creative power and on his ability to divine a path. His opinion of life, which is at the bottom of his attitude to life and is neither shaped into words nor expressed in thought, is his own masterpiece. Thus the child arrives at his law of movement which aids him after a certain amount of training to obtain a style of life, in accordance with which we see the individual thinking, feeling, and acting throughout his whole life.

COMMENT *Here again Adler takes the position of "soft" determinism by attributing the origin of the law of movement to the "free creative power" of the child. This he did not explain further. He did, however, state: "Since even physics has withdrawn the ground of causality from under [the mechanistically thinking psychologists] by supporting a statistical probability for the course of events, the attacks on Individual Psychology for its denial of causality in psychological events need no longer be taken seriously" (1933a, p. 8). Murphy's discussion of the emergence of the personality structure has a marked similarity to Adler's position. Murphy concludes: "The physicist . . . simply describes mathematically the region within which prediction can be made. . . . With our much more limited knowledge of biological and psychological laws, it might be wise to accept the same principle" (84, p. 645).*

2. SELF-CONSISTENCY[9]

Once the goal of superiority has been made concrete, there are no mistakes made in the style of life. The habits and symptoms of the individual are precisely right for attaining his concrete goal, for they are beyond all criticism. Every problem child, every neurotic, every drunkard, criminal, or sexual pervert is making the proper movements to achieve what he takes to be the position of superiority. It is impossible to attack his symptoms by themselves; they are exactly the symptoms he ought to have for such a goal. A boy at one school, the laziest boy in the class, was asked by his teacher, "Why do you get on so badly with your work?" He answered, "If I am the laziest boy here, you will always be occupied with me. You never pay any attention to good boys, who never disturb the class and do all their work properly." So long as it was his aim to attract notice and rule over his teacher, he had found the best way to do it. Another boy was very obedient but seemed to be stupid. He had a brother two years older who was intelligent and active but always got into trouble because of his impudence. One day the younger brother was overheard saying to the older brother, "I'd rather be as stupid as I am than be as impudent as you are." His stupidity was really quite intelligent if we grant him the goal of escaping trouble. Because of his stupidity less was demanded of him, and if he made mistakes he was not blamed for them. Granted his goal, he would have been a fool not to be stupid.

With every individual, we must look below the surface. We must look for the underlying coherence, for the unity [or self-consistency] of the personality. This unity is fixed in all its expressions. If we take an irregular triangle and place it in different positions, each position will seem to give us quite a different triangle; but if we look hard we shall discover that the triangle is always the same. So, too, with the prototype: Its content is never exhausted by any single expression, but we can recognize it in all its expressions.

3. CONSTANCY[10]

When the prototype—that early personality which embodies the goal —is formed, the line of direction is established and the individual becomes definitely oriented. It is this fact which enables us to predict what will happen later in life. The individual's apperceptions are from then on bound to fall into a groove established by the line of direction. The child will not perceive given situations as they actually exist, but under the prejudice of his own interests.

From now on, the world is seen through a stable schema of apperception: Experiences are interpreted before they are accepted, and the interpretation always accords with the original meaning given to life. Even if this meaning is very gravely mistaken, even if the approach to our problems and tasks brings us continually into misfortunes and agonies, it is never easily relinquished.

By the time a child is five years old his attitude to his environment is usually so fixed and mechanized that it proceeds in more or less the same direction for the rest of his life. His apperception of the external world remains the same. The child is caught in the trap of his perspectives and repeats unceasingly his original mental mechanisms and the resulting actions.

The first realization we obtained was that the strongest impulses toward building the mental life have their origin in earliest childhood. In itself this was, to be sure, no particularly bold discovery, for similar observations have been made by investigators of all times. What was new in our formulations was that we sought to bring the childhood experiences, impressions, and attitudes, so far as they could still be traced, into connected relationship with later manifestations of the mental life by comparing the childhood experiences with later situations and attitudes. In so doing, it became particularly significant that one can never regard single manifestations of the mental life as separate entities, but that one can gain understanding of them only if one understands all manifestations of a mental life as parts of an indivisible whole and then attempts to uncover the line of movement, the schema of life (*Lebensschablone*), the style of life, and recognizes that the secret goal of the child's attitude is identical with the individual's attitude of later years.

What an individual may change is the way in which he makes his goal concrete, just as he may change one expression of his concrete goal, his occupation. We can never say to a man, "Your striving for superiority would be satisfied if you did this or that . . ." The striving for superiority remains flexible. Indeed, the nearer to health and normality an individual is, the more he can find new openings for his strivings when they are blocked in one particular direction. It is only the neurotic who feels, of the concrete expressions of his goal, "I must have this or nothing."

Yet while the outer form, the concretization, the verbalization of the mental phenomena, and the appearance may change, from the point of view of the mental movement no changes take place. The goal and dynamic, everything which moves the mental life in the direction of the goal, remain unchanged.

For example, if a patient shows an anxious character, always filled with distrust and aiming at separation from others, it could easily be established that the same movements were already a part of him in his third or fourth year, except that they were of childlike simplicity and more easily discernible. That is why we have made it a rule always to concentrate our attention at first on the childhood of the patient.

People find it very difficult to free themselves from the schema into which they have grown during the first years of life. There are only a few who have been able to shed this schema, even though mental life in other situations in adulthood appears differently and thus conveys a different impression. This different impression is not tantamount to a change in the schema of life. The mental life still rests on the same foundation, the individual still shows the same line of movement and lets us divine the same goals in both ages, in childhood as in adulthood.

COMMENT *The stress on the importance of early childhood for later development is obviously similar to Freud's.* Freud, however, considered that at this stage certain objective events mold the child, whereas Adler believed that at this stage the child creatively forms his subjective opinion of the world and himself, albeit utilizing his surrounding objective situation.

According to Freud: "The first years of infancy (up to about the age of five) are, for a number of reasons, of special importance. This is, in the first place, because they contain the first expansion of sexuality, which leaves behind decisive determinants for the sexual life of maturity; and, in the second place, because the impressions of this period come up against an unformed and weak ego, upon which they act like traumas. The ego cannot defend itself against the emotional storms which they call forth except by repression, and in this way it acquires in childhood all its predispositions to subsequent illnesses and disturbances of function" (41, p. 201).

Adler's reason for going back to the patient's childhood is to obtain, as he said in the above, a simpler, more easily discernible picture of the style of life, which could on principle, however, be learned also in other ways. It was therefore irrelevant for Adler whether memories were true or not, or whether they were earlier or later memories (see p. 352). In any event, they would express the basic attitude, which remains relatively constant throughout the years.

4. FACTORS MAKING FOR CONSTANCY AND CHANGE[11]

The child builds up his whole life, which we have called concretely style of life, at a time when he has neither adequate language nor adequate concepts. When he grows further in the sense [of his style of life], he grows in a movement which has never been formulated into words and therefore, unassailable to criticism, is also withdrawn from the criticism of experience. We cannot say that this is a repressed unconscious. Rather, we must say that something has not been understood or that something has been withheld from the understanding.

Because the individual adopts a certain particular approach, a certain attitude, a certain relation toward the problems of the outside world (the outside world includes the experience of one's own body), anything that does not fit this early-adopted attitude is more or less excluded, or it is wholly or in part stripped of its intellectual content and objective meaning and is interpreted in accordance with the individual's view of the world. The same thing happens with regard to the inseparably associated emotional factors and the attitudes growing out of them. We can observe in the whole life style, in every element of behavior—in thoughts, emotions, and actions—simply the direction selected by the individual for his striving. What is left over after this process of elimination by the life style remains as part of the mental life and operates "unconsciously," as some authors are wont to put it, or as we would say, "not-understood." The individual with the life style in question withdraws the impressions fashioned by it from his further criticism. The neurotic [for example] can maintain his mistaken picture of the world only with the help of such auxiliary forces and devices as he has withdrawn from critical review.

It is very obvious that we are influenced not by facts but by our opinion of facts. Our greater or lesser certainty of having formed an opinion which corresponds to the facts depends upon our experience, which is always inadequate, upon the absence of contradiction with our opinions, and upon the success of our actions according to our opinion. This is especially true for inexperienced children and asocial adults. It is easy to understand that these criteria are frequently inadequate because our action circle is often restricted. Furthermore, smaller failures and contradictions can often be straightened out more or less easily, without any effort or with the help of others. This assists us in keeping permanently to our life plan, once it has been formed. Only greater failures force a sharper reflection, and even this becomes fruitful only in those persons who participate in the cooperative solution of life's problems and who are free of goals of a personal superiority.

Only at the point where we come immediately up against facts which disclose to us a contradiction to our opinion are we inclined, as a result of immediate experience, to correct our views in small matters and allow the law of causality to influence us. But we do not change our opinion of life.

The style of life of an individual is wholly accomplished in earliest childhood and is not changed so long as the individual does not understand the unavoidable discrepancies regarding the inescapable demands of social problems. I do not doubt that some persons through experience bring their mistaken style nearer to a social adaptation but always only if their common sense (a social function) is working for improvement. Otherwise the failures we observe do not change in the least degree.

COMMENT   Many of the statements by Adler regarding the dominating
          personal attitudes have since been worked out independ-
ently by Krech and Crutchfield for attitudes in general. Founded largely
on Gestalt theory (Köhler), field theory (Lewin), and purposive behaviorism (Tolman), their book stresses the subjectivistic, phenomenological approach throughout. Attitudes are seen as based not so much
on facts as on functional factors, which are responsible for the manner
in which these facts will be used (63, p. 168). The chapter on development and change of beliefs and attitudes describes very succinctly, and
in far greater detail than does Adler, the phenomenon of "self-preservation of beliefs and attitudes" through the devices of selectivity in perception and memory, cognitive constancy, and of withdrawal. "Attitudes
and beliefs create, as it were, the fuel upon which they grow . . .
Vicious circles are created. Beliefs and attitudes not only twist and warp
data and thus maintain themselves, but create new data for self-incorpora-
tion and thus grow in intensity" (63, p. 194).

E. Prediction and Its Limitations

COMMENT   In the following selections, Adler gives his views on the
          problem of general laws versus the unique law of the in-
dividual personality, that is, nomothetic versus idiographic lawfulness.
With regard to the specific case, nomothetic laws provide only probabilities, which are not considered adequate for individual prediction. The
particular law of the individual case is what Adler calls the individual's
"law of movement" which underlies the style of life. Knowledge of the
law of movement is the outcome of a complete understanding of the individual according to the principles of Individual Psychology, particularly understanding his unique goal of superiority and his typical way of
striving for it, as well as his opinion of himself and the world. On this
basis, individual prediction is possible. Successful prediction in turn becomes the criterion of understanding, "the sole criterion of understanding" (1923a, p. 25).

1. GENERAL LAWS[12]

Types, similarities, and approximate likenesses are often either entities
that owe their existence merely to the poverty of our language, which

is incapable of giving simple expression to the nuances that are always present, or they are results of a statistical probability. The evidence of their existence should never be allowed to degenerate into the setting up of a fixed rule. Such evidence cannot bring us any nearer to the understanding of the individual case. It can only be used to throw light on a field of vision in which the individual case in its uniqueness must be found. The observation of an increased inferiority feeling, for instance, tells us nothing as yet of the nature and characteristics of the individual case. It tells as little as does evidence of any defects in upbringing or in the social conditions. These defects manifest themselves in the behavior of the individual toward the outside world in an ever-varying form which is different for each individual because of the intervention of the creative power of the child and of his opinion springing from it.

There is always something subjective in the development of a child, and it is this individuality which pedagogues must investigate. This prevents the application of general rules in the education of groups of children and is the reason why the application of the same rule results differently with different children. When we see children reacting to the same situation in almost the same way we cannot say that it is because of a law of nature. We say that human beings are prone to make the same mistakes because of their common lack of understanding.

Each individual always manifests himself as unique, be it in thinking, feeling, speaking, or acting. We are always dealing with individual nuances and variations. It is partly due to the abstractness and limitations of language that the speaker, reader, and listener must have discovered the realm between the words in order to gain a true understanding of and the proper contact with the partner. When two do the same, it is not the same; but also when two think, feel, or want the same, differences exist. Therefore we cannot do entirely without guessing if we want to understand another person correctly. Whether a person merely takes a stand [on an issue] or forms his view of the world, the individuality of the style of life always stands out clearly.

I believe that I am not bound by any strict rule or prejudice but prefer to subscribe to the principle: Everything can also be different (*Alles kann auch anders sein*). The uniqueness of the individual cannot be expressed in a short formula, and general rules—even those laid down by Individual Psychology, of my own creation—should be regarded as nothing more than an aid to a preliminary illumination of the field of view in which the single individual can be found—or missed. Thus we assign only limited value to general rules and instead lay strong emphasis on flexibility and on empathy into nuances.

COMMENT *The phrase "or missed" is to be particularly noted, for it shows the flexibility with which Adler was prepared to expect the unexpected, even from the point of view of his own generalizations. Such generalizations, being merely statistical probabilities, may well be untrue for any one specific case: "The specific individual cannot be judged with the measure of probability" (1937a, p. 775).*

2. THE INDIVIDUAL'S LAW OF MOVEMENT[13]

Everyone carries within himself an opinion of himself and the problems of life, a life line, and a law of movement which keeps fast hold of him without his understanding it or giving himself an account of it.

The law of movement in the mental life of a person is the decisive factor for his individuality. The declaration of this law was actually the strongest step which Individual Psychology has taken. Although it was necessary to freeze the movement in order to see it as form, we have always maintained the viewpoint that all is movement. We have found that it must be that way to arrive at the solution of problems and the overcoming of difficulties.

Ways toward the goal of overcoming differ with each individual, so that we lack words to name more than that which is typical in each case and are forced to take refuge in lengthy descriptions. The individual is hardly ever able to state clearly where his way leads without individual-psychological insight, and he often states the contrary. Only the recognition of his law of movement gives us the explanation.

We are interested not so much in the past as in the future. In order to understand a person's future we must understand his style of life [which is based on his law of movement]. Because an individual has a style of life, it is sometimes possible to predict his future just on the basis of talking to him and having him answer questions. It is like looking at the fifth act of a drama, where all the mysteries are solved. We can make predictions in this way because we know the phases, the difficulties, and the questions of life. Thus from experience and knowledge of a few facts we can tell [for example] what will happen to children who always separate themselves from others, who are looking for support, who are pampered, and who hesitate in approaching situations.

If we know the goal of a person, we can undertake to explain and to understand what the psychological phenomena want to tell us, why they were created, what a person has made of his innate material, why he has made it just so and not differently, how his character traits, his feelings and emotions, his logic, his morals, and his aesthetics must be constituted in order that he may arrive at his goal. We could also understand why and to what extent he deviates from our—possibly the normal—movement, if we could perhaps determine that his goal is too far removed from ours or even too far from the absolute logic of human communal life. After all, we are able to infer the familiar composer from an unfamiliar melody, the architectural style from an ornament, always from the connection of the part with the whole. It is the same in the case of a person, except that rarely does anyone fashion his life in such an artfully perfect form. Paltry typologies tell us nothing about the individual mistake. If we could infer the individually comprehended goal from the ornaments and melodies of a human life and, on this basis, develop the entire style of life [and the underlying individual law of movement], we could classify a person with almost natural-science accuracy. We could predict how a person would act in a specific situation.

COMMENT   We should like to point out that this statement on prediction is phrased in the form of an hypothesis. In actual situations, however, one is usually not completely successful in either inferring "the individually comprehended goal" or in developing "the entire style of life." Thus prediction will not be sufficiently valid to permit taking for granted the response of an individual to a certain measure. Accordingly Adler suggests that the educator or therapist always checks up on the response of the individual to the influence that has been brought to bear (see p. 344).

F. Psychological Theory and the Style of Life

1. PSYCHOLOGICAL THEORY AND ITS ACCEPTANCE[14]

The influence of science on the educational, religious, or political attitude of individuals is just as undeniable as is the influence of literature and art on the development of mankind. In addition to the special position of science as a modifying force, it must also be taken into account as one of the general impressions which the individual receives in his striving to overcome his internal difficulties. These impressions are taken up, sifted, molded, or distorted in accordance with his biased perspective, with his "tendentious apperception," and with a picture of the world at which he arrived very early in life. Thus the shades of different tendencies and attitudes in individuals are understandable even when they originated amidst the greatest sameness of common formative conditions. Largely, an individual will understand only what he has been somehow cognizant of before. (I think it was Charcot who first said that.)

As soon as a scientific system is offered to the world, it appeals to individuals, both laymen and scientists, with a trend of mind similar to that of the author of the system and provides them with a scientific foundation for an attitude towards life which they had achieved previously. When a scientific system sanctions social deviations, the unity of the personality of its author and the seeming logic of the system, however patched up it may be, mislead individuals of a similar trend of mind to regard as normal their own social deviations, once they have thus been sanctioned.

A person's opinion of himself and the environment can best be deduced from the meaning he finds in life and from the meaning he gives to his own life, [his philosophy of life]. Here the possible dissonance to an ideal social interest, to living together, working together, and being a fellow man, will clearly show itself. We are now prepared to understand that it is important to learn something about the meaning of life and also wherein different individuals see the meaning of life.

The full meaning of life lies, of course, outside our experience. Yet if a meaning can be discerned which is at least partially valid [and which we have construed to be the striving for an ideal society], then it should obviously put in the wrong those who are in striking opposition to it. In other words, the author is modest enough to strive for an initial partial success, [namely, to demonstrate that the extreme cases of those who oppose social contribution as the meaning of life are in fact to be found among the failures in life]. This appears to him sufficiently supported by his experiences.

The author undertakes this task the more willingly since from here the hope beckons that, as this meaning of life is discerned clearly, at least to some extent, not only will there grow a scientific program for further research in its direction, but also the number of those will grow appreciably who, through this better discerned meaning of life, can be won over to it.

COMMENT   *It might be in place to summarize this section briefly. Different psychological systems appeal to people with different philosophies of life. Adler's psychology will appeal to those whose philosophy includes the idea of cooperation. If, however, it can be shown that a cooperative outlook on life is actually a condition for mental health, then possibly more people can be won over to this outlook.*

2. PSYCHOLOGICAL THEORY AND ITS AUTHOR[15]

By proving that every individual's conception of life is determined by, and is part of, the person's style of life, Individual Psychology has thrown light upon the rather bewildering fact that philosophers and psychologists differ widely in their interpretations of the inner world. It is plain that each of them regards mind and psyche from a viewpoint which is determined by his philosophy of life.

Thus an author whose wrong conception of life is like that of a pampered child will inevitably declare that all trouble arises because the individual is unable to get what he wants. He will take it for granted that all failures, neuroses, psychoses, delinquencies, suicides, and perversions are due to the fact that these people have suppressed their wishes. These authors will also find that the real world is hostile and destined to perish. Social interest is for them a mystical dogma forced upon people by illusions or fear. "Love thy neighbor as thyself" is for them merely ridiculous. But the relationship between the individual and the mother, the pampering person, they consider to be of the highest importance. Automatically they close their eyes to other conflicting views.

Authors afraid of losing ground or of being assailed by criticism attach importance only to those facts that are capable of receiving physical confirmation in laboratories and that can be recorded and reduced to figures. They feel protected by mathematical rules and they become irritable if they are without such symbols. Of course, mathematics gives a great feeling of security and provides support for many persons. But, when we study mind and psyche, we find that these are the gifts of evolution and have been spread over millions of years. They work like miracles, and all we can discover about them is the manner in which they function in relation to outside problems. We have to keep in mind, too, that the body and its inherited qualities are simply parts of the general environment.

And Individual Psychology? Has it not also its own particular conception of life? Has it not also a specific point of view regarding the behavior of the individual in his relation to outside problems? Of course it has. But in the first place we have tried to prove that our conception of life is more capable of objectivity than the conception of other psychologists. And secondly we know that we also are predisposed by our philosophy of life, while others do not know that they always find what they have known before. For this reason, Individual Psychology is more capable of detachment and self-control.

3. AUTOBIOGRAPHICAL NOTES[16]

When I was five I became ill with pneumonia and was given up by the physician. A second physician advised a treatment just the same, and in a few days I became well again. In the joy over my recovery, there was talk for a long time about the mortal danger in which I was supposed to have been. From that time on I recall always thinking of myself in the future as a physician. This means that I had set a goal from which I could expect an end to my childlike distress, my fear of death. Clearly I expected more from the occupation of my choice than it could accomplish: The overcoming of death and of the fear of death is something I should not have expected from human, but only from divine accomplishments. Reality, however, demands action, and so I was forced to modify my goal by changing the conscious form of the guiding fiction until it appeared to satisfy reality. So I came to choose the occupation of physician in order to overcome death and the fear of death.

On the basis of similar impressions a somewhat retarded boy decided to become a grave digger, in order, as he said, to bury the others and not to be buried himself. The rigid antithetical thinking of this boy who later became neurotic did not admit compromise solutions; his childish, saving fiction turned to the opposite, albeit in an unimportant detail.

The following experience dates from the time of my choosing my occupation, about my fifth year. The father of a playmate asked me what I wanted to become and I answered, "A doctor." To this the man, who possibly had had unfortunate experiences with physicians, answered: "In that case one should hang you right away from the nearest lamp post."

On account of my regulative [guiding] idea this comment left me, of course, completely cold. I believe I thought at the time that I would become a good physician, toward whom no one should have hostile feelings.

Soon after it struck me that this man, a lamp-maker, had his trade, rather than me, uppermost in his mind. After that the determination to become a doctor never left me. I never could picture myself taking up any other profession. Even the fascinating lure of art, despite the fact that I had considerable abilities in various forms of music, was not enough to turn me from my chosen path.

I did not enjoy staying at home. Perhaps because my attitude toward my mother was at fault, but also without doubt because I did my utmost to excel at running, jumping, and rushing around—activities of which my elder brother was constantly making me aware. I was always eager to get outdoors and was helped in doing this by the fact that almost next door to our home was an open, practically disused plot and a big field.

The field near our house was the meeting place of all the local children. Most of the people in our district were quiet, humble, and usually poor people who frequently asked me into their homes. Because of my friendliness and liveliness I was well received wherever I went. My elder brother was the only one with whom I did not get along well, and he never took any part in our games. At an early age I became part of a wide social milieu, and in our games both the boys and girls learned to look upon one another as communal equals.

It was not so much my childhood experiences in themselves that were important; rather the manner in which I judged and assimilated them.

COMMENT   At this point we should like to add a few data of Adler's life and the most outstanding impressions of him as a person. We have taken these data primarily from the biography by Bottome (15), but have also taken Furtmuller (44), Hertha Orgler (88), and Manes Sperber (97) into account.

Adler was born on February 7, 1870 in a suburb of Vienna, the second son in a family of six children. His father was a grain merchant, and comfortably situated. Adler attended the University of Vienna from which he received his medical degree in 1895. Two years later he married Raissa Timofejewna, who had come from Moscow to study at the university. In time they had four children.

At first Adler specialized in ophthalmology and then turned to general medicine, while interested right along in the psychological aspects of illness. There may well be a relationship between his early practice as an eye specialist and the many perceptual implications in his psychological theory. Later he established himself as a psychiatrist.

After his early association with Freud, which has been mentioned above, pp. 3; 56; and 73, and which ended in 1911, Adler formed his own group, which was at first called the Society for Free Psychoanalytic Research and which had its own publication. Within the year he changed the name to Individual Psychology and founded the society, and later the journal, bearing this name. During the first World War, Adler served in the Austrian army as a physician.

After the war he became interested in child guidance and established the first guidance clinics in connection with the Viennese school system. Ultimately these numbered some thirty (see p. 393). At the same time, Individual Psychology made great gains, reaching its height before the advent of Hitler, when there were thirty-four local groups in Central Europe and all over the world.

From 1925 on Adler regularly visited the United States and settled here in 1935. Here he continued his clinical and private practice, his lectures, his writings, and served as Professor of Medical Psychology at the Long Island College of Medicine. He died in Aberdeen, Scotland, on May 28, 1937, while on a lecture tour.

Individual Psychology groups continue to be active in England, Switzerland, Holland, France, and Austria and the American Society, with groups in New York, Chicago and Los Angeles, publishes the American Journal of Individual Psychology. An international association was reconstituted in 1954.

Adler's most outstanding personal characteristic was his interest in and sympathy with the "common man." From his student days on he was keenly interested in social problems and social betterment. While fresh from the university he wrote a pamphlet on The Health of Tailors, whose condition was apparently deplorable in Austria as elsewhere at that time (15, pp. 46–47). Also early in his life, he took a definite stand on the issue of school reform (1927f, p. 490). With these interests, it was only natural that he was in sympathy with the Social-Democratic movement, in which every kind of social reform found its strongest expression in the Austria of those days (1912a, p. 24n). When he took up the practice of general medicine in Vienna, it was in a lower middle-class neighborhood. As one expression of his basic attitude, Adler was free from any pomposity. He spoke the Viennese dialect. He loved Vienna and enjoyed the simple pleasures in life, such as food and sociability. He was very musical, had a good voice, and enjoyed especially singing the ballads of Schubert and Schumann to the accompaniment of a friend on the piano. His manner was generally simple, and he preferred to use non-technical language. He addressed teachers and adult education groups and all kinds of audiences in order to reach as many people directly as possible. His interest in people seemed inexhaustible. After his many lectures, he liked to be surrounded by the question-asking audience, and he would later continue the discussion at home or in a restaurant with a smaller circle of interested students and friends. In his later years, in New York, he was in his spare hours an avid and quite indiscriminate visitor of motion pictures, to observe people acting on the screen. It was his interest in people also which made him read the more sensational late evening newspapers. Once, while looking out of his hotel window in New York, observing the traffic light altering its colors at regular intervals, he remarked: "This is the poetry of the big city." His harmony with the world was one of adaptability.

FOOTNOTES TO CHAPTER SEVEN

1. 1, 2, 3: *The Science of Living* (1929c), pp. 98, 98–99, and 100.
2. 1 and 6: *Der Sinn des Lebens* (1933a), pp. 8 and 133; 2: "Der nervöse Charakter" (1931b), 1–14; 3: "The fundamental views of Individual Psychology" (1935a), p. 7; 4: *What Life Should Mean to You* (1931a), p. 96; 5: "Nochmals—die Einheit der Neurosen" (1930e), pp. 201–216.
3. 1 and 2: "The structure of neurosis" (1932b), p. 5; 3: "Individualpsychologie" (1926b), p. 400; 4: *The Education of Children* (1930a), p. 5.
4. 1: "Persönlichkeit als geschlossene Einheit" (1932a), pp. 81–88; 2 and 3: "Psychiatric aspects regarding individual and social disorganization" (1937a), pp. 775 and 777. 4: "Individualpsychologie" (1926b), p. 402.
5. 1 and 2: "Die Individualpsychologie, ihre Voraussetzungen und Ergebnisse" (1914f), pp. 1 and 1–2; 3: *Education of Children* (1930a), p. 23; 4: "Persönlichkeit" (1932a), pp. 81–88.
6. 1: "Persönlichkeit" (1932a), pp. 81–88; 2: "Structure of neurosis" (1932b), p. 12; 3 and 4: *What Life Should Mean to You* (1931a), pp. 57 and 58–59.
7. 1: *Die Technik der Individualpsychologie. Tl. 2.* (1930d), p. 8; 2 and 3: *Sinn des Lebens* (1933a), pp. 10 and 12; 4, 6, 7: *Education of Children* (1930a), pp. 30, 6, and 29; 5: *Science of Living*

1929c), pp. 35–36; 8: "Nochmals—die Einheit" (1930e), pp. 201–216; 9:"IP" (1926b), p. 399; 10: "Fundamental views" (1935a), p. 8; 11 to 15: "Der Komplexzwang als Teil der Persönlichkeit und der Neurose" (1935b), pp. 1–6.

8. 1, 2, 4, 7: Sinn des Lebens (1933a), pp. 7–8, 49, 125–126, and 97; 3: Science of Living (1929c), p. 34; 5: "Religion und Individualpsychologie" (1933c), p. 74; 6: "Psychische Kausalität" (1923c), p. 38.

9. 1 and 2: What Life Should Mean to You (1931a), pp. 61–62 and 59–60.

10. 1: Science of Living (1929c), p. 35; 2 and 5: What Life Should Mean to You (1931a), pp. 12–13 and 59–60; 3: Education of Children (1930a), pp. 135–136; 4, 6, 7, 8: Menschenkenntnis (1927a), pp. 3, 4, 4, and 4.

11. 1, 3, 4: Sinn des Lebens (1933a), pp. 10, 16, and 12; 2: "The neurotic's picture of the world" (1936d), pp. 7–8; 5: "Psychiatric aspects" (1937a), p. 777.

12. 1 and 4: Sinn des Lebens (1933a), pp. 17 and 7; 2: Education of Children (1930a), p. 138; 3: "Religion" (1933c), p. 59.

13. 1, 2, 3: Sinn des Lebens (1933a), pp. 16, 122, and 49–50; 4: Science of Living (1929c), pp. 99–101; 5: "IP" (1926b), p. 400.

14. 1 and 2: "Prevention of neurosis" (1935c), pp. 4 and 4–5; 3, 4, 5: Sinn des Lebens (1933a), pp. 10–11, 11, and 11.

15. 1 to 4: Social Interest (1933b), pp. 154, 154, 154–155, and 155. These passages not included in the original, Sinn des Lebens (1933a).

16. 1, 2, 3: "Aus den individualpsychologischen Ergebnissen bezüglich Schlafstörungen" (1913a), p. 125; 4 to 7: "Autobiographical notes" 1939), pp. 12, 10, 10, and 11 (to 1939).

CHAPTER EIGHT

PSYCHOLOGY OF USE

COMMENT   *"Psychology of use" is the term Adler chose for his functional or dynamic psychology. In the preceding chapter, we
have seen that for Adler the unitary self, with its striving for a unique
goal in a uniquely perceived world, was sovereign in the personality structure. The present chapter will show how, under these conditions, all
psychological and bodily processes and characteristics become tools for
the self, subordinated to and part of the style of life. Thus the chapter will
show Adler's dynamic psychology as a truly personalistic psychology adhering to the principle of "soft" determinism.*

*Despite the stress on a creative self as the intervening variable, Adler
did not overlook the significance of objective conditions in providing
probabilities. Far from doing so, he made important contributions to their
description. Regarding heredity and physical determinants, for example,
he pointed out the importance of organ inferiorities, and regarding environment, the importance of birth order (see Chapter 15). One may
consider it a tribute to his appreciation of all the factors which the field
theorist and the "soft" determinist must keep in mind simultaneously,
a position which in Adler's day was less well understood than today, that
he was misinterpreted both as overstressing biological factors and as an
out-and-out environmentalist, while he was most often rejected for his
emphasis on the third factor, the creativity of the individual as the intervening variable.*

A. The Use of Heredity and of Environment

1. USE VERSUS POSSESSION[1]

The direction and the directed utilization of instincts and drives, as well as impressions from the environment and education, are the artistic work of the child and cannot be understood in the sense of a psychology of possession (*Besitzpsychologie*) but only of a psychology of use (*Gebrauchspsychologie*).

Possession psychologists attempt to trace every kind of symptom to the obscure regions of an uncertain heredity or to such environmental influences as are generally regarded as unsuitable. But this does not mean anything for the individual case, because the child receives, digests, and responds to such influences with a certain arbitrariness. Individual Psychology is the psychology of use and emphasizes the creative appropriation and exploitation of all these influences. Those who regard the ever-differing problems of life as remaining the same, who do not perceive their uniqueness in each case, can easily be misled to believe in efficient causes, drives, and instincts as the demonic rulers of our destiny. Only those who do not perceive that ever-new problems emerge for each generation can believe in the effectiveness of an hereditary unconscious.

The psychologies of possession are concerned with showing what a person brings with him into the world and retains as his possession. From his inheritance, they seek to derive everything that is psychological. Seen from the standpoint of common sense, this is an awkward position. In other matters in life, we are not inclined to draw all our conclusions from a person's possessions, but only from the use he makes of the possessions. We are much more interested in the use than in the possession. Individual Psychology—and I should like to say that there are other schools of psychology which must also be regarded as psychologies of use —considers the attitude of an individual to the problems of life in order to understand him, and therefore considers the use he makes of his capacities.

The raw material with which the Individual Psychologist works is the relationship of the individual to the problems of the outside world. The Individual Psychologist must observe how a particular individual relates himself to the outside world. This outside world includes the individual's own body, his bodily functions, and the functions of his mind. He does not relate himself to the outside world in a predetermined manner as is often assumed. He relates himself always according to his own interpretation of himself and of his present problem. His limits are not only the common human limits, but also the limits which he has set himself. It is neither heredity nor environment which determines his relationship to the outside. Heredity only endows him with certain abilities. Environment only gives him certain impressions. These abilities and impressions, and the manner in which he "experiences" them—that is to say, the interpretation he makes of these experiences—are the bricks which he uses in his own "creative" way in building up his attitude toward life. It is his individual way of using these bricks, or in other words his attitude toward life, which determines this relationship to the outside world.

It should be unnecessary to add that use is limited by capacity. Use always remains within the frame of human capacities, although we cannot make any definite statement as to the range of these capacities.

COMMENT   *This last paragraph must be considered a rebuttal to a misunderstanding to which Adler had laid himself open when he said: "Everybody can accomplish everything" (1929c, p. 227). But he did not mean this statement literally; rather he called it a maxim, that is, a rule of conduct. "It is a sign of an inferiority complex when a boy or girl despairs of following this maxim and feels unable to accomplish his goal on the useful side of life" (1929c, p. 227). Another time he stated: "The theory of heredity must never be emphasized in education or in the theory and practice of psychology. Except in cases of sub-normal children, it is proper to assume that everyone can do everything necessary. This is not, of course, to deny the differences of inherited material, but what is important is always the use which is made of it" (1929b, p. 4).*

2. HEREDITY[2]

It goes without saying that the inheritance, primarily of physical attributes but also of specifically human potentialities, is not subject to any doubt whatsoever. But what matters ultimately is what the child, the individual, does with the equipment he inherits. That is his own creative achievement. It is certainly human chromosomes, the individual's physical endowment, his endocrine glands, and his blood constituents, which enable him to move, to function, and to look like a human being. But how and for what purpose or objective he molds and shapes these various formative factors becomes manifest only through the millions of variations in individual styles of life. Although these may frequently appear to be disintegrated, a closer understanding will show each single case to be a unified variant determined by the life goal of the individual, which is closely connected with his conception of the world.

Heredity may be regarded as a supply of bricks which, with all their different qualities, are used by each individual in his infancy to build up his style of life. Resemblances and statistical probabilities can be frequently ascertained and counted upon, but never identical likeness. To make this clearly understood, let me point out here, despite my disinclination to use metaphors in scientific discussions, that a hammer may be regarded by everybody as a useful instrument, fashioned by the inherited and cultivated ingenuity of the human race. It was invented originally to drive a nail. Under given circumstances, however, it may also be used for other purposes, such as a missile, a paper weight, or a murderous weapon. A hammer is thus an environmental factor, a product and a phase of experience of the individual, just as are the properties of the body and the inherited potentialities of the human individual.

Unprejudiced research is not in a position to observe an individual's disposition or constitution but only the use he makes of them. These factors appear to him as alluring or stimulating opportunities. It would be erroneous to assume that they act as causes, for, with deepened understanding, we see that a different use is made of the same stimuli by different individuals. Therefore we are justified in assuming merely that on a statistical basis it is probable that these factors will evoke certain seemingly typical uses. So much we may understand. Any assertion beyond this we may regard as unscientific.

3. ENVIRONMENT[3]

Individual Psychology has been misunderstood to be an environmentalistic theory, tracing the entire psychological structure of a person to environmental influences. To examine this misunderstanding more closely, one would have to ask: Who seeks, who answers, who utilizes the impressions from the environment? Is man a dictaphone or a machine? There must be something else at play.

A consideration similar to that applied to hereditary factors is highly advisable also in the discussion of environmental factors. Here, obviously, we have to deal with the inheritance of social relationships. They, too, just as inherited physical properties, may represent allurements toward a certain form of response. To establish his relationship to the problems of the outside world and to mold these relationships in accordance with his style of life is the achievement of the child, the "father of the man" in a moving, changing world. Some understanding of this fact is to be found among authors who attribute all outcomes, particularly all failures, to environment and education. None of them, however, has asserted, let alone demonstrated, that sameness in environment and education could create absolute "equality." Environmental influences, the example of the attitude of relatives, and educational factors act only as allurements for the individual child which he takes up in accordance with or against the intention of the educator, and this in a thousand varieties.

These indisputable facts frequently cause the following ambiguous play. Whatever cannot be evaluated as environmental influence is evaluated as hereditary influence, while whatever cannot be referred to obscure hereditary factors, is attributed to environment. One thing, however, is certain. Hereditary and environmental factors are directed by the child, fumbling and groping around in the dark, as it were, toward possibilities of success, toward the successful solution of his problems. Naturally when examined with a maturer knowledge, they very frequently cannot [properly] be regarded as possibilities of success. I have pointed out previously that success may mean to some individuals the suppression of the weak, to some the leaning on others, and to some the elimination of important problems of life when these seem to portend possibilities of defeat. We can understand such interpretations of success, although of course we do not approve of them.

No experience is a cause of success or failure. We do not suffer from the shock of our experiences—the so-called trauma—but we make out of them just what suits our purposes. We are self-determined by the meaning we give to our experiences, and there is probably always something of a mistake involved when we take particular experiences as the basis for our future life. Meanings are not determined by situations, but we determine ourselves by the meanings we give to situations.

In drawing a comparison [between the neurotic and] the healthy psyche, it seemed at first, as it would to anyone, that particular experiences or fantasies in childhood give rise to the development of the neurosis. Indeed the first psychoanalytic investigations, especially of Freud and Breuer, emphasized that the traumatic influence of a sexual experience, with its direct and indirect consequences of repression and displacement, played the most important role among the causes of the neurosis. Yet the sexual and other childhood impressions which are brought to light by the examination of the neurotic do not differ particularly in degree or extent from the normal. Sometimes one finds more of them, sometimes less, but always an amount which is also reached by healthy individuals.

Unhappy experiences in childhood may be given quite opposite meanings. One man with unhappy experiences behind him will not dwell on them except as they show him something which can be remedied for the future. He will feel, "We must work to remove such unfortunate situations and make sure that our children are better placed." Another man will feel, "Life is unfair. Other people always have the best of it. If the world treated me like that, why should I treat the world any better?" It is in this way that some parents say of their children, "I had to suffer just as much when I was a child, and I came through it. Why shouldn't they?" A third man will feel, "Everything should be forgiven me because of my unhappy childhood." In the actions of all three men, their interpretations will be evident. They will never change their actions unless they change their interpretations. It is here that Individual Psychology breaks through the theory of determinism.

It is not the child's experiences which dictate his actions; it is the conclusions which he draws from his experiences. When we inquire into the story of a problem child, we see difficulties in the relation between himself and his mother. We can, however, see the same difficulties among other children, but they have answered them in a better way. This brings us back to the fundamental view of Individual Psychology: There are no reasons for the development of character; rather, a child can make use of experiences for his goal and turn them into reasons. We cannot say, for example, that if a child is badly nourished he will become a criminal. We must see what conclusion the child has drawn [from this experience].

B. Cognitive Processes

1. PERCEPTION AND HALLUCINATION[4]

a. *Perception*. According to an expression of Charcot which refers to scientific research, one always finds only that which one knows. This observation, when applied to everyday life, implies that our whole sphere of perception is limited by a number of existing psychological mechanisms and readinesses, as is also expressed in Kant's theory of a priori forms of perception. Here we must also call attention to Bergson's fundamental teachings, without being able to insert his important viewpoints.

The special abilities of the psyche which play the main part in bringing about our picture of the world have in common that their selectivity, acuteness, and effect are determined by the goal, which is envisioned by everyone. This explains why everyone perceives in particular only a certain part of life, of the environment, of an event. Man utilizes only what and how his goal demands. Therefore the process of perception can be comprehended only when one has gained a picture of the hidden goal of a person and has understood everything in him as influenced by this goal.

Perception can never be compared with a photographic apparatus; it always contains something of the individual's uniqueness. Not everything one sees is also perceived, and if one asks for the perceptions of two persons who have seen the same picture, one receives the most varied answers. The child perceives in his environment only that which for some reason fits his previously formed uniqueness. Perceptions are not strictly identical with reality, for man is able to transform his contact with the external world according to the demands of his uniqueness. Thus what a person perceives, and how he does so, constitutes his particular uniqueness. Perception is more than a mere physical process. It is a psychological function, and, from the way in which a man perceives, one can draw profound conclusions regarding his inner self.

COMMENT   *Since he held that both the personality and the individual mode of perception, in mutual interaction, arise simultaneously, Adler could state above that, on the one hand, the inner self, that is, the personality, can be understood from the way in which a man perceives, while on the other hand, perception can be comprehended only through previous knowledge of the man's goal and its all-pervading influence, his personality. This is very similar to the conclusion at which Jerome S. Bruner arrived in his paper on "Personality dynamics and the process of perceiving," based on experimental work in the field: "I find it hard to decide whether I have been discussing the role of personality factors in the process of perceiving or the role of perceptual factors in per-*

sonality functioning" (20, p. 145). For the subjectivity of perception, see pp. 182–183 and 248.

b. *Hallucination*. Regarding hallucinations, research has generally been concerned with the question of what they are, and the result has been the meaningless tautology that they are excitations of the visual area. [In contradistinction to this approach] we presuppose that it is largely impossible to name and to know the true nature of hallucinations, a presupposition which applies to all the fundamental facts of biology and physics, such as the objective fact of life, of assimilation, and of electricity. To us an hallucination is an expression which contradicts logic and the truth of social life, as memory also does, but to a lesser extent. A person who hallucinates removes himself from the realm of social interest, circumvents logic, curtails the sense of the truth, and strives for other than customary goals.

The goal cannot be directly inferred from the hallucination. Torn from its context, the hallucination, like any psychological phenomenon, is ambiguous. Its true meaning, its significance, its whence and why can be understood only from the individual as a whole, from his personality. To us hallucination signifies an expression of the personality in a particular position.

2. LEARNING[6]

COMMENT   *Most characteristic of Adler's views on learning is the expression "self-training," which is consistent with his recognition of the sovereignty of the self. While he greatly emphasizes the importance of learning and training, as briefly shown below, he always focuses on the interest, activity, spontaneity, and creativity of the learner as the ultimately crucial factor in the process.*

We do not always learn from experience. Of course we learn to avoid certain difficulties and we acquire a certain conduct towards them, but the line along which we move is not changed thereby. Out of the fulness of his experiences a person will make only very specific practical applications which, upon closer investigation, can always be shown to be such as somehow fit his life line and reaffirm him in his life schema [style of life]. The [German] language says with singular sensitivity that we make our experiences (man macht seine Erfahrungen), by which it indicates that everyone is master of the way in which he utilizes his experiences. We can indeed observe every day how people draw the most varied conclusions from their experiences.

The assertion that the life line of a person remains unchanged may appear incomprehensible to some because, after all, a person has so many experiences during his life which effect a change in his conduct. But we should consider that any experience is ambiguous. There are hardly two people who will make the same practical application of one and the same experience.

Why do people retain certain experiences and not others? What do we retain as habit? What do we imitate in the first place? Is man not guided and limited in his drive to imitate by virtually compelling laws? The observation of adolescents and children and also of adults who, for some reason, are particularly given to imitation, shows that no one imitates anything which does not suit him in some way.

Educational influences are likely to be accepted only when they seem to hold a promise of success for the individual's style of life. This fact must be considered an objection to behaviorism and reflexology. It will probably never be possible to produce conditioned reflexes which would lead to a feeling of defeat.

The individual sees all his problems from a perspective which is his own creation. Thus he also sees the environment which trains him with his own self-created perspective and accordingly changes its effect upon him for better or worse.

If a boy is timid, he will not care for physical achievements, or rather, he will not think of them as possible for himself. In consequence, it will not occur to him to train his muscles in an efficient way, and he will exclude all the impressions from outside that would ordinarily be a stimulus to muscular development. Other children, who allow themselves to be influenced and interested in the training of their muscles, will go farther ahead in physical fitness. He, because his interest is blocked, will remain behind.

By watching children [at play], we can often see them training for an occupation in adult life. When a child wishes to be a teacher, we can notice how he brings younger children together and plays school with them. A girl who looks forward to being a mother will play with dolls and train herself to a greater interest in babies. She is training herself in identification and in fulfilling the tasks of a mother.

Among outstanding men, we generally find an "early start." They played the piano at the age of four, or they wrote stories for the other members of the family when they were still very small. Their interest was long and continuous. Their training was spontaneous and widespread.

We believe that the question of genius can throw light on the whole subject [of learning]. Geniuses went a difficult way and they had many obstacles to contend with. Often they started with gravely imperfect organs. In almost all outstanding people, we find some organ imperfection. We gather the impression that they were sorely confronted at the beginning of life but struggled and overcame their difficulties. We can notice especially how early they fixed their interests and how hard they trained themselves in their childhood. They sharpened their senses, so that they could make contact with the problems of the world and understand them. From this early training we can conclude that their art and their genius was their own creation, not an undeserved gift of nature or inheritance.

3. MEMORY[6]

In our endeavors to throw light on the impregnable unity of the mental life I had to come to grips with the function and structure of memory. Here I was able to confirm the observations of earlier writers, namely, that memory is by no means to be regarded as the gathering place of impressions and sensations, that impressions are not retained as mneme, but that in the function of memory we are dealing with a partial force of the self-consistent mental life, the self. As such, memory, like perception, has the function of fitting impressions to the style of life and using them accordingly. To use a cannibalistic simile, one might say that the function of memory is to devour impressions and digest them. Anything that is not palatable to the style of life is rejected, forgotten, or saved as a warning example. The style of life decides. A good deal is digested only to a half, a quarter, or a thousandth part. Sometimes only the feelings and attitudes which accompany the impressions are digested. With these there are occasionally mingled memories of words or ideas or parts of them.

When we forget the name of a person otherwise well known to us, he need not always be someone whom we dislike, nor need he remind us of anything disagreeable. His name and personality may lie, either at the present time or permanently, outside our interest as this is enforced by our style of life. When we forget the name, we often know everything else about the person that seems to us of importance. He stands before us, and we can place him and say a great deal about him. Precisely because we cannot remember his name, he stands completely in the field of our consciousness.

COMMENT *Regarding the forgetting of names Freud had said: "If any-one forgets an otherwise familiar proper name . . . it is not hard to guess that he has something against the owner of the name and does not like to think of him" (38, p. 48). Yet in the same book he modified this statement. The forgetting of names does also "occur on occasions where the intervention of an unpleasantness-motive cannot be established" (38, p. 67). But when Freud gives an example we still see this motive, as when he says one may forget the name of a stranger when it is the same as that of a loved one because one begrudges this name to the stranger.*

Memory lets parts of an impression or all of it disappear for the intention described above or for some other reason. It is an artistic ability which conforms to the style of life of an individual. The impression as a whole thus includes much more than the experience which has been clothed in words. The individual apperception furnishes memory the perception in accordance with the uniqueness of the individual. The uniqueness of the individual takes over the impression which has been formed in this way and equips it with feelings and an attitude. Both the feelings and the attitude, in their turn, obey the individual's law of movement.

What remains from this digestive process is what we call recollection, whether this is expressed in words, in feelings, or in an attitude toward the external world. This process comprises approximately what we understand by the function of [apperceiving] memory. An ideal, objective reproduction, independent of the uniqueness of the individual, does not exist. We must expect, therefore, to find just as many forms of memory as we recognize forms of styles of life.

The mechanism of the apperceiving memory with its host of experiences transforms itself from an objectively operating system into a subjectively active schema, modified by the fiction of the future personality. It becomes the task of this schema to bring about connections with the environment which serve to enhance the self-esteem, to give directives and hints to the preparatory actions and thoughts, and to bring these in contact with the hard core of existing readinesses.

The apperceiving memory which influences our picture of the world so immensely, works as if with a schema, a schematic fiction. The selection and molding of our sensations, perceptions, experiences, and memory correspond to this fiction, as does the training of all our innate tendencies and abilities, until they are changed into the appropriate psychological and technical skills, automatisms, and readinesses. Our conscious and unconscious memory and its individual structure function in accordance with the personality ideal and its standards. [For the diagnostic significance of recollections, see pp. 350–356.]

According to the present practice of psychology, which might be called mal-practice, if someone has a poor memory or can recall only a few words, it would be concluded that his ability to remember is limited, that he is suffering from an hereditary or pathological deficiency in this ability. Incidentally, such a conclusion usually contains that which the premise has already expressed in other words. The procedure of Individual Psychology is quite different. After organic causes have been ruled out, we would raise the question: At what does the weakness of the memory aim? What is it after? We can only infer this goal from an intimate knowledge of the whole individual, so that an understanding of the part grows out of an understanding of the whole. We should then find something like the following which would represent a large number of cases: This person is about to prove to himself and to others that he should desist from some action or decision. He wants to keep the real motives unnamed or unconscious, and finds that these can be effectively replaced by weakness of memory.

Forgetfulness is brought about by a narrowing of attention, just as is the losing of important objects. The possibility of greater attention, that is, of interest, is present, but it is dimmed by a certain displeasure which initiates, encourages, or creates the losing or forgetting. This is the case, for example, when children lose their books. Usually one will easily be able to ascertain that they have not yet become quite accustomed to school conditions. There are housewives who are continuously misplacing or losing their keys. In their case, too, we will usually find that they are women who cannot come to friendly terms with the housewife's occupation. Forgetful people are the kind who do not like to rebel openly, but who, through their forgetfulness, betray a certain lack of interest in their tasks.

4. SUGGESTIBILITY[7]

The question as to how one person can influence another is to be answered in the sense that here, too, we are dealing with context phenomena (*Zusammenhangserscheinungen*). Our whole life runs its course on the presupposition that mutual influence is possible. This is particularly accentuated in certain relationships, as between teacher and pupil, parent and child, husband and wife. Owing to social interest, there exists in everyone to a certain extent a tendency to meet half-way the influence of another person. The degree to which an individual may be influenced depends, among other factors, upon the extent to which his rights seem safeguarded by the person exercising the influence. A lasting influence upon someone to whom one does wrong is impossible.

In hypnosis a suggestion is effective only if it meets with someone who is willing to accept it. In no case does the limit of the readiness to be hypnotized depend on the will of the hypnotizer. It depends on the psychological attitude of the medium.

The nature of suggestion can be understood only if one classifies it in the broadest sense under the impressions. Man not only receives impressions but continues to be under their influence. When the impressions are demands of another person or attempts to convince or persuade, we may speak of suggestion. Suggestion is a matter of modifying or strengthening an already effective attitude which manifests itself clearly in its bearer.

Individuals react differently to impressions from the outside. In general, those who are especially susceptible to suggestion and hypnosis are inclined to overestimate the opinions of others, that is, to have a low opinion of the correctness of their own views. They adapt themselves easily to the opinion of other persons because they overvalue their importance. Those who are relatively immune to suggestion are likely to take everything that comes from the outside as an insult, to consider only their own opinion as right and to reject everything another person offers them. Both extremes actually have a feeling of weakness.

Among people who fail in life and whose failures we designate by such terms as neurosis, psychosis, delinquency, [we often find people who nurture the opinion that they are particularly suggestible] but we seldom find any susceptibility to suggestion when it comes to matters in the nature of cooperation and sharing with our fellow men. When we do encounter suggestibility in the direction of cooperation among problem children of little activity, it is often followed by resentment and secret revolt. Occasionally it also happens during psychotherapy that a patient seems to be willing to follow a suggestion although we know he is not because he does nothing toward improving his behavior. For the most part, we find those individuals complaining about being suggestible who in reality are quite the opposite, so that we may assume they talk about their suggestibility in order to protect themselves. In general it may be said that suggestibility appears only where it fits in with the style of life.

5. FANTASY[8]

It would be a great mistake to separate the function of fantasy from the whole of the mental life and its ties with the demands of the external world, let alone to contrast it with the whole, that is, with the self. Fantasy is a part of the individual style of life, which it characterizes. As a psychological movement, fantasy leaves its mark on all other parts of the mental life. Its task, under certain circumstances, is to express itself in thoughts, while at other times it hides in the realm of feelings and emotions or is embedded in the attitude of the individual. Like every other psychological movment, it aims at the future, since it also moves with the stream toward the goal of perfection. From this point of view it becomes increasingly clear how meaningless it is to see a wish fulfillment in the movement of fantasy or of its derivatives, night and daydreams, and to believe that by doing so, one has come closer to an understanding of fantasy. Since every psychological expressive form moves from below to above, from a minus to a plus situation, we can, of course, consider every psychological expressive movement as a wish fulfillment.

Every attempt to solve a problem, since it involves the unknown of the future, sets the fantasy to work. The creative power to which we have assigned the formation of the style of life in childhood continues to work here. The guidance of fantasy rests with the style of life. In the products of fantasy, whether the individual recognizes the coherence or is completely ignorant of it, we can find the expression of the style of life. Thus these products can be used as entrance gates to gain insight into the workshop of the mind.

COMMENT *This and a similar statement under perception (see p. 210 above) provides the systematic opening for the so-called projective techniques. According to Adlerian theory, these should, how-*

ever, be called tests of perception or of fantasy, corresponding to the older names for these devices, or better still tests of apperception, since they clearly involve the schema of apperception. Apperception, is, of course, the term chosen by Henry A. Murray for his well-known Thematic Apperception Test (85). In this connection, we should like to point out that Raymond B. Cattell recently described the presently current term of projective technique as "a serious misnomer . . . misleading to research design and clinical diagnosis" (23, p. 56). Instead, Cattell accepts apperception test as one of the most accurate alternatives (23, p. 94). This term would be in accord with Adlerian theory.

In daydreams of children and of adults, fantasy takes precisely that concrete direction which is supposed to serve the overcoming of a felt weakness. Disconnected to a certain extent from common sense, daydreams tend in the direction of the goal of superiority. This is easily understood as an attempt to compensate, to maintain the psychological equilibrium, which, however, is never accomplished in this way. The process is somewhat similar to that which the child takes in creating his style of life. Where he feels the difficulty, fantasy helps to give him an illusory view of the enhancement of his self-esteem, usually spurring him on at the same time. Certainly there are plenty of cases, however, where this latter incitement is lacking, where the fantasy, so to speak, is the compensation. Obviously such a situation is to be regarded as antisocial, even though it may be devoid of any activity or of any aggression against the environment.

Whenever the ambition of a person finds reality intolerable, he flees to the magic of fantasy. We do not want to forget, however, that when fantasy is rightly coupled with social interest, the really great achievements are to be expected, for fantasy, by rousing expectant feelings and emotions, has the same effect as increasing the gas pressure in a machine that is running: The performance is increased.

Night dreams, like daydreams, are phenomena accompanied by the desire to anticipate and appear when man is occupied with paving a path into the future and with walking it securely. The striking difference is that daydreams can still be understood while this is rarely the case with night dreams. For the present, it should be mentioned merely that in night dreams we again find the power line of an individual who wants to have a firm hold on the future, who is facing a problem, and who is attempting its solution. [For a full discussion of dreams see pp. 357–365.]

c. Character Traits and Expressive Movements

1. CHARACTER TRAITS[9]

The goal influences the philosophy of life, the pace and the schema of life of an individual and guides his expressive movements. The character traits are thus only the outer forms of the movement line of a person. As such they convey to us an understanding of his attitude toward the environment, his fellow man, the community at large, and his life problems. They are phenomena which represent means for achieving self-assertion. They are devices which join to form a method of living.

A character trait is comparable to a guiding line which is attached to the individual as a pattern, permitting him to express his self-consistent personality in any situation without much reflection. Character traits do not correspond to innate forces and substrata; they are acquired, although very early, in order to make it possible to retain a definite pace. For example, laziness is not innate. A child is lazy because this attribute appears to him as a suitable means to make life easier and at the same time to maintain his significance, for the power position of an individual exists, in a certain sense, also when he moves along the line of laziness. He can always refer to it as an innate defect, leaving his inner value intact. The end result of such a self-reflection is always approximately as follows: "If I did not have this defect, my abilities could develop brilliantly; but unfortunately I do have this defect." Another child who, in an unbridled striving for power, is engaged in a constant struggle with his environment will develop character traits which appear necessary for such a struggle: ambition, envy, distrust. It is generally believed that such phenomena are completely merged with a personality, that they are innate and unalterable. But closer examination shows that it is only that they appear necessary for the movement line of the individual and are adopted for this reason. They are not primary but secondary factors, forced by the secret goal of the individual, and must be understood teleologically.

All character traits reveal the degree of social interest. They run along the line which, according to the opinion of the individual, leads to the goal of superiority. They are guiding lines interwoven with the style of life which has formed them and which, again and again, brings them to light.

2. EXPRESSIVE MOVEMENTS[10]

The bodily postures and attitudes always indicate the manner in which an individual approaches his goal. A person who goes straight on shows courage, whereas an adult who is anxious and hesitant has a style of life that prohibits direct action, and something of a detour appears in every action. We can detect by the way in which an individual gives his hand whether he has social feeling and likes to be connected with others. A perfectly [ideally] normal handshake is rather rare; it is usually overdone, underdone, or betrays a pushing-off or pulling-to tendency. It is noticeable in a streetcar that some people lean sideways, showing that they wish to be supported and are quite oblivious of the convenience of others. The same social insensibility is seen in those who cough in front of others, quite thoughtless of infecting them. Some, in entering a room, seem to keep instinctively at the greatest possible distance from everyone else. All these things reveal, more directly than their conversation, the attitudes that individuals assume towards life.

Among the authors who have well understood the foundations and certain expositions of the problems treated here we must mention primarily Ludwig Klages. In his *Problems of Graphology* and in *The Principles of Characterology*, he reports specific results of his theory of expressive movements. But already in 1905 he had developed thoughts regarding the form of personal expression which we wish to cite here (with the author's permission) on account of their significance and classical form.

"Every inner activity, in as far as it is not counteracted by opposing forces, is accompanied by a movement which is analogous to the original activity. This is the basic law of expression and its interpretation. To the most general characteristics of the inner activity, for example, the following movements must correspond: to striving, advancing movements; to resistance, retreating movements; to inner progress, a continuation of movement; to standstill, interruption of movement; to feelings of resistance, inhibition and tension, those movements will correspond which are directed against physical resistance and thus arouse increased pressure sensations (making a fist).

"Of the greatest importance to psychology are metaphors which name inner processes according to certain functions and organs of the body. For example, irony is brought in relation to the teeth by giving it the attribute 'biting;' pedantry is brought in relation to the bones by calling it 'calcified.' Among such phrases the ancient differentiation between 'head' and 'heart' is of greatest significance, for example, 'he has no head' versus 'he has no heart,' one referring to the absence of insight, the other to the absence of kindness."

In continuation of these thoughts, Klages arrives at the conclusion that "expressive movement is a general simile in terms of action." Considerations which were in many respects similar led me later to the conclusion that expressive movement, action, emotion, physiognomy, and all other psychological phenomena, including the pathological ones, are a simile of the unconsciously posited and effective life plan.

In order to arrive at a more effective result, the psyche speaks an organ dialect. In mimic and physiognomy, in the expressive movements of the emotions, in rhythms of the dance and of religious ecstacy, in pantomime, in art, and most eloquently in music, this organ dialect renounces language as a means of communication in order to impress us the more. Such effects are easily permitted by the communality of a given culture and the similarity of the human sense organs. These effects do not render the unambiguity of the word, but rather the stronger resonance of pictorial language, and thus betray their tendency to prevail as special devices where the spoken word fails to gain dominance and superiority beyond the limits of the ordinary.

COMMENT *The selection above is from the original paper on organ dialect (1912c), where this term was used broadly to include nonverbal communication. Adler's later meaning of organ dialect was restricted to the functions of the body (see below).*

3. SLEEP POSTURES[11]

By comparing the sleeping postures of patients in various hospitals with the reports of their daily life, I have concluded that the mental attitude is consistently expressed in both modes of life, sleeping and waking.

Very little children sleep upon their backs, with the arms raised, and when we see a child sleeping in this position, we may assume that he is healthy. If the child changes this position and sleeps with the arms down, for example, some illness is to be suspected. Similarly, if an adult is accustomed to sleep in a certain position and suddenly changes it, we may assume that something is altered in his mental attitude.

When we see a person sleeping upon the back, stretched out like a soldier at attention, it is a sign that he wishes to appear as great as possible.

If he lies curled up like a hedgehog with the sheet drawn over his head, he is not likely to be a striving or courageous character but is probably cowardly. A person who sleeps on his stomach betrays a stubbornness and negativity.

Some people turn a gradual somersault in sleep and awake with their heads at the bottom of the bed and their feet on the pillow. Such people are in unusually strong opposition to the world. Other patients make a halfturn and sleep with their heads hanging down over the edge of the mattress; they develop headaches from this practice, which are generally used to escape the demands of the following day. All sleep postures have a purposive nature. Restless sleepers, who keep moving all night, show that they are dissatisfied and want to be doing something more than they are. It may also be a sign that they want to be watched by another person, usually by the mother. When children cry in sleep, it is for the same reason. They do not want to be alone but would like to ensure notice and protection. The quietest sleepers are those who are most settled in their attitude to the problems of life. Their lives being well organized by day, they can use the night for its proper purpose of rest and recreation, and their sleep is generally free from dreaming.

D. Organ Dialect

COMMENT   The interaction of body and mind as a unit, the psychosomatic problem, was Adler's original concern in his Study of Organ Inferiority (1907a). In this early monograph it was the organ inferiority which, through the "psychological superstructure," gave rise to certain compensatory psychological and bodily processes. Although Adler referred "all phenomena of neuroses back to organ inferiority" (1907a, p. 63), it should be mentioned that even then he was far from stating the reverse, namely, that all organ inferiority leads to failure.

In his subsequent shift of emphasis from the primacy of bodily processes to the primacy of psychological processes, the organ inferiority lost its causal position and assumed two new functions. First, it became one of the important objective factors which provide certain probabilities for the individual's development (see pp. 368-369), such factors being ultimately subject to the individual's own interpretation. Second, the inferior organ, as the point of least resistance, became the preferred means by which the psyche expressed itself through the body. This second function is the topic of the present section.

1. ORGAN FUNCTIONS AS EXPRESSIVE BEHAVIOR[12]

Through recognition of the law of movement, we arrive at the purpose and meaning of expressive movements, which may be words, thoughts, feelings, and actions. But the body is also subject to the law of movement. This is disclosed when we consider the meaning of its functions. These speak a language which is usually more expressive and discloses the individual's opinion more clearly than words are able to do. Still it is a language, the language of the body, which I have called organ dialect. For example, a man who pretends to be courageous and possibly even believes in his courage shows by his trembling and palpitation that he has lost his equanimity. A child who behaves obediently but wets the bed at night thereby manifests clearly his opinion not to wish to submit to the prescribed culture.

Enuresis generally serves the purpose of attracting notice, of subordinating others, and of occupying their attention in the nighttime as well as the day. Sometimes it is to antagonize them. The habit is a declaration of enmity. From every angle, we can see that enuresis is really a creative expression, for the child is speaking with his bladder instead of his mouth.

We should like to point briefly to the following further examples of organ dialect. The refusal of normal functions may be an expression of defiance; pain, an expression of jealousy and desire; insomnia, of ambition; over-sensitivity, anxiety, and nervous organic disorders, of craving for power. Occasionally sexual excitations arise in this connection as co-ordinated forms of expressive movements.

To a certain degree, every emotion finds some bodily expression. The individual will show his emotion in some visible form, perhaps in his posture and attitude, perhaps in his face, perhaps in the trembling of his legs and knees. Similar changes could be found in the organs themselves. If he flushes or turns pale, for example, the circulation of the blood is affected. In anger, anxiety, sorrow, or any other emotion, the body always speaks. The mind is able to activate the physical conditions. The emotions and their physical expressions tell us how the mind is acting and reacting in a situation which it interprets as favorable or unfavorable.

2. THE MECHANISM OF ORGAN DIALECT[13]

The means by which the body is influenced have never been completely explored, and we shall probably never have a full account of them. A mental tension affects both the central nervous system and the autonomic nervous system. Where there is tension, there is action in the central nervous system; the individual drums on the table, plucks at his lip or tears up pieces of paper; he has to move in some way; chewing a pencil or a cigar gives him an outlet. These movements show us that he feels himself too much confronted by some situation. By means of the autonomic system, the tension is communicated to the whole body. It is the same whether he blushes when he is among strangers, begins to tremble, or exhibits a tic; they are all results of tension. And so, with every emotion, the whole body is itself in tension. The manifestations of this tension, however, are not as clear at every point, and we speak of symptoms only in those points where the results are discoverable.

The body, through the autonomic nervous system, the vagus nerve, and endocrine variations, is set into movement which can manifest itself in alterations of the blood circulation, of the secretions, the muscle tonus, and of almost all the organs. As temporary phenomena the changes are natural and only show themselves differently according to the style of life of the person concerned. If they persist, one speaks of functional organ neuroses. These, like the psychoneuroses, owe their origin to a style of life which, in the case of failure, shows an inclination to retreat from the problem at hand and to safeguard this retreat by clinging to the bodily and psychological shock symptoms which have arisen. This is the way the psychological process reflects itself in the body. [For a discussion of psychosomatic disorders see pp. 308–314.]

3. CHOICE OF THE ORGAN[14]

Those things which stir a person particularly or which may even drive him toward his specific organ dialect are derived from his previous history, essentially from his main interests and his bodily disposition, in so far as it has coordinated itself to a final goal in a compensatory fashion. For example, individuals with sensitive visual organs will manifest even in their manner of expression an accumulation of concepts referring to seeing, insight, and perception.

Altogether, the reflection of man's inferior, more sensitive organs plays a part in his conceptual world. In the neurotic symptoms this relationship becomes concretized. Thus, in the case of an inferior respiratory apparatus, nervous asthma may help to express distress in which one "runs out of air." Constipation may express, among other things, stoppage of expenses. Nervous trismus (lockjaw) by way of detours of thought, but still in accordance with an "inner slogan" (Robert Kann), may express the stopping of any intake, possibly also including conception. In the manifestation of the "inner slogan" we find almost always that the organ which is encroached upon is the one which is so predisposed. Thus the assumption of a "displacement" becomes unnecessary.

Already in childhood, sensations emerge from the inferior organ which are used by the will to power, and remain with the neurotic individual as long as he is not cured. The digestive apparatus, the heart, the skin, the sexual apparatus, the locomotor organs, the sensory apparatus, or the pain tracts may become excited by the inclination to dominate, depending on their adequacy and usefulness for expressing the desire for power. In accordance with the life line, the secret plan of life of the patient, these organs may show the forms of hostile aggression, of standing still, or of flight.

Each individual's body speaks in a language of its own. When one man is in a situation in which he is afraid, he trembles; the hair of another will stand on end; a third will have palpitations of the heart. Still others will sweat or choke, speak in a hoarse voice, or shrink physically and cower away. Sometimes the tonus of the body is affected, the appetite lost, or vomiting induced. With some it is the bladder which is mainly irritated by such emotions, with others the sexual organs. Many children feel stimulated in the sexual organs when taking examinations. It is well known that criminals will frequently go to a house of prostitution, or to their sweethearts, after they have committed a crime.

All of these responses belong to different types of individuals and could probably be discovered to be to some extent hereditary. Physical expressions of this kind will often give us hints of the weaknesses and peculiarities of the family tree. Other members of the family may make a very similar bodily response.

It is always necessary to look for these reciprocal actions of the mind on the body, and of the body on the mind, for both of them are parts of the whole with which we are concerned.

4. PHYSICAL DEVELOPMENT AS FORM OF EXPRESSION[15]

In all probability, the mind governs and influences the whole building-up of the body. We have no direct proof of this hypothesis, and it is difficult to see how proof could ever be established. The evidence, however, seems clear enough.

The style of life and a corresponding emotional disposition exert a continuous influence on the development of the body. A courageous individual will show the effects of his attitude in his physique. His body will be differently built up. The tonus of his muscles will be stronger, the carriage of his body will be firmer. Posture probably influences very considerably the development of the body and perhaps accounts in part for the better tonus of the muscles. The expression of the face is different in the courageous individual, and, in the end, the whole cast of features. Even the conformation of the skull may be affected.

We can often observe bodily expressions which are plainly the end results of mental failings, where the right way to compensate for a difficulty has not been discovered. We may be sure, for example, that the endocrine glands themselves can be influenced in the first four or five years of life. Imperfect glands never have a compelling influence on conduct. On the other hand, they are being continuously affected by the whole environment, by the direction in which the child seeks to receive impressions, and by the creative activity of its mind.

5. FEELINGS[16]

The feelings of an individual bear the impress of the meaning he gives to life and of the goal he has set for his strivings. To a great extent they rule his body and do not depend on it. They depend primarily on his goal and his consequent style of life. The feelings are never in contradiction to the style of life. We are no longer, therefore, in the realm of physiology or biology. The rise of feelings cannot be explained by chemical theory and cannot be predicted by chemical examination. In Individual Psychology, while we presuppose the physiological processes, we are most interested in the psychological goal. It is not so much our concern that anxiety influences the sympathetic and parasympathetic nerves. We look, rather, for the purpose and end of anxiety.

In every individual, we see that feelings have grown and developed in the direction and to the degree which were essential to the attainment of his goal. His anxiety or courage, cheerfulness or sadness, have always agreed with his style of life: Their proportionate strength and dominance has been exactly what we could expect. A man who accomplishes his goal of superiority by sadness cannot be gay and satisfied with his accomplishments. He can only be happy when he is miserable. We can notice also that feelings appear and disappear at need.

6. EMOTIONS[17]

The emotions are accentuations of the character traits as we have described them. They are psychological movement forms, limited in time. [We distinguish between socially disjunctive and socially conjunctive emotions.] The disjunctive emotions (*trennende Affekte*), such as anger, sorrow, or fear, are not mysterious phenomena which cannot be interpreted. They appear always where they serve a purpose corresponding to the life method or guiding line of the individual. Their purpose is to bring about a change of the situation in favor of the individual. They are intensified movements at which an individual arrives only when he has renounced another possibility of asserting himself, or, in other words, when he no longer believes that there is any other possibility. One aspect of the emotion, then, is a feeling of inferiority or inadequacy which forces its bearer to pull together all his strength and to carry out greater movements than usual. Through such heightened effort his own person is placed into the foreground and made victorious. Thus, as there is no rage without an enemy, this emotion can only have victory over him for its goal. It is a popular method, still possible in our culture, to assert oneself through such increased movements. There would be far fewer outbursts of temper if the possibility were not offered of assuring oneself significance in this way.

In an outburst of temper the individual wishes to overcome his imperfections as quickly as possible. To hit, accuse, or attack another individual seems to be the best way. The anger, in its turn, influences the organs. It mobilizes them for action or lays an additional stress on them. Some people when they are angry have stomach trouble at the same time, or grow red in the face. Their circulation is altered to such a degree that a headache ensues. We shall generally find unadmitted rage or humiliation behind attacks of migraine or habitual headaches, and, with some people, anger results in trigeminal neuralgia or fits of an epileptic nature.

In the socially conjunctive emotions (*verbindende Affekte*), we clearly see the social relationship. The emotion of joy, for example, cannot stand isolation. In its expressions of seeking company and embracing another, it shows the inclination to play the game, to communicate, and to share the enjoyment. The entire attitude is engaging. It is extending the hand so to speak, a warmth which radiates toward the other person and is intended to elevate him as well. All the elements of union are present in this emotion. The ascending line is not missing here either. Here we have an individual who, from a feeling of dissatisfaction, arrives at a feeling of superiority. Joy is indeed the correct expression for the overcoming of difficulties. It goes hand in hand with laughter in its freeing effect, representing the keystone of this emotion, as it were. It points beyond oneself and solicits the fellow feeling of the other person. Malicious joy at the misfortune of others is, of course, a disjunctive emotion by which one seeks superiority over the other person. Sympathy is the purest expression of social interest. Where we find it, we may generally rest assured that there is social interest. This emotion reveals the extent to which an individual is able to empathize with the situation of a fellow man.

COMMENT With his insistence on the self-consistency of the personality, Adler suggests an approach to the problem of a theory of emotion which is the very opposite of theories which see emotion as a disorganized response. Such disorganizational theories of emotion were reviewed some twenty years later in a paper by Robert W. Leeper in which he supports the motivational approach. Leeper concludes that if we conceived of emotional processes as motivational, "we might come to see . . . that part of the task of education is the development of healthy emotional processes as one of the indispensable assets, after all, of human life" (65, p. 20). But how is this task to be accomplished? According to Adler, healthy emotional processes would have to be developed through the strengthening of social interest.

E. Homogenization of Psychological Processes

COMMENT With the self dominant in the personality structure and all psychological processes considered as being in the service of the self, these processes naturally become alike in this respect. In other words, from the point of view of the highest abstraction, which is the individual law of movement, all psychological processes are alike in that they are but functionaries of the individual in his situation as he sees it. From this point of view, certain obvious antithetical pairs of behavior, such as conscious-unconscious or remembering-forgetting, lose their sharp distinctions altogether and become homogenized into continua.

While Adler maintained that such antitheses have no existence in reality, he showed that antithetical thinking is highly characteristic of the primitive mind and the neurotic character. Thinking in antitheses is in *itself an indication of the neurotic's erroneous perception of reality, of the neurotic schema of apperception. It has grown from the neurotic's greater need for safeguards, of which thinking in terms of rigid classes is one. This problem is dealt with on page 248.*

1. ARISTOTELIAN CLASSIFICATION[18]

The primitive orientation in the world which corresponds to the antithetical assertions of Aristotle, as well as to the Pythagorean tables of opposites, originates in the feeling of insecurity and represents a simple device of logic. What I have described as polar hermaphroditic opposites, Lombroso as bipolar and Bleuler as ambivalent, leads back to this mode of apperception which functions according to the principle of antithesis. We should not fall into the common error of regarding this as an essence of things, but must recognize in it the primitive working method, a point of view which measures a thing, a force, or an experience by an opposite which is fitted to it.

COMMENT   *In this 1912 passage, Adler raises a point which was to be worked out later by Lewin in his paper on "Aristotelian and Galileian Modes of Thought" (67). According to Lewin, the criterion of a good theory is that "the places of dichotomies and conceptual antitheses are taken by more and more fluid transitions, by gradations which deprive the dichotomies of their antithetical character, and represent in logical form a transition stage between the class concept and the series concept" (67, p. 10). In the light of such parallel thinking of Lewin and Adler, it was possible to borrow Lewin's term of homogenization as the most adequate heading for the present part.*

In the thinking of primitive peoples and of ancient philosophers, we always meet this desire to put concepts in strong antithesis, to treat them as contradictions. The antithetic attitude can be illustrated very clearly among neurotics. People often believe that left and right are contradictions, that man and woman, hot and cold, light and heavy, strong and weak are contradictions. From a scientific standpoint, they are not contradictions, but varieties. They are degrees of a scale, arranged in accordance with their approximation to some ideal fiction. In the same way, good and bad, normal and abnormal, are not contradictions but varieties. Any theory which treats sleep and waking, dream thoughts and day thoughts as contradictions is bound to be unscientific.

2. SLEEPING AND WAKING[19]

In sleep, sense perceptions, though not absent, are diminished and our contact with reality is lessened. When we dream we are alone. Demands of society are not so urgently present with us. In our dream thought, we are not stimulated to reckon so honestly with the situation around us. Yet we are still in contact with reality. If we are disturbed with problems, our sleep is disturbed also. The fact that during sleep we can make the adjustments which prevent us from falling out of bed shows that connections with reality are still present. A mother can sleep through the loudest noises in the street and yet awaken at the slightest movement of her child.

Our distinctive method of dream-interpretation [see pp. 358–361] is founded upon this recognition of the unity of the waking and sleeping life. This is an advance upon the valuable discoveries of Lichtenberg and of Freud that dreams always contain signs of vital problems which the dreamer does not recognize in his waking life, discoveries which our work amply confirms. But the dream is not merely the substitute satisfaction of wishes unfulfilled in waking—especially not of Freud's "infantile sexual desires"—but it is a function of the entire style of life, more dynamically related to the future than to the past, a fact intuitively known in antiquity when dreams were regarded as prophetic and not as historical. The dreamer is engaged in molding his attitude and disposition to the coming events of his life, storing up a certain reserve of feeling and emotion which could not be acquired in the daytime by contact with reality and by logical thinking. In dreams, therefore, we never find any other tendencies or movements than those manifested in the style of the waking life when the latter is coherently grasped.

If the dream life is separated from the day life, and the satisfaction given by a dream takes place in a life of its own, we can perhaps understand the purpose of dreams for the dreamer. But then we have lost the coherence of the personality. Dreams have now no purpose for the waking man. From a scientific point of view, the dreamer and the waking man are the same individual, and the purpose of dreams must be applicable to this one coherent personality.

The dream is not a contradiction to waking life. It must always be in the same line as other movements and expressions of life. If, during the day, we are occupied with striving towards the goal of superiority, we must be occupied with the same problem at night. Every one must dream as if he had a task to fulfill in dreaming, as if he had to strive towards superiority also in his dreams. The dream must be a product of the style of life, and it must help to build up and enforce the style of life.

3. REMEMBERING AND FORGETTING[20]

Looking back, everybody remembers certain important things, and indeed what is fixed in memory is always important. There are schools of psychology which act on the opposite assumption. They believe that what a person has forgotten is the most important point. But there is really no great difference between the two ideas, for even when a person can tell us his conscious remembrances, he still does not know what they mean. He does not see their connection with his actions. Hence the result is the same, whether we emphasize the hidden or forgotten significance of conscious memories, or the importance of forgotten memories.

When a patient looks back into his past, we can be sure that anything his memory will turn up will be of emotional interest to him, and thus we will find a clue to his personality [see pp. 351–352]. It is not to be denied that the forgotten experiences are also important for the style of life, but many times it is more difficult to find out the forgotten remembrances, or, as they are called, the unconscious remembrances. Both conscious and unconscious remembrances have the common quality of running towards the same goal of superiority. It is well, therefore, to find them both if possible, for both are in the end about equally important, and the individual himself generally understands neither. It is for the outsider to understand and interpret both of them.

4. TRUTH AND IMAGINATION[21]

Some persons claim that they can remember back to their first year. This is scarcely possible, and the truth is probably that these are fancied memories, not true remembrances. But it does not matter whether they are fancied or true since they are parts of the personality. Some persons insist that they are not sure whether they remember a thing or whether their parents have told them about it. This, too, is not really important, because even if their parents did tell them, they have fixed it in their minds and therefore it helps to tell us where their interest lies.

5. AMBIVALENCE AND INDECISION[22]

Is it at all thinkable that an individual, an indivisible entity, which we feel and understand to be a unity and of which we can predict (and this must be esteemed the sole criterion of understanding) how he will behave in a given situation—is it thinkable, that such an individual strives after several goals? We have never found it to be so. But what about *double vie* or ambivalence? Do we not in this case discern two aims? Do we not see vacillation and indecision?

Once when Socrates saw a sophist with his robe full of holes he said to him: "Young man of Athens, your vanity peeps from the holes in your robe!" Unassumingness and vanity side by side! Have we here an honest ambivalence? Is it not rather a ruse to drive with two horses instead of one, to be distinguished even by that very unassumingness? In the *double vie* these two roles reinforce one another to bring about their aim of excelling others. Just so does a speculator on the stock exchange sometimes act the bull and at other times the bear, as the occasion may require, in either case his object being to gain money, that is, power.

Our understanding of the psychological structure of indecision is pertinent here. Even in indecision there are not two different goals, but a single goal, and that is, "But stay!" [The single goal of indecision is the *status quo*.] The same reflection is true of all so-called nervous symptoms. Like a hidden brake they put a check on the forward movement, they side-track the advance.

6. CONSCIOUSNESS AND UNCONSCIOUSNESS[23]

Man knows more than he understands. Just as his power of knowing is awake in the dream when his understanding is asleep, so it is in his waking life. Man understands nothing about his goal, but still he pursues it. He understands nothing about his style of life, yet he is continually bound to it. For example, when a man is very dissatisfied with his wife, another woman often seems more attractive to him. But he does not see the connection, to say nothing of understanding the implied accusation or revenge. Only when seen in coherence with his style of life and the problem before him can his knowledge of the things close at hand become an understanding of these things.

The unconscious is nothing other than that which we have been unable to formulate in clear concepts. It is not a matter of concepts hiding away in some unconscious or subconscious recesses of our minds, but of parts of our consciousness, the significance of which we have not fully understood.

We cannot oppose "consciousness" to "unconsciousness" as if they were two antagonistic halves of an individual's existence. The conscious life becomes unconscious as soon as we fail to understand it, and as soon as we understand an unconscious tendency it has already become conscious.

The biological significance of consciousness as well as unconsciousness rests in the fact that these states enable action according to a self-consistently oriented life plan. This view coincides in part with the significant theories of Steinthal, Vaihinger, and Bergson. Even consciousness is merely a device of the psyche, as becomes clearly evident from the analysis of obsessions, madness, hallucination, and psychosis in general, although the plan of operation does not become conscious and intelligible in these cases. Thus every conscious manifestation of the psyche points to the unconscious, fictional, final goal, just as does the unconscious striving, in so far as one comprehends it rightly. The frequent antithesis of conscious and unconscious impulses is an antithesis of means only, but irrelevant for the final purpose of enhancing the self.

This final goal and every exaggerated variety of it must remain unconscious and not understood, if, by its opposition to reality, it would make action impossible. Where consciousness becomes necessary as a means of life, as a safeguard for the unity of the self and for the self-ideal, it will appear in the proper form and degree. Even the fictional goal of the neurotic life plan may in part become conscious if this process is suited to achieve an enhancement of the self-esteem. This is especially true in psychosis. But as soon as the neurotic goal might undo itself by becoming conscious, usually because it conflicts too greatly with social interest, it forms the life plan in the unconscious.

It is a general human phenomenon to lay aside thoughts which stand in our way, and take up those which advance our position. All individuals consider for the most part only those things which are useful for their view and attitude. In other words, that becomes conscious which advances us, and that remains unconscious which might disturb our argumentation.

Psychotherapy can take up from here by calling the guiding idea of greatness into consciousness [making it understood] and rendering it ineffective through criticism. The neurotic system is possible only as long as the guiding self-ideal remains unconscious [is not understood].

If one explains to a patient that the mainspring of his behavior is something which he has had to conceal for the very purpose of retaining his behavior, then, of course, one disturbs his entire psychological mechanism, because now that train of thought which disturbs his plan becomes clear to him.

The contrast to the view of Freud and other authors is clear. It is actually the compulsion toward the unity of the self, that is, the fictional goal, which dominates the extent of the conscious as well as that of the unconscious.

If one proceeds correctly, one will always find the self, the whole, while from an incorrect view a conflict may seem to be present, such as between the conscious and the unconscious. Freud, the representative of the incorrect view, is today rapidly approaching a better understanding when he speaks, as he does, of the unconscious in the ego. This, of course, gives the ego an entirely different face, the face which Individual Psychology saw first.

FOOTNOTES TO CHAPTER EIGHT

1. 1, 2, 3, 5: *Der Sinn des Lebens* (1933a), pp. 16–17, 98, 122, and 122; 4: "The Fundamental views of Individual Psychology" (1935a), p. 5.
2. 1 and 2: "Prevention of neurosis" (1935c), p. 6; 3: "The Structure of neurosis" (1932b), p. 6.
3. 1: "Persönlichkeit als geschlossene Einheit" (1932a), p. 81; 2 and 3: "Prevention of neurosis" (1935c), pp. 6–7 and 7; 4, 6, 7: *What Life Should Mean to You* (1931a), pp. 14, 13–14, and 123–124; 5: "Über neurotische Disposition" (1909), p. 55.
4. 1: *Über den nervösen Charakter* (1912a), p. 35; 2 and 3: *Menschenkenntnis* (1927a), pp. 35 and 35–36; 4 and 5: "Zur Theorie der Halluzination" (1912d), p. 38.
5. 1 and 2: *Menschenkenntnis* (1927a), pp. 7 and 6–7; 3: "Über die Homosexualität" (1918b), p. 130; 4: "Prevention of neurosis" (1935c), p. 7; 5: "Fundamental views" (1935a), p. 5; 6 to 9: *What Life Should Mean to You* (1931a), pp. 40, 245–246, 170, and 247–248.
6. 1 to 4: *Sinn des Lebens* (1933a), pp. 133–134, 134, 134, and 135; 5 and 6: *Nervoser Charakter* (1912a), pp. 35 and 40; 7: "Die Individualpsychologie, ihre Voraussetzungen und Ergebnisse" (1914f), p. 3; 8: *Menschenkenntnis* (1927a), p. 77.

7. 1 to 4: *Menschenkenntnis* (1927a), pp. 47–48, 50, 52, and 52; 5: "The neurotic's picture of the world" (1936d), pp. 9–10.

8. 1 to 4: *Sinn des Lebens* (1933a), pp. 159, 160, 162–163, and 163; 5: *Menschenkenntnis* (1927a), pp. 45–46.

9. 1 and 2: *Menschenkenntnis* (1927a), pp. 128 and 128–129; 3: *Sinn des Lebens* (1933a), p. 189.

10. 1: *Problems of Neurosis* (1929b), p. 151; 2 to 6: "Organdialekt" (1912c), pp. 136, 136, 138, 139, and 134.

11. 1 to 4: *Problems of Neurosis* (1929b), pp. 152, 151–152, 152, and 152–153.

12. 1: *Sinn des Lebens* (1933a), p. 50; 2 and 4: *What Life Should Mean to You* (1931a), pp. 38–39 and 40–42; 3: "Organdialekt" (1912c), p. 135.

13. 1: *What Life Should Mean to You* (1931a), p. 42; 2: *Sinn des Lebens* (1933a), pp. 48–49.

14. 1, 2, 3: "Organdialekt" (1912c), pp. 131, 132, and 135; 4, 5, 6: *What Life Should Mean to You* (1931a), pp. 41, 41, and 43.

15. 1, 2, 3: *What Life Should Mean to You* (1931a), pp. 39–40, 43, and 40.

16. 1 and 2: *What Life Should Mean to You* (1931a), pp. 29–30 and 31.

17. 1 and 3: *Menschenkenntnis* (1927a), pp. 214–215 and 223–224; 2: *What Life Should Mean to You* (1931a), p. 42.

18. 1: *Nervöser Charakter* (1912a), pp. 19–20; 2: *What Life Should Mean to You* (1931a), pp. 95–96.

19. 1, 3, 4: *What Life Should Mean to You* (1931a), pp. 99, 97, and 98; 2: *Problems of Neurosis* (1929b), pp. 162–163.

20. 1 and 2: *The Science of Living* (1929c), pp. 108 and 118–119.

21. 1: *Science of Living* (1929c), p. 120.

22. 1, 2, 3: "Progress in Individual Psychology" (1923a), pp. 25, 25–26, and 26.

23. 1 and 10: *Sinn des Lebens* (1933a), pp. 170 and 160–161; 2: "Structure of neurosis" (1932b), p. 10; 3: *Problems of Neurosis* (1929b), p. 163; 4, 5, 7, 9: "Zur Rolle des Unbewussten in der Neurose" (1913e), pp. 163, 164, 164, and 164; 6 and 8: *Menschenkenntnis* (1927a), p. 83.

PART II

ABNORMAL PSYCHOLOGY AND RELATED FIELDS

PART II

ABNORMAL PSYCHOLOGY AND
RELATED FIELDS

CHAPTER NINE

THE NEUROTIC DISPOSITION

COMMENT   Adler's theory of neurosis and other behavior disorders is
in essence the following: (1) An individual with a mistaken
opinion of himself and the world, that is, with mistaken goals and a mistaken style of life, (2) will resort to various forms of abnormal behavior
aimed at safeguarding his opinion of himself (3) when confronted with
situations which he feels he cannot meet successfully, due to his mistaken
views and the resulting inadequate preparation. (4) The mistake consists in being self-centered rather than taking the human interrelatedness
into account. (5) The individual is not consciously aware of these
processes.

The present chapter is concerned with the first point above. This Adler
called variously the neurotic disposition, the neurotic character, the
nervous modus vivendi, the neurotic style of life, or the pampered style
of life. Due to the crucial significance of the neurotic disposition for the
actual neurosis, he at times made no distinction between the two, using
the terms neurotically disposed and neurotic interchangeably.

Neurotic behavior and the origin of the symptoms will be discussed
in Chapters 10 and 11, respectively. The origin of the neurotic disposition
will be dealt with in Chapter 15.

In the present chapter and Chapter 10, all side-headings are followed by
dates to facilitate the understanding and appreciation of the fundamental
concepts presented by keeping the reader chronologically oriented.

A. The Neurotic Disposition

COMMENT   In the following selections from two of Adler's last papers
the neurotic disposition is called the pampered style of life.
The individual with the pampered style is "comparatively inactive, filled

with a personal ego-centric striving for superiority, and is therefore retarded in the development of his social interest" (see below). In the
normal individual, by contrast, the striving for superiority is centered on
the tasks which confront him, which means that his social interest has
been developed; and he is comparatively active in solving his problems.
For this kind of activity, which is combined with social interest, Adler
frequently used the word courage. The distinction between these two
styles of life is meant to offer only points of orientation; the difference is
not abrupt, but gradual. Furthermore, and very importantly so, within
this broad frame, each individual case will be found to have developed its
own unique style of life, the origin of which is ultimately to be sought
in the individual's own creativeness.

In the following opening sentence Adler speaks of the "concept of life
as motion," an idea which often recurs in his writings. To the clinical
psychologist this conception will actually be a very familiar one. He will
remember that in the Rorschach technique any perception of a living
form is scored as a movement response.

1. OVERCOMING AND SOCIAL INTEREST (1935) [1]

All life functions are properly developed for the victorious overcoming contact with the outside world. Our physical and psychological functions are evaluated as appropriate, healthy, and normal only when they
are fit for the overcoming of normal, external, oppositional factors.

Along with the striving for the overcoming of difficulties, obstacles,
and so on, we think we have been able to demonstrate the existence of
another power in the structure of life. This second power may be named
social interest. Viewed from the present level of our understanding both
powers seem to be factors in the process of evolution. It is conceivable
that the striving to overcome is probably the older.

In a neurosis we are always confronted with a highly placed goal of
personal superiority. When applying the principles of Individual Psychology to the investigation of such a case, this goal of superiority can
always be demonstrated as permeating all phases of life and all attitudes
of an individual to his problems, from his earliest childhood on. For
therapeutic purposes, this has to be shown to the individual carefully
and kindly. That such a highly placed goal of personal superiority be-
tokens a lack of the proper measure of social interest and precludes the
development of a healthy interest in others is understandable. The striving

for personal superiority and the nondevelopment of social interest are both mistakes. However, they are not two mistakes which the individual has made; they are one and the same mistake.

2. DEGREE OF ACTIVITY (1935) [2]

There is, however, a third thing which comes to the attention of the investigator. We always find that in cases of neurosis we are dealing with comparatively less active individuals who naturally, by virtue of the unchanging or unchanged style of life, were even in their childhood characterized by the lack of activity required and desirable for the correct solution of their problems. This examination of the individual's activity cannot be carried out in figures and numbers. That is just as impossible as the quantitative examination of the degree of social interest or of the striving for personal power. Such appraisal can be secured only by creative or artistic empathy and by ascertaining the continuity of these phenomena in the individual under consideration.

Neurosis is the natural, logical development of an individual who is comparatively inactive, filled with a personal, egocentric striving for superiority, and is therefore retarded in the development of his social interest, as we find regularly among the more passive pampered styles of life.

What happens, however, to children who manifest the pampered style of life, but seek their chances of success in a more active way? They, too, do not look upon others as fellow-beings. They, too, live under the pressure of a conception of the world in which they expect to receive everything from others, or in which, owing to their greater activity, they take everything from them. But the comparatively more active children are much less in danger of becoming neurotics. At a given moment, always dependent upon an exogenous factor, that is, a difficult situation, they tend to become criminals.

3. THE PAMPERED STYLE OF LIFE (1935, 1936) [3]

It is comparatively easy now to ascertain that the neurotic has been a child to whom leaning on other people offered a possibility of success. Such a child experienced, developed, and secured for himself during several years of his life an enriched and elevated position by obtaining everything easily, with the help of others, and by expecting everything from others. Thus he came to a standstill in the development of his social interest and acquired a picture of the world that promised him an easy and quick fulfillment of his wishes. In such a case the development of great activity is not very urgent. In a word, from the beginning of his life the neurotic manifests the pampered style of life, which is not adequate for the solution of the social problems of life. And the potentially neurotic child later, when confronted by a difficult situation, often becomes the neurotic patient.

Extreme discouragement, continuous hesitation, oversensitivity, impatience, exaggerated emotion and phenomena of retreat, physical and psychological disturbances showing the signs of weakness and need for support as found in the neurotic, are always evidence that a patient has not yet abandoned his early-acquired pampered style of life. These show that a patient endowed with a comparatively small degree of activity, and not possessing sufficient social interest, has pictured to himself a world in which he is entitled to be first in everything.

The pampered style of life as a living phenomenon is the creation of the child, though its formation is frequently aided by others, of course. Consequently this style of life can be found occasionally in cases where we cannot speak with any justification of pampering, but where on the contrary, we find neglect.

I should like to stress here that the pampered style of life should not be read into the attitude of the mother or the grandmother. It is the creation of the child, and is very frequently found even where there is no evidence whatever of pampering by another person.

COMMENT In another paper, appearing the same year, Adler went still further in this direction, stating that "this pampered style of life is found almost more frequently in neglected children or in those who feel themselves neglected" (1936b) than in others.

Originally Adler had used the term pampered to describe an influence upon an individual, that is, an actual stimulus condition. In its present usage, however, the term pampered, as a modifier of the style of life, is employed to describe a form of response of the individual. To clarify this distinction Adler used to say that a person with a pampered style of life is one who wants to be pampered rather than necessarily one who actually has been pampered. One must keep in mind that between the pampering situation and the pampered response Adler interposes the creative activity of the individual as the important intervening variable.

4. PSYCHOLOGICAL TOLERANCE (1923) [4]

In view of their great psychological cost, neuroses and psychoses may be described as nervous breakdowns. The extent of the breakdown is appraised by the extent to which the patient is prevented from normal participation in society, its demands and its benefits. It is the exclusive and isolated individuals, whose contact with life has always been loose because of their exaggerated personal ambition, who will resort to such abnormal distance from the demands of society. These are the neurotically disposed individuals. They are characterized by a false attitude toward all life problems, the social, the vocational, and the sexual problem. The false attitude consists in regarding these demands as merely personal, private affairs and overlooking the common relationship and general implications.

This is the reason why in the face of threatening or actual defeat such people will easily lose courage. [The amount of threat a person can bear without losing courage may be called *psychological tolerance*.] Psychological tolerance depends on the strength of social ties. If the tolerance is exceeded, this will in turn reflect itself in the attitude toward the demands of life. "One cannot ask so much of me; one must take my disorder into account." "What couldn't I accomplish if I were well." Everyone has something of such an attitude. The psychological tolerance is undermined by failures, some of which are certainly to be expected. Encouragement can strengthen the tolerance and prevent, ease, or defer the outbreak of a neurosis.

B. The Exaggerated Goal of Self-Enhancement

COMMENT   *In the preceding outline of the neurotic disposition the egocentric striving for personal superiority was considered one of its important dynamic characteristics. This striving is described in more detail in the present selections from Adler's earlier writings. According to these, the neurotically disposed individual sets his goal higher than does the normal person and strives for it more rigidly. Both of these characteristics are explained as compensations for an increased inferiority feeling.*

What is missing in these early formulations is Adler's concept of social interest. It seemingly did not appear in print until 1918 approximately (1918a).

From that time on the nondevelopment of social interest is considered together with increased inferiority feelings as the explanation for the egocentric striving and the emphasis is shifted from the manner and intensity of this striving to the socially useless direction which it takes. The addition of the concept of social interest, however, did not supercede the earlier contributions or diminish their significance. Rather, the later theory subsumes the earlier contributions.

1. INFERIORITY FEELING AND COMPENSATION (1913) [5]

In the *Study of Organ Inferiority* (1907a) I showed that innate constitutional anomolies are not to be regarded merely as phenomena of degeneration, but also as often leading to compensatory achievement and overachievement. They also lead to significant correlated phenomena to which increased psychological activity contributes essentially. This compensatory psychological effort often strikes out along new and different paths in order to deal with the tensions of life and so cover up a felt deficiency.

The most common form in which the feeling of inferiority, which appears in childhood, attempts to escape its unmasking consists in the construction of a compensatory psychological superstructure aimed at regaining stability and superiority with trained readinesses and safeguards. This is the nervous *modus vivendi*. Any departure from the normal can subsequently be explained by the greater ambition and the stronger caution. But all the devices and arrangements, nervous character traits as well as nervous symptoms, derive their significance from preliminary trials, experiences, empathies and imitations—such as are not entirely foreign to the life of a healthy individual. They speak a language which, if properly understood, always expresses the idea: here is an individual who is striving incessantly from the sphere of insecurity and the feeling of inferiority towards a godlike dominance over his environment, is struggling for his significance, is attempting to force it.

The actual form of expression and the deepening of this guiding thought could also be designated as *will to power* (Nietzsche).

2. HIGHER GOAL-SETTING (1913) [6]

When we look back upon the results gained so far, we obtain a fundamental view regarding the interrelation of the child's inferiority feeling, his reassuring and orienting goal-setting, and his efforts and safeguards for coming closer to the goal. An increased insecurity feeling in childhood causes a higher and more unalterable goal-setting, a striving which goes beyond human measure, and at the same time brings about the best-suited efforts or safeguards for attaining the goal. This combination gives us a picture of those phenomena which we call neurosis, and from which the neurotic character rises strikingly and more prominently with either its whipped-up activity or its semblance of irreparable passivity, sometimes behind the mask of indecision and hesitation.

In this psychological schema there are two approximately fixed points: the low self-estimation of the child who feels inferior, and the over-life-size goal which may reach as high as godlikeness. Between these two points there rest the preparatory attempts, the groping devices and tricks, as well as the finished readinesses and habitual attitudes. It is from these that the above-mentioned goal, which is actually hidden, may be inferred.

One of the forms of these preparatory attitudes are the character traits. They give structure and form to the personality, and are the proper mediators between past and future. As mental readinesses they serve the person's guiding ideal. Depending on their nature, they may initiate either contact with the environment or a fight against it, or may force a hesitating or avoiding attitude in the face of a decision. The child's feeling of insecurity needs such guiding lines and available readinesses.

When increased inferiority feeling is added, these guiding lines are brought out more sharply and raised to categorical imperatives. What was once useful to such children, they try to perpetuate and deify on account of its reassuring effect. Clear defeats can force a change of front and therewith a veiling, but not a change of character traits.

COMMENT   *Lewin arrived at essentially similar conclusions regarding higher goal-setting, when summarizing many years of work by himself and his students on the level of aspiration in normal subjects. "A successful individual typically sets his next goal somewhat, but not too much, above his last achievement. In this way he steadily raises his level of aspiration. Although in the long run he is guided by his ideal goal, which may be rather high, nevertheless his real goal for the next step is kept realistically close to his present position. The unsuccessful individual, on the other hand, tends to show one of two reactions: he sets his goal very low, frequently below his past achievement . . . or* he sets his goal far above his ability. This latter conduct is rather common. Sometimes the result is a gesturelike keeping up of high goals without serious striving; it may at other times mean that the individual is following blindly his ideal goal, losing sight of what in the present situation is possible" (71, as quoted in 63, p. 410).

3. THE ACCENTUATED DOGMATIZED GUIDING FICTION (1912)[7]

It is the feeling of insecurity which forces the neurotic to a stronger attachment to fictions, guiding lines, ideals, and principles. These guiding principles are envisaged by the normal person also. But to him they are a figure of speech (modus dicendi), a device for distinguishing above from below, left from right, right from wrong; he does not lack the open-mindedness, when called upon to make a decision, to free himself from these fictions and to reckon with reality. Just as little do the world's phenomena resolve themselves for him into rigid antitheses; on the contrary he strives constantly to keep his thoughts and actions detached from the unreal guiding line and to bring them into harmony with reality. The fact that he uses fictions at all as a means to an end arises from the usefulness of the fiction in casting up the accounts of life. The neurotic, however, like the dependent child still removed from the world, and like the primitive mind of early man, clings to the straw of his fiction, hypostasizes it, that is, arbitrarily ascribes reality to it, and seeks to realize it in the world. For this the fiction is unfit; it is still more unfit when, as in the psychoses, it is elevated to a dogma or anthropomorphized. "Act 'as if' you were lost, 'as if' you were the biggest, 'as if' you were the most hated." The symbol as a modus dicendi dominates our speech and thought. The neurotic takes it literally, and the psychotic attempts its realization. In my contributions to the theory of the neuroses this point is constantly emphasized and maintained.

More firmly than the normal individual does the neurotic fixate his God, his idol, his personality ideal, and cling to his guiding line, and with deeper purpose he loses sight of reality. The normal person, on the other hand, is always ready to dispense with this aid, this crutch. In this instance, the neurotic resembles a person who looks up to God, commends himself to the Lord, and then waits credulously for His guidance; the neurotic is nailed to the cross of his fiction. The normal individual, too, can and will create his deity, will feel drawn upward. But he will never lose sight of reality, and always take it into account as soon as action and work are demanded. The neurotic is under the hypnotic spell of a fictional life plan.

I readily follow here the ingenious views of Vaihinger, who maintains that historically ideas tend to grow from fictions (unreal but practically useful constructs) to hypotheses and later to dogmas. In Individual Psychology this change of intensity differentiates in a general way the thinking of the normal individual (fiction as an expedient), of the neurotic (attempt to realize the fiction), and of the psychotic (incomplete but safeguarding anthropomorphism and reification of the fiction: dogmatization).

An example of this progression would be the intensification of cautiousness into anxiety, and occasionally the reification of the anticipation of disaster into melancholia. These three steps of achieving security may be clarified as follows. Caution: (normal, fiction) 'as if' I could lose my money, 'as if' I could be below. Anxiety: (neurotic, hypothesis) 'as if' I were going to lose my money, 'as if' I were going to be below. Melancholia: (psychotic, dogma) 'as if' I had lost my money, 'as if' I were below. In other words, the stronger the feeling of insecurity, the more accentuated the fiction becomes through increasing abstraction from reality, and the more it approaches dogma. The patient nourishes and feigns within himself everything which brings him nearer to his guiding line, which in turn gives him security and thus is effective, albeit in a reduced circle. In this process reality becomes devaluated in various degrees, and the corrective paths which are adapted to society prove themselves increasingly insufficient.

COMMENT *The views of Vaihinger given by Adler above are what Vaihinger calls "the law of ideational shifts." According to Vaihinger both fictions, and to a lesser degree, hypotheses involve a state of psychological tension. "This condition of tension, involving as it does a feeling of discomfort, quite naturally explains the tendency of the psyche to transform [every fiction and] every hypothesis into a dogma" (111, p. 125). Adler applies Vaihinger's way of thinking to differentiate between the normal and abnormal forms of achieving security through compensation. This implies two further dimensions: flexibility—rigidity, and contact with reality—distance from it. The abnormal individual satisfies his greater need for security at the price of losing his flexibility and his connectedness with reality. Greater distance from reality has been covered in the passages above; rigidity is taken up in the passage below.*

4. THE ANTITHETICAL MODE OF APPERCEPTION (1912) [8]

The neurotically disposed individual has a sharply schematizing, strongly abstracting mode of apperception. Thus he groups inner as well as outer events according to a strictly antithetical schema, something like the debit and credit sides in bookkeeping, and admits no degrees in between. This mistake in neurotic thinking, which is identical with exaggerated abstraction, is also caused by the neurotic safeguarding tendency. This tendency needs sharply defined guiding lines, ideals, and bogeys in which the neurotic believes, in order to choose, foresee, and take action. In this way he becomes estranged from concrete reality, where psychological elasticity is needed rather than rigidity, that is, where the use of abstraction is needed rather than its worship and deification. After all, there is no principle to live by which would be valid to the very end; even the most correct solutions of problems interfere with the course of life when they are pushed too far into the foreground, as for example, if one makes cleanliness and truth, the goal of all striving.

In the psychological life of the neurotic we find the inclination to stylize experiences and persons in the environment to a very pronounced degree, exactly as we find it in primitive thought, mythology, legend, cosmogeny, theogeny, primitive art, psychotic productions, and the beginnings of philosophy. In this process phenomena which do not belong together must, of course, be sharply separated by abstractive fiction. The urge to do this comes from the desire for orientation which, in turn, originates in the safeguarding tendency. This urge is often so considerable that it demands artificial dissection of the unity, the category, and even the self into two or several antithetical parts.

The neurotic carries the feeling of insecurity constantly with him. Therefore, "analogical thinking," that is, the attempted solution of problems according to the analogy of former experiences, is more strongly and distinctly expressed in him than in normal individuals. His fear of the new (the *misoneism* of Lombroso) and of decisions and tests which are always present, originates from his deficient self-confidence. He has chained himself so much to guiding lines, takes them so literally, and seeks to realize them so much, to the exclusion of any alternative, that unknowingly he has renounced the unprejudiced, open-minded approach to questions of reality.

COMMENT *In the above Adler describes the neurotic's view of the world as what one might call a caricature of an Aristotelean class theory. This is, of course, the direct opposite of what he considered the correct view, which recognizes no classes, but only interacting forces.*

According to Adler the neurotic's way of thinking is characterized by antitheses, dichotomies, and prejudice. All of these are seen as dogmatized fictions to which the neurotic clings as a crutch (see above) to support him in his efforts at coping with the world in the face of his feeling of insecurity. Here Adler anticipated important recent research on social prejudice. In summarizing these studies Allport states they have shown "beyond a doubt that prejudiced attitudes may serve as a psychological crutch for persons crippled in their encounters with life. . . . From this point of view prejudice would seem to be largely a device for handling basic insecurity" (5, p. 12). The similarity of Allport's terminology here with that of Adler is striking.

5. THE MASCULINE PROTEST (1912, 1913) [9]

The understanding of the world according to concrete pairs of opposites corresponds to the primitive attempts of the child to orient himself in the world and to safeguard himself. Among these pairs I have regularly found: (1) above-below and (2) masculine-feminine. In the sense of the patient, but not in the general sense, memories, impulses, and actions are always arranged according to a classification of *inferior = below = feminine* versus *powerful = above = masculine*. This classification is important. Because it can be falsified and advanced at will, it affords a distortion of the picture of the world by which it is always possible for the neurotic to retain his standpoint of having been humiliated. It lies in the nature of things that here the patient's experiences of his constitutional inferiority come to his assistance, as does the increasing aggression of his environment which is continuously irritated by his neurotic behavior.

The neurotic's striving for security, his very safeguards, can be understood when the original antithetic value-factor, namely that of insecurity, is taken into consideration at the same time. Both security and insecurity are the result of a dichotomizing judgment which has become dependent upon the fictional personality ideal and furnishes biased subjective value judgments. The feeling of security and its opposite pole, the feeling of insecurity, arranged according to the antithesis of inferiority feeling and personality ideal, are, like the latter, a fictional pair of values. They are the kind of psychological construction concerning which Vaihinger points out "that in them reality is artificially divided, that they have meaning and value only when together, but that, when taken singly, they lead through their isolation to meaninglessness, contradictions, and illusionary problems." In the analysis of psychoneuroses it often becomes apparent that these antitheses are analogous to the antithesis of man—woman taken for real. The dynamics of the neurosis can therefore be regarded, and are often so understood by the neurotic, 'as if' the patient wished to change from a woman to a man or wanted to hide his unmanliness. These tendencies, in their varied fullness, give the picture of what I have called the masculine protest.

The schematic formula "I want to be a real man," then serves as an abstract and concretized goal of the neurotic. This outcome is a compensation for the underlying feeling of inferiority which is equated with femininity. The schema according to which the neurotic here apperceives and proceeds is formulated with planful falsification, is antithetical throughout and intrinsically hostile. As the unconscious assumptions of the neurotic goal-striving (in male and female patients alike) we can regularly recognize the following two: (1) Human relations are under all circumstances a struggle for superiority. (2) The feminine sex is inferior and serves in its reaction as a measure of masculine strength.

c. The Underdeveloped Social Interest

COMMENT   *In time, social interest, or rather the underdevelopment of social interest, became the key concept in Adler's theory of abnormal psychology. While social interest has already been treated at some length (see Chapter 5), the complexity of this concept and its significance for understanding the abnormal dynamics are treated in the present selections. It will be seen that underdevelopment of social interest exerts a negative influence on perception, reasoning, and value formation. Its influence on perception becomes apparent in the use of such expressions as the "private view of the world," "not seeing in the same way" as other people, the neurotic's "picture of the world," his "private map," the necessity for learning to "re-see the world." In understanding and reasoning, the absence of social interest leads to forms which make sense to the neurotic, but which no longer correspond to common sense. Thus the neurotic has a "private intelligence," but he is not reasonable, in that his conclusions do not appear logical to other people as well. In this constellation the neurotic's value judgments also become corrupted. He will be found striving for superiority on the socially "useless side," that is on the valueless side, valueless from the point of view of society. Ultimately such striving becomes valueless to the patient himself because all values are in the last analysis social values.*

1. THE PRIVATE FRAME OF REFERENCE (1927) [10]

We have often proposed a simple device for determining the intensity of the neurosis, aside from its wider relationships. It is to ask ourselves under what conditions the patient's ailment would have meaning or justification. In this way we are able to gain a certain amount of insight. We start from the point that we are dealing with a person who has set for himself other tasks and another ultimate purpose than that which we would expect of him or which life would require of him. We maintain that the ideal, typical, ultimate purpose of a human being, irrespective of health or sickness, is to solve his life problems. The neurotic, however, has set for himself entirely different tasks. Why, for example, should a boy be lazy although this yields him nothing but unpleasantness? We will be able to understand this only if we ask ourselves whether his purpose may not be quite different, and whether he may not possibly be acting quite correctly with respect to this ultimate purpose. Only then can we note that the symptoms which we observe are actually quite correct, but that this person has a style of life which differs from the normal.

The neurotic has, of course, a notion of the frame of reference of normal life, for every one knows what the demands of life require of one. Yet despite this knowledge, his behavior takes place according to another frame. Here then we have two frames of reference. The one is the normal, the socially average, which includes all logic and all reason, and within which we would expect those movements of an individual which we call normal. The other is the neurotic, a private frame of reference. An example of such a private frame of reference would be a very pampered child who shows behavior which from the start requires that everything should be handed to him on a platter and that there should always be someone at his service, so that he may obtain without effort what others have to work for. Often we meet people who know the significance of the socially normal frame of reference very well, who even have the will to act accordingly, but at the same time show by their behavior that they follow a quite different frame of reference in reality.

2. NEUROSES AND JOKES (1927)[11]

If we employ the view of the private frame of reference, we find that the neurosis and the joke have similar characteristics. While the listener uses a normal frame of reference, the one who tells the joke suddenly introduces a new frame of reference, which is related to the first in a few points, but otherwise shows the matter in an entirely new light. In the following familiar joke we can show how these two frames of reference clash, and thus produce the comical and remarkable effect. "A horse trader wants to praise his horse and says, 'If you mount it at 6 o'clock in the morning, you can be in Pressburg at 9 o'clock.' Whereupon the customer replies, 'What should I do in Pressburg at 9 o'clock?' " Their minds do not meet. What happens, is a sudden split according to two points of view. The essential part of the joke is this dual frame of reference, and here we see the relationship with that other device, the neurosis.

Actually a large number of nervous symptoms seem like a poor joke. They try to trip us up, and sometimes surprise us as a joke does. One cannot maintain that this is due to lack of intelligence. Among our patients there are very intelligent people. Rather we must speak of a subjugated intelligence. Whenever a person wants to avoid the solution of his normal problems, he is forced to subjugate his intelligence because it would speak in favor of carrying out the solution.

Neuroses and jokes, like all other psychological processes, are related to social interest. We find in both also the striving for significance, which here tends towards the depreciation of others; undoubtedly the joke represents a revolt against the socially normal frame of reference. But a joke can only be good if the two frames of reference appear to have approximately equal general validity. If one frame of reference is obviously invalid, the joke is no longer a good one. The neurosis is rather to be compared with a poor joke, because its particular frame of reference appears, from the point of view of Individual Psychology, as invalid.

We have always been inclined to use jokes to clarify his error to the neurotic. In this way we can show him that he has a second frame of reference within which he acts, and that he tries to bring his problem in line with logic in accordance with this false system. Here is a main point of attack of therapy; we attempt to undo the false values which are at the basis of the actions of the neurotic.

3. PRIVATE SENSE VERSUS COMMON SENSE (1931, 1936) [12]

We must distinguish between "private intelligence" and "common sense," and must understand reason as being connected with common sense—sense that can be shared. According to private intelligence an individual may attempt through a personal, private view of the world to assert himself and enhance his own sense of superiority by injuring that of someone else. Private intelligence is at work whenever a person tries, unfairly, to turn to his own advantage the social contributions of another person. But here, we shall have to add a qualification: the injury inflicted is not deliberately intentional. [See pp. 148–151.]

An anecdote is told of the leader of a small religious sect. One day she called her followers together and informed them that the end of the world was due on the next Wednesday. Her followers were much impressed, sold their property, abandoned all worldly considerations, and waited in excitement for the promised catastrophe. Wednesday passed without unusual occurrences. On Thursday they called in a body to ask an explanation. "See what difficulties we are in," they said. "We abandoned all our security. We told everybody we met that the end of the world was coming on Wednesday, and when they laughed at us we were not discouraged but repeated that we knew it on infallible authority. Wednesday has gone by and the world is still here around us." "But my Wednesday," said the prophetess, "is not your Wednesday." In this way, by a private meaning, she secured herself against challenge. A private meaning can never be put to the test. The mark of all true "meanings of life" is that they are common meanings, that is, meanings in which others can share and which others can accept as valid.

To speak, to read, and to write all presuppose a bridge with other men. Language itself is a common creation of mankind, the result of social interest. Understanding is a common matter, not a private function. To understand is to understand as we expect that everybody should understand. It is to connect ourselves in a common meaning with other people, to be controlled by the common sense of all mankind. There are some people who are seeking mainly for their own interests and for personal superiority. They give a private meaning to life; life should exist for them alone. This is no understanding, however; it is an opinion which no one else in the whole wide world could share. We find, therefore, that such people are unable to connect themselves with their fellow men. Often when we see a child who has trained towards interest in himself, we find that he has a hangdog or vacant look in his face; and we can see something of the same look in the faces of criminals or of the insane. They are not using their eyes to connect with others. They are not seeing in the same way.

For the neurotic, coming to understand his own picture of the world—a picture which he built up early in childhood and which has served as his "private map," so to speak, for making his way through life—is an essential part of the process of cure. When one is attempting to redirect his life to a more nearly normal way of living, he will need to understand how he has been seeing the world. He will have to re-see the world and alter his old private view in order to bring it more into harmony with a "common view" of the world—remembering that by common view we mean a view in which others can share. It is not likely that others would share his private opinion, that at all times and in all situations, he should, by right, occupy the position of ascendancy and be the recipient of special privileges.

COMMENT   *The phrase "private world" was used by Adler in 1930 (see pp. 390–391). It employs the qualification private in the sense in which he speaks here of private intelligence, private map, and private view of the world. It has since become a familiar addition to the psychiatric and psychological vocabulary.*

Undoubtedly Phyllis Bottome helped popularize the term when she chose Private Worlds for the title of a novel centered around a mental institution(16). She was strongly influenced by Adler and, as the reader has learned, became his biographer. The book appeared in 1934, was widely read and made into a successful motion picture. Actually, Bottome used private in a broader sense than Adler generally did, to include all of Adler's subjective schema of apperception (see pp. 181–184), the normal as well as the abnormal. Thus the psychiatrists in Bottome's novel as well as the patients had their private worlds.

4. STRIVING ON THE SOCIALLY USELESS SIDE (1929, 1931) [18]

Each individual strives from a feeling of weakness and inferiority, as this is shown also in bodily development, towards a goal of an "ideal end-form," that is, toward overcoming all difficulties of life. This can take place in a satisfactory way and can lead to a proper feeling of worth only on the useful side, in the developed social interest, where the individual senses himself as valuable. Valuable can mean nothing other than valuable for human society. In the neurosis one will always find an increased inferiority feeling which stems from earliest childhood. In accordance with this feeling the patient constantly seeks an easier way (with regard to society, occupation, sexuality), wants to reduce his sphere of activity considerably, and often expresses these desires in the death wish. Also on the useless, antisocial side of life, his increased inferiority feeling incites him towards a goal of personal superiority, or the semblance of superiority, generally looked for at the expense of others. The most serviceable moods and affects for this purpose, such as fear, rage, sadness, and guilt feelings, show in their own dynamics the tense attempt to advance from "below" to "above," from an increased inferiority feeling towards superiority over the other, the opponent. Thus, in each expressive movement, one can observe, in addition to the degree of social interest, the individual striving towards superiority. We shall be satisfied only when we have seen this dual dynamic in the neurotic symptom as acting in exactly the same way as in any other expression of life.

How may people who have mistaken the way to superiority be helped? It is not so difficult if we recognize that the striving for superiority is common to all men. We can then put ourselves in their position and sympathize with their struggles. The only mistake they make is that their strivings are on the useless side of life. It is the striving for superiority which is behind every human creation and it is the source of all contributions which are made to our culture. The whole of human life proceeds along this great line of action—from below to above, from minus to plus, from defeat to victory. The only individuals who can really meet and master the problems of life, however, are those who show in their striving a tendency to enrich all others, who go ahead in such a way that others benefit also. All human judgments of value and success are founded, in the end, upon cooperation; this is the great shared commonplace of the human race. We shall never find a man who is completely devoid of social feeling. The neurotic and the criminal also know this open secret; we can see their knowledge in the pains they take to justify their style of life or to throw responsibility elsewhere. They have lost courage, however, to proceed on the useful side of life. An inferiority complex tells them, "Success in cooperation is not for you." They have turned away from the real problems of life and are engaged in shadow-fighting to reassure themselves of their strength. [See pp. 157–159.]

D. Inferiority and Superiority Complexes

COMMENT *The inferiority complex is the term with which Adler's name is most often connected, yet it was in all probability not coined by him. Used by him variously to convey three different meanings, it represents no particularly new contribution to the theory of Individual Psychology in any way commensurate with its popularity.*

According to Oliver Brachfeld, Adler's first use of the term occurred in 1926 when, "in the course of his first lecturing tour in the United States, he realized that he had been called the 'father of the inferiority and superiority complex' . . . He had to bow to the power of this word, which he had begun by rejecting because of its definitely Freudian ring" (17, pp. 112–113 & 102). Brachfeld's statement is supported by the fact that the first use of the term attributed to Adler is found in an interview in the New York Times in the fall of 1925 (1925). Furthermore Adler referred in 1930 to "what is called in America, under the influence of Individual Psychology, the 'superiority complex' . . . the outcome of the 'inferiority complex' " (1930d, p. 122). Later the term also caught the public's attention in the German-speaking countries, and this to such an extent that the nickname, "Minko," became current to denote the Minderwertigkeitskomplex (1933g).

When Adler adopted the term in his writings he used it first as a synonym for the feeling of inferiority in general, the normal as well as the abnormal (1925, 1929a, p. 108; 1930d, p. 122). Although he subsequently limited the meaning of the term to the abnormally increased inferiority feeling, the first usage left its mark. Thus we find, for example, that when in 1927 Edna Heidbreder constructed a scale for measuring the trait of inferiority feeling, she entitled her paper "The Normal Inferiority Complex" (49).

Within a few years Adler used the term in two other senses. The first refers to abnormally increased inferiority feelings; this meaning we shall call, for the sake of clarity, the "inferiority [feeling] complex." The second refers to the means by which an individual "explains to himself and others that he is not strong enough to solve a given problem in a socially useful way" (1935b, p. 2). This usage does not denote the increased inferiority feeling itself but rather its outcome. It serves as an excuse, as many symptoms do, and we shall differentiate it from the first meaning by calling it the "inferiority [symptom] complex."

The superiority complex is likewise an outcome of the increased inferiority feeling; through this complex the individual demonstrates to himself and others his personal superiority, albeit in a socially useless way. The superiority complex was treated by Adler consistently as representing one form of faulty compensation for increased inferiority feelings, that is, as a symptom.

Insofar as the inferiority complex is a feeling complex, it belongs with the neurotic disposition. Insofar as it became a symptom complex, it might more properly belong, together with the superiority complex, in the next chapter, which deals with the significance of the symptoms. But we considered it preferable to treat all three complexes in one place.

1. INFERIORITY [FEELING] COMPLEX (1929, 1931)[14]

It is important to realize that it is not the sense of inferiority which matters but the degree and character of it. The abnormal feeling of inferiority has acquired the name of "inferiority [feeling] complex." But complex is not the correct word for this feeling of inferiority that permeates the whole personality. It is more than a complex, it is almost a disease whose ravages vary under different circumstances.

Every neurotic has an inferiority [feeling] complex. No neurotic is distinguished from other neurotics by the fact that he has an inferiority [feeling] complex and the others have none. He is distinguished from the others by the kind of situation in which he feels unable to continue on the useful side of life, by the limits he has put to his strivings and activities.

Inferiority feelings are in some degree common to all of us, since we all find ourselves in positions which we wish to improve. If we have kept our courage, we shall set about ridding ourselves of these feelings by the only direct, realistic and satisfactory means—by improving the situation. No human being can bear a feeling of inferiority for long; he will be thrown into a tension which necessitates some kind of action. But suppose an individual is discouraged; suppose he cannot conceive that if he makes realistic efforts he will improve the situation. He will still be unable to bear his feelings of inferiority; he will still struggle to get rid of them; but he will try methods which bring him no farther ahead. His goal is still "to be superior to difficulties," but instead of overcoming obstacles he will try to hypnotize himself, or autointoxicate himself, into feeling superior. Meanwhile his feelings of inferiority will accumulate, because the situation which produces them remains unaltered. The provocation is still there. Every step he takes will lead him farther into self-deception, and all his problems will press in upon him with greater and greater urgency. The real feelings of inferiority will remain. They will be the same old feelings of inferiority provoked by the same old situation. They will be the lasting undercurrent of his psychic life. In such a case we may truly speak of an inferiority [feeling] complex.

2. INFERIORITY [SYMPTOM] COMPLEX (1929, 1935, 1933) [16]

Everyone, as we have said, has a feeling of inferiority. But the feeling of inferiority is not a disease; it is rather a stimulant to healthy, normal striving and development. It becomes a pathological condition only when the sense of inadequacy overwhelms the individual and, far from stimulating him to useful activity, makes him depressed and incapable of development.

The inferiority [symptom] complex describes the attitude of an individual who by this complex expresses that he is not in the position to solve an existing problem. It must not be confused with the inferiority feeling. The inferiority [symptom] complex is the presentation of the person to himself and others that he is not strong enough to solve a given problem in a socially useful way. Needless to say, no point of rest is given in this way. The total mood with all its thought, feeling, and action material is continued into failure.

I have struggled a long time for a solution of the important question which arises in this connection, namely, how the inferiority feeling with its bodily and psychological consequences in the clash with a life problem develops into the inferiority [symptom] complex. I found the solution as in all other problems within the purview of Individual Psychology by seeking the explanation of the part by reference to the whole and of the whole by reference to the part. The inferiority [symptom] complex, that is, the persistence of the consequences of the feeling of inferiority and the retention of that feeling, finds its explanation in greater lack of social interest.

COMMENT *This understanding of the inferiority complex as a symptom is the one which has since become accepted among Individual Psychologists. According to Alexandra Adler: "We say that a person is suffering from an 'inferiority complex' when he reacts fatalistically* to a crippling situation, real or fancied, without attempting to correct or improve it. This should not be confused with the 'feeling of inferiority' which is present in everyone in certain situations, particularly in every child—a feeling which normally incites an individual to achieve future successful development" (1, p. 15). According to Rudolf Dreikurs: "The term 'inferiority complex' applies to an entirely different psychological mechanism [than inferiority feeling]. A discouraged individual may use a real or assumed deficiency for the purpose of special benefit, generally as an excuse or an alibi for non-participation and withdrawal, or as a means to get special services or considerations. This is the only type of inferiority of which the individual is fully aware, as he tries to impress others and his own conscience with the magnitude of his defect. The 'inferiority complex' does not lead to any compensation [it being a conscious symptom and as such the compensation itself, albeit an unsatisfactory one]. It is a deadlock for any further development" (28, p. 45).

3. SUPERIORITY COMPLEX (1929, 1931, 1933) [16]

We have seen how every symptom of an individual's life is expressed in a movement—in a progress. Thus the symptom may be said to have a past and a future. Now the future is tied up with our striving and with our goal, while the past represents the state of inferiority or inadequacy which we are trying to overcome. That is why in an inferiority [feeling] complex we are interested in the beginning, while in a superiority complex we are more interested in the continuity, in the progression of the movement itself. Moreover, the two complexes are naturally related. We should not be astonished if in the cases where we see an inferiority [feeling] complex we find a superiority complex more or less hidden. On the other hand, if we inquire into a superiority complex and study its continuity, we can always find a more or less hidden inferiority [feeling] complex.

We must bear in mind, of course, that the word complex as attached to inferiority [feeling] and superiority merely represents an exaggerated condition of the sense of inferiority and the striving for superiority. If we look at things this way it takes away the apparent paradox of two contradictory tendencies, the inferiority [feeling] complex and the superiority complex, existing in the same individual. As normal sentiments the striving for superiority and the feeling of inferiority are naturally complementary; we should not strive to be superior and to succeed if we did not feel a certain lack in our present condition. Now inasmuch as the so-called complexes develop out of the natural sentiments, there is no more contradiction in them than in the sentiments.

If a person is a show-off it is only because he feels inferior, because he does not feel strong enough to compete with others on the useful side of life. That is why he stays on the useless side. He is not in harmony with society. It seems to be a trait of human nature that when individuals— both children and adults—feel weak, they cease to be interested socially but strive for [personal] superiority. They want to solve the problems of life in such a way as to obtain personal superiority without any admixture of social interest. A superiority complex is a second phase. It is a compensation for the inferiority [feeling] complex.

Many neurotics, if they were asked whether they felt inferior, would answer, "No." Some would even answer, "Just the opposite. I know quite well that I am superior to the people around me." We do not need to ask; we need only watch the individual's behavior. It is there that we shall notice what tricks he uses to reassure himself of his importance. If we see someone who is arrogant, for example, we can guess that he feels, "Other people are apt to overlook me. I must show that I am somebody." If we see some one who gesticulates strongly when he speaks, we can guess that he feels, "My words would not carry any weight if I did not emphasize them." Behind every one who behaves as if he were superior to others, we can suspect a feeling of inferiority which calls for very special efforts of concealment. It is as if a man feared that he was too small and walked on his toes to make himself seem taller. Sometimes we can see this very behavior if two children are comparing their height. The one who is afraid that he is smaller will stretch up and hold himself very tensely; he will try to seem bigger than he is. If we asked such a child, "Do you think you are too small?" we should hardly expect him to acknowledge the fact.

The superiority complex is one of the ways which a person with an inferiority [feeling] complex may use as a method of escape from his difficulties. He assumes that he is superior when he is not, and this false success compensates him for the state of inferiority which he cannot bear. The normal person does not have a superiority complex, he does not even have a sense of superiority. He has the striving to be superior in the sense that we all have ambition to be successful; but so long as this striving is expressed in work it does not lead to false valuations, which are at the root of mental disease.

The superiority complex, as I have described it, appears usually clearly characterized in the bearing, the character traits, and the opinion of one's own superhuman gifts and capacities. It can also become visible in the exaggerated demands one makes on oneself and on other persons. Disdain; vanity in connection with personal appearance, whether in the way of elegance or neglect; an unfashionable mode of attire; exaggerated masculine conduct in women or feminine behavior in men; arrogance; exuberant emotion; snobbishness; boastfulness; a tyrannical nature; nagging; a tendency to depreciate; inordinate hero-worship, as well as an inclination to hobnob with prominent persons or to domineer over people who are weak or ill or of lesser stature; emphasis on one's own idiosyncrasies; the misuse of valuable ideas and movements in order to depreciate others: all these may direct attention to a possible superiority complex. Also heightened affects like anger, desire of revenge, grief, habitually loud laughter, inattentive listening, and looking away when meeting people, directing the conversation to oneself, habitual enthusiasm over trivial matters, point quite often to a feeling of inferiority ending in a superiority complex. Credulous assumptions, too, crediting oneself with the possession of telepathic or similar powers, or of prophetic inspiration, justifiably arouse the suspicion of a superiority complex.

I should like to warn those who are devoted to the idea of human welfare not to use this idea as a superiority complex of their own, or to thrust it thoughtlessly on everyone. The same warning applies to the knowledge of the inferiority complex and its concealing superstructure. One only makes oneself suspect of both complexes, if one throws these terms around rashly, and in doing so achieves nothing but often justified opposition. When one has correctly established such facts, one should not forget the universal faultiness of man, through which even noble and valuable persons may fall into the error of the superiority complex. To say nothing of the fact that, as Barbusse puts it so well, "Even the most kind-hearted man cannot always rid himself of the feeling of contempt."

FOOTNOTES TO CHAPTER NINE

1. 1, 2, 3: "Prevention of neurosis" (1935c), pp. 8, 8, and 8–9.
2. 1, 2, 3: "Prevention of neurosis" (1935c), pp. 9, 9, and 9–10.

3. 1 and 4: "Prevention of neurosis" (1935c), pp. 9 and 10; 2 and 3: "The neurotic's picture of the world" (1936d), pp. 4 and 6–7.

4. 1 and 2: "Die Tragfähigkeit der menschlichen Seele" (1923b), pp. 42 and 42.

5. 1 and 2: "Individualpsychologische Behandlung der Neurosen" (1913c), pp. 22 and 22; 3: Über den nervösen Charakter (1912a), 4th ed., p. 19.

6. 1 to 4: "Der nervöse Charakter" (1913b), pp. 145, 145, 145, and 146.

7. 1 to 4: Nervöser Charakter (1912a), pp. 22, 40, 86, and 83.

8. 1, 2, 3: Nervöser Charakter (1912a), pp. 30, 30, and 16.

9. 1 and 2: Nervöser Charakter (1912a), pp. 20 and 56; 3: "Individualpsychologische Behandlung" (1913c), p. 24.

10. 1 and 2: "Zusammenhänge zwischen Neurose und Witz" (1927c), pp. 94–96.

11. 1 to 4: "Neurose und Witz" (1927c), pp. 94–96.

12. 1: "Trick and neurosis" (1931f), p. 5; 2 and 3: What Life Should Mean to You (1931a), pp. 8–9 and 254–255; 4: "Neurotic's picture" (1936d), p. 13.

13. 1: "Die Individualpsychologie in der Neurosenlehre" (1929f), pp. 81–88; 2: What Life Should Mean to You (1931a), pp. 68–69.

14. 1: The Science of Living (1929c), p. 74; 2 and 3: What Life Should Mean to You (1931a), pp. 49 and 51–52.

15. 1: The Science of Living (1929c), pp. 96–97; 2: "Der Komplexzwang als Teil der Persönlichkeit und der Neurose" (1935b), pp. 1–6; 3: Der Sinn des Lebens (1933a), p. 76.

16. 1, 2, 3, 5: The Science of Living (1929c), pp. 78–79, 79, 83 and 85, and 97; 4: What Life Should Mean to You (1931a), pp. 49–50; 6 and 7: Sinn des Lebens (1933a), pp. 81–82 and 82.

CHAPTER TEN

NEUROTIC SAFEGUARDING BEHAVIOR

COMMENT *The preceding chapter was concerned essentially with the neurotic dynamics, that is, the striving for an exaggerated goal of superiority on the socially useless side. The present chapter deals with typical forms of neurotic behavior as the outcome of such motivational tendencies. The common function of neurotic behavior in all its varied forms is, according to Adler, to provide safeguards for the self-esteem which is bound up with the hidden goal of superiority.*

The first section of the present chapter discusses the function of the neurotic symptoms as safeguards and as excuses. As safeguards they serve an unconscious, hidden, function; as excuses a conscious function. The two functions often exist side by side. The next two sections describe the two possible forms which neurotic behavior, that is, behavior on the unconstructive or useless side, can take. The one form is that of aggression, the other that of withdrawal, which Adler called seeking distance.

A. The Function of the Neurotic Symptoms

1. SAFEGUARDS (1913)[1]

All neurotic symptoms have as their object the task of safeguarding the patient's self-esteem and thereby also the life-line [later, style of life] into which he has grown. To prove his ability to cope with life the patient needs arrangements and neurotic symptoms as an expedient. He needs them as an oversized safeguarding component against the dangers which, in his feeling of inferiority, he expects and incessantly seeks to avoid in working out his plans for the future.

Upon closer observation we find that in the neurotic all lines of direction are provided from various sides with warning signs and encouragements, with mementoes and invitations to action, so that one can speak of a far-flung net of safeguards. His mental life is a superstructure over a threatening childhood situation, although in the course of years this superstructure has become externally changed and better adapted to reality than the developmental stage of the child permitted. All this constitutes a rigid system, which permeates every psychological phenomenon of the neurotic. Once the system has been understood, the phenomena appear as figures of speech expressing the direction lines again and again. His path is unalterably safeguarded by his particular schemas of character traits, emotional readinesses, and symptoms.

COMMENT   This interpretation of the symptoms was one of the main controversial issues which led Adler to separate from Freud in 1911, the other having been the significance of sex in the neurosis. For Freud "the essential preliminary condition for the development of symptoms" was repression (38, p. 259), and the symptom itself was "a substitute for some other process which was held back by repression" (38, p. 262). "The symptom has its origin in the repressed, it is as it were the representative of the repressed in relation to the ego" (41, p. 82). According to Adler's safeguarding theory, the symptom had its origin in the self or the "ego," if one wishes to use this term. Adler accepted repression, if at all, only as one of the many safeguarding devices. "If drive-repressions appear, these are only incidental phenomena which form under the accentuated pressure of the masculine protest and of the striving for significance and the safeguarding tendencies" (1911b, p. 110), all functions of the self or "ego." This view was quite unacceptable to Freud at a time when an "odium of analytical unorthodoxy . . . attached to the study of the ego" (32, p. 4).

Fifteen years later, however, Freud revised his theory on this point. He then presented, on his own, the view that (1) repression is not always or necessarily the precondition for the development of symptoms, (2) repression itself is but one of the ego defenses, and (3) all symptoms are a form of defense. Thus he now accepted three important points which he had strongly contested at first, when they were presented by Adler.

It is true that as early as 1894 and 1896 Freud had used the term defense (Abwehr) in connection with neuroses and psychoses (36, I, pp. 59–75 and pp. 155–182). But this was in a very limited sense, applying only to certain specific forms of such disorders, and so we find that by 1905 he had replaced defense by the concept of repression (36, I, p. 279). When defense became Freud's new generic principle in the 1920's it no longer had the above mentioned limited meaning of his 1890 papers, but was a "general designation for all the techniques which the ego makes use of in conflicts which may lead to a neurosis" (40, p. 158). Freud had found "good enough grounds for reintroducing the old concept of defence . . . and for subsuming repression under it as a special instance" (40, p. 157).

Despite the similarity which from then on existed between Freud's "defense mechanisms" and Adler's earlier "safeguarding devices," a fundamental difference of basic theory remained. Freud's defenses provide "protection of the ego against instinctual demands" (40, p. 157); whereas Adler's safeguards protect the self-esteem from threats by outside demands and problems of life. These respective explanations are consistent with Freud's biological and Adler's social orientation.

When the term ego defense is used today, this is most often in the sense of the Adlerian safeguarding device, that is, in the sense of safeguarding the subjective self and self-ideal from threatening outside situations. This meaning received acceptance even in psychoanalytic circles when Anna Freud in 1936 recognized that, at least in children, defenses are not limited to "the warding off of internal instinctual stimuli," but may also apply to dangers which have their source in the outside world (32, pp. 73–74).

2. EXCUSES (1929, 1936) [2]

The patient [unknowingly] selects certain symptoms and develops them until they impress him [consciously] as real obstacles. Behind his barricade of symptoms the patient feels hidden and secure. To the question, "What use are you making of your talents?" he answers, "This thing stops me; I cannot go ahead," and points to his self-erected barricade. We must never neglect the patient's own use of his symptoms. To be overworked by grappling with his own neurotic difficulties is not only an extenuating circumstance, it is also the patient's inner relief from his striving for superiority. He really expects less of himself. Such a self-protective style of life may also take a form in which the individual feels himself overwhelmed with social difficulties.

The entire interest of the neurotic is turned to the shock results, the symptoms. The actual task which threatened loss of prestige is almost forgotten. The patient declares that he is unable to solve his task "on account of the symptoms, and only on account of these." He expects from the others the solution of his problems, or the excuse from all demands, or, at least, the granting of "extenuating circumstances." When he has his extenuating alibi, he feels that his prestige is protected. His line of success, embedded into the life process, can remain uninterrupted —by paying the price. The important principle of life, the desire to solve a problem successfully, is no longer threatened.

3. THE PRICE OF THE SYMPTOMS (1930, 1933, 1936) [8]

Without doubt the neurotic does suffer, but he always prefers his present sufferings to those greater sufferings he would experience were he to appear defeated in regard to the solution of his problems. He would rather put up with these sufferings than have his worthlessness disclosed. Whereas he will persist in saying "I should like to get well again, I want to get rid of the symptom" and will even go to consult a doctor, he does not know that there is something else which would make him suffer still more, namely, being proven worthless. We see now what a neurotic state actually is. It is an attempt to avoid a greater evil, an attempt to maintain the semblance of value at any price, and paying the costs. But at the same time the neurotic would like to reach his goal without any cost at all.

The suffering of the patient is real, usually exaggerated as a protection against loss of prestige. It is a general abuse in the psychiatric literature to think that the patient fled into the neurosis as if he were in love with his symptoms, as if he did not want to give up his symptoms. Quite on the contrary, he would like to give them up, if that would not mean risking an apparently greater evil: the danger of death, through loss of prestige.

Why does the patient suffer? Let us assume that he would enjoy his symptoms. Then we should possibly have a case of melancholia or schizophrenia. This would mean that the patient had detached himself from the ties of social interest so completely that he lost the logic or reason which binds us all. But this is not the case in neuroses. In compulsion neurosis, for example, the patient himself regards his thoughts as foolish. Foolish, however, as they may be from the point of view and the goal of a fellow man, they are none the less perfectly suited as a means of the patient to detach himself from the task of which he is afraid and to justify his position on the useless side of life. He would lose this justification if he were happy in his neurotic actions. Therefore, he suffers.

COMMENT *Although Adler describes the symptoms as a purposive creation of the individual, this must not be taken as a conscious process. If it were conscious, it would destroy the self-consistency of the individual's personality structure, or style of life. If the patient realized that his "barricade" were "self-erected," as Adler describes it above, or that he were paying a price for his alibi, or that he were using his symptom for postponing a test he fears, the symptom's purpose of serving as an excuse would automatically be defeated. Therefore all this remains unconscious. To quote Adler: "A character trait will be wholly or partly 'in the unconscious' depending on what the self-consistency of the personality requires" (1912a, p. 217).*

Adler was sometimes misinterpreted as ignoring unconscious factors. But this was decidedly not the case, although he did tend to avoid the use of the term unconscious, substituting such words as "hidden" or "not understood," in order to avoid any reification of the "unconscious."

B. Safeguarding through Aggression

COMMENT *It was Adler, not Freud, who introduced the concept of an aggression drive, as has been shown in Chapter 1. Although Adler gave up this concept and employed the term aggression only rarely, aggression as a form of behavior continued to play a large part in his understanding of the neuroses. Adler subsumed aggression under the larger concept of striving for overcoming, where aggression is but one of the forms this striving may take when the social interest remains underdeveloped, and where it may often manifest itself in very subtle ways.*

In the following the depreciation tendency, open accusation of others, and self-accusation or guilt are presented as forms of aggression for the purpose of safeguarding the self-esteem.

1. DEPRECIATION (1911, 1912)[4]

False valuations, whether over- or under-valuations, are of the greatest concern for the psychological dynamics in normal life and for the neurosis, and require the most searching interest of Individual Psychology.

"The fox and the sour grapes" is an instructive example. Instead of becoming conscious of his own inferiority, the fox devalues the grapes and so remains in good humor. He is set on ideas of grandeur. This kind of psychological process serves primarily the purpose of clinging to the fiction of one's "free will" and, in connection with this, of one's own value. Over-valuations of one's own achievements and goals serve the same purpose; they are enforced through the flight from the dark feeling of one's inferiority, and are arranged by, and originate in, the exaggerated safeguarding tendency against the feeling of being "below."

In this depreciation tendency of the neurotic, which cannot be overrated, we find the origin of the important reinforcement of certain character traits representing further readinesses intended to injure other persons, such as sadism, hatred, always wanting to have the last word, intolerance, and envy. Active homosexuality, perversions which disparage the partner, and sex murder also follow from the depreciation tendency, as concretized symbolism of conquest according to the schema of the sexual superiority of the male. In brief, the neurotic may enhance his self-esteem by disparaging the other person, in the most serious cases becoming lord over life and death, his own life as well as that of the other person.

a. *Idealization.* It is one of the most effective attitudes of the neurotic to measure thumbs down, so to speak, a real person by an ideal, since in doing so he can depreciate him as much as he wishes.

A short girl prefers tall men; or a girl falls in love only when the parents have forbidden it, while treating the attainable [partner] with open disdain and hostility. In the conversation and thoughts of such girls the limiting word "only" always crops up. They want only an educated man, only a rich man, only a real he-man, only platonic love, only a childless marriage, only a man who will grant his wife complete freedom. Here one sees the depreciation tendency so strongly at work that, in the end, hardly a man is left who would satisfy their requirements. Usually they have a ready-made, often unconscious, ideal to which traits of the father, a brother, a fairy-tale hero, a literary or historical character are admixed. The more we become familiar with these ideals, the greater becomes our conviction that they have been posited as a fictional measure by which to depreciate reality.

The depreciation of the partner is the most usual phenomenon in neurotics. In some cases this may be obvious. In others this may be so deeply hidden that many readers may search their case material in vain for verification of this statement. One finds so many masochistic and "feminine traits," far-reaching tendencies toward submission and hypnotizability! The hysterical desire for the great strong man before whom one can bow has always captured our attention. How many of the neurotic patients are full of admiration for their physician and pile hymns of praise on him! This may appear like being in love, but the bitter end follows. Such patients cannot tolerate subordination, and the next step in their reasoning is: "What a weakling I am. Of what submission am I capable. By all means I must safeguard myself against falling." This situation may be compared to that of a man preparing for a high jump, who takes a few steps backwards and crouches way down low in order to jump all the higher. In the same way the neurotic crouches at first, only to disregard subsequently the other person all the more.

b. *Solicitude.* I have found a further interesting kind of disparagement among neurotic patients in their solicitude, their anxious behavior, and their fears for the fate of other persons. They act as if without their aid the others would be incapable of caring for themselves. They always give advice, want to do everything themselves, find new dangers, and never rest until the other person, confused and discouraged, confides himself to their care. Neurotic parents thus create much damage; many frictions in love and marriage also arise in this fashion. The neurotic aspires to make the laws for the others. One of my patients who had been run over twice during his childhood, associated his damaged self-esteem with this recollection. Whenever he crossed the street in the company of someone else, he anxiously led the other person by the arm as if he did not credit him with the ability to get there without help. Many people are worried when their relatives travel by rail, or go swimming or boating; they give incessant instructions to the nurse maid; and continue their depreciation tendency by exaggerated criticisms and reproofs. In every school and office one finds nervous teachers and superiors given to such nagging disparagements.

2. ACCUSATION (1912, 1914, 1929) [5]

Neurosis invariably gives relief to the subject, not, of course, in the light of objectivity and common sense, but according to his own private logic. It secures some triumph or at least allays the fear of defeat. Thus neurosis is the weapon of the coward and the weak. We cannot ignore the heavily-veiled aggressive or vindictive element in most neuroses.

In the investigation of a neurotic style of life we must always suspect an opponent, and note who suffers most because of the patient's condition. Usually this is a member of the family. There is always this element of concealed accusation in neurosis, the patient feeling as though he were deprived of his right—that is, of the center of attention—and wanting to fix the responsibility and blame upon someone. By such hidden vengeance and accusation, by excluding social activity whilst fighting against persons and rules, the problem child and the neurotic find some relief from their dissatisfaction. There are cases in which the revenge motive is fairly obvious, as it was with a neurotic woman I treated whose marriage was entirely unhappy, and who yet would never divorce her husband, preferring to remain a continual accusation against him. It must be remembered, however, that neurotics generally, like perverts, drunkards, and morphia-maniacs, have not wholly denied their social feeling.

These logical interpretations are frequently intermixed with compensating ambition or, as in children, with aggression towards the parents. "It is the fault of my parents, my fate; because I am the youngest, was born too late; because I am a Cinderella; because I am perhaps not the child of these parents, of this father, of this mother; because I am too small, too weak, have too small a head, am too homely; because I have a speech defect, a hearing defect, am cross-eyed, nearsighted; because I have misshaped genitals, because I am not manly, because I am a girl; because I am by nature bad, stupid, awkward; because I have masturbated; because I am too sensuous, too covetous, and naturally perverted; because I submit easily, am too dependent and obedient; because I cry easily, am easily moved; because I am a criminal, a thief, an incendiary, and could murder someone; my ancestry, my education, my circumcision are to blame; because I have a long nose, too much hair, too little hair; because I am a cripple; because I have been pampered, and because I have been discriminated against." Such are the attempts of the child to unburden himself by blaming fate—just as in the Greek dramas and fate tragedies—to save his self-esteem, and to attribute blame to others. These attempts are regularly met with in the psychological treatment of the neuroses, and can always be referred back to the relationship between the inferiority feeling and the ideal.

The life plan of the neurotic demands categorically that if he fails, it should be through someone else's fault and that he should be freed from personal responsibility; or that, if his triumph is prevented, it should be by a fatal detail only. The common human element in this desire is striking. When the individual helps it along with his devices, then the entire content of life is permeated by the reassuring, anesthetizing stream of the life-lie which safeguards the self-esteem. Every therapeutic cure, and still more, any awkward attempt to show the patient the truth, tears him from the cradle of his freedom from responsibility and must therefore reckon with the most vehement resistance.

I regard it as an extremely useful guide for the illumination of a psychogenic disease picture to raise the question of "the opponent." The answer to this question shows us the patient no longer in an artificial isolation, but in his socially given system. The belligerent tendency of the neurosis and psychosis can then be easily understood. The specific disorder, which otherwise could be taken as the end of the consideration, is now put into its rightful place as a means, a method of life, a symptom of the path which the patient takes to arrive at his goal of superiority or at least to feel that it is his due.

In certain forms of psychosis, and also in neurotic patients the attack and accusation are not aimed at a single person, but at a number of people, the opposite sex, occasionally at the whole of humanity, or the entire world order. This behavior becomes very clearly evident in paranoia. On the other hand, in dementia praecox the condemnation of the world is intended by the complete turning away from it. The battle of the hypochondriac and melancholic is more hidden, and limited to a few persons.

3. SELF-ACCUSATION AND GUILT (1912 TO 1933) [6]

Prominent among the forms of neurotic behavior which safeguard the superiority fiction are cursing oneself, reproaching oneself, self-torture, and suicide. This may seem strange, until we realize that the whole arrangement of the neurosis follows the trait of self-torture, that the neurosis is a self-torturing device for the purpose of enhancing the self and depreciating the immediate environment. And indeed the first stirrings of the aggression drive directed against one's own person originate from a situation in which the child wants to hurt the parents or wants to attract their attention more effectively.

Often one finds in the psychology of masturbation an admixture of atonement or of an intention to hurt someone, the latter like a defiant revolt against the parents or against life itself, the former as a cheap pretence or hypocritical act. To injure another person through atonement is one of the most subtle devices of the neurotic, as when, for example, he indulges in self-accusations. Ideas of suicide reveal the same mechanism, which becomes particularly clear in suicide pacts. In depression related traits are also found.

A depressed woman who domineered over her husband developed a guilt complex, which often happens in such a situation. She remembered that she had deceived her husband with another man some twenty-five years before, during all which time this event had played no further part in her life. But all at once she told her husband and accused herself. This so-called guilt complex, which we should wholly misunderstand by the Freudian interpretation, was quite clearly an attack upon the husband who was no longer obedient. She could hurt him by confession and self-accusation. Who is so simple as to think that it is a case of the majesty of the truth vindicating itself after a quarter of a century? The truth is often a terrible weapon of aggression. It is possible to lie, and even to murder, with the truth. Nietzsche, with a most penetrating vision and from the same standpoint as we take for Individual Psychology, described the feeling of guilt as mere wickedness. And in the majority of neurotic cases the fact is that a guilt complex is used as a means to fix its maker on the useless side of life.

The following is a case of religious guilt feelings in a very ambitious eighteen-year-old girl. She was a very good and capable girl, and especially conscientious about carrying out all her religious obligations. One day she began to reproach herself for not having been sufficiently pious, for having transgressed religious commandments, and for having often entertained sinful thoughts. When she finally carried things so far as to spend all day accusing herself, her family began to be seriously concerned about her state of mind. Actually there was not the least thing with which one could reproach her. One day her spirtual adviser attempted to relieve her of her entire burden of sins by explaining to her that these were no sins at all, and that she was free. The next day the girl planted herself before him in the street and shouted out that he was unworthy of entering the church because he had taken such a great burden of sin upon himself.

COMMENT Guilt, which has just been shown as aggressive behavior, can also serve in the interest of gaining distance, that is, withdrawing. The same is also true of anxiety behavior, which is described below under distance behavior and which frequently has a component of aggression. Since all forms of behavior are in the service of the goal to be attained, it is indeed possible that guilt or anxiety, or other forms of behavior, may at one time be used for withdrawing and at another time for aggression, or for both purposes simultaneously. The following passage is an illustration of guilt as distance behavior, and thus constitutes the transition from this section to the next.

Preference for the hinterland of life is notably safeguarded by the individual's mode of thinking and argumentation, occasionally also by compulsive thinking, or by fruitless guilt feelings. It is not the guilt feelings, however, that bring about distance; rather the defective inclination and preparation of the whole personality find such feelings advantageous for preventing any advance. Groundless self-accusation on account of masturbation, for example, supplies a suitable pretext for practicing it. Looking back on his past everyone would like to have many things undone. But in the case of the neurotic such regrets serve as an excellent excuse for not cooperating. The attempt to trace failures like neurosis or crime to such tricky guilt feelings means to misjudge the seriousness of the situation.

c. Safeguarding through Distance

1. THE FOURFOLD MODUS OF DISTANCE (1914) [7]

In the neurosis we meet with generally human traits, although without inner balance and to a stronger degree. The essential tendency of the neurotic is the striving from the feeling of inferiority toward "above." If we adhere to this view, we find as the resultant combination of these two moods [the feeling of inferiority and the striving toward "above"] a neurotic constant back-and-forth, a half-and-half, the conduct of powerless exaltation, where at one time the trait of powerlessness, at another time the trait of exaltation becomes more prominent. This process is most clearly visible in manic-depressive insanity. As in neurotic indecision or compulsion neurosis or phobia, the result is a "nothing," or almost a "nothing." In the more favorable cases the patient seems to make his actions contingent upon preparing a situation which appears more difficult than it actually is and upon furnishing a proof of illness.

This peculiar process is demonstrable in all neuroses and psychoses, and has been described by me in detail as the "hesitating attitude." Favorable circumstances permit me now to strengthen this view further. At the same time that one recognizes in the attitude and the devices of the neurotic his demand for a superior flawlessness, one is regularly surprised to find that he interrupts the expected direction of his action at a certain point of his aggression. We are always struck by the fact that the patient at this particular stage is certain to interpose a "distance" between himself and the expected action or decision. Usually the entire disturbance is like stage fright. Simultaneously with the purposeful setting up of a distance, which frequently also becomes manifest through a bodily expressive movement, the patient secludes himself from the world and reality in various degrees. Every psychiatrist will be able to fit this picture easily into his experiences, especially if he keeps in mind the many degrees in which seclusion is encountered. For greater clarity I wish to describe a fourfold modus of this behavior.

a. *Moving Backward*. This category includes suicide, suicide attempts; severe cases of agoraphobia; fainting, psychoepileptic attacks; compulsive blushing and severe compulsion neurosis; *asthma nervosum*; migraine and severe hysterical pains; hysterical paralysis; abulia; mutism; severe anxiety attacks of all kinds; refusal to take food; amnesia, hallucination; psychosis; alcoholism, morphinism; vagabondage and criminal tendencies. Anxiety, falling, and criminal dreams are frequent in such cases and indicate exaggerated forethought, the fear of what might conceivably happen. The concept of external compulsion is tremendously extended, and every social, even every personal obligation, is warded off with exaggerated sensitivity. In severe cases every useful activity is prevented. Through the proof of illness the patient can, on the positive side, enforce his own will, and on the negative side, remain victorious over the normal social obligations. This is also true for the following three categories.

b. *Standing Still*. It is as if a witches' circle had been drawn around the patient, which prevents him from moving closer toward the reality of life, from facing the truth, from taking a stand, from permitting a test or a decision regarding his value. Occupational tasks, examinations, social, love, and marital relations serve as exciting causes as soon as they appear as problems of life. Anxiety, a weak memory, insomnia with subsequent incapacity for work, compulsion phenomena, impotence, *ejaculatio praecox*, masturbation, perversions, asthma, hysterical psychosis—these are all safeguarding arrangements to prevent transgression of the boundaries. The less severe cases of the first category [moving backward] also belong here. The frequent dreams of being hampered, of failing in one's purpose, of missing a train, or of examinations often represent concretely the patient's life-line and the way in which he breaks off at a certain point and constructs the distance. Niebuhr writes in his *History of Rome*, III, 248: "National, like personal, vanity is more ashamed of the kind of failure which reveals limits of strength than of the greatest dishonor which results from lazy and cowardly omission of all efforts. Through the former, vain aspirations are destroyed; in the latter they continue."

c. *Hesitation and Back-and-Forth*. These forms secure the distance, and often end with the excuse of the above disorders or of a "too late." They are clearly efforts to waste time, a fertile field for compulsion neuroses. Usually the following mechanism can be found: first a difficulty is created and sanctioned, and then its conquest is attempted, in vain. Washing compulsion, pathological pedantry, fear to touch (a spatial expression of the arrangement of distance), coming too late, retracing one's steps, destroying work begun (Penelope), or always leaving something unfinished are found very often. Equally often one sees that the patient, under an "irresistible" compulsion toward some unimportant activity or amusement, delays a piece of work or a decision until it is too late. Or, shortly before the decision, an artificially constructed impediment is apt to occur (for example, stage fright). This behavior shows a clear relationship to the preceding category [standing still], except that there the decision is completely prevented. A frequent type of dream, representing a groping attempt of the life-plan, is a back-and-forth of some kind or a coming-too-late. The superiority and safeguarding of the patient can be seen from a fiction which is often expressed or remains unexpressed, but is never understood. This fiction begins with an "if" clause: "If I didn't have . . . (this affliction), I would be the first." As a rule the if-clause contains an unfulfillable condition, or the patient's own arrangement, which only he can change. It is understandable that he will not give up this life-lie as long as he maintains his life-plan.

d. *Construction of Obstacles*. These are less severe cases, in which the individual always manages somehow to be active in life and may even be prominent. Some cases develop spontaneously; others develop from more severe cases with the aid of some medical cure. In the latter the physician as well as the patient believes that a left-over from the disorder has remained. But this left-over is only the old distance, which the patient now uses differently, and with greater social interest. Whereas formerly he created the distance in order to break off, he now creates it in order to overcome it. The meaning or the goal of this attitude is easily divined: the patient's self-esteem is protected in his own judgment, and usually also his prestige in the estimation of others. If the decision falls against him, he can refer to his difficulties and to the proof of his illness which he has himself constructed. If he remains victorious, what could he not have done if he were well, when, as a sick man, he achieved so much—one-handed, so to speak! The arrangements of this category are: less severe anxiety or compulsion conditions; fatigue (neurasthenia); sleeplessness; constipation, stomach and intestinal disorders which consume strength and time and also require a pedantic, time-consuming routine; compulsive pedantries; headaches; poor memory; irritability, moodiness; pedantic demands for submission of the environment, and continuous preparation for conflicts with it; masturbation and pollutions from which superstitious conclusions are drawn; etc. In this way the patient always puts himself to the test of whether he is really capable and arrives consciously or implicitly at the conclusion of a pathological insufficiency. Often this result lies implicitly, but understandably, in the neurotic arrangement which is fostered by the life-plan of the patient. The battle of the patient with his symptom, to which are added his complaint, his desperation, and possible guilt feelings in the stage of the fully-developed neurosis, is suited primarily to emphasize strongly the significance of the symptom in the eyes of the patient and of his environment.

2. ANXIETY (1927) [8]

Once a person has acquired the attitude of running away from the difficulties of life, this attitude may be greatly strengthened and safeguarded by the addition of anxiety. There are, indeed, people whose first impulse is anxiety whenever they are faced with any undertaking such as leaving home, separating from a companion, applying for a job, or when love beckons. They are so little connected with life and with their fellow men that any change in their accustomed situation brings them fear. Consequently, any development of their personality and capability remains inhibited. Although the anxious individual does not always begin to tremble and run away immediately, his pace is slowed down, and he finds all kinds of pretexts and excuses. Sometimes he will be quite unaware that his anxious attitude came to the fore under the pressure of a new situation.

In individuals with an attitude of hostility toward their environment we often find traits of anxiety which lend a particular coloring to their character. Anxiety is an extraordinarily far-flung phenomenon which accompanies a person from his earliest days, often into his old age. It embitters his life to a marked degree, renders him quite unsuited for making contacts, and thus also for laying the basis for a peaceful life and for fruitful accomplishments. Fear can extend itself to all relationships of human life. One can be afraid of the outer world or of one's own inner world, and hence, one may either avoid society because one fears it, or one may be afraid of being alone. In the anxious person we shall meet again the well-known type who feels himself forced by necessity to think more of himself and consequently has little left over for his fellow man.

As though in confirmation of this view one often finds that such people are inclined to think of the past or of death, which has about the same effect. To think about the past is an unobtrusive, and therefore popular, means of shirking. Also, fear of death or disease is often found in people who look for an excuse to forego all achievement. Or they emphasize that all is vanity, after all, that life is short, and one cannot know what will happen. The consolation of religion with the hereafter can have the same effect, by making a person see his actual goal only in the hereafter and the existence on earth as a very superfluous endeavor, as a valueless phase of his development.

3. EXCLUSION TENDENCY (1930 TO 1936) [9]

COMMENT *The following represents a later version of the observations presented under the Fourfold Modus of Distance, together with some additional material.*

The neurotic's faulty picture of the world is constantly being so shaken by reality that he feels threatened from many sides. Consequently he narrows down his sphere of activity; he always presents pedantically the same opinions and the same attitudes which he accepted early in his life. Eventually, as a result of the "narrowing down" process, he shows an inferiority complex with all its consequences. Then, in order to escape this inferiority complex and because he finally sees himself threatened by the problem of death, he convulsively constructs a superiority complex. This is a compensatory movement.

For the safeguarding of his picture of the world and for the defense of his vanity, the neurotic erects a wall against the demands of actual community life. Without clearly realizing it himself, he excludes or shoves aside all disturbing problems of life, while he abandons himself utterly to his feelings and to the observation of his symptoms. These symptoms are the result of the shock which he experiences when, in a difficult situation, he feels himself too weak to arrive at the high goal which he, in his vanity, has set for himself; when he feels too weak to play a pre-eminent role commensurate with that which should be his according to his picture of the world. Thus he is able to avoid the shock of imminent problems and to relegate these problems to the background. Such a procedure of exclusion naturally appears to him the lesser of two evils.

The neurotic's life style and his picture of the world are parts of one integral system. He sees everything with the eyes of his vanity. He approaches every situation and problem of life with fearful anticipation as to whether his prestige will be assured, seldom finds this to be the case, and therefore feels compelled to withdraw from the problems of life. His retreat is effected by means of his symptoms; and the symptoms are the results of shock effects. These shock effects he has found useful in obtaining relief from a difficult situation. There is then no incentive for him to give up the shock effects which have served a purpose for him; so he holds on to them.

To some degree or other, every neurotic restricts his sphere of action, his contacts with the whole situation. He tries to keep at a distance the real confronting problems of life and confines himself to circumstances in which he feels able to dominate. In this way he builds for himself a narrow stable, closes the door, and spends his life away from the wind, the sunlight, and the fresh air.

The so-called Oedipus complex is in reality nothing more than a special instance of the "narrow stable" of the neurotic. If an individual is afraid to meet the problem of love in the world at large, he will not succeed in ridding himself of this problem. If he confines his field of action to the family circle, it will not surprise us to find that his sexual strivings also are elaborated within these limits. Because of his feeling of insecurity he has never spread his interest outside the few people with whom he is most familiar. He fears that with others he would not be able to dominate in his accustomed way. We could probably induce an Oedipus complex in any child. All we should need is for his mother to spoil him, and refuse to spread his social interest to other people, and for his father to be comparatively indifferent or cold. [See pp. 375–376.]

This picture of restricted movement is given by all the symptoms of neurosis. In the speech of the stammerer we can see his hesitating attitude. His residue of social feeling drives him to make connection with his fellows, but his low opinion of himself, his fear of coming to the test, conflict with his social feeling, and he hesitates in his speech. Children who are "backward" at school, men and women who have found no occupation by the age of thirty or more, or have shelved the problem of marriage, compulsion neurotics who must carry out the same action again and again, insomniacs who weary themselves for the tasks of the day —all of these reveal the inferiority complex which forbids them to make progress in solving the problems of life. Masturbation, premature ejaculation, impotence, and perversion all show a halting style of life, consequent on a fear of inadequacy in the approach to the other sex. The concomitant goal of supremacy will suggest itself if we ask, "Why so afraid of inadequacy?" The answer can only be, "Because the individual has set for himself so high a goal of success."

In the narrowness of the "abnormal" frame of reference the variety, the change of phenomena, and the adaptation to new life problems and demands of the day are excluded. But to some extent such exclusion, and therefore such repetition, is found in everyone. Contrary to the view of many recent characterologies, what we call character is the always repeated way, the guiding line, the way in which one behaves towards the problems of life on the strength of one's style of life. The style of life itself can come about only through the exclusion of forms of expression which are less suited, and through a kind of abstraction. It is exactly the same with regard to style in painting, in architecture, or in music. We could understand neither a healthy nor a sick person, if we had not comprehended, consciously or unconsciously, his habitual, always-repeated forms of expression. Any experience and concept formation always occurs under the necessity of exclusion. But the nervous individual formulates his style of life more rigidly, more narrowly; he is nailed to the cross of his narrow, personal, noncooperative fiction, as I explained originally in 1912 in my book *The Nervous Character*.

FOOTNOTES TO CHAPTER TEN

1. **1 and 2:** "Individualpsychologische Behandlung der Neurosen" (1913c), p. 25.
2. **1:** *Problems of Neurosis* (1929b), p. 13; **2:** "Das Todesproblem in der Neurose" (1936b), pp. 1–6.
3. **1:** *Social Interest* (1933b), pp. 164–165; **2:** "Todesproblem" (1936b), pp. 1–6; **3:** *Das Problem der Homosexualität* (1930c), pp. 50–51.
4. **1 and 5:** "Beitrag zum Verständnis des Widerstands in der Behandlung" (1911c), pp. 102n and 104; **2, 3, 4, 6:** *Über den nervosen Charakter* (1912a), 4th ed., pp. 29, 109, 123, and 168.
5. **1 and 2:** *Problems of Neurosis* (1929b), pp. 80 and 81–82; **3:** *Nervöser Charakter* (1912a), p, 36; **4, 5, 6:** "Lebenslüge und Verantwortlichkeit in der Neurose und Psychose" (1914c), p. 178.
6. **1 and 2:** *Nervoser Charakter* (1912a), pp. 201 and 202; **3:** *Problems of Neurosis* (1929b), p. 24; **4:** *Menschenkenntnis* (1927a), p. 214; **5:** *Der Sinn des Lebens* (1933a), p. 74.
7. **1 to 6:** "Das Problem der 'Distanz'" (1914b), pp. 73, 73–74, 74, 74, 74–75, and 75–76.
8. **1, 2, 3:** *Menschenkenntnis* (1927a), pp. 189, 188–189, and 189.
9. **1, 2, 3:** "The neurotic's picture of the world" (1936d), pp. 3–4, 11, and 13; **4, 5, 6:** *What Life Should Mean to You* (1931a), pp. 53, 54, and 54–55; **7:** "Nochmals—Die Einheit der Neurosen" (1930e), pp. 201–216.

CHAPTER ELEVEN

THE ONSET OF THE NEUROSIS

COMMENT In the preceding chapter were discussed the main characteristics of neurotic behavior, its functions in general,
and the principal forms which it may take. The present chapter will
focus more specifically on the problem: by what processes and under
what conditions is the neurotically disposed individual prone to develop
an actual neurosis with specific symptoms? The problem is handled in
the following steps, which roughly coincide with the four sections of the
chapter. (1) The basic process is the creative ability by which the individual, under certain conditions, reaches for suitable neurotic behavior
and symptoms to protect his unconscious self-ideal and to provide himself with excuses. (2) This process is supported by the individual's organic
condition, his previous experiences, and particularly his oversensitivity,
a general trait of the neurotic disposition. (3) The individual takes recourse to neurotic symptoms when confronted with problems which he
interprets as threatening, that is, as too difficult to cope with. What will
assume the character of an exogenous factor is relative to the individual's
interpretation. There are, however, certain general situations which are
likely to become exogenous factors.

A. The Subjective Factor

1. CREATIVITY AND GOAL ORIENTATION[1]

We can understand symptom selection only if we regard it as a piece
of art. We must refrain from making judgments, and can only admire
how every human being is an artist on his life's road. In this creative act
which is before us, the creator of which is always the respective patient,
or whatever you wish to call him, one trait is invariably found, and that

is the striving for a kind of perfection. Whoever speaks of symptom selection must associate it with the idea that it is concerned with something purposive, with something that can be grasped and understood only from a teleological point of view.

The individual's artful construction of his form of life, which is not only reaction, but to a large extent action, follows by no means a causal process. The decisive factor is always the concretized fictional goal of life in the sense of a superiority, which in the case of the "abnormal" coincides with a greater lack in the ability to cooperate. In his inability to cooperate the discouraged neurotic fills in his frame of reference concretely in a narrowness which represents the last space of movement left to him, after he has excluded all ways to a better cooperation, in order to gain exaggerated security against an anticipated defeat.

The neurosis and psychosis are attempts at compensation, creations of the psyche which result from the accentuated and exaggerated guiding idea of the child who has an accentuated inferiority feeling. The insecurity of these children regarding their future and success in life compels them toward stronger efforts and safeguards in their fictional life-plan and toward detours around the problems of life. The more fixed and rigid their guiding image, the more dogmatically will they draw the guiding lines of their life. The more cautious they become in doing so, the further do they spin their thoughts out into the future. The necessary character traits are an organization of these thoughts at the peripheral end where the clash with the environment is to take place; they are outposts of the psychological readinesses of such persons. The neurotic character with its enormous sensitivity, makes contact with reality in order to change it or to subjugate it in accordance with the personality ideal. When defeat threatens, the neurotic symptoms and readinesses become effective, inhibiting the progress of action.

The guiding fiction selects only the useful psychological elements, and organizes self-consistently only those abilities and memories which turn out to be well-suited for the finale. In the neurotic reorganization of the psyche, the guiding fiction is the absolute ruler and uses the experiences according to their suitability as if the psyche were static, real material.

2. METAPHORICAL THINKING[2]

If I have a goal before me to avoid achievement and I am trained from childhood on through my timidity to let someone else do the work for me, to accompany me, to protect me, to deprive this person of his freedom and make him subordinate to me, then I must, of course, being on this road, fortify it as much as possible so that I can reach my goal in security. How do I create anxiety which permits me to exclude necessary achievements, and forces another person to ease that burden of anxiety for me? The patients tell very plainly how they do it, although they do not understand what they say. "I feel the floor swaying; I think of the death of my husband, or of my own death; I feel that I shall faint, that I may get a heart attack." Especially in pampered people the thought of the death of others plays an unbelievable part because in this event their support might be lost. The patient is continuously occupied with the thought of how miserable he then would be. Through this thought, which touches the very necessities of his life, he is able to create by the use of empathy an anxiety such as if the person concerned had already died. He identifies with a situation which could possibly happen in the future. This can best be observed in depressed or melancholic individuals who live as if the misfortune had already happened.

Thus, for example, a patient with agoraphobia will combine unconsciously and emotionally in a junctim (1) the thought of being alone or with strange people, of shopping, of going to a theatre or to a party with (2) the phantasy of a stroke, an ocean voyage, a delivery in the street, or infection from germs on the street. A junctim is the purposively slanted association of a thought and a feeling complex, which actually have little or nothing in common, for the sake of intensifying an affect. It is similar to the metaphor.

Similarly, where we have a patient suffering from anxiety attacks, seeking a proof of illness in order to escape the decision of an examination, of a love relationship, or any enterprise, the neurotic caution will urge toward associating his situation with the idea of an execution, a prison, a shoreless sea, being buried alive, or death. To avoid a decision regarding the success of a love relationship the following association of ideas may expediently take place: man with murderer or burglar; woman with sphinx, demon, or vampire.

Every possible defeat is often felt as the more threatening by associating it with the thought of death or pregnancy (found among male neurotics as well). The emotion thus derived forces the patient to avoid an enterprise. At times the mother or the father are elevated through phantasy to the roles of lover or spouse until this tie is firm enough to safeguard the avoidance of the marriage problem.

3. THE NEUROTIC ARRANGEMENT[3]

COMMENT   Neurotic "arrangement" is a term which Adler used often, especially in his earlier work. It is the way in which he describes the crucial factor x in the formula for neurosis given below. Arrangement might be defined as provoking experiences and exploiting them. One might say that the meaning of provoking is to arrange for experiences, while the meaning of exploiting is to rearrange experiences beyond the normal evaluation, to a point of distorting their values.

In order to present a clear, although only schematic, picture of the peculiar way in which the neurotic and psychotic orient themselves in the world I should like to submit two formulas. The first would represent the popular view of neurosis, whereas the second, with which it should be compared, corresponds better to the above views and to reality. The first formula would be: Individual heredity; physique (Kretschmer), alleged sexual components (Freud), introversion and extroversion (Jung) + Experiences: sexual and incest experiences (Freud) + Environment + Demands of life = Neurosis. Here the individual is thought of as impaired by physical inferiority, or heredity, or sexual constitution, by emotion and by his character. Furthermore the experiences, environment, and external demands are thought of as pressing on the patient like a burden until they force him into the "flight into sickness." This view is obviously wrong. Nor can one maintain it through using the auxiliary hypothesis that the neurosis compensates for an actual minus situation in respect to wish-fulfillment or "libido."

An appropriate formula would have to read somewhat as follows: Evaluation (Individual + Experiences + Environment) + x = Personality ideal of superiority. Here x stands for an arrangement and biased interpretation of experiences, character traits, emotions, and symptoms. The life problem of the neurotic is not: "What must I do to fit into the demands of society and thereby achieve a harmonious existence?" but: "How must I fashion my life to satisfy my superiority tendency, to transform my inferiority feeling into a feeling of godlikeness?"

The only point we consider fixed is the personality ideal. To approach godlikeness the neurotic evaluates his individuality, his experiences, and his environment according to his slant. But this is far from sufficient to keep him on his life-line and bring him closer to his goal. Therefore he provokes further experiences and exploits them. [This is represented by the x in the formula.] He does this to facilitate his preconceived utilization of such experiences, namely to feel himself slighted, cheated, or a sufferer, in order to create for himself the familiar and desired basis for aggression. From this it follows that the neurotic creates from reality and his own potentialities the number and kind of character traits and emotional readinesses which are in accord with his personality ideal. In the same manner the patient grows into his symptoms, which arise from the sum total of his experience in the very form which appears necessary and useful for his self-enhancement. This modus vivendi has been conceived and retained by a self-determined goal and does not contain the slightest trace of a predetermined, innate (autochthonous) teleology.

According to the purposive nature of the neurotic life-plan the question of conservation or loss of psychological energy loses all meaning. The patient will always have produced just enough psychological energy to maintain his course toward superiority, masculine protest, and god-likeness.

COMMENT   *Adler's replacement on the right side of the equation of "Neurosis" by "Personality Ideal" corresponds to the shift from the mechanistic to the finalistic view of causality. Accordingly, one must read the second formula, not from left to right but from right to left, to establish the causal sequence. It is not the objective conditions on the left which cause the neurosis, but it is the neurotic personality ideal which distorts all objective data and gives rise to the "arrangements," the symptoms. Despite various contributing factors the ideal or goal is ultimately self-determined in accordance with Adler's general position (8).*

The first formula, which Adler presents as the popular view and with Freudian labels, is indeed essentially the same as a formula presented by Freud (38, p. 316). Freud's formula reads:

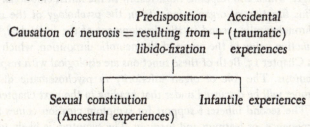

$$\text{Causation of neurosis} = \begin{array}{cc} \text{Predisposition} & \text{Accidental} \\ \text{resulting from} + & \text{(traumatic)} \\ \text{libido-fixation} & \text{experiences} \end{array}$$

$$\begin{array}{cc} \text{Sexual constitution} & \text{Infantile experiences} \\ \text{(Ancestral experiences)} & \end{array}$$

The basic difference between Adler and Freud, as we understand it, is shown by these two formulas. A full appreciation of their significance affords an understanding of Freud as the depth psychologist of "objective," positivistic psychology and of Adler as the depth psychologist of "subjective," personalistic, phenomenological psychology—a difference which was presented in the Introduction and which represents the essence of our interpretation of Adler.

By implication, the two formulas also bring out the difference in function attributed to the self by Freud and by Adler. In the Freudian formula a specific external agent, the trauma, sets off the disturbance which is fostered by constitutional factors and infantile experiences; the self is merely the ground on which the internal and external forces interact. According to Adler's formula with its subjective emphasis on every factor, the self necessarily becomes decisive; it is not only active, but creative. The self creates the personality ideal, evaluates experiences, and makes "arrangements." In this connection we wish to point out again that the individual engages in all these processes unconsciously, that is, in Adler's definition, is not aware of what he is doing, or does not understand it.

B. Supporting Factors

COMMENT The creation of the symptoms receives support from three factors inherent in the individual. The first is the biological condition, where organ inferiority particularly lends itself as a crystallization point for symptoms. While any individual when meeting an impasse will respond emotionally, that is, with bodily and mental agitation, the neurotically disposed individual tends to fixate such agitation. The least resistance to such fixation of a shock effect is offered by the inferior organ which also responds most readily in the initial emotional agitation. This function of organ inferiority in the psychology of the neurosis is chronologically second in the development of the individual, its earlier function being in the origin of the neurotic disposition, which is treated in Chapter 15. Both of these functions are etiological with respect to the neurosis. The role of organ inferiority in psychosomatic disturbances proper will be discussed under that heading in the next chapter.

The second inherent support for symptom creation comes from past experience, or learning and memory. The symptom is likely to take the form of a response which the individual has experienced in the past as serving his purposes.

The third support comes from the area of perception, in the form of oversensitivity, which Adler described as the most distinguishing trait of the neurotically disposed individual. Due to his living "as if in enemy country" he needs "to hear further and to see further." Thus he is likely to perceive critical situations where the normal individual would not, and to magnify out of all proportion those situations which would normally seem critical.

1. ORGAN INFERIORITY[4]

Some symptoms of a physical nature recur constantly, or even become chronic, although no organic cause is behind them. Often, however, they disclose an inferior organ, an organic place of least resistance (locus minoris resistentiae). We also note that in these inferior organs later in life definite manifestations of organic damage may come to light. But it is also possible that the child quite naturally will take a particular interest in tending and developing this place of least resistance toward greater creative achievement. Children who suffer in some way from weakness of vision may take a particular interest in observing perspective, color and line. There is no doubt that they suffer from an unusually strong tension, which sometimes can be put to great advantage. Sometimes, however, they give up very soon because they have tried and met with no success.

When the neurotic is brought face to face with a problem with which he is not prepared to cope, he suffers a shock and responds with a shock reaction. In such exogenous situations he develops the shock symptoms that correspond to his physical type and to his particular life style, while emphasizing especially those which seem to justify him in evading the imminent problem which carries with it the threat of defeat.

The organs most disturbed by this tension are those which have been made susceptible by some inherited weakness. Hence we find, where a whole family is liable to a particular organic weakness, that several members suffer from organic illnesses, and others from neurotic symptoms of that same organ. In such cases we must not overlook the contributory factor of imagination. In distinction from other psychologists, however, we find that the only symptoms imitated are those which are alignable to the neurotic goal of superiority.

2. LEARNING AND MEMORY[5]

When the pampered individual has tried out a certain method and found it successful, he will use it again and again. If a certain symptom is selected in childhood and found workable, the neurotic adult will often employ it in his later life as a means of furthering his asocial ends. This cannot be interpreted as "regression"; it is a definite employment of past experiences for present and future gain. If symptoms disappear, it is always because the individual is now in a situation in which they are no longer of any benefit to him. When one wants to achieve something, or when one thinks about something, one can utilize only what has been a part of previous experience. Thus the individual must reach back to a situation where his refusal to cooperate had met with the most favorable circumstances.

Whether the neurotic dominates by bullying or by whining will depend on his training: he will choose the device which he has tested best and found most effective for his purposes. Sometimes, if he is dissatisfied with one method, he will try the other. In either case the goal is the same —to gain a feeling of superiority without working to improve the situation. The discouraged child who finds that he can tyrannize best by tears will be a cry-baby; and a direct line of development leads from the cry-baby to the adult depressed patient. Tears and complaints—the means which I have called "water power"—can be an extremely useful weapon for disturbing cooperation and reducing others to a condition of slavery.

The form and content of the neurotic guiding line come from the impressions of the child who feels slighted. These impressions, which necessarily grow out of an original feeling of inferiority, call to life an aggressive attitude, the purpose of which is to overcome a great insecurity. Within this aggressive attitude we may place all the attempts of the child which promise an enhancement of his self-esteem. Successful attempts urge toward repetition, and unsuccessful ones serve as warning mementos. All neurotic symptoms come from these preparatory means which strive toward the final goal of superiority. They are mental readinesses, always ready to initiate the struggle for self-esteem; they are in the command of the guiding fiction, which attempts its realization by means of reactions which are available from childhood.

Every one of the abstract guiding lines of the neurosis, and of the psychological mechanisms on which they are based, can be or can become available to consciousness in the form of a memory image. This image, which is a manifestation of the safeguarding tendency, can arise from the retention of a childhood experience, or it may be the product of fantasy. Sometimes it is not formed until a later period, or it becomes changed, often when the neurosis has already been developed. It may represent a symbol, a label, so to speak, for a particular mode of response. Obviously the result of a kind of thought-economy, in the sense of entailing the least expenditure of energy (Avenarius), it is never significant for its content, but only as an abstract schema or the remains of a psychological occurrence. This schematic fiction is never to be regarded as other than allegorical, no matter how concretely it may behave. It reflects a real component of experiences together with a "moral," both of which are retained by the memory function in the interest of security of action. They may take the form of a memento, to maintain the guiding line better, or of a prejudice, to prevent deviating from it.

No memory image or fantasy from childhood has ever had a pathological effect, that is, as a psychological trauma. Such memory images are brought up from material long past only when the neurosis develops, when the feeling of a strong decrease in the self-esteem leads to the masculine protest and to a closer adherence to the long-standing, compensatory guiding lines which are already apparent in the memory itself. The memory images assert themselves then because of their usefulness in making the neurotic behavior possible and in interpreting it. Here we find primarily readinesses for pain, anxiety, and the affects which are based on such memories. These memories are filled out in a hallucinatory fashion, and are like optical and accoustic hallucinations. They will usually be typical memories most closely related to the guiding line, because they represent or lead to the small and large detours which the neurotic, who clings to his guiding line, must take to raise his self-esteem. This is why Individual Psychology attaches great importance to the understanding of earliest childhood recollections, and it has shown that they represent revealing signs from the period when the style of life was constructed.

3. OVERSENSITIVITY[6]

The neurotic psyche discloses itself most readily in oversensivity. The clinical treatment of neurotics has always taken this phenomenon into account, but did not sufficiently appreciate its psychological significance nor explore its determination in the individual case in order to remove it. I can name only two authors who mention the very far-reaching importance of this phenomenon. The historian Lamprecht has observed the significance of "irritability" for folk-psychology, and Bleuler makes "affectivity" the center of the neuroses, especially paranoia (Bleuler. *Suggestibilität, Affektivität und Paranoia*).

As a rule oversensitivity is found with equal clarity in all neurotics. The patient, when asked, usually admits that he feels easily hurt by a word or a facial expression. When he denies oversensitivity, we can find out from his relatives that they have noticed it and made strong efforts not to arouse it. The fact that oversensitivity is found in healthy persons as well does not prove anything; we need only consider that there are numerous borderline cases of neurosis among them.

The expressions of oversensitivity are interesting enough. They become apparent precisely as soon as there is a situation in which the patient considers himself neglected, hurt, small, or besmudged. It often happens that, supported by unimportant incidentals, he arbitrarily invents such a situation. He often tries with much discernment to give a logical representation of his viewpoint, which only the experienced psychotherapist can see through. Or the patient seeks recourse in a delusion, as in paranoia and also in some neuroses—to make the inexplicability of his behavior understandable.

One is surprised at the accumulation of disparagements and humiliations to which such patients are exposed until one discovers that they run after their slaps in the face, so to speak. This tendency originates in the unconscious, and usually, together with other tendencies, brings about the masochistic character of the neurosis, presenting the patient as a hypochondriacal, hurt, persecuted, disparaged, unappreciated person for whom there is only sorrow, misery, and "bad luck." Lack of joy in life; the continuous expectation of accidents, delays, failures, disparagements, which can be recognized in the very facial traits of the patient; superstitious fear of numbers and unlucky days; inclination towards telepathy, with a premonition of some evil; distrust in his own strength which awakens doubt about everything; distrust in others which is socially disturbing and disrupts every group—these at times characterize the oversensitive patient. The neurosis may receive a particular coloring through various degrees of inhibition of aggression, through shyness, timidity, anxiety, and excitement in new unaccustomed situations, which may even go as far as to produce physical and psychological paralysis. [Like someone exposed in a hostile world, someone for whom this earth is not good enough, the neurotic thinks always of himself, his distress, his deficiencies, and never of what he could contribute.*]

Thus oversensitivity becomes "pre-sensitivity." On the other hand we also find in the neurosis phenomena which can be described as "post-sensitivity." Such patients cannot get over a painful impression and are unable to free themselves from a lack of satisfaction. [They are unable to reconcile themselves with life and its institutions, that is, with other people.*] They give the impression of stubborn, defiant individuals, unable to create a substitute satisfaction through "culturally directed aggression," but insisting rigidly and firmly on "having it their way." They show this tendency in every situation and throughout their lives. Righteous fanatics and litigators always show this trait.

The feeling of his weakness so dominates the neurotic that, without his knowing it, he harnesses all his strength to build a protective superstructure. It is in doing so that his sensitivity becomes sharpened. He learns to pay attention to relationships which would escape others; he exaggerates his caution; he foresees all possible results when he begins an action or an ordeal; he tries to hear further and to see further; he becomes petty, insatiable, stingy; he attempts to stretch the limits of his influence and power ever further in time and space and thereby loses the impartiality and composure which alone guarantee psychological health and efficiency.

c. Objective Factors and Their Relativity

COMMENT   *Trauma and conflict are treated alike by Adler, in that he ascribes no truly etiological significance to either the traumatic situation, as already briefly mentioned, or to the conflict situation as such. Both occur in the lives of all individuals. But whereas the normal individual "digests" his traumas and solves his conflicts, the neurotically disposed individual is likely to magnify and retain such experiences, even to "run after them." This he does in order to provide himself with an alibi by which he safeguards his self-esteem. He feels his self-esteem threatened because he is unprepared in the first place to deal with life in general. This is, in turn, because he does not fully realize the fact of human interrelatedness and does not accept its inexorable consequences for his behavior. Therefore Adler recognizes only one conflict as sig-*

* Added from a later edition.

nificant, namely, the incongruity of the mistaken style of life with the fact of human interrelatedness, or as he calls it, the demands of social living.

All exogenous factors become quite relative to the purposes of the neurotically disposed individual and in this way do not differ functionally from the inherent supporting factors discussed above, namely, organ inferiority, learning and memory, and oversensitivity. This relativity is summarized under the heading, "Clinging to Shock Effects." On the other hand there is no full-fledged neurosis without a precipitating exogenous factor. The last section enumerates typical occasions which frequently function as exogenous factors in the onset of neuroses.

1. THE RELATIVITY OF ADVERSE EXPERIENCES[7]

There is, of course, no question of a causal condition [for the neurosis]; the patient is not obligated to his symptom. Rather it is as if he let himself be tempted and seduced into his symptom. It is a seduction of the human mind which, however, is so natural that we can empathize with it.

All experience is for the neurotic merely the material or means to gain for his faulty perspective renewed inducements in the direction of his neurotic guiding lines. This is proven by his falsifying distortion of the environment which can go as far as a complete shutting off; by the wilful, always biased development of the emotions and sensations, together with the resulting reactions; and by the planful interplay of recollection and amnesia, of conscious and unconscious impulses, of knowledge and superstition.

The cause of a neurosis is not that a person has experienced something, but that he cannot digest an experience due to the lack in his style of life of the ability to cooperate. Or it may also be that [as a child] he made one of the stereotyped experiences (secret observation of a love scene between the parents, castration threat) into the cause without sufficient reason, sufficient from the common-sense point of view. Other children, due to their greater social interest, that is, their lower inferiority feeling and their sounder schema of apperception, remain, on the contrary, without harmful impressions from the same experiences. Therefore, I was rightly able to maintain in contrast to Freud that "the neurotic does not suffer from reminiscences, he makes them" [1914g, p. 44]. He raises them to rank and dignity.

When the child, erring in his pampered style of life, has constructed his picture of the world almost as if he were living in a dream, then every one of his later experiences is seen, felt, interpreted, and responded to in the light of this same attitude toward life. It is not the experiences as such, it is not their objective significance which then have an effect on him, but the conception, evaluation, and meaning which he gives to these experiences; he always interprets experiences according to his already existing attitude and life style.

COMMENT *The relativity of trauma or frustration was illustrated strikingly by A. H. Maslow in his well-known paper on "Frustration, Threat and Deprivation," where he states: Only "a deprivation which is at the same time a threat to the personality, that is, to the life goals of the individual, to his defensive system, to his self-esteem, or to his feeling of security" will have "frustrating" effects (77, p. 364). Maslow came to a similar conclusion regarding the relativity of "conflict" and its effects when he pointed out: "We must define the situation . . . by its psychological meaning to the particular subject involved" (76, p. 86).*

2. THE RELATIVITY OF CONFLICT[8]

Everyone has conflicts that cause him greater or less agitation; everyone feels them in body and mind. If there were no inexorable demands of an ideal community, if everyone were able in life to satisfy his mistaken law of movement—or to express it more fancifully: his drives, his conditioned reflexes—then there would be no conflict. But no one could make such an absurd demand. It is only put forward timidly when the connection between the individual and the community is overlooked, or when an attempt has been made to separate them. Everyone submits more or less willingly to the iron law of the ideal community. Only a child who has been utterly spoiled will expect and demand: *res mihi subigere conor,* in Horace's words of reproof, freely translated: to make use of the contributions of the community for my own ends without adding anything myself. Only he who has sufficiently embodied in himself and in his law of movement the goal toward the community, will be able to solve his share of conflicts in the sense of the community.

The neurotic, from childhood on, is trained in his law of movement to retreat from tasks that he fears might, through his failing in them, injure his vanity and interfere with his striving for personal superiority, for being the first, a striving that is all too strongly dissociated from social interest. Furthermore, his life motto "all or nothing" usually only slightly modified, the oversensitivity of a person continuously threatened with defeats, the intensified affects of one who lives as though he were in a hostile country, his impatience, and his greed evoke more frequent and stronger conflicts than would be necessary. This in turn makes the retreat which his style of life has prescribed for him easier. The neurotic person, like everyone else, has his conflicts. But it is his way of trying to solve them which distinguishes him clearly from all other people.

Individual Psychology is not the attempt to describe man in conflict with himself. What it describes is always the same self in its course of movement which experiences the incongruity of its life style with the social demands. Here the self tries erroneously to maintain its life style instead of developing it higher so as to accord with these demands, that is, instead of developing in the direction of a stronger social interest. In this way defiance, personal ambition, the feeling of defeat, and flight from the community cannot be explained as psychological attitudes resulting from a lack of conquest of the self. Rather, these attitudes are parts of the life style and are resources, guiding lines, and means used by an individual with little inclination towards society in meeting problems of life which require more social interest than he is able to muster. They are means which can finally save at least the semblance of a personal superiority for the individual, on the useless side of life.

Since people in general, being largely pampered, regard every unfulfilled or unfulfillable wish as a suppression, I should like to repeat here: Individual Psychology demands the suppression of neither justified nor unjustified wishes. But it does teach that unjustified wishes must be recognized as violating social feeling, and that by a surplus of social interest they can be made, not to become suppressed, but to disappear.

COMMENT   *Thus successful psychotherapy is not the result of better repression by a so-called strengthened ego. Rather, it is the outcome of an insightful reorganization of dynamic factors. By the very nature of reorganization, the old organization disappears when the new organization emerges. This restatement of Adler in terms of Gestalt theory suggests itself through the close relationship between the two approaches.*

3. CLINGING TO SHOCK EFFECTS[9]

We classify neurotic symptoms into physical shocks of certain organs and into psychological shocks such as manifestations of anxiety, compulsive thoughts, and manifestations of depression. They are all persistent symptoms. If we assume that they have not developed without some meaning, and try to see them in their context, we find that they originated when the patient was confronted with a problem which was too difficult for him. The symptoms persist because the problem persists. In this way the persistence of neurotic symptoms appears to be established and explained.

The onset of the symptoms takes place when a person is confronted by a certain problem. We have made extensive studies to find out wherein the difficulty of the solution of problems lies. The results have shown that people are always confronted with problems which require a social preparation for their solution. Thereby Individual Psychology has permanently illuminated the whole area. Such preparation must be acquired in earliest childhood because further development is possible only from an initial understanding.

The problem may be a disappointment in friendship. Which of us has never experienced this, or has not received a shock from it? But the shock is still no sign of neurosis. It is a sign of neurosis, and actually becomes a neurosis, only when it persists, when it develops into a chronic condition. In that case the individual in question avoids suspiciously all personal intimacy and shows clearly that he is always prevented from coming into closer contact with other persons by shyness and embarrassment, and by bodily symptoms like palpitations of the heart, perspiration, gastrointestinal troubles, and urgency to urinate. In the light of Individual Psychology such a condition speaks clearly of an insufficiently developed contact-feeling with others. This is also shown by the fact that his disappointment will actually lead him to isolation. When, to give another example, someone loses money in business and feels the shock of this loss, he has not yet become a neurotic. This becomes a neurotic phenomenon only when he remains in that state, when he feels the shock and does nothing else. This can only be explained if we understand that such a person has not acquired a sufficient degree of cooperative ability, and that he goes forward only on the condition of being successful in everything he attempts. Everyone will experience shock effects if he is exposed to a concentrated barrage of fire. But he will become stuck with these effects, and they will become permanent, only when he is not prepared for the tasks of life, that is, when he is a person who has not been a real co-worker from his childhood on.

The neurotic safeguards himself by his retreat, and he safeguards his retreat by intensifying the physical and psychological shock-phenomena that have arisen in the clash with a problem that has threatened defeat.

The neurosis is the patient's automatic, unknowing exploitation of the symptoms which have arisen from the effects of a shock. This exploitation is more feasible for those persons who have a great dread of losing their prestige and who have been tempted already in childhood, in most cases by being pampered, to take this course.

4. THE EXOGENOUS FACTOR[10]

COMMENT   *Despite the fact that in his theory of the neuroses Adler attributed the ultimately decisive significance to subjective factors, he was far from overlooking the importance of the exogenous factor. Without an exogenous factor, that is, under sufficiently protected conditions, a neurotically disposed individual could go through life without ever developing a full-fledged neurosis. When the actual neurosis takes its onset, however, "the exogenous factor, the proximity of a task that demands cooperation and fellowship, is always the exciting factor of the symptoms" (see below). "We must remember that it is the exogenous situation which sets the match to the fire" (1934b, p. 4).*

The exogenous factor must inevitably be an essential part of the patient's total situation. This follows from Adler's field-theoretical tenet that "it is the way in which an individual relates himself to the outside world which interests the Individual Psychologist" (1936d, p. 3). Accordingly Adler also included "a comprehensive understanding of the nature of the exogenous factor" as one of the five "most trustworthy approaches to the exploration of the personality" (see pp. 327–328).

As soon as the patient fears or experiences a disparagement in a situation and turns to flight, his readinesses for sensation and response, accentuated by childlike analogies, and his symbolized thoughts become active as a means of expression. He who, so to speak, is inoculated with inferiority feelings shows himself susceptible to any reduction of his self-esteem. Accordingly, the typical occasions for the onset of a neurosis and psychosis are easily guessed and proven. They are: (1) uncertainty of one's sexual role and of one's masculinity; (2) onset of menstruation; (3) menstrual period; (4) the time of sexual intercourse, of masturbation; (5) marriageability and marriage; (6) pregnancy; (7) childbirth and lactation; (8) climacteric, diminution of potency, aging; (9) examinations, choice of occupation; (10) mortal danger and loss of someone close.

All these stages and experiences call forth intensifications or changes in the preparatory attitudes to life. The common bond which holds them together is the expectation of a new reality [which is always of a social nature, for which the neurotic is not properly prepared due to his lack of developed social interest *] and which therefore always means to him a new struggle, and a new danger of succumbing. Immediately he proceeds to intensive safeguards, the most extreme of which is suicide. Onsets of psychoses and neuroses represent accentuations of his neurotic readiness, in which safeguarding character traits, offered as excuses, are to be found. These are: increased oversensitivity, greater caution, rage, pedantry, defiance, thrift, dissatisfaction, and impatience. Since these traits can easily be verified, they are particularly suited to establishing the psychogenic nature of a disorder. To be relieved of impending demands of life, to delay the solution of a life-question, or to gain extentuating circumstances then becomes the secondary ideal goal. This is demanded by the egotism of the patient and by his lack of interest in others.

COMMENT   *The list of the ten "typical occasions for the onset of a neurosis" given above is a relatively early formulation and is presented largely in terms of physiological mile-stones. Later Adler formulated the exogenous factor in terms of life-problems, which he grouped into three main categories. These we have already met in the form of the three social ties (see pp. 131–132).*

Three problems are irrevocably set before every individual. These are: the attitude toward one's fellow man, occupation, and love. All three are linked with one another by the first. They are not accidental, but inescapable problems. The greater the error in respect to these problems made by the bearer of an erroneous style of life, the more complications will threaten him. These complications seem to stay away only so long as he is not tested for the capacity of his social interest. The exogenous factor, the proximity of a task that demands cooperation and fellowship,

* Added from a later edition.

is always the exciting factor of the symptoms, the behavior problem, the neurosis, the suicide, the crime, the drug addiction, and the sexual perversion.

FOOTNOTES TO CHAPTER ELEVEN

1. **1:** "How the child selects his symptoms" (1936c), p. 67; **2:** "Nochmals —Die Einheit der Neurosen" (1930e), pp. 201–216; **3 and 4:** *Über den nervöser Charakter* (1912a), 4th ed., p. 218.

2. **1:** "Symptom selection" (1936c), pp. 74–75; **2, 3, 4:** "Individual-psychologische Behandlung der Neurosen" (1913c), pp. 26, 26, and 27.

3. **1 to 4:** "Individualpsychologische Behandlung" (1913c), pp. 27–28, 28, 28, and 28.

4. **1:** "Symptom selection" (1936c), p. 69; **2:** "The neurotic's picture of the world" (1936d), p. 4; **3:** *Problems of Neurosis* (1929b), p. 11.

5. **1:** "Symptom selection" (1936c), manuscript p. 14; **2:** *What Life Should Mean to You* (1931a), p. 53; **3, 4, 5:** *Nervoser Charakter* (1912a), pp. 16, 44, and 45.

6. **1 to 5:** "Über neurotische Disposition" (1909), pp. 57, 58, 58, 58, and 58; **6:** *Nervoser Charakter* (1912a), p. 5.

7. **1:** "Die Zwangsneurose" (1918c), p. 143; **2:** "Das Problem der 'Distanz'" (1914b), p. 72; **3:** "Nochmals—Die Einheit" (1930e), pp. 201–216; **4:** "Neurotic's picture" (1936d), p. 7.

8. **1, 2, 4:** *Der Sinn des Lebens* (1933a), pp. 111–112, 113, and 194; **3:** "Religion und Individualpsychologie" (1933c), pp. 75–76.

9. **1 to 5:** *Sinn des Lebens* (1933a), pp. 106–107, 107, 107–108, 113, and 117.

10. **1 and 2:** *Nervoser Charakter* (1912a), pp. 21 and 22; **3:** *Sinn des Lebens* (1933a), p. 9.

CHAPTER TWELVE

THE DYNAMIC UNITY OF MENTAL DISORDERS

COMMENT *The preceding three chapters comprise Adler's theory of the neurosis, except for the origin of the neurotic disposition which will be found in Chapter 15. It is a unified theory, which Adler considered applicable to all mental disturbances and which must be understood as a modification of a still more general theory of personality. This thought is expressed in the first section of the present chapter. The remaining sections represent applications of this unified theory to the understanding of various specific mental disorders as these are commonly classified on the basis of symptoms.*

A. Unity and Diversity

1. UNITY[1]

The psychoneurosis is forced by vanity and has the ultimate purpose of safeguarding a person from a clash with his life tasks, that is, with reality, and of sparing him the danger of having the dark secret of his inferiority revealed. Only by this fundamental understanding has the unity of the neurosis and psychosis become established.

All mistaken answers [to the tasks of life] are degrees of an infinite series of failures or abnormalities, or of the attempts of more or less discouraged people to solve their life-problems without the use of cooperation or social interest. Only if one would regard warm and cold as rigid contrasts, could one also regard the infinite series of relationships as if their more extreme differences would constitute discrete opposites. These are, however, actually only differences in degree of the ability to cooperate. Thus what appear as discrete disease entities are only different symptoms which indicate how one or the other individual considers that he would dream himself into life without losing the feeling of his personal value.

Several psychiatrists have already pointed out this relationship of individuality and psychosis [and neurosis]. The development of psychiatry also shows a progressive blurring of the boundaries between specific diagnostic categories. Ideal types are disappearing from literature and practice. We seem to be generally approaching a basic view to which Individual Psychology has contributed notably: namely, that the neurotic method of life reaches with an apparently inescapable and individually founded lawfulness for the means of a useful neurosis or psychosis in order to succeed. The findings of Individual Psychology are well-suited to the support of this view for they show that the patient develops his inner world, which contrasts with reality, on the foundation of a wrong perspective although this perspective, which dictates his attitude toward society, is always understandable in terms of what is commonly human.

I have found and described certain dynamic forces of the neuroses and psychoses as follows: (1) the inferiority feeling of the child; (2) the safeguarding tendency and striving for compensation; (3) a fictional goal of superiority, erected in childhood and thereafter functioning in a teleological fashion, (4) resulting tested methods, character traits, affects, symptoms, and attitudes in answer to the demands of social interrelatedness; (5) all of these utilized as the means for fictional self-enhancement in relation to the environment; (6) the seeking of detours and distance from the expectations of the community in order to escape a real evaluation and personal liability and responsibility; (7) the neurotic perspective and biased devaluation of reality, which may go as far as madness; (8) the elimination of almost all possibilities of human relations and cooperation. These forces have led me and many other investigators to the positing of one explanatory principle which has proved itself valuable and indispensable in the widest sense for the understanding of the neuroses and psychoses.

There are no pure cases. There are only mixed cases in which it can be seen that at one time one aspect, at another time another aspect of the whole psychic process comes to the foreground.

The method of Individual Psychology has brought us satisfactory elucidations regarding the nature of neuroses, the structure of its symptoms, and the means of a sovereign therapy. The seemingly nonsensical behavior in neurasthenia, degeneration psychosis, compulsion neurosis, hysteria, and paranoia appears understandable and well-determined. The accomplishments of men of genius, criminal actions, and creations of the folk psyche are accessible to psychological analysis and turn out to be comparable in their psychological structure to that of the neurotic symptoms. This comparability of psychological results and their surprising identity give us such confidence in dealing with the difficult subject of the theory of neurosis that even strong objections by qualified critics could not disconcert us, let alone unjustified complaints or unqualified rejection.

Naturally, anyone who stands for the unity and uniform structure of the psychoneuroses will have to explain each particular case individually.

COMMENT   In the above Adler established a common principle for all mental life. Although Freud had notably pointed out similarities between the normal and the abnormal and maintained common etiologies for diverse symptoms, he criticized Adler for going much too far in this direction. In 1914 Freud wrote: "Psycho-analysis has never claimed to provide a complete theory of human mentality as a whole, but only expected that what it offered should be applied to supplement and correct the knowledge acquired by other means. Now Alfred Adler's theory goes far beyond this point; it seeks at one stroke to explain the behavior and character of human beings as well as the neurotic and psychotic manifestations in them" (36, I, p. 338).

Twenty years later Freud still criticized Adler specifically for his view of the unity of maladjustment as follows: "Whether a person is a homosexual, or a necrophilist, or an anxiety-ridden hysteric, or a shut-in obsessional, or a raving madman—in every case the Individual Psychologist of the Adlerian persuasion will assign as the motive force of his condition the fact that he wants to assert himself, to overcompensate for his inferiority, to be on top, to move over from the feminine to the masculine line" (41, pp. 193–194). By such uniform etiological diagnosis Freud is reminded of an unscrupulous country doctor who makes the same diagnosis of all the various ailments of his peasant patients.

It is precisely this analogy from medical practice to psychotherapy, drawn by Freud, which becomes highly questionable in the light of considerable present-day opinion. Firstly, whereas in medical therapy the etiological diagnosis is all-important for determining the therapeutic steps to be taken, in psychotherapy the treatment is essentially the same regardless of the diagnosis of a disease entity. The fact that psychotherapy does not vary with the categorical diagnosis, but only with the severity of the case, implies a common etiology. In this connection it may be recalled that the recent client-centered therapy of Rogers employs no diagnosis. Secondly, there would seem to be widespread recognition today of the unreliability of psychiatric diagnosis according to disease entities.

Freud was, of course, not the only one to criticize Adler for seeming oversimplification. Adler's response to an early critic is characteristic: "Bleuler speaks—strangely enough—in a disparaging sense of the fact 'that one can explain everything with this view.' To me and to others it will be valuable for just this reason" (1914e, p. 185n).

2. DIVERSITY[2]

COMMENT   Originally Adler stressed the dynamic unity of all mental disturbances, combining them under the term neurosis. In his later years he made two distinctions which, however, still left the idea of essential unity intact as a superordinated concept. The first distinction is according to relative strength of social interest and will be presented in the two selections which follow. The second distinction is according to degree of activity. This has already been treated under Degree of Activity in Maladjustment (pp. 165–166), to which the reader is referred.

Neurosis is always behavior which can be expressed in two words, the words "Yes—but." This is the best and easiest definition because it distinguishes a neurosis from all other types of failure and the neurotic from the normal person. What does "yes" mean? What does "but" mean? To explain this would need a long lecture, but perhaps it can be said in a short and simple way. By "yes" I mean that the neurotic person recognizes common sense [an expression of social interest]. He sees that there is a particular problem before him and he says yes, but he does not follow it up. It is always followed by "but." So he does not accomplish what is expected of him. In this but you find the whole strength of the neurotic symptoms. They are much stronger than what is represented by the yes. Therefore, the neurotic always falls short of the problems of life because he is more interested in what he has expressed by the but than in what is expressed by the yes. He understands social interest, and that makes him different from the psychotic person, for instance, but he does not go all the way.

Every neurotic professes the best of intentions. He is quite convinced of the necessity for social interest and for meeting the problems of life. Only in his case there is an exception to this universal demand. What excuses him is the neurosis itself. His whole attitude says, "I am anxious to solve all my problems, but unfortunately I am prevented." In this he differs from the criminal, whose professions of bad intentions are often quite open and whose social interest is concealed and suppressed. It is difficult to decide which offers the greater injury to human welfare, the neurotic whose motives are so good, but whose actions apart from these good motives would seem spiteful, egotistic, and designed to hold up the cooperation of his fellows; or the criminal, whose hostility is so much more open and who takes pains to subdue the relics of his social interest.

B. Anxiety Neurosis[3]

COMMENT *When Adler uses the term anxiety, it is generally as a descriptive term for a conscious symptom, such as a phobia, as shown in this section. In Chapter 10 such anxiety was shown to be a form of safeguarding behavior.*

Occasionally, however, Adler did use the word anxiety in an explanatory sense, as when he stated that a compulsion safeguards the individual from "falling victim to anxiety" (see p. 305). In such usage the context always makes it clear that the anxiety is the fear of being proven worthless or the fear of defeat. Generally Adler described such anxiety as "increased feelings of inferiority" and its consequences, the "feeling as if one lived in enemy country," and the "feeling of insecurity and inadequacy." Hence Adler himself did not often use the term anxiety in this second sense. It was left for Karen Horney to call this whole syndrome of feelings "basic anxiety" which she defined as "the feeling of being isolated and helpless in a potentially hostile world" (53).

Fear of defeat is the only reason for the will to escape. At the same time it is the hardest of all reasons to admit. Therefore we frequently find at this point some fictional form of anxiety, which the patient interprets to himself variously but never truly—never, that is, as the simple fear of defeat. Agoraphobia, anxiety neurosis, and all the forms of phobia may originate at this point; but, whichever it may be, it fulfills its purpose of blocking the way to further activity. Thus what was desired is attained: the ordeal is evaded without disclosing, even to its owner, the hated feeling of inferiority. All the other neurotic symptoms and functional disturbances such as compulsion ideas, fits, fatigue, sleeplessness, neurotic heart, headaches, migraine and so on, develop out of the severe tension of this very difficult concealment.

The manifestations of fear of open places are interesting because we soon discover that such people always have the feeling that they are the object of some hostile persecution. They believe that something distinguishes them quite markedly from others. This belief is sometimes expressed in fantastic ideas, such as the fear of falling, which means for us only that they feel themselves to be very high. In these symptoms, in the excesses of anxiety, the same goal of superiority and power is expressed as we always find when an individual is placed under pressure and a sad fate moves into threatening proximity. In many people, anxiety means only that someone must be present to occupy himself with them. If things have gone so far that a person can no longer leave his room, then everything must be subordinated to his anxiety. It is he who imposes the law on others; everybody must come to see him, while he is excused from having to go to anyone. Thus he becomes the king who dominates the others.

With this approach anxiety cannot be taken as rising from the repression of sexuality or from disastrous birth-experiences. Rather, a child who is accustomed to being accompanied, helped, and supported by his mother may find anxiety, whatever its source, a very efficient weapon for controlling his mother. A patient suffering from agoraphobia loses the feeling of anxiety when he is at home or is dominating another person. All neurotic patients exclude every part of life in which they do not feel strong enough to be the conqueror.

A married woman of twenty-five suffered from an anxiety neurosis. Her violent attacks of anxiety occurred when her husband was delayed in coming home. She had felt curtailed in her life with her family, and her husband was the first person who had treated her with overindulgence. But now his business obligations made it impossible for him to devote himself so much to her. She now wanted to be connected only with her husband and to exclude everyone else. By the development of an anxiety neurosis she was hindering her husband's business, no one could demand anything from her, and her husband had to obey. But she paid for this success by very painful anxieties, so much so that her husband had been able to persuade her to come and see me.

c. Compulsion Neurosis

1. FIGHTING WINDMILLS[4]

Discouragement, the surest sign of a neurotic, forces him to put a distance between himself and absolutely necessary decisions. To justify this distance he resorts to arrangements which pile up in front of him like a mountain of junk. Thus the neurotic separates himself from the front of life. His staying in the hinterland has a compulsive character determined by his trembling ambition. Nowhere does the mountain of self-arranged difficulties become so obvious as in the compulsion neurosis.

The usual forms of compulsion neurosis are compulsion to wash, pray, or masturbate, moral compulsive ideas of all kinds, and brooding. From the standpoint of systematic classification, the field of compulsion neurosis could be enlarged considerably since we find the same mechanism also in the symptom area of nocturnal enuresis, neurotic refusal of food, compulsive hunger, and perversion. In one sense every individual has something in his psychological make-up which reminds one of compulsion neurosis and which may lead to considerable disturbances, for example, excessive confidence in supernatural help, as if the individual wanted to have everything given to him; counting syllables, reading signs, and counting windows. All of these appear quite senseless, but can be reported by many persons who have remained normal.

The compulsion neurotic feels compelled to do something, to perform a compulsive action, which he himself feels is absurd and recognizes as being out-of-joint with social living. Yet he must yield to the compulsion, or else fall victim to anxiety. The compulsion neurotic has a feeling of insecurity and inadequacy, a feeling of "not being able."

The patient who feels a compulsion to jump out of windows has built up this compulsion into a safeguard. He acquires a sense of superiority by successfully overcoming the urge, and employs the whole situation as an excuse for his lack of success in life. He then believes that only his compulsive idea prevents him from fulfilling an actually triumphant mission. Thus he covers his inferiority complex with a superiority complex and appears magnificent enough in his own eyes.

The compulsion neurotic retires, so to speak, to a secondary field of action where he expends all his energies instead of devoting them to solving his primary problem. Like a veritable Don Quixote he fights windmills, concerning himself with matters which have no proper place in our social world, and only serve to dally away time. For time appears to him as his most dangerous foe, always making some demand on him, and always impelling him to solve problems which he feels are beyond his powers.

Related to compulsion neurosis is what I should like to call *conflict neurosis*. Such cases almost incessantly get into quarrels and conflicts with their environment. To maintain such a position of belligerence they may resort to all kinds of suspicions and accusations, which may be based on some general, flowery, ethical principles. The cause is always a cowardly withdrawal from the real problems of life, the external conflicts providing a diversion and an excuse from the imminent tasks. The relationship to paranoia is obvious.

2. RATIONALITY[5]

In an individual who suffers from compulsion neurosis the rational aspect is the most strongly stressed. This tendency to rationalize and formulate, to pay attention to formal routine and orderly arrangement, is not restricted to the obsessional ideas, but reveals itself in other phases of the patient's life as well. But his highly developed ideational life runs counter to social interest, and hence to common sense.

The compulsion neurotic begins early to employ and train an absurd process of reasoning in order to allow himself a sense of great personal importance and worth without achieving anything objectively tangible. A properly conducted inquiry into his past history will reveal certain characteristic traits: a pedantic striving for faultlessness and perfect accuracy; a tendency to sidestep difficult tasks by confusing them with unrelated, simple tasks; the practice of formalized religious exercises and rituals, with the idea of "tempting God;" the habit of stressing the difficulty of situations in order to make a greater triumph of their solution; a desire to elude rivalries; a pride in a grotesquely exaggerated family tradition.

Often he has a marked feeling for words, is fond of brooding over ideas, loves to play with maxims and precepts, and acts as if he firmly believed that "in the beginning was the Word." Such a person may achieve fine things, provided he turns these inclinations to the advantage of society. Otherwise they are futile and result in empty form. This is the case with the compulsion-neurotic in his phrase-mongering, addiction to compulsive prayers and to repetition of ritual-like performances; love of formulas; overt curses and libels; and earnest faith in the potency of his anathemas. Certain repetitive actions can easily be understood as expressing an obsessional idea, for instance, the washing compulsion shouts louder than words that everyone but the patient is dirty.

3. MISTAKEN INTERPRETATIONS[6]

The belief in the magical efficiency and omnipotence of words and ideas, this recourse to "primitive, archaic thought," is not an atavism and does not stem from the "collective unconscious," but represents an ever-feasible, childish device for achieving a sense of power.

Neither can we properly speak of a "conflict" in these cases, since the patient never deviates from the road of evasion, which he paves with good intentions or feelings of guilt. "Conflict" only means a standstill.

Sometimes the patient makes a great display of guilt feelings in reference to his compulsion. By acknowledging his guilt and raising trivialities to a rank of importance and dignity, he has the assurance of appearing more genteel and more honest than any of his fellows. Beyond this, these much bewailed trivialities have no "deeper" significance. This becomes evident from the fact that in compulsion neurosis as in depression the patient contents himself with merely expressing a sense of guilt, while he would never think of exercising "active contrition" in the form of improved behavior.

The writers on this topic always seem to consider the compulsion as if it resided in the obsessions or compulsive ideas. They regard obsession or obsessional action as if it were wholly divorced from the normal processes of thought; as if thinking were "charged" with compulsion which rises up from time to time, like a demon from a pit, to overpower and take possession of its victim; as if the compulsion had an individuality of its own. Freud, with incomparable grace and ease, invests each of his postulated instincts with human attributes. But the compulsion does not reside in the compulsive idea or action; it originates outside these, in the sphere of our normal social life. This is the source of the patient's neurotic compulsion or urge. He must evade the realities of life, since he feels incompetent to face them, and since his high-flown ambition must elude any sort of palpable failure. He retreats farther and farther before the bayonets of life, which he feels are closing in on him from without, until he finds a secluded cranny of life, where he is put to no real test, and can make use of the motions that give him a feeling of complete superiority.

4. A CASE[7]

A young singer, who seemed confident that he had a fine voice but felt thrust into the background by his father and his older brother, engaged in an incessant struggle against the impulse to jump out of the window. He believed that it was only his puzzling obsession which prevented him from becoming "the greatest tenor." He was free of it only so long as someone was at his side, and this, of course, was impossible in a theater or on the concert platform where he would have had to appear if he were to go on with his profession of concert singer. So we can see that his compulsive idea served as a means of putting at a distance the test of his greatness. He was really not sure that the test would result in his favor. He felt that he must surpass his father and brother in some way. Now if he prevented himself from ever coming to the test he could always save his vanity from being hurt. And he could maintain his personal prestige in his own eyes by having arranged a situation in which he could say and believe, "I could have been greater than they if I had not been burdened with this fear. But I was."

D. Psychosomatic Disorders

1. PSYCHOSOMATIC DISORDERS AS ORGAN DIALECT[8]

Some day it will probably be proved that every organ inferiority may respond to psychological influences and speak the organ language, that is, a language expressing the attitude of the individual toward the problems confronting him. The appreciation of this is important for the understanding of symptom selection and, particularly, of what we still call hysteria or functional neurosis. Sometimes one organ, sometimes another, is outstandingly responsive to the pressure of outside influences. In this connection it must always be remembered that the organic structure is a unity, and that a shock in one area throws the whole body into vibration.

Through the autonomic nervous system the irritation is transmitted in accordance with the individual's disposition and organic peculiarities [see pp. 224 and 287]. His organs begin to respond. The irritation always excites the whole organism, although we are able to observe the excitation only in those parts which manifest it more clearly.

COMMENT *Here Adler expresses the view which forms one of the important conceptions in Kurt Goldstein's organismic theory of human biology. According to Goldstein: "The pattern of the excitation which occurs in the system, as the result of a stimulus, cannot be sufficiently characterized by noting merely the state of excitation in the 'near part.' The rest of the system, the 'distant part,' . . . is also in a very definite state of excitation" (48, p. 109). Goldstein regards "this configuration of excitation, the foreground-background relation, as the basic form of the functioning of the nervous system" (48, p. 110). Thus Goldstein adapts the figure-ground principle of the Gestalt school to bodily functions, which Adler implies in the above. This is one of the many similarities between Goldstein and Adler, arising from their common point of view as physicians close to Gestalt psychology, emphasizing the unity of the organism.*

The functional disturbance can be seen in the lowering of the muscular tone or in its stimulation; in the hair standing on end, in perspiration, in disorders of the heart, the stomach and the bowels, in urgency to urinate, in breathing difficulty, in constriction of the throat, in sexual excitation, or its opposite, in headaches, migraine, blushing or turning pale. Through recent research, especially that of Cannon and Maranon and others, it has become established that the sympathetico-adrenal system plays an important part in these changes, as do also the cranial and sacral parts of the autonomic nervous system. These systems respond differentially to the various emotional states. Thus, also, our old assumption has been confirmed, namely, that the functions of the endocrine glands, the thyroid, the adrenal, the hypophysis, and the sex glands, are influenced by the external world. They respond to the psychological impressions according to the intensity with which these are felt subjectively and according to the style of life of the individual. They respond in the normal case to re-establish the bodily equilibrium; but where the individual is lacking in aptitude toward the problems of life, this response is of an extreme, overcompensatory nature.

When the vascular system is affected by the psyche, the skin is often affected too. It is recognized that skin diseases may be provoked in that way. Structural changes may also result from psychic irritation, as is seen particularly clearly in cases of scoliosis. Such cases as I have seen were predisposed to these troubles, but usually only became afflicted when the patient lost his poise and self-confidence on being confronted by a particular situation. There are pains which become localized on the anterior wall of the chest when the patient is in a state of depression. Cases of flatfoot are very similar; the sufferers are often depressed individuals. There can be but one explanation of this, namely, that depression can cause a loss of muscle tone. This fact is apparent in every man alive; whether he is flatfooted or not, his whole poise and bearing are characteristic of "the man within"; he speaks with his muscular apparatus. It is essential to understand this physical speech, which I have called "organ dialect."

2. A CASE[9]

A girl who had been very pretty, spoiled by her mother and ill-used by a drunken father, became an actress and had many love affairs, which culminated in her becoming the mistress of an elderly man. Such an obvious exploitation of an advantage indicates deep feelings of insecurity and cowardice. This relationship, however, brought her trouble; her mother reproached her, and although the man loved her, he could not get a divorce. During this time her younger sister became engaged. In the face of this competition, she began to suffer from headaches and palpitation, and became very irritable towards the man.

In a certain type we find that headaches are regularly produced by severe tensions of anger. The emotion accumulates so to speak during a period in which the patient shows no symptoms. The emotional tension may actually result in circulatory changes producing attacks of trigeminal neuralgia, migraine, and epileptiform seizures. An illustration of such circulatory disturbances is provided by the well-known respiratory spasms and sensations of choking induced by violent rage. The tendency to anger is related to excessive ambition; both originate in a competitive striving to escape from a sense of being overcome. They occur in unsocial natures, who feel uncertain of attaining their goal by patient striving, and often try to escape to the useless side upon an outburst of temper. Children make use of such explosions to conquer by terrifying, or at least to feel superior; and in a similar way they use the consequences, their headaches.

The girl's condition was the result of a neurotic method of striving to hasten her marriage, and was not at all ineffective. The married man was greatly worried by her continuous headaches, came to see me about my patient, and said that he would hurry the divorce and marry her. Treatment of the immediate illness was easy—in fact, it would have cleared up without me, for the girl was powerful enough to succeed with the help of her headaches.

I explained to her the connection between her headaches and the competitive attitude to her sister: it was the goal of her childhood not to be surpassed by her younger sister. She felt incapable of attaining her goal of superiority by normal means, for she was one of those children whose interest has become absorbed in themselves, and who tremble for fear that they will not succeed. She admitted that she cared only for herself and did not like the man she was about to marry.

Her palpitation was due to the fact that she had twice been pregnant and both times had resorted to abortion, when she justified herself to the doctor by saying that her heart was too weak for her to bear children. It was true that her heart was irritated by tense situations and suppressed anger, but she used this symptom increasingly and exaggerated it to justify her intention never to have children. Self-absorbed women generally show their lack of human and social interest by an unwillingness to have children; but sometimes, of course, they desire children for reasons of ambition or for fear of being considered inferior.

3. INSOMNIA[10]

A description of the symptoms of insomnia will not give any essentially new information. The main emphasis—and it seems rather trite to mention it—always falls on the insufficient rest and the resultant tiredness and inability to work. But here let me say that many patients who enjoy undisturbed sleep also complain of tiredness. The nature of the illness of which insomnia is a symptom can be easily described: insomnia is found at times in all psychological diseases. Especially the severest psychological disorders, the psychoses, are usually preceded by exceptionally severe insomnia.

If you want to find out how insomnia fits in with the whole personality, ask the patient: "What would you do if you could sleep?" Then he will tell of what he is afraid. For example, if he could sleep he could work better and could take his examination. He is so afraid of his problem that he is tense; therefore he cannot relax and, thus, he cannot sleep.

Everyone who does not sleep has a purpose, in which he is supported by not sleeping. You will always find another person involved, and insomnia is an effective way of striking at this other person, who usually is near by. Married men and women strike at wives and husbands.

Sometimes insomnia is a tool of ambition. A person who cannot sleep feels that he must be shown special consideration, for everyone can see that he could accomplish much more if he could only sleep. Therefore, he has a certain privilege and cannot be measured with the same gauge as others. We doubt whether he really could accomplish more, and in the therapy we make him understand that it is not entirely true that he would accomplish more if he would sleep. Amount of sleep and accomplishments are not related and cannot be measured by each other. Insomnia occurs only in a situation in which a person is confronted with a problem for which he is not prepared.

4. DISORDERS OF SEXUAL FUNCTIONS[11]

The dialect of the sexual organs is especially expressive and very often leads the patient to the doctor. Each case has its peculiarities, but in practically every one the patient is expressing by the disorder of his sexual functioning, a stoppage, hesitation, or escape in the face of the three life-problems. The various forms of impotence are traceable to a common root in a disinclination and lack of training for relations with other persons. This is always demonstrable when we leave the sexual symptoms temporarily out of account and study the nature of the patient's social contacts. In women the same dialect appears as vaginismus [painful spasmodic contraction of the vagina]. This is an avoidance of man, which is accompanied by other mental symptoms, signifying the woman's aversion either to a certain man or to men in general. Besides this active avoidance there are the passive forms of sexual rejection, frigidity and the display of passivity. This lack of function reflects the woman's idea of not being present during intercourse, as though the event were only the man's affair. In all cases of frigidity I have found that the woman felt the female role as one of humiliation and curtailment. It is important to verify this precisely and apart from the sexual life.

Premature ejaculation, lack of sex interest and satisfaction, vaginismus and frigidity, are all signs of a determination to exclude actions which the individual is apparently willing to perform. The individual is like a stammerer in the sexual sphere.

Normally, of course, the sexual objective is in harmony with the conscious life-goal, is indeed one aspect of it, and as soon as approach to this objective becomes possible, it produces the thoughts and feelings which are appropriate, excluding all contradictions and conflicting tasks. But in the neurotic, thoughts and feelings are produced which belong to other duties or functions of life; irrelevant considerations are admitted which inhibit, traverse, or pervert normal conduct along the sexual line. The impotence, or whatever sexual disability is thus produced, is dictated by a neurotic goal of superiority and a mistaken style of life. Investigation always reveals a fixed intention to receive without giving, and a lack of social interest, courage, and optimistic activity.

The neurotic goal of superiority is always more or less identified with the masculine role owing to the privileges, both real and imaginary, with which our present culture has invested the male. A girl's feeling of inferiority may be markedly increased when she realizes that she is a female, and a boy's also when he doubts his maleness. Both compensate by an exaggeration of what they imagine to be masculine behavior. This form of compensation, which may have the most varied and intricate consequences according to circumstances, is what I have called the masculine protest.

I was the first to describe the attitude of protest on the part of a woman against her sexual role as the masculine protest. It frequently gives rise to menstrual troubles and functional disorders in the sexual sphere. It always springs from the dissatisfaction with a sexual role which already in the girl's family was regarded as subordinate, an evaluation which is considerably supported by the imperfection of our culture.

When the climacteric in a woman is marked by retrogression, this is also determined by the woman's disposition, and by her opinion of the climacteric as a danger or an illness.

Pseudo-pregnancy is another subject within this sphere for which the following case is an example. A patient had had sexual relations with a man for many years, and he had told her he would marry her if she should ever become pregnant. Her abdomen began to swell just as in pregnancy and continued to do so for six or seven months. But a gynecologist found her not to be pregnant at all; the swelling was the non-conscious creation of the woman.

The sex glands can be put in a passive state by emotional influences in accordance with the individual's disposition and attitude. A youngster who feels he is unmanly may accordingly live a life not conducive to the development of the sex glands. He eliminates certain activities which would be required for the normal glandular development. This can result in feminine appearance in later years. I have seen such youngsters become more masculine looking once they have been brought into proper contact with other boys. We also find that in individuals who have an unusually strong leaning toward the other sex the sex glands develop an increased activity and efficiency if this attitude persists.

E. Schizophrenia

1. THE GOAL OF GODLIKENESS[12]

The loftiest goals are to be found in the most pathological cases, that is, in the psychoses. In cases of schizophrenia we often find the desire to be Jesus Christ. In manic-depressive cases also, in the manic phases, the patient frequently wishes to be the saviour of mankind, whilst in the depressive phases he often complains of being the greatest evil on earth. In paranoia the patient not only strives to be the center of attention, but actually believes he is that already. Individual Psychology has shown that the goal of superiority can only be fixed at such altitudes when the individual has, by losing all interest in others, also lost interest in his own reason and understanding. Moreover the height of the goal now confronts the individual with such difficulties that common sense has become useless to him, incapable of solving them. This goal of personal superiority blocks the approach to reality. The end result, and logical culmination of such a life-line is, of course, total isolation in an asylum.

We can find in all goals one common factor—a striving to be godlike. Sometimes we find children who express themselves quite openly in this way, and remark, "I should like to be God." Many philosophers have had the same idea. In old religious disciplines the same objective is visible; disciples should educate themselves in such a way that they become godlike. Whether it is our earthly life we desire to perpetuate, or we imagine ourselves as coming to earth again and again through many incarnations, or we foresee an immortality in another world, these prospects are all based upon the desire to be like God. The same goal of godlikeness comes out in the desire to know everything, to possess universal wisdom, or in the wish to perpetuate our life. This ideal of godlikeness appears also in the idea of "superman"; and it is revealing—I shall not say more—that Nietzsche when he became insane signed himself in a letter to Strindberg, "The Crucified." Often insane people express their goal of superiority in an undisguised form. They will assert, "I am Napoleon," or "I am the Emperor of China." They wish to be the center of attention through the whole world, to be looked on from all sides, to be connected with the whole world by wireless and overhear all conversations, to predict the future, to be the bearers of supernatural power.

COMMENT *While in the above paragraph Adler points out that the goal of godlikeness is not unique with the schizophrenic, he has shown elsewhere wherein the difference between the normal and pathological goals of godlikeness consists. Where the goal of godlikeness is still within the range of the normal, it functions as an undogmatic, flexible fiction; but in the psychotic it becomes a rigid, concretized dogma (see pp. 246–247).*

2. EXTREME ISOLATION[13]

Every development in an individual's life is determined by his ultimate goal, by which the successive phases of his life are organically connected. When a mother, whose son has suddenly become schizophrenic at the age of eighteen, says that he was perfectly normal until that age, we cannot agree with her. And we find, upon inquiry into the boy's past life, that he was of a domineering disposition and did not play with his schoolmates. Such a childhood is a bad preparation for facing the real problems of life. In this case it was a preparation for schizophrenia, which thus was not a sudden development but the result of a life-attitude, and only showed itself when he had to face a really difficult situation.

Sometimes a child, badly prepared for adult life, feels himself in a panic at the approach of the problems of occupation, social life and society, and love and marriage. He loses all hope of ability to meet them. With regard to society, he is bashful and reserved, he isolates himself and stays at home. With regard to occupation, he can find no work that attracts him and is sure that he would be a failure in everything. With regard to love and marriage, he is embarrassed with the other sex and afraid to meet it. If he is spoken to, he blushes; he cannot find words to reply. Every day he is in deeper and deeper despair. At last he is completely blocked towards all the problems of life and no one can understand him any longer. He does not look at others, speak to them, or listen to them. He does not work or study. He is always engaged in fantasy. Only a shabby remainder of sex activity is left. This is insanity, dementia praecox.

Insanity is the highest degree of isolation; it represents a greater distance from fellow men than any other expression except, perhaps, suicide. But even insanity is not incurable if the interest in others can be aroused. It is an art to cure such cases, and a very difficult art. We must win the patient back to cooperation; and we can do it only by patience and the kindliest and friendliest manner.

3. A CASE[14]

Once I was called in to do what I could for a girl with dementia praecox. She had suffered from this condition for eight years and for the last two years had been in an asylum. She barked like a dog, spat, tore her clothes and tried to eat her handkerchief. We can see how far she had turned away from interest in human beings. She wanted to play the role of a dog, and we can understand this. She felt that her mother had treated her as a dog; and perhaps she was saying, "The more I see of human beings, the more I should like to be a dog." When I first spoke to her, on eight successive days, she did not answer a word. I continued to speak to her, and after thirty days she began to talk in a confused and unintelligible way. I was a friend to her, and she was encouraged.

If a patient of this type is encouraged he does not know what to do with his courage. His resistance against his fellow men is very strong. We can predict the conduct he will try when his courage comes back to some degree but he still does not wish to be cooperative. He is like a problem child; he will try to be a nuisance, will break anything he can lay his hands on, or will hit the attendant. When I next spoke to this girl she hit me. I had to consider what I should do. The only answer that would surprise her was to put up no resistance. You can imagine the girl—she was not a girl of great physical strength. I let her hit me and looked friendly. This she did not expect and it took away every challenge from her. She still did not know what to do with her re-awakened courage. She broke my window and cut her hand on the glass. I did not reproach her, but bandaged her hand. The usual way of meeting such violence, to confine her and lock her in her room, was the wrong way. We must act differently if we wish to win this girl. It is the greatest mistake to expect an insane person to act as a normal person. Almost everyone is annoyed and irritated because the insane do not respond like ordinary beings. They do not eat, they tear their clothes, and so on. Let them do it. There is no other possibility of helping them. I still see this girl from time to time, and she has remained in good health for ten years. She earns her own living, is reconciled to her fellows, and no one who saw her would believe that she had ever suffered from insanity.

4. PARANOIA[15]

COMMENT *In the following the reader will note a considerable similarity between the structure of paranoia and that of compulsion neurosis, a similarity which has been pointed out by Adler above (see p. 306).*

Those persons are inclined toward paranoia who after a relatively energetic start characteristically become discouraged and stop at some distance from their goal. They tend to engage in elaborate ideational and more active enterprises in a secondary theater of operations (Nebenkriegsschauplatz), in a mock battle against self-created difficulties. Thereby they gain the unconscious pretense by which they cover up, justify, or delay endlessly their potential defeat in life. The paranoid system is safeguarded against the greatest objections from reality. Therefore it is more planful than that of other psychoses and can be shaken only under favorable conditions, as, for example, in the beginning. The relatively high level of activity explains why the collapse usually does not occur until the later years, and this in turn lends to the delusion the features of a certain maturity.

The activity is usually of a very belligerent kind. The patient blames others for the lack of success in his exaggerated plans, and his active striving for complete superiority results in an attitude of hostility toward others. This expresses itself in ideas of reference, delusions of persecution, and delusions of grandeur. In all these three conditions the patient sees himself as the center of the world. The ideas of the paranoiac are difficult to correct because he needs them in their very form to fortify his position. At the same time they permit him to retain the fiction of his superiority without submitting it to the test.

His hallucinations are connected with a strong empathy into a role and represent encouraging or warning voices. They arise always when the patient wants something unconditionally, yet at the same time wants to be considered free from responsibility. Like dreams, they must be understood as a metaphor; while they need not be intelligible to the patient, they depict the tactics he wants to use toward a specific problem. The hallucination, again like certain dreams, turns out to be a device for objectifying subjective impulses, to the apparent objectivity of which the patient is absolutely committed. The compulsion towards freedom from responsibility does not permit that the volition should be guided by objective determination and replaces it by voices and visions which appear quite foreign to the patient. To this is added, as a fortification for the system, the biased, tendentious selection of recollections and evaluation of experiences, biased, that is, in favor of the delusion.

COMMENT *Here we should like to point out that when Adler speaks of hallucination as "a device for objectifying subjective impulses" he describes in fact what is today generally understood by "projection," although he never uses this term. It is interesting to recall that it was in relation to paranoia that Freud originally used the term projection in 1896 (36, I, p. 180).*

The paranoid attitude not only casts the mind but also the body into a role which fits the delusion. Stereotyped forms of speech, posture, and movement are connected with the guiding idea; incidentally these are found more abundantly in borderline cases and within the frame of dementia praecox. Depressive traits are frequently admixed to paranoia, and thus we find particularly complaints about poor sleep, inadequate nourishment, etc. These complaints are subsequently used in the direction of delusions of persecution, poisoning, or grandeur. The delusion of grandeur manifests itself at times only in the form of the patient's emphasis on the uniqueness of his suffering.

The self-evaluation of the paranoiac is exaggerated to godlikeness, but is erected as a compensation for a deep feeling of inferiority. This weakness is disclosed in his rapid renunciation of social demands and of his own plans, change of the theater of operations to the unreal, strong inclination toward the construction of paranoid preoccupying pretenses, and in blaming of others as a matter of principle. His distrust and disbelief in other people, and in their knowledge and ability, make possible the construction of cosmogenic, religious, and political ideas of his own invention in opposition to commonly held views. Since the patient obviously lacks self-confidence, he needs all this to maintain his own balance and his superiority.

To lose time in order to gain time, this is the guiding idea of the individual inclined to paranoia; it enforces all his delaying activities, including frequent change of occupation and vagrancy.

F. Melancholia and Related Disorders

1. MELANCHOLIA AS AGGRESSION[16]

Melancholia develops in individuals whose method of living has from early childhood on been dependent upon the achievements and the support of others. Such individuals will always try to lean on others and will not scorn the use of exaggerated hints at their own inadequacy to force the support, adjustment, and submissiveness of others. When a difficulty arises, they will evade the main issue, the continuation of their development, or even the adherence to their own sphere of action. According to the melancholic perspective, life resembles a difficult and enormous hazard, the preponderent majority of men are hostile, and the world consists of uncomfortable obstacles. By concretizing their subjective inferiority feeling, melancholiacs openly or implicitly raise the claim to a higher "disability compensation."

Their self-esteem from childhood on is clearly low, as can be concluded from their unceasing attempts to achieve greatest importance. They frequently point out how they missed an opportunity of an extraordinary development, thus disclosing an affinity with paranoia. In what really represents a disguised idea of greatness, the patient bewails the terrible fate which will overwhelm his family when he is gone; or he speaks in a self-accusatory way about his part in the destruction of the world, in the outbreak of the World War, or in the death and ruination of certain people. Melancholiacs accuse themselves openly of all kinds of inferiority and take upon themselves ostentatiously the blame for all failures and errors.

Together with these self-accusations and self-reproaches we always find disguised references to heredity, to parents' errors in bringing them up, and to willful lack of consideration on the part of relatives and superiors. This accusation of others, another similarity with paranoia, can be deduced from the situation which marks the onset of the melancholia.

Actually there is no psychological disease from which the environment suffers more and is more reminded of its unworthiness than melancholia. A proof for the aggressive nature of melancholia is found in the occasional murder impulses and the frequent penctration of the melancholic attitude by paranoid traits. Then "the guilt of the others" becomes very clear, as in the case of a patient who believed she was doomed to death by cancer because her husband had forced her to visit a relative who suffered from cancer. As a rule, however, the difference between the melancholic and the paranoid attitudes seems to be that in the former the patient apparently feels himself guilty, whereas the paranoiac accuses others, provided he is unable to enforce his superiority otherwise. We wish to note incidentally that these two types of blaming are commonly human and show themselves to be widespread, once one has acquired a keen eye for them.

The history of our patients shows us very clearly that melancholiacs never really become attached to anything; they soon feel uprooted, and they easily lose the belief in themselves and others. Even in their healthy days they show an ambitious but hesitating attitude, are afraid of any responsibility, and work on a life-lie the content of which is their own weakness, but the effect of which is the battle against others. It is a great mistake to attribute benevolence and kindness to melancholia.

The most prominent offensive weapons of the melancholic type are complaints, tears and depression, through which he shows his weakness and need for help. This peculiar form of aggression, caused by the early-acquired deficiency in social activity, proceeds in a way not unlike suicide, from an injury inflicted upon oneself to a threat toward the environment or to acts of revenge.

2. THE MELANCHOLIC FICTION[17]

Once the social determination and belligerent attitude of melancholia are understood, one will also see the goal of superiority by which the patient is hypnotized. The path which he takes in reaching his goal seems strange at first, it must be admitted. He makes himself small, anticipates a situation of the deepest misery, and draws from the empathy with this situation the emotion of grief and the attitude of a broken man. We may compare this to the actor of whom Hamlet says, "What's Hecuba to him, or he to Hecuba, That he should weep for her?" (*Hamlet*, Act II, Scene 2.) This may seem to be a contradiction to the ideal of greatness which we have asserted. But actually his weakness, which may go so far as annihilation, becomes a formidable weapon for securing significance and avoiding responsibility.

The psychological relationship to phobia and hypochondriasis is unmistakable, only that in melancholia insight into the disease vanishes and any criticism of the delusion is excluded, for the purpose of a stronger attack and because of a more comprehensive inferiority feeling. This is accomplished through a strong anticipation of an unavoidable disaster and resolute empathy into the threatening danger. The categorical imperative of melancholia becomes: "Act, think, and feel as if the horrible fate that you paint on the wall had already befallen you or were inevitable." The main prerequisite of melancholia is the godlike, prophetic look. The relationship with neurosis and psychosis in general becomes clear if we consider the pessimistic perspective as the common bond. In each case the symptom or attack of the patient signifies that he is removed from the present through anticipation, and from reality through empathy into a role [of a person who is already perishing].

Melancholia thus presents itself as an attempt and device to achieve the goal of superiority by detours. As in any neurosis and psychosis this is done through voluntary payment of the "cost of war." Thus this disease also resembles suicide attempts, in which it sometimes ends. Thought and speech inhibitions, stupor, and physical bearing make the picture of the "hesitating attitude" particularly tangible. Intended as disturbances of social functions, they also point to the restriction of social interest. Anxiety serves its usual purpose as safeguard, weapon, and proof of illness; violent attacks of rage at times break through as expressions of the fanaticism of weakness and as signs of the hidden activity; the delusions point to the sources of the biased tendentious fantasy which, in the service of the disease, furnishes and arranges the emotions for the patient. The suffering is most pronounced in the morning hours, which means, as soon as the patient is supposed to enter life.

3. ORGANIC ACCOMPANIMENTS[18]

Organs, insofar as they can be influenced, come under the power of the melancholic goal, adjust their functions to the total role, and thus help to establish the physiognomy of clinical melancholia. Incidentally, the malfunctioning of the organs must, from our point of view, represent the definite consequence of an inherited organ inferiority. Here, as well as in connection with eating, the patient often shows a series of self-induced disturbances which take place without sufficient self-criticism, but systematically and methodically. Eating is restricted by calling up thoughts suggestive of disgust or anxious suspicions (poison) and besides, like all other functions, is under the pressure of the biased tendentious melancholic empathy ("as if nothing were of use, as if everything must end badly"). Sleep is disturbed by compulsory brooding, by thinking of not sleeping. Bowel and urinary functions can become pathological by contrary influences or by making continual claims upon them, in some cases producing a condition of irritation in the respective organs. Heart activity, breathing, posture, and occasionally the tear glands come under the pressure of the melancholic fiction which strongly tends to a complete empathy into a situation of despair. The melancholia subsides as soon as the patient, by a proof of illness, has attained in one way or another the fictional feeling of having regained superiority and protection against possible misfortunes.

4. A DREAM IN MELANCHOLIA[19]

A melancholiac revealed the entire arrangement of his sickness by a dream which he had at the beginning of his treatment. He had fallen sick when he was transferred from a leading position to another place where he would have to make good all over again. Twelve years before, when he was twenty-six years old, he had become melancholic on a similar occasion. His dream was as follows: "I am in the boarding house where I regularly have my lunch. A girl who has interested me for a long time is waiting on the table. Suddenly I notice that the world is coming to an end. At that moment the thought strikes me that now I could rape the girl because I would be free of responsibility. After the deed it turned out that the world had not come to an end after all." The interpretation is not hard to find. We learn that the patient avoids, among other things, any decision in love because he fears the responsibility. He has often played with thoughts of the end of the world (enemy of mankind!). In sexual disguise the dream points to the necessity for believing in the end of the world in order to be triumphant. Thus he produces a situation where he is free from responsibility. The dream shows the patient on the way to reaching his goal by a fictional arrangement, an "as if," a trial attempt at doing violence to others.

5. MANIA[20]

Mania, in common with melancholia and the severer neuroses, is a barricade erected by the patient to block his own approach to the real business of life, and it is sometimes preliminary to the establishment of psychosis in the form of manic-depressive insanity. The first formidable phase of mental disorder, as we have seen, occurs invariably when some urgent problem presses for solution and the patient has lost courage. In mania there is an effort to overcome this cowardice, and the patient pushes himself forward, exaggerates his actions, and talks and laughs with needless excitement. He is high-spirited and irritable, has great projects, is very superior and boastful of his power, and displays strong sexual inclinations. These patients need watching or they may do damage, but this phase of their illness is a sudden blaze which soon consumes its fuel. The natural and usual sequel is a phase of melancholia in which the patient must on no account be restrained as he barricades himself from expression all too surely. Such alternations in manic-depressive insanity are manifested by individuals who showed slight phases of conduct of the same pattern in their earlier life. They begin with an excitement which rapidly wanes into a depression. This tendency is evident even in their handwriting, in which the first letter of a word is written very large, while the others decrease in size and drop below the line. Brilliant beginnings and sudden anticlimaxes are repeated at intervals throughout their life-histories.

The apparently "normal" phases, or apparently "sane" parts in the psychosis serve the purpose generally of obligating others, of giving them hope in order that the patient may combat them further. This is similar to the neurotic's being-in-love. In the forward as well as the backward movement of the psychological wave the hostile, belligerent trait, which at times ends in suicide, can clearly be recognized. Thus psychosis altogether appears to us as the mental suicide of an individual who does not believe himself adequate to the demands of society and to his own goals. In his backward movement there lies a secret *actio in distans*, a hostility against reality, while the forward movement always indicates through its exaltation an inner weakness and a bluff to overrun the others.

6. SUICIDE[21]

The observations of Individual Psychology have shown that every step of an individual is directed toward the successful solution of a presently imminent task. What the individual considers success is always a matter of his subjective opinion. Suicide is a solution only for one who in the face of an urgent problem has arrived at the end of his limited social interest.

Such persons as children were always poor losers. While they seldom made a direct attack against others, they always showed a style of life which attempted to influence others through increased complaining, sadness, and suffering. A tendency to collapse under psychological pain when confronted with difficult life situations often stood out in addition to increased ambition, vanity, and consciousness of their value for others. Fantasies of sickness or death, through which the pain of others reaches its highest degree, went parallel with this firm belief in their high value for others, a belief which they usually had acquired from the pampering situation of their childhood. I have found similar traits in the early history of melancholiacs, whose type borders on that of the suicide, and also of alcoholics and drug addicts. Reduced to the simplest form, the life style of the potential suicide is characterized by the fact that he hurts others by dreaming himself into injuries, or by administering them to himself. One will seldom go wrong in determining against whom the attack is aimed when one has found who is actually affected most by it.

A youth seventeen years old, the youngest in his family, and excessively spoiled by his mother, had to stay behind in the care of an elder sister when his mother set out on a journey. One evening, when left alone in the house by his sister, at a time when he was struggling with apparently insurmountable difficulties at school, he committed suicide. He left the following letter behind: "Don't tell mother what I have done. Her present address is ———. Tell her, when she comes back, that I no longer had any enjoyment in life. Tell her to put flowers on my grave every day." An old woman with an incurable illness committed suicide because her neighbor would not part with his wireless set. The chauffeur of a wealthy man, learning on his master's death that he was not to receive the bequest that had been promised him, killed his wife and daughter and committed suicide.

FOOTNOTES TO CHAPTER TWELVE

1. 1: *Über den nervösen Charakter* (1912a), 4th ed., p. 219; 2: "Nochmals—Die Einheit der Neurosen" (1930e), pp. 201–216; 3: "Lebenslüge und Verantwortlichkeit in der Neurose und Psychose" (1914c), p. 177; 4: "Melancholie und Paranoia" (1914e), p. 185; 5: "The structure of neurosis" (1932b), p. 10; 6 and 7: "Über neurotische Disposition" (1909), pp. 54 and 72.
2. 1: "Lecture to the Medical Society of Individual Psychology, London" (1934a), pp. 11–12; 2: *What Life Should Mean to You* (1931a), pp. 186–187.

3. 1 and 4: *Problems of Neurosis* (1929b), pp. 10–11 and 154; 2: *Menschenkenntnis* (1927a), p. 191; 3: *What Life Should Mean to You* (1931a), pp. 30–31.

4. 1 and 2: "Die Zwangsneurose" (1918c), pp. 140 and 140, 141–142; 3, 4, 5: "Compulsion Neurosis" (1931e), pp. 4, 7 and 6, and 5; 6: *Nervoser Charakter* (1912a), p. 187.

5. 1, 2, 3: "Compulsion" (1931e), pp. 19, 7, and 19–20.

6. 1 to 4: "Compulsion" (1931e), pp. 5, 7, 7, and 7–8.

7. "Compulsion" (1931e), p. 11.

8. 1, 2, 4: "Physical manifestions of psychic disturbances" (1934b), pp. 3, 6, and 7; 3: *Der Sinn des Lebens* (1933a), pp. 74–75.

9. 1 to 5: *Problems of Neurosis* (1929b), pp. 57–58, 58–59, 59, 59–60, and 60.

10. 1: "Nervöse Schlaflosigkeit" (1914d), p. 115; 2, 3, 4: "Sleeplessness" (1944), pp. 60, 61, and 64.

11. 1 to 4: *Problems of Neurosis* (1929b), pp. 156–158, 49–50, 50, and 42; 5: *Sinn des Lebens* (1933a), p. 42; 6, 7, 8: "Physical manifestations" (1934b), pp. 5, 4, and 5.

12. 1: *Problems of Neurosis* (1929b), pp. 128–129; 2: *What Life Should Mean to You* (1931a), pp. 60–61.

13. 1: *Problems of Neurosis* (1929b), p. 18; 2 and 3: *What Life Should Mean to You* (1931a), pp. 184 and 255.

14. 1 and 2: *What Life Should Mean to You* (1931a), pp. 256 and 256–257.

15. 1 to 6: "Melancholie" (1914e), pp. 191–192, 192–193, 194, 193–194, 193, and 195.

16. 1, 2, 3, 6: "Melancholie" (1914e), pp. 186, 187, 187, and 188–190; 4 and 5: "Lebenslüge" (1914c), pp. 180 and 184.

17. 1 and 3: "Lebenslüge" (1914c), pp. 179–180 and 183; 2: "Melancholie" (1914e), p. 188.

18. 1: "Melancholie" (1914e), pp. 190–191.

19. 1: "Lebensluge" (1914c), p. 181.

20. 1: *Problems of Neurosis* (1929b), p. 27; 2: "Melancholie" (1914e), pp. 192–193.

21. 1 and 2: "Selbstmord" (1937b), pp. 49–52; 3: *Social Interest* (1933b), pp. 133–134.

7. Contain...

CHAPTER THIRTEEN

UNDERSTANDING AND TREATING THE PATIENT

COMMENT *When Adler postulated the unity of the neuroses, by which he meant the dynamic similarity of all failures in life, categorical diagnosis necessarily lost its significance for him, and it became essential for him to grasp each individual case in its uniqueness. It is a characteristic of field theory in general, as distinguished from class theory, that the underlying explanatory constructs are relatively few and that consequently, in dealing with a concrete instance, the burden rests on the understanding of the unique interplay of the forces involved in that one instance.*

The question now arises, how did Adler deal with the specific case? The answer resolves itself into three parts: by understanding the specific, unique life-style of the patient; by enabling the patient himself to understand his life-style and the mistakes it contains; and by strengthening, through the therapeutic relationship, the rudiment of social interest which Adler always assumed to be still present. The rationale of therapy according to Adler is that once the patient has gained in courage, as an accompaniment of the increased social interest, and has gained an understanding of his mistakes, he will no longer make them.

1. Understanding the specific life-style of the patient, his specific problem situation, and the specific significance of his symptoms: *This is accomplished by an initial, tentative understanding of the patient, which is gained through empathy, intuition, and guessing. On this basis Adler formed what we might call a hypothesis of the patient's life-style and situation. At one time, when addressing a group of medical men, he termed this step of forming the hypothesis, the general diagnosis, and termed the verification of the hypothesis, the special diagnosis. This second step consists in a careful interpretation of all the expressions of the*

patient, to see what bearing these have on the hypothesis. "In the special diagnosis you must learn by testing . . . At first you have to guess at the cause. But then you have to prove it by other signs. If these do not agree, you must be severe enough with yourself to reject your first hypothesis and seek another explanation" (1931d, pp. 17–18).

2. Explaining the patient to himself: The understanding the therapist has gained must be communicated to the patient in such a way that he will accept this interpretation, despite his initial negativism and lack of cooperation, which are generally part of the neurotic syndrome. The therapist convinces the patient by being able to explain in the light of the patient's self-consistent, goal-directed style of life all of the patient's actions, even to the point of predicting them correctly.

3. Strengthening social interest: The therapist must discover whatever social interest there is in the patient and make contact with it, must strengthen this social interest by giving the patient the experience of a "fellow man" and of cooperation in the joint task of the treatment, and must spread this newly awakened social interest beyond himself to others. This procedure Adler explains as the "belated assumption of the maternal function" (see p. 341).

A. Understanding the Patient

1. METHODS FOR UNDERSTANDING[1]

Individual Psychology is committed to the principle of investigating the system of a psychological disorder along the path which the patient himself has taken. Our work has shown what great significance must be ascribed to the individual material which the patient has at his disposal and, still more, to his own evaluation of this material. Therefore an understanding of the individual and an individualizing examination became a main requirement.

All the methods of Individual Psychology for understanding the personality take into account the individual's opinion of his goal of superiority, the strength of his inferiority feeling, the degree of his social interest, and the fact that the whole individual cannot be torn from his context with life—or better said, from his context with society.

According to my experience, so far the most trustworthy approaches to the exploration of personality are given in a comprehensive understanding of (1) the earliest childhood recollections, (2) the position of the child in the birth order, (3) childhood disorders, (4) day and night dreams, and (5) the nature of the exogenous factor that causes the illness. All the results of such an investigation, which also include the attitude toward the physician, must be evaluated with the greatest caution, and their course must always be examined for consistency with other findings. In this way we will succeed in obtaining a faithful picture of the self-consistent style of life of an individual and in comprehending in the case of a failure the degree of his deviation, the nature of which always turns out to be a lack of the ability to make contact.

COMMENT   *The five specific diagnostic approaches listed above are presented in detail as follows: the exogenous, pathogenic factor, pages 296–297; earliest recollections, pages 350–357; dreams, pages 357–365; birth-order position, pages 376–382; and childhood behavior disorders, pages 386–392. Finally, an informal list of questions by Adler as a diagnostic interview guide for use with adult patients is presented at the end of Chapter 16, and is preceded by a more detailed schedule for use with child patients.*

The present section is concerned with the general principles of understanding the life style.

2. EMPATHY, INTUITION, AND GUESSING[2]

The partially unconscious course of the neurosis, which contradicts reality, is explained primarily by the unswerving tendency of the patient to arrive at his goal. The contradiction to reality, that is, to the logical demands of society, is related to the limited experiences and the peculiar human relationships which were effective at the time of the construction of the life-plan in early childhood. Insight into the meaning of this plan is best acquired through artistic and intuitive empathy with the essential nature of the patient. One will then notice how, unintentionally, one makes comparisons between oneself and the patient, between different attitudes of the same patient, or between similar attitudes of different patients. To give an orientation to one's observations, which include the patient's symptoms, experiences, manner of life, and development, I use three devices. The first assumes that the life-plan originated under aggravated conditions, such as organ inferiorities, pressure in the family, pampering, rivalry, or a neurotic family-tradition, and directs my attention to childhood reactions similar to the present symptoms. The second device assumes an equation [see p. 284] in which the personality ideal is the determining factor of the neurosis and according to which I enter my observation. The third device looks for the largest common denominator for all accessible expressive movements. [Adler added this third device in the 1930 revision.]

Until recent times it was chiefly the poets who best succeeded in getting the clue to a person's style of life. Their ability to show the individual living, acting, and dying as an indivisible whole in closest connection with the tasks of his environment rouses our highest admiration. This power was due to their gift of divination. Only by guessing did they come to see what lies behind and between the expressive movements, namely, the individual's law of movement. Many people call this gift *intuition* and believe that it is the special possession only of the greatest minds. In reality this gift is most human. Everyone makes use of it constantly in the chaos of life, before the abysmal uncertainty of the future. Correct guessing is the first step toward the mastery of our problems. But this correct guessing distinguishes especially the man who is a partner, a fellow man, and is interested in the successful solution of all human problems.

Some day soon it will be realized that the artist is the leader of mankind on the path to the absolute truth. Among poetic works of art which have led me to the insights of Individual Psychology the following stand out as pinnacles: fairy tales, the Bible, Shakespeare, and Goethe.

3. EXPRESSIVE BEHAVIOR AND SYMPTOMS[3]

The glance, the gait, the vigor or weakness of the patient's approach can reveal a great deal. Much may be missed if one becomes accustomed to rules such as assigning a particular place, like a couch, or keeping to a certain time. The first interview, although entirely unconstrained, should already be a test. Even the handshake may suggest a definite problem. One often sees that pampered persons like to lean against something, and that children cling to their mothers. But, just as with everything that requires the ability to guess, so here also one should avoid strict rules and should verify instead. I see an advantage in not interrupting the patient's movements. Let him get up, come and go, or smoke as he likes. I have even occasionally given patients the opportunity to go to sleep in my presence when they proposed this, thus making my task more difficult. Such an attitude spoke as clearly as hostile words. A patient's sidelong glance also clearly indicates his slight inclination to cooperate. This can become conspicuous in other ways as well, as when the patient says little or nothing, when he beats about the bush, or when by incessant talking he prevents the consultant from speaking. For the patient the consultation is a social problem, like every encounter of one person with another. Everyone will introduce himself according to his law of movement. The expert can often tell something of the patient's social feeling at the first glance.

I have found it of considerable value to conduct myself as during a pantomime, that is, for a while not to pay any attention to the words of the patient, but instead to read his deeper intention from his bearing and his movements within a situation. In doing so one will sense the sharp contradiction between the seen and the heard expressions and recognize clearly the meaning of symptoms.

We must remember that the patient has no understanding of his own forms of expression and is thus unable to conceal his true self. We see his personality in action and revealed, not by what he says or thinks about himself, but by his acts interpreted in their context. Not that the patient deliberately wants to lie to us, but we have learned to recognize a vast gulf between a man's conscious thoughts and his unconscious motivations, a gulf which can best be bridged by a disinterested but sympathetic outsider. The outsider, whether he be the psychologist, or the parent, or the teacher, should learn to interpret a personality on the basis of objective facts seen as the expression of the purposive, but more or less unconscious, strivings of the individual.

We look upon symptoms as creations, as works of art. Thus when we try to prove something from any particular symptom we can do so only if we look upon the symptom as a single part of a complete whole, that is, we must find in every symptom something that lies deeper than the outward and visible signs, something that underlies the actual manifestation and the form of the complaint itself. We must look behind the headache, the anxiety symptom, the obsession idea, behind the fact of an individual being a thief or a loafer in school. For behind lies something more, something personal and entirely individual. The more we understand of the structure of the psyche, the more will we realize that no symptom observed in two different cases has ever exactly the same significance. But there is one assumption we can make in all cases: a symptom is connected with the individual's struggle to reach a chosen goal.

4. THE ORGANIC COMPONENT[4]

In the first interviews with the patient we must make sure whether it really is a case of neurosis or one of organic disorder. If I do not suspect a real organic disorder, I may temporarily exclude that aspect of the case from consideration, and proceed to investigate the circumstances and style of life. If on the other hand, it is evidently a case of organic disorder, I must consider whether the complaint and suffering are greater than the illness itself would justify, that is, whether there is a combination of organic and psychic illness. In such cases I have often found more pain than the illness warrants, or unaccountable excitement which may increase the fever. In organic illness, also, the appetite varies according to the general outlook, and a serious illness may be prolonged or even fatally influenced if the patient turns pessimistic or becomes psychologically lethargic.

5. VERIFYING THE UNDERSTANDING[5]

To verify my findings, I check one indication by another [for internal consistency], eliciting information of many various kinds. We can thus more easily comprehend the style of life; and if we always check and verify each impression by others, we shall not be misled into mere generalizations.

There are a number of tests for the correctness of a neuropsychiatric opinion. (1) The psychiatrist examines the patient in the presence of the family physician, without asking leading questions or doing any systematic questioning. Yet he must proceed so that the whole personality is illuminated. The family physician, without having been given any explanation previously, will from the questions and answers of the examination usually see the coherence which comes to light, whereas the patient will remain completely unaware of it.

(2) The above method is not incontestable, therefore a second test for the correctness of our view of the symptom is necessary. Set aside the symptom and the actual reason for the treatment completely, and concern yourself only with the personality of the patient. Try to gain information about him, to explore his nature, his intentions in life, and his attitude toward the demands of his family and society. Soon you will achieve a fairly sharply outlined character-picture into which the various traits can be fitted. (3) Look for an assumption according to which the

behavior of the patient becomes understandable. If you have made the correct assumption, you will find that the patient also uses it as his starting point, although he does not comprehend its significance. (4) Ask the patient: What would you do if you were completely well? Most certainly he will name precisely that demand of society which we would expect him to avoid.

I try to note what activities, of a kind normally to be expected, are being excluded by the patient. As soon as I feel I have grasped his circumstances, I inquire whether the patient's thoughts, feelings, actions, and characteristics are all working in the same direction, towards the exclusion or at least the postponement of a present problem. The discussion invariably reveals an accented "if." "I would marry if . . ." "I would resume my work if . . ." "I would take my examination if . . ." and so on. The neurotic has always collected some more or less plausible reasons to justify his escape from the challenge of life, but he does not realize what he is doing.

(5) The correctness of the results is further checked if the guiding lines, which we have deduced from the essential nature of the patient, afford us an understanding of the symptom as necessary, somehow usable, and expedient.

Since the struggle to reach a position of vantage is the key to the whole personality, we shall meet it at every point of the individual's psychological life. To recognize this fact gives us two further great aids in our task of understanding an individual style of life. (6) We can begin wherever we choose: every expression will lead us in the same direction—towards the one motive, the one melody, around which the personality is built. (7) We are provided with a vast store of material. Every word, thought, feeling, or gesture contributes to our understanding. Any mistake we might make in considering one expression too hastily can be checked and corrected by a thousand other expressions. We cannot finally decide the meaning of one expression until we can see its part in the whole; but every expression is saying the same thing, every expression is urging us towards the solution. In a way we are like archaeologists who find fragments of earthenware, tools, the ruined walls of buildings, broken monuments, and leaves of papyrus; and from these fragments proceed to infer the life of a whole city which has perished. Only we are dealing not with something which has perished, but with the inter-organized aspects of a human being, a living personality which can continuously set before us new manifestations of its own meaning.

B. Explaining the Patient to Himself

1. THE PATIENT'S MISTAKE[6]

The apperception-schema of the patient evaluates all impressions as if they were fundamental matters and dichotomizes them in a purposeful manner into above-below, victor-vanquished, masculine-feminine, nothing-everything, etc. It is due to such a schema that one finds traits in the neurotic similar to those found in the beginnings of culture, where necessity also forced people to such safeguards. This is why we call the neurotic schema primitive. It would be fantastic to suspect in such analogies anything more than mimicry, let alone a repetition of phylogenesis. This apperception-schema must always be traced and unmasked as being immature and untenable, but suited to the purpose of continued fighting.

At the same time there must be uncovered, step by step, the unattainable goal of superiority over all; the purposive concealment of this goal; the all-dominating, direction-giving power of the goal; the patient's lack of freedom and his hostility toward mankind, which are determined by the goal. Similarly we find the proof, as soon as sufficient material is at hand, that all neurotic character traits, the neurotic affects and symptoms, serve as means to continue along the prescribed path and to make that path more secure.

So long as he does not understand this error, so long as he regards his fictional world as the right one, so long as he finds the real objective world unbearable for his vanity, he will remain a neurotic. If he can abandon his dream of a world, a dream which was born of his vanity and which justifies his vanity, then more and more will it be possible for him to begin to feel himself an equal among equals, and less and less will he feel dependent upon the opinions of others. His courage, too, will mount and his reason and "common sense" will increase and gain control where heretofore he has been under the sway of his "private sense."

In a somnambulistic sort of way the neurotic person is so much involved in the world he has created during his early childhood that he needs the help provided by discussions under objective Individual Psychological direction to enable him to understand himself sufficiently so that he can increase his ability to cooperate. The cure or reorientation is brought about by a correction of the faulty picture of the world and the unequivocal acceptance of a mature picture of the world.

2. HELPING INSIGHT[7]

The uncovering of the neurotic system, or life-plan (or style of life) for the patient, is the most important component in therapy. The reason for this is that the life-plan in its entirety can be kept intact only if the patient succeeds in withdrawing it from his own criticism and understanding. The uncovering of the neurotic life-plan proceeds apace in friendly and free conversation, in which it is always indicated that the patient take the initiative. I have found it best merely to search for the patient's neurotic line of operation in all his expressions and thoughts and to unmask it, and at the same time train the patient unobtrusively to do the same.

The physician must be so convinced of the uniqueness and exclusiveness of the neurotic direction line, that he is able to foretell the patient's disturbing devices and constructions, always to find and explain them, until the patient, completely upset, gives them up—only to put new and better hidden ones in their place. How often this will occur is impossible to say beforehand. But ultimately the patient will give in. He will do so the more readily, the less his relation to the physician has permitted the feeling of a defeat to develop. Just as the neurotic devices lie along the path to the feeling of some superiority, so there are also definite subjective sources of error which are utilized and conserved for the very reason that somehow they deepen the feeling of inferiority and thus furnish stimuli and incentive for further precautions. Such errors together with their purpose must be brought within the vision of the patient.

Among my patients, children and adults, I have never yet found one to whom it would not have been possible to explain his erroneous mechanism. To be sure, my patients are almost always intelligent.

3. EXPLAINING[8]

I always use the simplest and most direct method possible in the treatment of neurotics, but it would be of no use to tell a patient, for example, "You are a domineering woman, and you are now trying to rule by means of illness," for she would be offended. I must win her first, and take her part as far as possible. Every neurotic is partly right. In this particular case, if the woman did not feel deprived of value by her advancing age—a real privation of women in our present culture—

she would not cling to her prestige in such unseemly ways. But it is only very gradually that I can bring her to face the truth about what she is doing.

In cases of alcoholism and drug addiction [to give another example], it would be useless merely to take away the poison and say some encouraging words. The patient must realize why he took to drink. But insufficient also would be his recognition of the general principles of Individual Psychology, that those who turn inebriate have lost social courage and interest, or succumbed to fear of an imminent defeat. It is easy for the physician to say, and even for the patient to believe, that he turned to drink because of a sense of inferiority which originated in childhood, yet nothing will come out of the mere phraseology. The physician must grasp the special structure and development of that individual life with such accuracy, and express it with such lucidity, that the patient knows he is plainly understood and recognizes his own mistake.

When patients or practitioners come to me and say: "We have explained everything," or "We quite understand, and yet we cannot succeed," I consider their statements ridiculous. Always if I go into such a case of unsuccessful treatment I find that neither physician nor patient have understood the matter nor explained anything. Sometimes the patient has felt inferior and suppressed by the physician, and resisted all true explanation. Occasionally the tables have been turned and the patient has been treating the doctor! Not infrequently an inexperienced practitioner teaches the patient the theories of Individual Psychology in such phrases as "You lack social courage, you are not interested in others, you feel inferior," and so forth, which may be worse than useless. A real explanation must be so clear that the patient knows and feels his own experience instantly.

Nobody who has understood anything of Individual Psychology would attempt to cure by upbraiding the patient, as if we could do good by taking up a moralistic attitude. A patient has to be brought into such a state of feeling that he likes to listen, and wants to understand. Only then can he be influenced to live what he has understood.

That the patient is under no circumstances to be offended, I need not tell psychologically trained physicians. But this may occur without the knowledge of the physician, as when the patient may purposely revaluate harmless remarks which the physician may make as long as he does not clearly understand the nature of the patient. Therefore, particularly at the beginning, reserve is called for, and it is essential to grasp as quickly as possible the neurotic system. With some experience this may usually be discovered on the first day.

4. THE ACTUAL CURE[9]

The actual change in the nature of the patient can only be his own doing. I have found it most profitable to sit ostentatiously with my hands in my lap, fully convinced that no matter what I might be able to say on the point, the patient can learn nothing from me that he, as the sufferer, does not understand better, once he has recognized his life-line.

From the very beginning the consultant must try to make it clear that the responsibility for his cure is the patient's business, for as the English proverb very rightly says: "You can lead a horse to water, but you can't make him drink." One should always look at the treatment and the cure not as the success of the consultant but as the success of the patient. The adviser can only point out the mistakes, it is the patient who must make the truth living.

[The alleviation of symptoms, as against a complete cure, is also the patient's own doing.] In a considerable portion of neurotics, the turning to a physician, sometimes even to another person, is of itself enough to drive the patient on further. In approximately half of the neurotics, the call on the physician signifies their decision to get better, that is, to give up a symptom which has become superfluous or [too] disturbing. It is this 50 per cent of "cures" that enables all schools of psychiatry to continue to live.

c. The Therapeutic Relationship

1. DEPRECIATION TENDENCY AND RESISTANCE[10]

I expect from the patient again and again the same attitude which he has shown in accordance with his life-plan toward the persons of his former environment, and still earlier toward his family. At the moment of the introduction to the physician and often even earlier, the patient has the same feelings toward him as toward important persons in general. The assumption that the transference of such feelings or that resistance begins later is a mere deception. In such cases the physician only recognizes them later. Often it is then too late, if the patient in the mean-time has terminated the treatment while enjoying his hidden superiority, or has created an unbearable situation by a worsening of his symptoms.

It is the depreciation tendency [see pp. 267-269] which underlies the phenomenon Freud described as resistance and erroneously understood as the consequence of the repression of sexual impulses. The neurotic comes to the physician with this tendency, and he carries it away with him after the treatment, but considerably diminished, more like that of the normal person. The increased insight into himself then stands like a guardian over the patient and forces him to find more useful paths for his desire to be above, and to dampen his depreciation tendency.

COMMENT   *At the time when Adler wrote the above, 1912, Freud was explaining resistance as a repression phenomenon. "The pathogenic process which is demonstrated by the resistances we call re-pression" (38, p. 259). Toward the end of his life, however, Freud had come closer to seeing resistance as an expression of noncooperation. In 1937 he wrote: "These phenomena [including resistance] are unmistaka-ble indications of the existence of a power in mental life which, accord-ing to its aim, we call the aggressive or destructive instinct and which we derive from the primal death-instinct of animate matter" (36, V, p. 346).*

The following must be understood as forms of the depreciation tend-ency, which may at times be directed against the psychotherapist: ex-pressions of doubt, criticism, forgetfulness, tardinesses, any special re-quests by the patient, relapses after initial improvement, persistent silence, as well as stubborn retention of symptoms. These are often most subtle expressions. The therapist must have broad experience with and knowledge of the depreciation tendency not to be taken by surprise.

Since the physician obstructs the neurotic strivings of the patient, the physician is regarded as an obstacle, an obstruction, preventing the at-tainment of the superiority-ideal along the path of the neurosis. There-fore every patient will attempt to depreciate the physician, to deprive him of his influence, and to conceal from him the true state of affairs; the patient will always find new twists aimed at the psychotherapist. Especially as improvement progresses, will the patient attempt more energetically to jeopardize the success of the treatment by being un-punctual, wasting time, or staying away. When there is a standstill, there is usually hearty friendship and peace—except that the neurotic symp-toms continue. At times a specially marked hostility arises which, like all the phenomena of resistance, can be neutralized only if the patient's attention is drawn again and again to the essential similarity of all of his behavior.

A patient who had been under treatment for two months came to me one day and asked whether she could not come the next time at four o'clock instead of three. No matter how insistently patients in such cases plead the necessity of their requests, we are justified in assuming that this is an indication of intensified aggressiveness directed against the physician. The patient claimed that she would have to go to the dress-maker at three o'clock, a rather weak reason which was only slightly strengthened by the fact that owing to the length of the treatment, her free time was somewhat restricted. As I was not free at the hour she requested, I tentatively suggested five to six. This the patient rejected because her mother would be free at five and expected her at a friend's house. So we see that we are justified in assuming that the patient is showing resistance to the treatment.

The so-called *resistance* is only lack of courage to return to the useful side of life. This causes the patient to put up a defense against treatment, for fear that his relation with the psychologist should force him into some useful activity in which he will be defeated. For this reason we must never force a patient, but guide him very gently towards his easiest approach to usefulness. If we apply force he is certain to escape.

2. DISARMING THE PATIENT[11]

It is very necessary to keep from the patient any point from which he could attack. I can only give a few hints here designed to prevent the physician from falling into the position of being treated by the patient. For example, one should never, not even in the most certain cases, promise a cure, but rather only the possibility of a cure. One of the most important devices in psychotherapy is to ascribe the work and the success of the therapy to the patient at whose disposal one should place oneself in a friendly way, as a coworker.

For successful treatment it is absolutely necessary that the physician have a great deal of tact, renounce superior authority, be equally friendly at all times, be alertly interested, and have the cool-headed feeling that he is facing a sick person with whom he must not fight, but who is always ready to start a fight.

"To knock the weapons out of his hand," that is, to have the abnormal means of the neurotic appear ineffectual is the goal of every psychotherapeutic tactic. A patient once asked me, smiling, "Has anyone ever taken his life while being treated by you?" I answered him, "Not yet, but I am prepared for this to happen at any time."

A girl of twenty-seven who came to consult me after five years of suffering said: "I have seen so many doctors that you are my last hope in life." "No," I answered, "not the last hope. Perhaps the last but one. There may be others who can help you too." Her words were a challenge to me; she was daring me not to cure her, so as to make me feel bound in duty to do so. This is the type of patient who wishes to shift responsibility upon others, a common development of pampered children. It is important to evade such a challenge. The patient may have worked up a high tension of feeling about the idea that the doctor is his "last hope," but we must accept no such distinction. To do so would be to prepare the way for a disappointment, or even suicide.

To predict the possibility of an aggravation of the disease in cases of fainting spells, pains, or agoraphobia, saves a great amount of work at the beginning, because the attacks, as a rule, then do not take place. This fact corroborates our view about the marked negativism of neurotics. To show pleasure at a partial success or to boast about it would be a great mistake; the situation would soon take a turn for the worse. It is therefore better to turn one's manifest interest to the difficulties patiently, without annoyance, and in a calm scientific manner.

A basic principle for the therapist is never to allow the patient to force upon him a superior role such as that of teacher, father, or saviour, without contradicting and enlightening the patient. Such attempts represent the beginning of a movement on the part of the patient to pull down, in a manner to which he has been previously accustomed, all persons standing above him, and by thus administering a defeat, to disavow them. [See pp. 268–269.] To insist upon any superior rank or right is always disadvantageous with neurotic patients.

Special caution is called for in persuading the patient to any kind of venture. If this should come up, the consultant should say nothing for or against it, but, ruling out as a matter of course all generally dangerous undertakings, should only state that, while convinced of the success, he could not quite judge whether the patient was really ready for the venture. Spurring the patient on before he has acquired a greater social interest will usually have to be atoned for by a strengthening or a recurrence of the symptoms.

My own practice, also, is never to advise marriage or free relations. I find that it always leads to bad results. A patient who is told that he should marry or seek sexual experience is quite likely to develop impotence.

In the question of occupation, we can proceed more energetically. This does not mean requesting the patient to take up an occupation, but pointing out to him that he is best prepared for one or another occupation and could accomplish something in it.

The patient may bring complaints about his family. These must be anticipated in order to make it plain to him beforehand that his relations are to blame only so long as he makes them blameworthy by his conduct, and that they will immediately be blameless as soon as he feels himself well; further, that one cannot expect more knowledge from the patient's relatives than he himself possesses; and that he has on his own responsibility used the influences of his environment as building-bricks for constructing his mistaken style of life. It is also well to remind him that his parents, in the event of their being at fault, can appeal to the mistakes of their parents, and so on through the generations, so that for this reason there can be no blame in his sense of the word.

On the other hand, I always find the hostile relationship of the patient's relatives to the physician of advantage and sometimes have attempted to stir it up carefully. Since generally the tradition of the patient's entire family is similarly neurotic, one can greatly benefit the patient by disclosing and explaining this.

3. AWAKENING SOCIAL INTEREST[12]

Psychotherapy is an exercise in cooperation and a test of cooperation. We can succeed only if we are genuinely interested in the other. We must be able to see with his eyes and listen with his ears. He must contribute his part to our common understanding. We must work out his attitudes and his difficulties together. Even if we felt we had understood him, we should have no witness that we were right unless he also understood. A tactless truth can never be the whole truth; it shows that our understanding was not sufficient. We must cooperate with him in finding his mistakes, both for his own benefit and for the welfare of others.

All cases of failure which we have seen involve a lack of cooperation. Therefore cooperation between patient and consultant, as the first, serious scientifically conducted attempt to raise social interest, is of paramount importance, and from the start all measures should be taken to promote the cooperation of the patient with the consultant. Obviously this is only possible if the patient feels secure with the physician.

The task of the physician or psychologist is to give the patient the experience of contact with a fellow man, and then to enable him to transfer this awakened social interest to others. This method of winning the patient's good will, and then transferring it to his environment, is strictly analogous to the function of the mother, whose social task it is to interpret society to the individual. If the mother fails in this, the task is likely to fall much later to the physician, who is heavily handicapped for it. The mother has the enormous advantage of the physical and psychological relation; she represents the greatest experience of love and fellowship that the child will ever have.

For the psychologist the first rule is to win the patient; the second is never to worry about his own success; if he does so, he forfeits it. The psychotherapist must lose all thought of himself and all sensitiveness about his ascendency, and must never demand anything of the patient. Since his is a belated assumption of the maternal function, he must work with a corresponding devotion to the patient's needs. The patient's social interest, which is always present in some degree, finds its best possible expression in the relation with the psychologist.

The consultee must under all circumstances get the conviction that in relation to the treatment he is absolutely free. He can do, or not do, as he pleases.

4. ENCOURAGEMENT[13]

COMMENT   *The above is, of course, a description of what today would be called permissive atmosphere. In Adler the meaning of permissive atmosphere would be the unconditional expression of social interest on the part of the psychotherapist. The function of such an expression would be to decrease the patient's feeling of inferiority and thereby, at the same time, to activate the remnant of social interest in the patient and bring it to a stage of adequate development. Activating social interest may be taken as Adler's definition of encouragement, since he equates courage with activity plus social interest (see p. 166).*

The following case is an extreme example of this atmosphere. It is actually the same as that of the girl suffering from schizophrenia presented above (pp. 316–317), but in the present selection Adler has changed the description to that of a man in order better to disguise the identity of the patient. For this information we are indebted to Kurt A. Adler.

On one occasion I was actually menaced by a weakly man who suffered from dementia praecox and who was completely cured by me after having been declared incurable three years earlier. I knew that he expected to be given up and rejected by me also; this was in accordance with the notion of his fate which he had held since childhood. For three months he remained silent during the treatment. I used this time to give him cautious explanations of his life in so far as I knew about it. I recognized his silence and similar actions as an inclination to obstruct me. Finally as a culmination of his tactics he lifted his hand to strike me, against which I instantly resolved not to defend myself. After a further attack during which a window was smashed, I bound up his slightly bleeding wound in the friendliest way. (I know that my friends will not generalize from this case any more than from any other!) Later, when I was completely assured of the success of the treatment, I asked him: "How in your opinion did we both succeed in making you well?" His answer ought to make a very strong impression in interested circles. He replied: "That's quite simple. I had lost all courage to live. In our consultations I found it again." If one has recognized the Individual Psychology truth that courage is but one side of social interest, one will understand the transformation of this man.

In Individual Psychology treatment we have appreciable help [for building up courage] in that we are always able to draw attention to errors only and never to innate defects, to the possibilities of a cure and to equality with others, and also to the generally low level of social interest.

Altogether, in every step of the treatment, we must not deviate from the path of encouragement. This is in accordance with the conviction of Individual Psychology, by which so much untenable vanity feels offended, that "everybody can do everything" with the exception of amazingly high achievement, about the structure of which we cannot say very much anyway.

5. SOCIAL INTEREST IN OTHER FORMS OF PSYCHOTHERAPY[14]

One must strictly avoid arousing artificially, by continually pointing to suppressed sexual components, and in the face of an unchanged inferiority feeling and the relative insecurity of the patient toward the physician, the psychological tendency which Freud has called the *positive transference*. This is virtually demanded in the psychoanalytic treatment, but it only adds the new task of having to make this artificially created condition disappear again. By teaching the patient to take full responsibility for his conduct, the consultant will easily be able to prevent him from falling into the trap of positive transference, which seems to promise him an easy and immediate satisfaction of unfulfilled desires.

To spoil a patient who is accustomed to being spoiled [as in positive transference] may be an easy way to gain affections. But we shall not be able to help him either by spoiling or by slighting him. We must show him the interest of one man towards a fellow man; no interest could be truer or more objective.

In so far as what the Freudians call *transference* can be discussed apart from sexual implications, it is merely social interest.

Neurosis and psychosis are modes of expression for human beings who have lost courage. Anyone who has acquired this much insight into Individual Psychology will thenceforth refrain from undertaking with persons in this state of discouragement tedious excursions into mysterious regions of the psyche. Even such conjectures with regard to primary psychic processes as may chance to be correct would only serve as a welcome way of escape from the consideration of the problems of life. It is true that a powerful and helpful effect may be produced by this method; but, as in treatment by suggestion and hypnosis, this is simply the encouragement derived by the patient from the humane and patient work put in by the physician.

We are far from denying that other schools of psychiatry have their successes in dealing with neuroses, but in our experience they do so less by their methods than when they happen to give the patient a good human relationship with the physician, or above all, to give him encouragement. A quack or an osteopath may improve a person's attitude to life to a considerable extent; so also may a St. Anne de Beaupré, a Christian Scientist, or a Coué, or a visit to Lourdes. But we remain convinced that the cure of all mental disorder lies in the simpler, if more laborious, process of making the patient understand his own mistakes.

D. Special Aspects and Techniques of Treatment

1. DURATION AND EVALUATION[15]

If the patient at the first interview is in doubt as to whether he will undergo the treatment, let him make the decision in the next few days. The usual question about the duration of the treatment is not easy to answer. This question is quite justified, because a large number of those who visit me have heard of treatments which have lasted eight years and have still been unsuccessful. An Individual Psychology treatment, if properly carried out, should show at least a perceptible partial success in three months, often even sooner. One does well, in order to keep a door open for social interest from the start, to emphasize that the duration of the treatment depends on the cooperation of the patient; that the physician, if he is well-grounded in Individual Psychology, can find his bearings after half an hour; but that he must wait until the patient, too, has recognized his style of life and its mistakes. Still one can add: "If you are not convinced in one or two weeks that we are on the right path, I will stop the treatment."

Every interview should consider whether the patient is on the way to cooperation. Every gesture, every expression, everything he says or does not say is evidence thereof. A thorough understanding of his dreams likewise affords the opportunity to assess the success, the lack of success and the cooperation.

COMMENT *Adler was generally aware of the necessity for checking up on the results of any influence which is being exerted. For example, he wrote: " 'To educate' means not only to bring favorable influences to bear, but also to keep a sharp watch to see how the child uses them, in order to intervene further, if necessary" (1933c, pp. 73 and 90). This is a striking parallel to Lewin's reminder in reference to social psychology that the effectiveness of various techniques of change should be studied experimentally, which procedure he called action research. As Lewin expressed it: "We need reconnaissance to show us whether we move in the right direction and with what speed we move" (66, p. 38).*

2. PRACTICAL ASPECTS[16]

The unavoidable question of the fee often causes difficulties. I have had patients who have lost a considerable fortune in previous treatments. The consultant must bring himself into line with the customary fees. He should, however, in the interest of the required social feeling abstain from making unusually large demands, especially when these could be harmful to the patient. Gratuitous treatment should be given in a manner which does not allow the patient to feel that there is any lack of interest in his case, which is probably what he will be afraid of. The payment of a lump sum, even when that seems advantageous, or a promise to pay after successful treatment, should be declined, not because the latter is uncertain, but because it introduces artificially a new motive into the relationship between the doctor and his patient which makes success more difficult.

Making payments contingent upon the success of the treatment creates enormous difficulties for the patient. It is best to assume at every point that the patient, in his craving for superiority, will use any commitment by the physician, including length of treatment, to defeat the physician. Consequently all the necessary questions—the visiting time, the question of fees, free treatment, the physician's pledge to secrecy, etc.—should be regulated immediately and be strictly adhered to. To demand secrecy from the patient indicates lack of any knowledge of the psychology of the neurotic; on the other hand the physician must promise and keep strictest secrecy. It is under all circumstances a tremendous advantage if the patient goes to the physician.

Demands or expectations of any kind always harm the treatment. Even small favors which the patient often offers must be refused. Gifts should be declined in a friendly manner, or their acceptance postponed until after the treatment has been completed. There should be no mutual invitations or joint visits during the treatment.

In dealing with the parents and relatives of the patient one should never be critical; one should describe the case as worth considering and never as lost, even if one is not inclined to take it on. In an absolutely lost case, however, important circumstances may require stating the truth. When, during the course of treatment, unduly great difficulties appear, it seems advisable to declare oneself unable to deal with the case and to refer the patient to others who may be more capable.

3. THERAPEUTIC DEVICES AND TACTICS[17]

I have always found it an immense advantage to keep the level of tension in the treatment as low as possible, and I have virtually developed a method of telling almost every patient that there are jokes altogether like the structure of his peculiar neurosis, and that therefore the latter can also be taken more lightly than he does. References to fables and historical characters, and quotations from poets and philosophers help to strengthen the confidence in Individual Psychology and in its views.

One of my patients in a tension of feelings about going out-of-doors developed stomach and respiratory troubles. Many neurotics begin to swallow air when they get into a state of tension, which causes flatulence, stomach trouble, anxiety, and palpitation, besides affecting the breathing. When I made him realize that this was his condition he asked the usual question: "What shall I do not to swallow air?" Sometimes I reply: "I can tell you how to mount a horse, but I can't tell you how not to mount a horse." Or sometimes I advise: "If you want to go out, and feel in a conflict about it, swallow some air quickly." This man, like some other patients, swallowed air even in his sleep, but after my advice he began to control himself, and discontinued the habit.

Melancholiacs are often inclined to revenge themselves by committing suicide, and the doctor's first care is to avoid giving them an excuse for suicide. I myself try to relieve the whole tension by proposing to them, as the first rule in treatment, "Never do anything you don't like." This seems to be a very modest request, but I believe that it goes to the root of the whole trouble. If a depressed person is able to do anything he wants, whom can he accuse? What has he got to revenge himself for? "If you want to go to the theater," I tell him, "or to go on a holiday, do it. If you find on the way that you don't want to, stop it." It is the best situation any one could be in. It gives a satisfaction to his striving for superiority. He is like God and can do what he pleases. On the other hand, it does not fit very easily into his style of life. He wants to dominate and accuse others; if they agree with him, there is no way of dominating them. This rule is a great relief, and I have never had a suicide among my patients. It is understood, of course, that it is best to have someone to watch such a patient, and some of my patients have not been watched as closely as I should have liked. So long as there is an observer, there is no danger. Generally the patient replies, "But there is nothing I like doing." I have prepared for this answer, because I have heard it so often. "Then refrain from doing anything you dislike," I say. Sometimes, however, he will reply, "I should like to stay in bed all day." I know that if I allow it, he will no longer want to do it. I know that if I hinder him, he will start a war. I always agree.

Another rule is to attack the style of life of the patients still more directly. I tell them, "You can be cured in fourteen days if you follow this prescription. Try to think every day how you can please someone." See what this means to them. They are occupied with the thought, "How can I worry someone." The answers are very interesting. Some say, "This will be very easy for me. I have done it all my life." They have never done it. I ask them to think it over. They do not think it over. I tell them, "You can make use of all the time you spend when you are unable to go to sleep by thinking how you can please someone, and it will be a big step forward in your health." When I see them next day, I ask them, "Did you think over what I suggested?" They answer, "Last night I went to sleep as soon as I got into bed." All this must be done, of course, in a modest, friendly manner, without a hint of superiority. Others will answer, "I could never do it. I am so worried." I tell them, "Don't stop worrying; but at the same time you can think now and then of others." I want to direct their interest always towards their fellows. Many say, "Why should I please others? Others do not try to please me." "You must think of your health," I answer. "The others will suffer later on." It is extremely rarely that I have found a patient who said, "I have thought over what you suggested." All my efforts are devoted towards increasing the social interest of the patient. I know that the real reason for his malady is his lack of cooperation, and I want him to see it too. As soon as he can connect himself with his fellow men on an equal and cooperative footing, he is cured.

4. GROUP THERAPY[18]

COMMENT Group therapy would seem a logical development for Individual Psychology with its emphasis on "common sense"
versus "private intelligence," and with its understanding of all individual
problems as social problems which can only be solved by cooperation. Although Adler himself never practiced group therapy he suggested its use
for the treatment of criminals.

While I do not believe it would be possible to give every criminal an individual treatment, we could contribute much by a group treatment. I should propose, for instance, that we should have discussions with a great number of criminals on social problems, exactly as we have been considering them here. We should question them and let them answer; we should enlighten their minds and waken them from their life-long dream; we should free them from the intoxication of a private interpretation of the world and so low an opinion of their own possibilities; we should teach them not to limit themselves and diminish their fear of the situations and the social problems which they must meet. I am very sure that we could achieve great results from such group treatment.

COMMENT   *Whereas the above was only a suggestion, Adler did pioneer in a method which has certain aspects of group therapy. It is the method which he employed in his child-guidance clinics and consists in treating the children in front of and in cooperation with a group of adults. The common factor in this form of therapy and group therapy is that an individual's problems are discussed in front of a group and thus become objectified (see pp. 392–394).*

FOOTNOTES TO CHAPTER THIRTEEN

1. 1: "Das Problem der 'Distanz' " (1914b), p. 73; 2 and 3: *Der Sinn des Lebens* (1933a), pp. 25 and 26.
2. 1: "Individualpsychologische Behandlung der Neurosen" (1913c), p. 29; 2: *Sinn des Lebens* (1933a), pp. 20–21; 3: "Individualpsychologische Bemerkungen zu Alfred Bergers 'Hofrat Eysenhardt' " (1913d), p. 197.
3. 1: *Sinn des Lebens* (1933a), pp. 191–192; 2: "Individualpsychologische Behandlung" (1913c), p. 32; 3: *The Education of Children* (1930a), pp. 16–17; 4: "How the child selects his symptoms" (1936c), p. 67.
4. 1: *Problems of Neurosis* (1929b), pp. 70–71.
5. 1 and 4: *Problems of Neurosis* (1929b), p. 72; 2, 3, 5: "Die Zwangsneurose" (1918c), pp. 142–143, 143, and 143; 6: *What Life Should Mean to You* (1931a), pp. 71–72.
6. 1 and 2: "Individualpsychologische Behandlung" (1913c), p. 31; 3 and 4: "The neurotic's picture of the world" (1936d), pp. 13 and 3.
7. 1 and 2: "Individualpsychologische Behandlung" (1913c), pp. 29 and 31; 3: "Individualpsychologie und Wissenschaft" (1927d), p. 407.
8. 1 to 4: *Problems of Neurosis* (1929b), pp. 24, 74, 74, and 157; 5: "Individualpsychologische Behandlung" (1913c), p. 30.

9. **1:** "Individualpsychologische Behandlung" (1913c), p. 32; **2:** *Sinn des Lebens* (1933a), p. 193; **3:** *Praxis und Theorie* (1924), p. 217.

10. **1 and 4:** "Individualpsychologische Behandlung" (1913c), pp. 29 and 32; **2 and 3:** *Über den nervösen Charakter* (1912a), 4th ed., pp. 146 and 146–147; **5:** "Beitrag zum Verständnis des Widerstands in der Behandlung" (1911c), p. 101; **6:** *Problems of Neurosis* (1929b), p. 73.

11. **1, 5, 6, 11:** "Individualpsychologische Behandlung" (1913c), pp. 30, 30, 30, and 32; **2:** *Nervöser Charakter* (1912a), p. 146; **3:** " 'Verdrängung' und 'männlicher Protest' " (1911b), p. 109; **4 and 8:** *Problems of Neurosis* (1929b), pp. 8 and 9, and 73; **7, 9, 10:** *Sinn des Lebens* (1933a), pp. 198, 199, and 195.

12. **1:** *What Life Should Mean to You* (1931a), p. 72; **2 and 5:** *Sinn des Lebens* (1933a), pp. 193, 195; **3 and 4:** *Problems of Neurosis* (1929b), pp. 20–21 and 73.

13. **1, 2, 3:** *Sinn des Lebens* (1933a), pp. 194, 197, and 199.

14. **1:** *Sinn des Lebens* (1933a), pp. 193–194; **2:** *What Life Should Mean to You* (1931a), p. 72; **3 and 5:** *Problems of Neurosis* (1929b), pp. 73 and 40–41; **4:** "Progress in Individual Psychology" (1923a), p. 24.

15. **1 and 2:** *Sinn des Lebens* (1933a), pp. 196 and 198.

16. **1, 3, 4:** *Sinn des Lebens* (1933a), pp. 197, 197, and 192–193; **2:** "Individualpsychologische Behandlung" (1913c), p. 30.

17. **1:** *Sinn des Lebens* (1933a), p. 198; **2:** *Problems of Neurosis* (1929b), pp. 94–95; **3 and 4:** *What Life Should Mean to You* (1931a), pp. 258–259 and 259–260.

18. **1:** *What Life Should Mean to You* (1931a), p. 234.

CHAPTER FOURTEEN

EARLY RECOLLECTIONS AND DREAMS

COMMENT We have seen in the preceding chapter that Adler considered "the most trustworthy approaches to the exploration of the personality" of the patient to be: (1) earliest childhood recollections, (2) dreams, (3) place as a child in the family sequence, (4) childhood difficulties, and (5) the nature of the exogenous factor which occasioned the illness. The last three approaches refer to situational conditions and are dealt with elsewhere (see pp. 376–382, 386–392, and 296–297). Recollections and dreams are primarily productions of the individual and are both discussed here.

Recollections can be classified as productions of the individual, because according to Adler they are selections, distortions, or inventions of past events by the individual to fit his underlying mood, purpose, and interests, and would change accordingly, if not in respect to content, at any rate in respect to feeling tone. It is immaterial whether an earliest recollection would actually remain the earliest under all conditions of recall; and furthermore it is of no importance whether a recollection corresponds to objective events, or is an alteration of them, or is altogether a matter of fancy. In any case it reflects the individual's inner world, his style of life; and the stated earliest recollection in particular reflects the prototype of his style of life. If dreams have recently been called natural "projective" material, and justly so, this is equally true of recollections. The projective character of both rests in the fact that the subject believes he is reporting on an objective event, without being aware that his report is largely his own doing and therefore open to interpretation regarding his unconscious tendencies. Thus recollections and dreams, like any behavior, serve the therapist the dual purpose of affording him a more complete understanding of the case and a means for explaining the patient to himself.

A. Early Recollections

1. EXPRESSION OF THE STYLE OF LIFE[1]

Among all psychological expressions, some of the most revealing are the individual's memories. His memories are the reminders he carries about with him of his own limits and of the meaning of circumstances. There are no "chance memories": out of the incalculable number of impressions which meet an individual, he chooses to remember only those which he feels, however darkly, to have a bearing on his situation. Thus his memories represent his "Story of My Life"; a story he repeats to himself to warn him or comfort him, to keep him concentrated on his goal, and to prepare him by means of past experiences, so that he will meet the future with an already tested style of action.

A depressed individual could not remain depressed if he remembered his good moments and his successes. He must say to himself, "All my life I was unfortunate," and select only those events which he can interpret as instances of his unhappy fate. Memories can never run counter to the style of life. If an individual's goal of superiority demands that he should feel, "Other people always humiliate me," he will choose for remembrance incidents which he can interpret as humiliations. In so far as his style of life alters, his memories also will alter; he will remember different incidents, or he will put a different interpretation on the incidents he remembers.

Most illuminating of all is the way the individual begins his story, the earliest incident he can recall. The first memory will show his fundamental view of life, his first satisfactory crystallization of his attitude. It offers us an opportunity to see at one glance what he has taken as the starting point for his development.

I would never investigate a personality without asking for the first memory. In the main, people are perfectly willing to discuss their first memories. They take them as mere facts and do not realize the meaning hidden in them. Another point of interest in first memories is that their compression and simplicity allows us to use them for group investigations. We can ask a school class to write their earliest recollections; and, if we know how to interpret them, we have an extremely valuable picture of each child.

The discovery of the significance of early recollections is one of the most important findings of Individual Psychology. It has demonstrated the purposiveness in the choice of what is longest remembered, though the memory itself is quite conscious or easily brought out upon inquiry. Rightly understood, these conscious memories give us glimpses of depths just as profound as those which are more or less suddenly recalled during treatment.

We should not distinguish too sharply between old and new remembrances, for in new remembrances also the action line is involved. It is easier and more illuminating, however, to find the action line in the beginning, for then we discover the theme and are able to understand how the style of life of a person does not really change. In the style of life, formed at the age of four or five, we find the connection between remembrances of the past and actions of the present.

It is indifferent for the purposes of psychology whether the memory which an individual considers as first is really the first event which he can remember—or even whether it is a memory of a real event. Memories are important only for what they are "taken as"; for their interpretation and for their bearing on present and future life.

We do not believe that all early recollections are correct records of actual facts. Many are even fancied, and most perhaps are changed or distorted at a time later than that in which the events are supposed to have occurred; but this does not diminish their significance. What is altered or imagined is also expressive of the patient's goal, and although there is a difference between the work of fantasy and that of memory, we can safely make use of both by relating them to our knowledge of other factors. Their worth and meaning, however, cannot be rightly estimated until we relate them to the total style of life of the individual in question, and recognize their unity with his main line of striving towards a goal of superiority. The interest in being connected with the mother [for example] may appear even in the form of fictitious remembrances, as in the case of the patient who said to me: "You will not believe me, but I can remember being born, and my mother holding me in her arms."

2. INTERPRETATION[2]

To estimate its meaning we have to relate the early pattern of perception to all we can discover of the individual's present attitude, until we find how the one clearly mirrors the other.

Owing to the great number of spoiled children who come under treatment, we find that the mother is rarely absent from the earliest remembrance; indeed, if the life-style is one of a pampered child, the guess that the patient will recall something about his mother is usually correct. If the mother does not appear in the early recollections that, too, may have a certain significance; it may, for one thing, indicate a feeling of having been neglected by her. Very often the earliest memory of a spoiled child refers to its dispossession by the birth of a younger brother or sister. These recollections which record the feeling of being dispossessed vary from slight and innocent reminiscences, such as "I recollect when my younger sister was born," to instances highly significant of the particular attitude of the patient. A man once told me, "I was going to market with my mother and little brother. Suddenly it began to rain, and my mother took me up in her arms, and then remembering that I was the elder, she put me down and took up my younger brother." Successful as he was in his life, this man distrusted everybody, especially women.

A higher development of social interest is shown in the following: "I remember my mother letting me wheel my baby sister in the perambulator." In this instance, however, we might look also for signs of being at ease only with weaker people, and perhaps of dependence upon the mother.

The desire to be in company is not always a proof of a real interest in others. One girl, when asked for her first memory, replied, "I was playing with my elder sister and two girl friends." Here we can certainly see a child training to be sociable; but we obtain a new insight into her striving when she mentions as her greatest fear, "I am afraid of being left alone." We shall look, therefore, for signs of a lack of independence.

It must be remembered that old remembrances are not reasons, they are hints. They indicate the movement toward a goal and what obstacles had to be overcome. They show how a person becomes more interested in one side of life than another. We see that he may have a so-called trauma, along the lines of sex, for instance; that is, he may be more interested in such matters than in others. Some persons insist that the stomach is the most important organ, and we will find that old remembrances parallel later characteristics in such instances also.

Provided we possess the requisite experience and use the utmost care, we may in most cases discover from the earliest recollections the mistaken direction of the life path, the lack of social interest, or the contrary. (1)

Much comes to light through the choice of presentation of a "we" or "I" situation. (2) Much, too, comes to light from the mention of the mother. (3) Recollections of dangers and accidents, as well as of corporal and other punishments, disclose the exaggerated tendency to keep in mind particularly the hostile side of life. (4) The recollection of the birth of a brother or sister reveals the situation of dethronement. (5) The recollection of the first visit to the kindergarten or school shows the great impression produced by new situations. (6) The recollection of sickness or death is often linked with a fear of these dangers, and occasionally with the attempt to become better equipped to meet them, possibly as a doctor or a nurse or similarly. (7) Recollections of a stay in the country with the mother, as well as the mention of certain persons like the mother, the father, or the grandparents in a friendly atmosphere, often show not only a preference for these persons who evidently pampered the child, but also the exclusion of others. (8) Recollections of misdeeds, thefts, and sexual misdemeanors which have been committed usually point to a great effort to keep them from occurring again. (9) Occasionally one learns also of other interests, such as visual, auditory, or motor interests, which may give occasion to uncover failures in school and a mistaken occupational choice, and indicate an occupation which corresponds better to the preparation for life.

In this work the skeptical question arises whether we cannot easily make mistakes in the interpretation of recollections and their relation to the style of life in view of the ambiguity of single forms of expression. Our answer is that if we have found the real law of movement in an individual's recollections, we will find the same law confirmed in all his other forms of expression. In treatment we shall have to offer as many confirmations as necessary until the patient, too, becomes convinced of the correctness of our proof.

3. GUESSING FROM A RECOLLECTION[3]

Let me, for the sake of illustration, give a first memory and attempt to interpret it, as I do when I know nothing else of an individual—not even whether he is a child or an adult. The meaning we find in the first memories would have to be checked by other expressions of the personality; but we can use them as they stand [by themselves] for our training, and for sharpening our ability to guess.

A girl begins: "When I was three years old, my father . . ." [It is important to notice which people in the environment occur in first memories.] We can suppose that this girl was more interested in her father than her mother. If the child turns to the father, the mother has lost the game. The child has not been satisfied with its situation. This is generally the result of the birth of a younger child. If we hear in this recollection that there is a younger child, our guess will be confirmed.

"My father purchased for us a pair of ponies." There is more than one child, and we are interested to hear about the other. "He brought them by the halters to the house. My sister, who was three years older than I . . ." We must revise our interpretation. We had expected this girl to be the older sister, and she proves to be the younger. Perhaps the older sister was the mother's favorite, and it is for this reason that the girl mentions her father and the present of the two ponies.

"My sister took one strap and led her pony triumphantly down the street." Here is a triumph for the older sister. "My own pony, hurrying after the other, went too fast for me"—these are the consequences when her sister takes the lead!—"and trailed me face downward in the dirt. It was an ignominious end to an experience which had been gloriously anticipated." The sister has conquered, she has scored a point. We can be quite sure that this girl means, "If I am not careful, my older sister will always win. I am always being defeated, I am always in the dirt. The only way to be safe is to be first." We can understand, also, that the older sister had triumphed with the mother, and that this was the reason why the younger sister turned to her father.

"The fact that I later surpassed my sister as a horsewoman has never mellowed this disappointment in the least." All our suppositions are now confirmed. We can see what a race there had been between the two sisters. The younger felt, "I am always at the back, I must try to get ahead. I must surpass the others." This is the type I have described, so common among second children or youngest children, which always has a pacemaker for itself, and is always trying to overtake the pacemaker. This girl's memory reinforces her attitude. It says to her, "If any one is ahead of me I am endangered. I must always be the first." [See pp. 379–380.]

4. A CASE OF ANXIETY NEUROSIS[4]

A man about thirty-two years old, the eldest, spoiled son of a widow, proves unfitted for any profession because as soon as he begins to work he is seized with severe attacks of anxiety, though these improve immediately when one brings him home. He is a good-natured man, but he finds it difficult to gain contact with other persons. At school he became extremely excited before any examination, and often stayed away from school on the ground that he was tired and exhausted. His mother looked after him most affectionately. This method of retreating to his mother, well tested since he was a child, found notable support when the first girl to whom he took a liking rejected him. The shock he experienced as the result of this "exogenous" event confirmed him in his desire to retreat, so that he was never at ease unless he was with his mother. His earliest recollection from childhood was the following: "When I was about four years old I sat at the window and watched some workmen building a house on the opposite side of the street, while my mother knitted stockings."

Some may say that this is rather insignificant. But that is by no means the case. This man's choice of the earliest memory—whether it was really the earliest or not does not matter—shows us that some interest or other must have attracted him to it. The active work of his memory, guided by his style of life, selects an event which gives a strong indication of his individuality. The pampered child is revealed by the fact that the memory recalls a situation that includes the solicitous mother. But a still more important fact is disclosed: he looks on while other people work. His preparation for life is that of an onlooker. He is scarcely anything more than that. After such a patient has been cured, one will be on the lookout for employment in which he can put to use the better preparation of his powers of seeing and observing. Since we understand his case better than the patient, we must intervene actively and let him understand that while he can get on in any calling, if he wants to make the best use of his preparation he should seek some work in which observation chiefly is needed. This patient took up successfully a business dealing with objects of art.

5. A CASE OF GOOD ADJUSTMENT[5]

This is a written recollection of a girl in the third grade. "When I was four years old I couldn't draw well." We are not surprised at that, but are curious about other things. We want to learn just why this girl singles out drawing. It is probable that she has a particular interest in drawing and that she has struggled with it. We may conclude that her interest bore fruit; her handwriting, as I see it here, is a so-called beautiful handwriting. We should not wonder if she had struggled with her difficulties in the beginning, but had overcome these difficulties and conquered.

The recollection continues: "Often I wanted to draw a man. My mother would say: 'You make the nose like a cucumber.' I did not let this disturb me and went on drawing." Here we have the confirmation that she struggled and won. That has been the signpost in her life: One must struggle with the difficulties and then things will come out all right. "When it was all finished, I showed it to my mother. She said: 'Now you don't make the nose like a cucumber any more.' From that time on I was able to draw pretty men. I always remember that."

B. Dreams

1. FREUD'S THEORY OF DREAMS[6]

We find in science, in general literature, and in belles-lettres, many worthwhile views regarding dreams and their meaning. For example, as early as about 1850 the German poet, Hebbel, in his memories of childhood, says about dreams: "If a man would collect his dreams and examine them, and would add to the dreams which he is now having all the thoughts he has in association with them, all the remembrances, all the pictures he can grasp from them, and if he would combine these with the dreams he has had in the past, he would be able to understand himself much better by this than by means of any other kind of psychology." About fifty years later we find Freud coming forth as the first to have the courage to follow Hebbel's recommendation. Although much of Freud's interpretation of dreams is today no longer tenable, we must honor him for laying the foundation of the science of dream interpretation.

From the standpoint of Individual Psychology Freud's valid contributions may be summarized as follows: (1) He demonstrated that the affective or emotional attitudes in a dream indicate more nearly its real meaning than do the purely figurative or verbal elements. (2) Closely allied to the above is the distinction between the manifest and latent contents of the dream. The manifest content is the way the dream appears to the dreamer. The latent content consists of the associated thoughts, memories, and emotional attitudes. The latter is the dream interpretation. (3) Dreams are not unique as mental phenomena. They employ the same mental dynamisms as are used in slips of the tongue, daydreams, fantasies, and other waking behavior. (4) The method of verbal association is valid for obtaining the latent content of a dream.

Although Freud's theories represented a distinct advance in the interpretation of dreams, Individual Psychology cannot accept his point of view as final. Freud has claimed from the first that dreams are fulfillments of infantile sexual wishes. On the basis of actual experience this appears to assign to dreams a too limited scope.

The Freudians themselves found a sexual interpretation of dreams insufficient. Freud then suggested that he could also see in dreams the expression of an unconscious desire to die. Perhaps there is a sense in which this is true. Certain dreams, especially of neurotic persons, show an individual's lack of courage to meet his problems. This might be said to be the desire to die, but in saying that, we would actually be using terms in a highly figurative, metaphorical sense. It would not bring us any closer to finding how the whole personality is reflected in dreams.

It appears that Psychoanalysis, without understanding it, starts with the premises of a pampered child, who feels that his wishes must never be denied. Psychoanalysis works out these premises in the most thoroughgoing detail. But the striving for gratification, the basic assumption of Psychoanalysis, is only one of the countless varieties of the striving for superiority; we cannot take it as the central motive of all expressions of personality.

2. EXPRESSIONS OF THE STYLE OF LIFE[7]

In my investigations concerning dreams I had two great aids. The first was provided by Freud, with his unacceptable views. I profited by his mistakes. My second and much stronger support in the understanding of dreams came from an established fact, scientifically confirmed and illumined from many sides, the unity of the personality. The property of belonging to this unity must also characterize the dream. The supreme law of both life-forms, sleep and wakefulness alike, is this: the sense of worth of the self shall not be allowed to be diminished.

The findings of Individual Psychology point to the fact that all the behavior of a human being fits into a unit and is an expression of the individual's style of life.

The so-called conscious and unconscious are not contradictory, but form a single unity, and the methods used in interpreting the "conscious" life may be used in interpreting the "unconscious" or "semi-conscious" life, the life of our dreams. Only by considering dreams as one of the expressions of the style of life may an adequate interpretation of them be found.

It may be well to remark that the psychologist is not discouraged if somebody says to him, "I will not tell you any dreams for I cannot remember them. But I will make up some dreams." The psychologist knows that the person's imagination cannot create anything but that which his style of life commands. His made-up dreams are just as good as those he genuinely remembers, for his imagination and fancy will also be an expression of his style of life.

13. FORWARD-LOOKING, PROBLEM-SOLVING FUNCTION[8]

The traditional view of their prophetic nature may provide a partial solution of the problem of dreams. According to all historic dream interpretations, dreams sought to solve problems and sought guidance for the future. We recognize the significance of this, though, of course, we do not regard dreams to be prophecy.

A dream is a bridge that connects the problem which confronts the dreamer with his goal of attainment. In this way a dream will often come true, because the dreamer will be training for his part during the dream and will be thus preparing for it to come true.

The self draws strength from the dream fantasy to solve an imminent problem, for the solution of which its social interest is inadequate. The subjectively felt difficulty of the problem always acts as a test of social interest, and can be such a burden that even the best of us will begin to dream. Thus every dream-state has an exogenous factor. This, of course, means something more than and something different from Freud's "days' residue." The significance consists in that a person is put to the test and is seeking a solution. This seeking of a solution contains the "forward to the goal" and the "whither" of Individual Psychology in contrast to Freud's regression and fulfillment of infantile wishes. It points to the upward tendency in evolution and shows how each individual imagines this path for himself. It shows his opinion of his own nature and of the nature and meaning of life.

4. DREAM METAPHORS[9]

In dreams we fool ourselves into an inadequate solution of a problem, that is, inadequate from the standpoint of common sense, but adequate from the standpoint of our style of life. We do this by dismissing important facts and leaving only a small part of the problem which can, if everything is put into figurative metaphorical form, be solved easily. This dream process differs little from waking life. For example, a young man wants to get married but hesitates and expresses contradictory views regarding the important step he is considering. A friend may say, "Don't be a jackass!" The friend thus reduces the whole complicated problem to being a jackass or not, and thus enables the young man to find an easy solution of it.

The dream strives to pave the way towards solving a problem by a metaphorical expression of it, by a comparison "as if"; and in itself is a sign that the dreamer feels inadequate to solve the problem by common sense alone. Naturally the dreamer does not recognize the purpose of his own metaphor. If he understood it, it would be ineffective for its purpose. It is essentially a self-deception, in the interest of his own individual goal. We should expect, therefore, that the more the individual goal agrees with reality the less a person dreams; and we find that it is so. Very courageous people dream rarely, for they deal adequately with their situation in the daytime.

5. EMOTION-PRODUCING FUNCTION[10]

If we are really to discover the purpose of dreams, we must find what purpose is served by not understanding dreams or by forgetting them. It occurred to me one day that perhaps the real significance of a dream is that it is not to be understood; that perhaps there is a dynamism of the mind working to baffle us; and that it is not in the thoughts that we "fool" ourselves, but in the emotions and feelings aroused by the thoughts and pictures of a dream.

The purpose of the dream is achieved by the use of emotion and mood rather than reason and judgment. Reasoning alone could not purposely deceive us. Thoughts may give rise to errors in judgment, but this would be due to inadequate factual data. When our style of life comes into conflict with reality and common sense, we find it necessary, in order to preserve the style of life, to arouse feelings and emotions by means of the ideas and pictures of a dream which we do not understand.

In a dream, the individual's goal of achievement remains the same as in waking life, but a dream impels him toward that goal with increased emotional power. A man who wants to jump over a stream will perhaps count three before he jumps. Is there a necessary connection between jumping and counting three? Not the slightest. He counts, however, to stir up his feelings and to elicit all his powers. We have all the means ready in our minds to elaborate a style of life, to fix it, and to reinforce it; and one of the most important means of doing this is the ability to stir up feelings. We are engaged in this work every night and every day. Probably, waking or sleeping, we never see any picture without an emotional reaction. In dreams we produce the pictures which will arouse the feelings and emotions which we need for our purposes, that is, for solving the problems confronting us at the time of the dream, in accordance with the particular style of life which is ours.

Let us consider, for example, the dream of a married man who was not content with his family life. He had two children, but always worried that his wife was not taking care of them and was too much interested in other things. He was always criticizing his wife about these things and tried to reform her. One night he dreamed that he had a third child who got lost and was not to be found, and that he reproached his wife because she had not taken care of the child. The result of the dream was that he had created an emotion against his wife. No child had really been lost, but he got up in the morning criticizing and feeling antagonistic towards her. Thus people frequently get up in the morning, argumentative and critical as a result of an emotion created by the night's dream. It is like a state of intoxication and not unlike what one finds in melancholia, where the patient intoxicates himself with ideas of defeat, of death, and of all being lost.

6. A DREAM EXPRESSING FEAR OF MARRIAGE[11]

A case of anxiety neurosis taking the form of agoraphobia and accompanied by heart symptoms, occurred in a man of thirty-five. This man dreamed: "I crossed the border between Austria and Hungary, and they wanted to imprison me." This dream indicated the man's desire to come to a standstill, due to the fear that he would be defeated if he went on. Its interpretation very well confirms our understanding of anxiety neuroses. The man wanted to limit the scope of his activity in life, to "mark time" so as to gain time. He came to see me because he wished to marry, and the imminent prospect of doing so had brought him to a halt. The very fact that he came to consult me about his marriage clearly indicated his attitude towards it. Similarly, the way that he would behave in marriage was mirrored in the dream, in which he commanded himself, "Do not cross the border!" The prison in the dream also reflected the dreamer's view of marriage.

7. A DREAM DURING RECOVERY FROM DEPRESSION[12]

The aim of Individual Psychology treatment is always to increase an individual's courage to meet the problems of life. If this is done effectively, dreams can be expected to change during the course of treatment. The following dream of a depressed patient just before her cure serves as a good example: "I was sitting all alone on a bench. Suddenly a heavy snowstorm came on. Fortunately I escaped it, since I hurried indoors to my husband. Then I helped him to look for a suitable position in the advertisement columns of a newspaper." The patient was able to interpret the dream for herself. It shows clearly her feeling of reconciliation with her husband. At first she had hated him and had complained bitterly of his weakness and lack of enterprise in failing to earn a good living. The meaning of the dream is: "It is better to stay by my husband than to expose myself to dangers alone." Though we may agree with the patient in her view of the circumstances, the way in which she reconciles herself to her husband and her marriage still suggests too much the sort of advice which anxious relatives are accustomed to give. The dangers of being alone are overemphasized, and she is still not quite ready to cooperate with courage and independence.

8. COMMON DREAM ELEMENTS[13]

The interpretations given below to certain frequently found dream elements are only probable. Furthermore the elements in any one dream are not discrete; each is related to the other.

We need to warn ourselves that we cannot explain a dream without knowing its relationship to the other parts of the personality. Neither can we lay down any fixed and rigid rules of dream interpretation. The golden rule of Individual Psychology is: "Everything can be different." We must modify each dream interpretation to fit the individual concerned; and each individual is different. If we are not careful, we will only look for types or for universal symbols, and that is not enough. The only valid dream interpretation is that which can be integrated with an individual's general behavior, early memories, problems, etc. In each case the contents of the dream should be gone over with the patient and as many associations elicited from him as possible.

Dreams of falling: Dreams of falling are very common, especially among neurotic and psychotic persons. Why? Because fear of falling is always in their minds. It is the fear of loss of prestige. *Dreams of flying:* Another common and clear-cut dream symbol is that of flying. The key to such dreams is found in the feelings they arouse. They leave behind them a mood of buoyancy and courage; they lead from below to above; they picture the overcoming of difficulties and the striving for the goal of superiority as easy. They allow us to infer, therefore, an active individual, forward-looking and ambitious, who cannot get rid of his ambition even when he is asleep. They involve the problem: "Should I go on or not?" And the answer suggested is: "There are no obstacles in my way. I can do what others cannot do." *Dreams of paralysis:* When people dream frequently that they are paralyzed, it often symbolizes a warning that their current problem is insoluble. *Dreams of examinations:* With some individuals the meaning of such dreams would be: "You are not prepared to face the problem before you." With others it would mean: "You have passed examinations before, and you will pass the present test also." One individual's symbols are never the same as another's. What we must consider chiefly in the dream is the residue of mood and its coherence with the whole style of life.

Dreams about dead people suggest that the dreamer has not yet finally buried his dead and remains under the dead person's influence. *Missing a train* or an opportunity can be shown in most cases to be the expression of an established character trait, namely, escaping from a dreaded defeat by arriving too late or by letting an opportunity slip. *Dreams about being improperly clothed* followed by fright on that account can mostly be traced back to the fear of being detected in an imperfection. When the dreamer plays the part of a spectator it is almost certain that in waking life he would willingly be satisfied with the role of onlooker. *Sexual dreams* point in different directions; sometimes they show a comparatively inadequate training for sexual intercourse; at other times they reveal a retreat from a partner and a withdrawal upon oneself. *Homosexual dreams* are examples of what I have emphasized strongly enough to be the training against the other sex rather than an innate tendency. *Dreams of cruelty* in which the individual takes an active part betoken rage and a craving for revenge. *Dreams of soiling* have the same significance. Children who wet their beds often dream that they are urinating at the proper place. In this rather cowardly fashion they find it easy to express their grievance and their revenge at the feeling of being neglected. *Anxiety dreams* are frequently found to reflect heightened anxiety in the face of a defeat. *Pleasant dreams* reflect a more vigorous "fiat," or a contrast with the existing situation, meant to provoke all the stronger feelings of aversion.

Forgotten dreams permit the conjecture that their emotional tone is strong in the face of a common sense which is also strong. In order to bypass the latter, the thought material of the dream must be evaporated so that only the emotion and the attitude remain.

Recurrent dreams: In recurrent dreams we are able to find the style of life expressed with great clarity. They give us a definite and unmistakable indication as to the individual's goal of superiority. A repeated dream is a repeated answer to a repeatedly confronting problem. The style of life is best shown by dreams which are often repeated, or which have remained in the memory for many years. *Short dreams:* Short dreams indicate that the dreamer's current problems allow him to find a "short cut" between them and his style of life. Such dreams [of which the following is an example] are, by the way, much easier to analyze.

A red-haired patient suffered from air-swallowing among other symptoms. After the psychological mechanism of this behavior had been explained to him, he had a dream. He said: "I saw a red frog, bloated with air." This dream was a mystery to him which he could not understand. I interpreted it to him, explaining that while he was asleep he understood perfectly what he was doing, and that his dream was a way of saying: "I am like that red frog, suffering from my abnormal coloring and trying to blow myself up into a bigger being than I am."

Long dreams: Dreams which are long or very complicated are dreamed by patients who are seeking excessive security in their lives by means of circumventing detours, or by patients who are considering various solutions for their problems. Such dreams generally indicate hesitation and a desire on the part of the patient to postpone even his own self-deceptive solution in case it should appear not to work out rightly.

Absence of dreams: We have said that the more courageously and realistically one meets the problems of life the less need there is for dreaming. But this does not mean that an absence of dreams necessarily means an adjusted individual. It may mean that the contents are entirely forgotten and only the emotion remains. Or the absence of dreams may be a sign that an individual has come to a point of rest in his neurosis and has established a neurotic situation which he does not wish to change; this would be an adjustment to his style but not an adjustment to society. Or again, lack of imagination, such as is found among the feeble-minded, is often the reason for the rarity or absence of dreams, for a dream is a creation.

FOOTNOTES TO CHAPTER FOURTEEN

1. 1 to 4, 7: *What Life Should Mean to You* (1931a), pp. 73, 73–74, 75, 75, and 20; 5 and 8: "Significance of early recollections" (1929e), pp. 283, and 283 and 284; 6: *Science of Living* (1929c), p. 118.

2. 1 and 2: "Early recollections" (1929e), pp. 284, and 283 and 284; 3 and 4: *What Life Should Mean to You* (1931a), pp. 21 and 22; 5: *Science of Living* (1929c), pp. 129–130; 6 and 7: *Der Sinn des Lebens* (1933a), pp. 138–139 and 138.

3. 1 to 5: *What Life Should Mean to You* (1931a), pp. 75–76, 79–80, 80, 80, and 81.

4. 1 and 2: *Social Interest* (1933b), pp. 211–212 and 212–213.

5. 1 and 2: *Individualpsychologie in der Schule* (1929a), pp. 48 and 48–49.

6. 1 to 5: "On the interpretation of dreams" (1936a), pp. 4, 4, 4, 4–5, and 5.

7. 1: *Social Interest* (1933b), pp. 254 and 255; 2 and 3: "Interpretation of dreams" (1936a), pp. 4 and 6–7; 4: *Science of Living* (1929c), pp. 156–157.

8. 1: "Interpretation of dreams" (1936a), pp. 3–4; 2: *Science of Living* (1929c), pp. 158–159; 3: *Sinn des Lebens* (1933a), pp. 168–169.

9. 1 and 2: "Interpretation of dreams" (1936a), pp. 7 and 9.

10. 1, 2, 3: "Interpretation of dreams" (1936a), pp. 5–6, 6, and 7–8; 4: *Science of Living* (1929c), pp. 163–165.

11. 1: *Problems of Neurosis* (1929b), pp. 6–7.

12. 1: "Interpretation of dreams" (1936a), p. 15.

13. 1, 2, 3, 6, 8, 9: "Interpretation of dreams" (1936a), pp. 8, 13–14, 12–13, 13, 13, and 13; 4 and 5: *Social Interest* (1933b), pp. 263–265 and 263; 7: *Problems of Neurosis* (1929b), p. 135.

CHAPTER FIFTEEN

THE ORIGIN OF THE NEUROTIC DISPOSITION

COMMENT We began our presentation of Adler's theory of abnormal psychology with the neurotic disposition and have now arrived at the discussion of the problem: Under what conditions does the neurotic disposition or the neurotic style of life originate?

As to the origin of the style of life in general, normal as well as abnormal, Adler would say: The growing infant takes into account all the impressions he receives, those from his own body and those from the external environment, and under their influence creatively forms his opinion of himself and the world, together with his idea of his individual goal of success. This takes place gradually, during the middle of the preschool period. Once the child has thus formed a prototype of his style of life, all further impressions are strongly influenced by it.

A child is likely to develop a self-centered, noncooperative style of life with an unrealistic goal of superiority, i.e., the neurotic disposition, if he finds himself overburdened during this formative period. The present chapter discusses firstly the three childhood situations which are likely to overburden the child.

The second and third parts of the chapter deal with the roles of the significant persons in the child's early life and with his sibling situation. These two categories of situational factors are of themselves, of course, not pathogenic since they are common to all children, and to this extent the chapter deals with developmental psychology in general. The present context, however, stresses the errors which may arise from the situation and which may make for the neurotic disposition. The significant persons are the agents which effect the overburdening conditions of pampering and neglect. It will be recalled that the sibling situation was mentioned by Adler as one of the five specific aids for understanding the individual style of life of the patient (see pp. 327–328).

At times Adler seems to express himself in a deterministic fashion about all these influences. Such expressions must, however, be understood in the light of his over-all orientation which recognizes in objective factors only temptations or allurements to which the individual responds creatively. Although the probabilities provided by certain factors may be very strong, they nonetheless represent probabilities only rather than causes.

A. The Overburdening Childhood Situations

1. THE FAULTY STYLE OF LIFE[1]

All the early childhood situations influence the child and press him to take a stand towards these situations, a stand which will somehow allow him to retain and pursue a goal of superiority. This steady striving for self-enhancement will always take individually differing forms. From the beginning of the child's life a training comes about, as a result of which the child permits the growth of a role within himself of which he may be conscious or unconscious. After a while a certain mechanization sets in, so that he finds his way in accordance with his mechanized movements and forms of expressions. It is very much like what takes place when a child has memorized a poem. He does not need to find the words; the whole thing has become mechanized and is no longer conscious; the poem runs by itself, as it were. Once acquired, the style of life of a child and his self-evaluation remain constant as long as insight into the self is missing.

What may have happened at the time of the construction of the style of life, when the mechanization took place, within the first four to five years, that would cause a child later to prove himself more or less unsuited or to fail completely when his conduct of life is tested? We are able to determine that under all circumstances a lack of social interest was evident. We found that these children were overburdened during the first four to five years because at that time they went through situations which exerted on them a damaging, permanent impression. They acquired a faulty mode of apperception through which they perceive the world altogether differently and set themselves a goal altogether different from one of common experiences (Miterleben). When they are tested, they are always inclined to dodge onto the useless side of life.

Among these children we find three types, all of which are also characterized by a lack of courage: (1) children with inferior organs, (2) pampered children, (3) neglected and hated children.

2. ORGAN INFERIORITIES[2]

First let us take children with imperfect organs, or those suffering from diseases or infirmities during their infancy. Such children are overburdened, and it will be difficult for them to feel that the meaning of life is contribution. Unless there is someone near them who can draw their attention away from themselves and interest them in others, they are likely to occupy themselves mainly with their own sensations. Later on, they may become discouraged by comparing themselves with those around them, and it may even happen, in our present civilization, that their feelings of inferiority are stressed through pity, ridicule, or avoidance on the part of their fellows. These are all circumstances in which such children may turn in upon themselves, lose hope of playing a useful part in our common life, and consider themselves personally humiliated by the world.

Children with inferior organs will feel inadequate for the tasks of life, and the minus situation will be felt by a child with inferior organs more intensely than by the average child. The organic weakness, however, does not necessarily function as a minus situation. Rather the child experiences the weakness of his organic equipment for the average social tasks and feels impelled to reorganize it accordingly. The outcome depends on the creative power of the individual which expands outwardly according to no rule except the rule that the determining goal always is success. What constitutes success for him depends upon the individual's own interpretation of his position.

I was the first person, I think, to describe the difficulties that confront a child whose organs are imperfect or whose glandular secretions are abnormal. This branch of science has made extraordinary progress, but hardly along the lines in which I should have liked to see it develop. From the beginning I was seeking a method of overcoming these difficulties, and not a ground for throwing the responsibility for failure upon heredity or physical condition. No imperfection of organs compels a mistaken style of life, and we never find two children whose glands have the same effects on them. We can often see children who overcome these difficulties and who, in overcoming them, develop unusual faculties for usefulness. Many of the most eminent men, men who made great contributions to our culture, began with imperfect organs; often their health was poor, and sometimes they died early. It is mainly from those people who struggled hard against difficulties, in body as in outer circumstances, that advances and new contributions have come. The struggle strengthened them, and they went further ahead. From the body we cannot judge whether the development of the mind will be bad or good. These observations of Individual Psychology are not a very good advertisement for schemes of eugenic selection.

Hitherto, however, most children who started with imperfect organs have not been trained in the right direction, their difficulties have not been understood, and they have become interested mainly in their own persons. This is why we find such a great number of failures among children whose early years were burdened with imperfect organs.

The illness of a child, like an innate organ inferiority, can likewise become a dangerous obstacle for the development of social interest. This applies to early illnesses, like rickets, which impair the physical though not the mental development and may also lead to more or less serious deformities. Among the other illnesses of early childhood, those impair social interest the most in which the anxiety and worry of the persons around him give the child a strong impression of his own worth without his contributing anything himself. To this category belong whooping-cough, scarlet fever, encephalitis, and chorea.

3. PAMPERING[3]

COMMENT   *As shown in Chapter 9, there is a distinction between the pampering situation and the pampered response, or style of life, and either may occur independently of the other. The present selections deal with the pampering situation and with further aspects of the pampered response.*

The second type of situation which often provides the occasion for a mistake in the meaning given to life is that of the pampered child. He has been trained to expect that his wishes will be treated as laws, and to receive without giving. He is granted prominence without working to deserve it and will generally come to feel this prominence as a birthright. Others have been so subservient to him that he has lost his independence and does not know that he can do things for himself. His interest was devoted to himself, and he never learned the use and necessity of cooperation. When faced with difficulties he has only one method of meeting them, that is to make demands on others.

In pampered children the degree of social feeling, their interest in others, despite an occasional thin varnish, is so slight that even the casual observer becomes aware of it. Their entire behavior expresses either openly or covered by a flourish, the surprised, even indignant question: "Why should I love my neighbor?" Not even the mother remains spared from their lovelessness. She becomes a subservient object, an object of their lust, and often pays dearly for her egotistic stubbornness in having wanted to bring up her child for herself rather than for society. For each of these children there comes the time when even the most affectionate mother can no longer fulfill all his wishes. Then the revolt of the young despot breaks out, leading to various forms of tyranny against the weaker.

Grown-up pampered children are perhaps the most dangerous class in our community. Some of them may make great protestations of good will; they may even become very "lovable" in order to secure an opportunity to tyrannize; but they are on strike against cooperating, as ordinary human beings, in our ordinary human tasks. There are others who are in more open revolt; when they no longer find the easy warmth and subordination to which they were accustomed, they feel betrayed; they consider society as hostile to themselves and try to revenge themselves upon all their fellows. When society shows hostility to their way of living, as it almost undoubtedly will, they take this as further proof that they are personally ill-treated. This is the reason why punishment is always ineffective; it can do nothing but confirm the opinion, "Others are against me."

Every pampered child becomes a hated child. Our civilization is such that neither society nor the family wishes to continue the pampering process indefinitely.

4. NEGLECT[4]

The third situation in which a mistake can easily be made is that of a neglected child. Such a child has never known what love and cooperation can be; his interpretation of life does not include these friendly forces. When he faces the problems of life, he will overrate their difficulty and underrate his own capacity to meet them with the aid and good will of others. He has found society cold to him and will expect it always to be cold. Especially will he not see that he can win affection and esteem by actions which are useful to others. He will thus be suspicious of others and unable to trust himself. There is really no experience which can take the place of unselfish affection. Everybody has the capacity to be interested in others; but this capacity must be trained and exercised or its development will be frustrated.

If there were a pure type of neglected or hated or unwanted child, he would be blind to the existence of cooperation, isolated, unable to communicate with others, and completely ignorant of everything that would help him to live in association with human beings. But an individual in these circumstances would perish. The fact that a child lived through the period of infancy is proof that he has been given some care and attention. We are dealing therefore never with pure types of neglected children, but with those who had less than usual consideration or were neglected in some respects though not in others.

The neglected child is one who never quite found a trustworthy other person. It is a very sad comment on our civilization that so many failures in life come from orphans or illegitimate children and that we must group such children, on the whole, among the neglected children.

The traits of unloved children in their most developed form can be observed by studying the biographies of all the great enemies of humanity. Here the one thing that stands out is that as children they were badly treated. Thus they developed hardness of character, envy and hatred; they could not bear to see others happy.

Some people think that their children should not be any happier than they themselves were as children. Such a view does not spring from bad intentions. It simply reflects the mentality of those who have been harshly brought up themselves. They can produce any number of good reasons and maxims, as for example, "Spare the rod and spoil the child" and give us endless proofs and examples. But these do not quite convince us in as much as the futility of a rigid, authoritarian education is proved by the simple fact that it estranges the child from his educator.

These three situations—imperfect organs, pampering, and neglect—are a great challenge to give a mistaken meaning to life; and children from these situations will almost always need help in revising their approach to problems. They must be helped to a better understanding.

B. The Roles of the Family Members

1. THE MOTHER[5]

The mother represents the greatest experience of love and fellowship which the child will ever have. Her task is to relate the growing child to herself psychologically, as he was formerly related to her physically. But she must also nourish the child's growing consciousness with true and normal conceptions of society, of work, and of love. In this way she gradually transforms the child's love for her and dependence upon her into a benevolent, confident, and responsible attitude towards society and the whole environment. This is the two-fold function of motherhood: to give the child the completest possible experience of human fellowship, and then to widen it into a life-attitude towards others.

a. *Encouraging the Social Interest.* From the moment of birth the baby seeks to connect himself with his mother. This is the purpose of his movements. For many months his mother plays the overwhelmingly most important role in his life; he is almost completely dependent upon her. It is in this situation that the ability to cooperate first develops. The mother gives her baby the first contact with another human being, the first interest in someone other than himself. She is his first bridge to social life; and a baby who could make no connection at all with his mother, or with some other human being who took her place, would inevitably perish.

This connection is so intimate and far-reaching that we are never able, in later years, to point to any characteristic as the effect of heredity. Every tendency which might have been inherited has been adopted, trained, educated, and made over again by the mother. Her skill, or lack of skill, has influenced all the child's potentialities. By a mother's skill we mean her ability to cooperate with her child and to win the child to cooperate with herself. She can be skillful only if she is interested in her child and occupied in winning his affection and securing his welfare.

A woman who is dissatisfied with her role has a goal in life which prevents her from making the best connection with her children. Her goal does not run in the same way as their goals; she is often occupied in proving her personal superiority, and for this purpose the children can be only a bother and distraction.

Mothers without an actually deep-rooted love for children may watch over every trait of the child with never-resting concern for their own glory, sensing everywhere a threat to their inflamed vanity, just as one who lacks social interest will degenerate into busybodyness when he wants to prove his interest in others. Such mothers expect their child to laugh, speak, stand and walk, even cut his teeth, earlier than any other child; to be more beautiful, more intelligent, and to surpass all others. Their caresses, presents, outbursts of anger, and punishments serve their own stubborn ambition.

b. *Spreading the Social Interest.* The relationships of a mother are not simple. Even her connection with her children must not be over-stressed. This is true for their sake as well as for hers. Where one problem is overstressed all other problems suffer; and even the single problem with which we are occupied can be met better if we put less weight upon it. A mother is related not only with her children, but also with her husband and with the whole social life around her. These three ties must be given equal attention; all three must be faced calmly and with common sense. If a mother considers only her tie with her children, she will be unable to avoid pampering and spoiling them. She will make it hard for them to develop independence and the ability to cooperate with others. After she has succeeded in connecting the child with herself, her next task is to spread his interest towards his father; and this task will prove almost impossible if she herself is not interested in the father. She must turn the child's interest also to the social life around him, to the other children of the family, to friends, relatives, and fellow human beings in general. Her task is thus twofold. She must give the child his first experience of a trustworthy fellow being; and she must then be prepared to spread this trust and friendship until it includes the whole of our human society.

The task of the mother is to turn the child as early as possible into a coworker, a fellow man who helps gladly and gladly lets himself be helped in so far as his own strength is not adequate.

A mother often feels her child as a part of herself; through her children she is connected with the whole of life; she feels herself the master of life and death. If her goal is one of personal superiority, she may exaggerate this feeling that her child is a part of herself and press him into her service. She may then try to make the child wholly dependent upon herself and control his life so that he shall always remain bound to her.

The most frequent difficulty is that the mother excuses the child from giving her any help or cooperation; heaps caresses and affection on him;

and constantly acts, thinks and speaks for him, curtailing every possibility of development. Thus she pampers the child and accustoms him to an imaginary world which is not ours and in which everything is done for the child by others. In consequence the child declines to extend his social interest toward others and aims to withdraw from the father, the siblings, and other persons who do not meet him with the same amount of warmth. Again in this connection one must not underrate the child's free estimation and the participation of his free creative power, which account for the diversity of the results. The child makes use of external influences to mold them according to his own interpretation.

2. THE FATHER AND THE MARITAL SITUATION[6]

The task of a father can be summed up in a few words. He must prove himself a good fellow man to his wife, to his children, and to society. He must meet in a good way the three problems of life—occupation, friendship, and love—and cooperate on an equal footing with his wife in the care and protection of the family.

Unfortunately the organization of the family seems unable to separate itself from the thought of paternal leadership and authority. Since this authority rests only to a very slight degree on social interest, it tempts all too soon to an open or secret resistance, and probably never finds unconditional acceptance. Its worst disadvantage is that it sets the child an example of striving for power.

The role of the father may take very different forms. Sometimes he will try to bring the child to his side by blindly fulfilling every wish of the child. It is a fact established by Individual Psychology in contrast to other schools of psychology that the child always takes sides with the pampering parent, irrespective of the sex differences. Since the first phase of the social relations of the child is always fulfilled by close contact with the mother, closeness to the father must always be understood as a secondary phase, and as a sign that the mother has lost out in competing with the father for the child's love. Sometimes the father foregoes all educational influence and remains a stranger to the child. Sometimes he is used only as a means to scare the child and is called upon to execute punishments.

If the father is given the task of punishing the children, this is unfortunate because it prepares them to regard men as the final authorities and the real powers in life, and because it disturbs the relation of the children with their father, making them fear him instead of feeling him to be a good friend. Perhaps some women are afraid of losing their hold over their children's affections if they punish them themselves; but the solution is not to delegate the punishment to the father. The children will not reproach their mother any the less because she has summoned an executioner to her aid.

Where the marriage is unhappy, the situation is full of danger for the child. His mother may feel herself unable to include the father in the family life; she may wish to keep the child entirely to herself. If children find dissension between their parents, they are very skillful in playing them off against each other. The first cooperation among other people which the child experiences is the cooperation of his parents; if their cooperation is poor, they cannot hope to teach him to be cooperative himself. A child is very gravely handicapped if the marriage of his parents is not a cooperative part of social life, a product of social life, and a preparation for social life.

3. THE OEDIPUS SITUATION[7]

If a child remains tied to his mother as a pampered child, he will develop more or less as a parasite who expects from his mother the satisfaction of all his needs, occasionally also sexual needs. This occurs all the more readily since at the time of the awakened sex drive the pampered child has already learned to deny himself no wish because he expects the satisfaction of all wishes from his mother. What Freud has designated as the Oedipus complex, which appears to him the natural foundation of psychological development, is nothing but one of the many phenomena in the life of a pampered child who is the unresisting plaything of his intensified wishes.

The Oedipus complex, which incidentally is not very frequent, is but one result, one of hundreds of concretized life-forms, of much deeper-lying disturbances in the soul of a child who feels inferior and cannot find a better compensation due to his lack of social interest. To insinuate ideas of patricide to thoughts such as "father should go away," "I want to be alone with mother," "when father is in the hospital, then I can have a good time," signifies that one has not understood that the Oedipus complex is but a figure of speech. Even where there are such thoughts as "father should die," or where there are dreams of shooting the father, they mean no more than the exploration of all possibilities for being alone with the mother. These forms are the result of wrong upbringing and are always found only in pampered children. If such a child later in life also finds no better solution for his problems than the neurosis, this is further proof of how difficult it is to increase social interest after the fifth year of life.

The closer contact that girls frequently have with their father and boys with their mother cannot be attributed to sexuality. In this connection two points are to be noted. Fathers often show a tender feeling toward their daughters, just as they are accustomed to do towards girls and women in general. And both girls and boys, preparing themselves for their future life in all their games, make this same playful preparation also in their attitude to the parent of the opposite sex.

4. FAVORITISM[8]

We find often among patients that they were the favorites of their grandmothers or grandfathers and understand immediately how this contributed to their childhood difficulties. Favoritism either meant pampering or stirring up rivalries and jealousies toward the other children. Also, many children say to themselves, "I was the favorite of my grandfather," and feel hurt that they are not the favorite of other persons as well.

The dangers of favoritism can hardly be overdramatized. Almost every discouragement in childhood springs from the feeling that someone else is preferred. Sometimes the feeling is not at all justified; but on the other hand where there is real equality there should be no occasion for it to develop. It is not enough for parents to say that they have no preference. They must observe whether there is even a suspicion of such a preference in the mind of any of their children.

c. Birth-Order Position

1. THE RELATIVITY OF THE POSITION[9]

It is a common fallacy to imagine that children of the same family are formed in the same environment. Of course there is much which is the same for all children in the same home, but the psychological situation of each child is individual and differs from that of others, because of the order of their succession.

There has been some misunderstanding of my custom of classification according to position in the family. It is not, of course, the child's number in the order of successive births which influences his character, but the *situation* into which he is born and the way in which he interprets it. Thus, if the eldest child is feeble-minded or suppressed, the second child may acquire a style of life similar to that of an eldest child; and in a large family, if two are born much later than the rest, and grow up together separated from the older children, the elder of these may develop like a first child. Such differences also happen sometimes in the case of twins.

2. THE OLDEST CHILD[10]

The first-born child is generally given a good deal of attention and spoiling. Too often it is quite suddenly and sharply that he finds himself ousted from his position. Another child is born and he is no longer unique. Now he must share the attention of his mother and father with a rival. We can often find in problem children, neurotics, criminals, drunkards, and perverts that their difficulties began in such circumstances.

The first-born is in a unique situation; for a while he is an only child and sometime later he is "dethroned." This expression chosen by me depicts the change in the situation so exactly that later writers, as Freud, for example, when they do justice to such a case, cannot do without this figurative expression. The time that elapses before this "dethronement" is important for the impression it makes on the child and for the way this impression is utilized. If the time is three years or more, this event meets with an already established style of life and is responded to accordingly. When the time interval is less, the whole process takes place without words and concepts; hence it is not susceptible to a correction by later experiences but only by Individual Psychological understanding of the context. These wordless impressions, of which there are many in early childhood, would be interpreted differently by Freud and Jung. They would regard them not as experiences, but as unconscious instincts or as the atavistic collective unconscious, respectively. Impulses of hate, however, or occasional death wishes are the artificial products of an incorrect training in social interest. They are well-known to us, but we find them only in pampered children, and they are often directed by the first-born against the second child. Similar moods and ill-feelings are found also in later children, especially again if they were pampered. This is sufficient evidence for relegating to the region of fable the idea that a more severe birth trauma is the reason for failures among the first-born.

When other children lose their position in the same way, they will probably not feel it so strongly, since they have already had the experience of cooperating with another child. They have never been the sole object of consideration and care. Of course, if the parents have allowed the first-born to feel sure of their affection, if he knows that his position is secure, and, above all, if he is prepared for the arrival of a younger child and has been trained to cooperate in its care, the crisis will pass without ill effects.

Among such oldest children we find individuals who develop a striving to protect others and help them. They train to imitate their fathers or mothers; often they play the part of a father or a mother with the younger children, look after them, teach them, and feel themselves responsible for their welfare. Sometimes they develop a great talent for organization. These are the favorable cases, though even a striving to protect others may be exaggerated into a desire to keep those others dependent and to rule over them.

Among many peoples and classes an advantageous status of the oldest child has become traditional. Even where this tradition has not actually become crystallized, the oldest child is usually the one whom one accredits with enough strength and intelligence to be a coworker and supervisor. Imagine what it must mean to a child to be constantly entrusted with the full confidence of his environment.

Generally the first-born is not prepared for the new baby which in fact does deprive him of attention, love, and appreciation. He begins trying to pull his mother back to him and thinking how he can regain attention. He fights for his mother's love. In every case of such a fight, we must inquire into the individual circumstances. If the mother fights back at him, the child will become high-tempered, wild, critical, and disobedient. When he turns against his mother, it often happens that his father gives him a chance to renew the old favorable position. Oldest children frequently prefer their fathers and lean towards their side. Such a fight lasts a long time, sometimes through a whole life.

Oldest children generally show, in one way or another, an interest in the past. All their movements and expressions are directed towards the bygone time when they were the center of attention. They admire the past and are pessimistic about the future. Sometimes a child who has lost his power, the small kingdom he ruled, understands better than others the importance of power and authority. When he grows up, he likes to take part in the exercise of authority and exaggerates the importance of rules and laws. Everything should be done by rule, and no rule should ever be changed; power should always be preserved in the hands of those entitled to it. Influences like these in childhood give a strong tendency towards conservatism. In my experience the greatest proportion of problem children are oldest children; and close behind them come the youngest children.

3. THE SECOND CHILD[11]

The second child is in a quite different position. From the time he is born, he shares attention with another child, and is therefore a little nearer to cooperation than an oldest child. If the oldest is not fighting against him and pushing him back, he is very well situated. Throughout his childhood he has a pacemaker; there is always a child ahead of him, and he is stimulated to exert himself and catch up. A typical second child is very easy to recognize. He behaves as if he were in a race, is under full steam all the time, and trains continually to surpass his older brother and conquer him. The Bible gives us many marvelous psychological hints, and the typical second child is beautifully portrayed in the story of Jacob. He wished to be the first, to take away Esau's position, to best Esau and excel him. The second child is often more talented and successful than the first. If he goes ahead faster, it is because he trained more. Even when he is grown up and outside the family circle, he often still makes use of a pacemaker by comparing himself with someone whom he thinks more advantageously placed, and tries to go beyond him.

These characteristics leave their mark on all expressions and are easily found in dreams. Oldest children often dream of falling; they are on top, but are not sure that they can keep their superiority. Second children often picture themselves running after trains and riding in bicycle races. Sometimes this hurry in his dreams is sufficient by itself to allow us to guess that the individual is a second child.

Here we see the restlessness, a striving which is less aimed at facts than at semblances, but which is unconquerable until either the goal has been reached, i.e., the man ahead has been outdistanced, or in case of defeat, the retreat begins which often results in neurosis. The mood of the second-born is comparable to the envy of the dispossessed with the prevailing feeling of having been slighted. His goal may be placed so high that he will suffer from it for the rest of his life, and his inner harmony be destroyed in consequence.

This was well expressed by a little boy of four, who cried out, weeping, "I am so unhappy because I can never be as old as my brother."

In his later life, the second child is rarely able to endure the strict leadership of others or to accept the idea of "eternal laws." He will be much more inclined to believe, rightly or wrongly, that there is no power in the world which cannot be overthrown. Beware of his revolutionary subtleties! Though it is possible to endanger a ruling power with slander, there are more insidious ways. For example, by means of excessive praise he may idealize and glorify a man or a method until the reality cannot stand up to the ideal. Both ways are employed in Antony's oration in *Julius Caesar*. I have shown elsewhere (1918d) how Dostoievsky made masterly use of the latter means, perhaps unconsciously, to undermine the pillars of old Russia. Those who remember his representation of Father Zosima in *The Brothers Karamazov*, and who also recall the fact that he was a second son, will easily agree with my suggestion regarding the influence played by position in the family.

I need hardly say that the style of life of a second child, like that of the first, may also appear in another child, one in a different chronological position in the family, if the situation is of a similar pattern.

4. THE YOUNGEST CHILD[12]

All other children can be dethroned, but never the youngest. He has no followers but many pacemakers. He is always the baby of the family, probably the most pampered, and faces the difficulties of a pampered child. But, because he is so much stimulated and has many chances for competition, he often develops in an extraordinary way, runs faster than the other children, and overcomes them all. The position of the youngest has not changed in human history; the oldest stories of mankind tell how the youngest child excelled his brothers and sisters.

In every fairy tale the youngest child surpasses all his brothers and sisters; in German, Russian, Scandinavian, or Chinese fairy tales the youngest is always the conqueror. In the Bible we can find excellent descriptions of youngest children which coincide exactly with our experience, e.g., the stories of Joseph, David, and Saul. Although Joseph had a younger brother, Benjamin, he was born when Joseph was seventeen years old, so that as a child Joseph was the youngest.

Joseph's style of life is typical of a youngest child. Even in his dreams he asserts his superiority. The others must bow down before him; he outshines them all. His brothers understood his dreams very well, which was not hard for them, since they had Joseph with them, and his attitude was clear enough. The feelings which Joseph aroused in his dreams they also had felt. They feared him and wanted to get rid of him. From being the last, however, Joseph became the first. In later days he was the pillar and support of the whole family, as the youngest child so often is.

And yet, the second largest proportion of problem children comes from among the youngest, because all the family spoils them. A spoiled child can never be independent. Sometimes a youngest child will not admit to any single ambition, but this is because he wishes to excel in everything, be unlimited and unique. Sometimes a youngest child may suffer from extreme inferiority feelings; everyone in the environment is older, stronger, and more experienced.

5. THE ONLY CHILD[18]

The only child has a problem of his own. His rival is not a brother or sister; his feelings of competition are directed against his father. An only child is pampered by his mother. She is afraid of losing him and wants to keep him under her attention. He develops what is called a "mother complex"; he is tied to his mother's apron strings and wishes to push his father out of the family picture. Often an only child is scared to death lest he should have brothers and sisters following him. When friends of the family say, "You ought to have a little brother or sister," he dislikes the prospect immensely. He wants to be the center of attention all the time. He really feels that it is a right of his, and if his position is challenged, he thinks it a great injustice. In later life, when he is no longer the center of attention, he has many difficulties.

Another point of danger for his development is that he is born into a timid environment. We often find only children in a family where we could expect more children. But the parents are timid and pessimistic; they feel they will not be able to solve the economic problem of having more than one child. The whole atmosphere is full of anxiety and the child suffers badly.

If the children are spaced many years apart, each child will have some of the features of an only child.

6. OTHER SIBLING SITUATIONS[14]

An only boy brought up in a family of girls has a hard time before him. He is in a wholly feminine environment, since the father is absent most of the day. Feeling that he is different, he may grow up isolated. On the other hand, he may fight strongly against this atmosphere and lay great stress on his masculinity. He will feel that he must assert his difference and his superiority; but there will always be tension. His development will proceed by extremes, he will train to be either very strong or very weak.

In a rather similar way, an only girl among boys is apt to develop very feminine or very masculine qualities. Frequently she is pursued through life by feelings of insecurity and helplessness.

The preeminence of one of the siblings in early childhood, whether pronounced or unpronounced, often becomes the disadvantage of the other. With amazing frequency the failures of one child are found beside the excellencies of the other. The greater activity of the one may bring about the passivity of the other; the height, the good looks, or the strength of the one may cast a shadow on the other.

COMMENT *It will have become eminently clear throughout this volume that Individual Psychology is an interpersonal, social theory of personality—accounting for both healthy development and deviations in terms of relationships. In the above section which dealt with the influence on the style of life of the child's specific position in the family group, Adler comes particularly close to the areas in psychology known by J. L. Moreno's term of sociometry or by Kurt Lewin's term of group dynamics. Adler presented his views on the importance of the birth-order position, for the first time, to our knowledge, in 1918 (1918e).*

FOOTNOTES TO CHAPTER FIFTEEN

1. 1 and 2: *Individualpsychologie in der Schule* (1929a), pp. 21 and 32–33.
2. 1, 3, 4: *What Life Should Mean to You* (1931a), pp. 14–15, 15, and 15–16; 2: "The structure of neurosis (1932b), p. 6; 5: *Der Sinn des Lebens* (1933a), p. 148.
3. 1 and 3: *What Life Should Mean to You* (1931a), pp. 16 and 16–17; 2: "Verzärtelte Kinder" (1930g); 4: *Science of Living* (1929c), p. 40.
4. 1, 2, 3, 6: *What Life Should Mean to You* (1931a), pp. 17–18, 18, 18, and 18–19; 4 and 5: *The Education of Children* (1930a), p. 15.

5. 1: *Problems of Neurosis* (1929b), p. 21; 2, 3, 4, 6, 8: *What Life Should Mean to You* (1931a), pp. 120, 120, 123, 125–126, and 124–125; 5: "Verzartelte Kinder" (1930g); 7 and 9: *Sinn des Lebens* (1933a), pp. 145 and 29.

6. 1, 4, 5: *What Life Should Mean to You* (1931a), pp. 134, 135–136, and 132–133; 2: *Menschenkenntnis* (1927a), p. 227; 3: "Verzärtelte Kinder" (1930g).

7. 1 and 3: *Sinn des Lebens* (1933a), pp. 33 and 145; 2: "Nochmals—Die Einheit der Neurosen" (1930e), pp. 201–216.

8. 1: *Education of Children* (1930a), p. 203; 2: *What Life Should Mean to You* (1931a), p. 142.

9. 1 and 2: *Problems of Neurosis* (1929b), p. 96.

10. 1, 3, 4, 6, 7: *What Life Should Mean to You* (1931a), pp. 144, 145, 147, 145–146, and 146–148; 2: *Sinn des Lebens* (1933a), pp. 151–152; 5: *Menschenkenntnis* (1927a), pp. 123–124.

11. 1 and 2: *What Life Should Mean to You* (1931a), pp. 148–149 and 149; 3: *Menschenkenntnis* (1927a), pp. 124–125; 4, 5, 6: *Problems of Neurosis* (1929b), pp. 105, 106, and 106.

12. 1, 3, 4: *What Life Should Mean to You* (1931a), pp. 150, 151, and 151–152; 2: *Education of Children* (1930a), p. 130.

13. 1, 2, 3: *What Life Should Mean to You* (1931a), pp. 152, 152–153, and 153.

14. 1 and 2: *What Life Should Mean to You* (1931a), pp. 153 and 154, and 154; 3: *Sinn des Lebens* (1933a), p. 149.

CHAPTER SIXTEEN

UNDERSTANDING AND TREATING
THE PROBLEM CHILD

COMMENT *The previous chapter described situational factors in the origin of the neurotic disposition. The present chapter is concerned with the early manifestations of such a disposition, that is, behavior disorders in children and their treatment. It deals with (1) Adler's theory of maladjustment in the child, a counterpart to the neurotic disposition described in Chapter 9; (2) his interpretation of a number of common behavior disorders in children; (3) his method of treating the problem child, especially as this was carried out in the numerous child-guidance clinics which he founded; (4) the classroom procedures he suggested for educating the child toward social living; and finally (5) a questionnaire for the guidance counselor as an aid in understanding the child, and a much shorter form for use with adult patients.*

A. Understanding the Problem Child

1. THE DYNAMICS OF PROBLEM BEHAVIOR[1]

The educability of the child originates in the breadth of his innate, differentiated, and growing social interest. Through social interest he gains contact with the common ideals. In this way the demands of the community become his personal demands; that is, the immanent logic of human society, its tacit assumptions and necessities, become the individual task of the child.

The child's educability is shaken by two factors especially: (1) an increased, intensified, and longer lasting inferiority feeling; (2) a goal which no longer guarantees only reassurance, security, and equality, but which develops a striving for power aimed at superiority over the environment.

Such children become problem children because under all circumstances they feel themselves cheated by nature and, rightly or wrongly, often consider themselves discriminated against by man.

They always take a dim and pessimistic view of the world; have difficulty in finding the approach to their peers and adults; are always engaged in a battle with their environment, which often takes place in silence and under cover; think always of themselves and not of others; and are filled by a continuous hostility which they also assume in others. Their sensitivity, often imperceptible to others, is always heightened to the extreme. They yearn for the satisfaction of their altogether insatiable vanity, an insoluble problem which forces them to avoid normal ways. If they meet with difficulties such as are regularly to be found in school, the deviation sets in.

One speaks of a problem child only when it has been evident for some time that he has not been taking his part as an equal coworker. He lacks social interest. However, an amount of social interest which may be quite sufficient for average circumstances frequently becomes inadequate when unfair demands are made by the home or school. From such cases we can learn something of value for the more difficult cases. On the other hand, the presence of exceptionally favorable external circumstances may certainly keep a childhood disorder from coming into sight, while it would appear straightaway, if the child were tested more severely.

I have proposed a classification of problem children which proves useful in many respects: the more passive children, such as the lazy, indolent, obedient but dependent, timid, anxious, and untruthful children; and a more active type such as those who are domineering, impatient, excitable, inclined to affects, troublesome, cruel, boastful, liable to run away, thievish, easily excited sexually, etc. No hairs need be split in this connection, but attempts should be made to ascertain as nearly as possible the amount of activity present in each particular case. This is all the more important, since in the case of the mature failure nearly the same degree of mistaken activity can be expected and observed as in childhood. It is not surprising to find a much larger percentage of passive failures of childhood among neurotics and of active failures among criminals. [See pp. 165–166.]

2. THE DETERMINATION OF PROBLEM BEHAVIOR[2]

When a child's behavior grows worse, or new symptoms appear, the stimulating cause must be taken into consideration. But the word cause must be used reluctantly. When a stone falls to the ground, it must fall in a certain direction and with a certain speed. But in a psychological "fall," strict causality does not play a part; it cannot be claimed that because a younger child is born the older one must deteriorate. We can speak only of bigger or smaller mistakes on the part of the individual, which, after they are made, affect his future development. All this is due to the goal-setting activity of the psyche; and this involves judgment, that is to say, the possibility of making mistakes. In his second or third year, as a rule, the child begins to fix for himself a goal of superiority which is forever before him and towards which he strives in his own manner, usually involving incorrect judgment.

The development of the child is determined neither by his own intrinsic ability nor the objective environment, but by the interpretation that he happens to make of the external reality and of his relation to it. Therefore we must see the child's situation with the eyes of the child himself and interpret it with his own mistaken judgment. We must remember that the education of children would be impossible were it not for the fact that they make mistakes [rather than that they are strictly determined].

We will understand the child better if we do not examine him in one respect only, but at many points. We must make a horizontal examination, to see how his self-evaluation expresses itself in other instances, and a vertical examination, to compare present phenomena with the peculiarities of the child's past. Then we shall have a line which shows the development of the child's style of life, and can rest assured that all expressive movements from the present and the past will agree, provided we have understood them correctly. This is due to the self-consistency of the structure of human psychological life.

B. Specific Behavior Disorders

COMMENT   The interpretation of childhood behavior disorders has a place in the understanding of the adult as well as of the child. The reader will remember that such disorders were one of the five aids to the understanding of the mistaken style of life in the adult (see pp. 327-328). The rationale of this aid is Adler's conviction that the style of life, which is formed in the pre-school period, does not change except "by the individual's own recognition of his faults and errors" (1929g, p.

6). Once difficulties in the childhood of the adult patient have been established, this information, in addition to its diagnostic value, can be used to widen his understanding of himself. It helps the therapist to convince the patient that his present difficulty is not due to any "cause," but that both the present and the past difficulties have their common origin in the early-established neurotic disposition, which is based on an early mistake in judgment.

1. HABIT DISORDERS[3]

One can force any child into an attitude of opposition. If the parents are particularly interested in eating, the child will find his mode of struggle here. If they insist that the child go regularly to the toilet, you will find always that the children present difficulties in this respect. This is one of the reasons why certain faults persist. The child who sucks his thumb thereby expresses his tendency to struggle. It is the same with respect to masturbation.

The sex drive is evident in the first weeks of infancy. If it is not stimulated, its appearances will be natural and need cause no alarm. When we see signs of local irritation during the first year of life, we should cooperate with the child and interest him less in his own person and more in his environment. If attempts at self-gratification cannot be stopped, we can be sure that the child has intentions of his own. He is not the victim of his sex drive but is making use of it for his own purposes. Generally, the aim of little children is to gain attention. If their habits no longer serve their purpose of attracting attention, they will give them up.

A good example of hereditary capital and the use to which it may be turned was given me by my investigations into families which suffered from inferiority of the kidney tract. Very often children in these families suffer from enuresis. The organ inferiority is real; however, it is by no means sufficient to account for the enuresis. The child is not under the compulsion of his organs; he uses them in his own way. Some children, for example, will wet the bed at night and never wet themselves during the day. Sometimes the habit will disappear suddenly, upon a change in the environment or in the attitude of the parents. Often in such families everything to do with urinating is overstressed. A defiant child will always find his way to attack his parents at their point of greatest weakness.

To cling to such probably slight pleasures as retention of feces, thumb-sucking, and childish play with the genitals, which may sometimes be initiated for the purpose of getting rid of certain tickling sensations, is the peculiarity of pampered children who are unable to deny themselves any wish or enjoyment.

Attempts to explain such behavior disorders by deriving them from the sexual libido or from sadistic drives do not uncover more primitive or even deeper layers of the psychological life. Rather they put the cart before the horse in misunderstanding the fundamental mood of such pampered children, which is their accentuated need for affection. Such explanations are also mistaken in that they regard the evolutionary function of organs as if it had to be acquired anew in each case. The development of these functions is as natural a law and as natural an acquisition for humanity as the upright gait and speech. In the imaginary world of pampered children, however, these, like the prohibition of incest, may be avoided as an indication of the wish to be pampered. The purpose of this evasion may be the exploiting of other persons, or, in cases where the pampering has been withheld, revenge and accusation.

The pathological symptoms which we find in enuresis and persistent, unexplained constipation, are often based in a deeply rooted defiance in children who would use every occasion to withdraw from what seems to them coercion, because they regard every coercion as an injury and humiliation. They experience their refusal to fit smoothly into the demands of the culture as a satisfaction, as a weighty sign of their significance. We interpret it as a sign of their revolt. Bad habits are clear indications of a development in opposition to the demands of the community. The opponent is never absent!

The child soon recognizes how important the satisfaction [or restraint] of these drives is for the peace of mind of his parents, and hence commences to do business in the interest of his sense of power by appropriately utilizing and varying his drives.

2. FEARS[4]

In Individual Psychology we are no longer concerned with finding out causes of fear, but rather with identifying its purpose. All pampered children suffer from fear; by their fears they can attract attention, and they build this emotion into their style of life. They use fear to secure their goal of regaining connection with the mother. A timid child is one who has been pampered and wants to be pampered again. Pampered children are often afraid of being left alone, especially in the dark. It is, however, not the dark itself of which they are afraid; they utilize fear in the attempt to bring their mothers closer to them. Sometimes they have nightmares and cry out in their sleep. This use of anxiety is so obvious that we should be very surprised to hear of a pampered child who never made trouble during the night.

3. STUTTERING[5]

When a child shows difficulties in learning to speak, he occupies the center of attention. The result is, of course, that he will pay too much attention to his speech. He begins to control his expression consciously, something that children who speak normally do not do. But the conscious control of a function which should operate automatically results in its further restriction.

Those who have much to do with young children will have noticed that almost all children show a faint tendency to stutter when they begin to speak. The development of speech is, as we know, quickened and retarded by many factors, principally by the degree of social interest.

Many stutterers when they become angry can scold without a trace of stuttering. Stutterers also frequently speak flawlessly when reciting, or when they are in love. These facts indicate that the decisive factor lies in the stutterer's relationship to other people. The decisive moment is the confrontation, the tension aroused when he must establish a connection between himself and another person, or when he must achieve expression by means of speech.

4. OVERT AGGRESSION[6]

When the desire for self-assertion becomes extraordinarily intense, it will always involve an element of envy. Children of this sort easily develop the habit not only of wishing their competitors all kinds of evils, which often leads to neurosis, but also of actually doing harm, causing trouble, and even manifesting now and then downright criminal traits. They may slander, betray domestic secrets, and degrade the other fellow to enhance their own value, especially when they are being observed by others. No one must surpass them; it does not matter to them whether they rise in value or the other fellow falls. They will display a militant and defiant attitude in their external appearance, sudden outbursts of anger, and readiness to fight imaginary foes.

The desire for superiority will also manifest itself in play. An intense desire for superiority will not allow the child to play the part of a horse when others appear as drivers. He will always want to be the driver himself, to lead and to direct. When kept back by his past experience from assuming such a role, he will content himself with disturbing the games of others.

Aggressive behavior is an indication of a hostile environment. A child is constantly quarreling with others because he is afraid that if he is not the aggressor the others will attack first. Such children are disobedient; they believe obedience to be a sign of subordination. They are often dirty, untidy, bite their nails and pick their noses, and are very stubborn. They think that the courteous return of a greeting is a degradation; they answer impertinently. They never complain because they regard sympathy of others as a personal humiliation. They never cry in front of others, and sometimes laugh when they should cry, which looks like a lack of feeling, but is only an indication of a fear of showing weakness. No act of cruelty has ever been done which has not been based upon a secret weakness. The person who is really strong has no inclination to cruelty.

5. DAYDREAMING AND ISOLATION[7]

There is a type of child who is reserved, impervious to knowledge, discipline, or correction, who lives in a world of his own fantasy and at no time displays a striving for superiority. With enough experience, however, it is possible to perceive that this is also a form of striving, even though an absurd one. Such a child has no faith in his ability to achieve success by the usual means, and as a result avoids all means and opportunities for improvement. He isolates himself and gives the impression of a hardened character. This hardness, however, does not include his whole personality; behind it one usually finds an extraordinarily sensitive, trembling spirit which needs this outer callousness to protect itself from hurt. One finds that he daydreams constantly and creates fantasies in which he always appears great or superior. Children who daydream a lot cannot adjust themselves to reality and are unable to make themselves useful. Children sometimes choose the middle road; they retain their daydreaming while making a partial adjustment to reality. Others make no adjustment at all and withdraw more and more from the world into a private world of their own creation; while still others want to have nothing to do with products of the imagination and occupy themselves only with reality, stories of travel, hunting, or history.

6. LAZINESS[8]

Laziness is another type of behavior, which, on the face of it, seems to contradict the view that all children have an innate striving for superiority. In fact a lazy child is scolded for not striving for superiority, for having no ambition. But if we examine his situation more closely, we shall see how the ordinary view is mistaken. The lazy child possesses certain advantages. Many children adopt a lazy attitude as a means of easing their situation. Their families usually say: "What couldn't he do if he were not lazy?" The children content themselves with the recognition that they could accomplish everything if only they were not lazy. This is balm for the child who has too little confidence in himself. It is a substitute for success, not only in the case of children, but for adults as well. When such children really do something, their small deed assumes extra significance in their eyes. Lazy children are like tight-rope walkers with a net underneath the rope; when they fall, they fall softly. It is less painful to be told that one is lazy than that one is incapable. In short, laziness serves as a screen to hide the child's lack of faith in himself, prohibiting him from making attempts to cope with the problems confronting him.

Laziness indicates the hesitating attitude. We can deduce from it that the child no longer believes that he can advance. He has lost all courage. He knows that he can no longer advance on the useful side. The value system of laziness will show itself on the useless side of life.

Some children who do not seek escape by laziness avoid useful activity by playing sick. Other children are unusually excited at examination time, feeling they will be shown some preference on account of their nervous tension. The same is true of crying; both crying and excitement are pleas for privilege.

7. LYING AND STEALING[9]

In regard to lying and its psychological structure one can say that obviously there must be a heavy hand somewhere which the child fears. Normally all children would tell the truth if they felt themselves sufficiently strong. Lying is a compensation to keep the inferiority feeling from manifesting itself. There are two principal forms of lies, lying out of fear, and lying in order to appear greater than one considers oneself in reality. The tendency toward imagination develops out of great weakness.

The psychological structure of stealing can be understood from the fact that here someone feels himself impoverished and tries to cover this deficit by enriching himself. He does not do it in a way which is in accord with the useful side of life, but by an artifice which very much resembles a lie. Stealing is always an attempt to escape a stronger person, or a cunning means to catch up with him.

Many children who feel themselves deprived try to corrupt others with presents in order to gain their love and tenderness. This is one of the most frequent motivations for stealing among children, a motivation often overlooked in children's courts.

c. Treating the Problem Child

COMMENT *Adler's method of treating the child differed from his method for the treatment of adults, described in Chapter 13, primarily in that he dealt with most of his child patients in clinics which were conducted in front of an audience. The sequence of the procedure was as follows. Before seeing the child he read and interpreted to the audience the case history which had been prepared by the referring school. Then the parent, usually the mother, was introduced, and finally the child was brought in. Accordingly the present section is concerned with (1) a description of the history and public character of these clinics, (2) interpretation of the case history to the audience, (3) Adler's approach to the parent, and (4) his approach to the child.*

1. CHILD GUIDANCE CLINICS[10]

In 1898 I wrote my first article developing my idea of the relation between medicine in the larger sense and the school. Later, in connection with an extension class, I conducted a clinic. But it was only a small beginning and a very unsatisfactory one in the face of the great need for child guidance. Thus was born the plan to teach the teachers, for through the school I could reach hundreds of children at once.

Then came the war [World War I], postponing all my plans. After the war Vienna became a very free place, with a school plan based on the belief that freedom and self-confidence should be the aims of education. In the years since the war, I have been able to establish twenty-two mental hygiene clinics for public school children. The clinical directors are all my pupils, physicians trained as psychologists and educators. For three years I have lectured to the teachers-in-training on problem children. There have come into my classes more than six hundred public school teachers, a great part of the present teaching staff in the schools of Vienna.

COMMENT *This was in 1927. By 1934 the number of clinics had increased to over thirty, when they were closed by the semi-dictatorship of Schuschnigg which preceded the coming of Hitler (15, p. 122). Since the second World War and as of 1954, five Individual Psychology child guidance clinics have again been functioning in Vienna in connection with adult education centers, and Individual Psychology is being taught in the Pedagogical Institute of the City of Vienna, by Oskar Spiel.*

As mentioned above, Adler soon realized that he could influence many more children if he were able to teach the teachers how to help the problem child in school. Thus he came to conduct his clinics in front of audiences of teachers at least as early as 1922 (1922b, p. 120). Out of this practice there apparently grew the realization that the presence of an audience held therapeutic values in itself, and from this experience the principle developed to hold all Individual Psychology clinics in public. For a brief description of this procedure we shall quote from the corroborative accounts of others, since we were unable to find more than a mere mention of it in Adler's writings.

Regine Seidler and Ladislaus Zilahi write: "The work in our child-guidance clinics proceeds in most cases with the doors wide open. This public character of the clinics has often been attacked. Our experience has shown, however, that the appearance of the child before a large gathering has a stimulating effect upon him. The public character of the procedure suggests to the child that his trouble is not a private affair, since strangers are also interested in it" (94).

The rationale of treatment before a group is described further by Doris Rayner in a paper based on her work and observations in the Individual Psychology clinic directed by Leonhard Seif in Munich: "Individual Psychologists feel that the open clinic is of more help to children and to parents than is the private interview, besides being a means of education for the group. The child realizes that his difficulty is a community problem. Consciously or unconsciously, he concludes that the attitude of the group is the same as that of the doctor; so when he finds that here for the first time is a man who does not blame him, who has confidence in him, who admits having made faults himself, he knows that the doctor is speaking for the group, and comes to feel the confidence and support of society. The parents also feel this, that it is not only one man who is advising them to let the child go hungry, go late for school, make faults unreproved and unpunished, but that a number of ordinary people like themselves would not blame them for relaxing their well-meant discipline, but even support these weird suggestions and understand their problems from their own experience" (89, pp. 25–26).

An additional aspect of this form of treatment is active audience participation as described in the following account by Martha Holub: "Sometimes only one person may be called on, as when we discuss with such a person, to all appearances in a general way, problems which are actually problems of the child in question. Sometimes everyone is asked to cooperate, as when we pass around the child's drawings or notebooks. Above all we like to use the public to demonstrate to the child our own imperfection, the imperfection of the adults, a method which is used so successfully by Ida Loewy. Take the case of a child who is very much ashamed about the many C's on his report card. We ask to hear from all those in the group who have never had a C in school, and nobody raises his hand" (52, pp. 96–97).

In this way, then, Adler pioneered in a form of group psychotherapy in his child-guidance clinics.

2. INTERPRETATION OF THE CASE HISTORY[11]

For teaching purposes, in order to give the right conception of how we go about our work, I always like to discuss the description of a case with which I am not familiar. It may be that I shall make some mistake in interpretation that later will reveal itself as such; but that should not discourage me. I fancy myself to be in the position of an artist, who, when he begins a piece of work, must first rely to a degree upon his past experience and acquired skill, before he begins actually to weigh and balance, sharpen or soften or alter the features, and strike a true likeness. When I first take up the case history of a difficult child, my aim is always to discern the basic underlying factors, which are the goal and the guiding idea around which the whole life-style has been developed and organized. Once we have an understanding of that, we can see that everything which has occurred did not necessarily have to occur [from the objective point of view], but that it was merely one of the possible things that could happen under the circumstances. We can then go so far as to put ourselves in the place of the patient and feel, think, and act with him. We can transpose ourselves into the role that the child has played and make the honest admission that under the same conditions, with the same picture of the world and with the same erroneous goal of a personal superiority [that is from the child's subjective point of view], we ourselves would have taken practically the same course of action. With this approach we lose much of our inclination to judge and condemn, and that is a fortunate loss.

What is most important is that we are enabled to see the connection of all the surface phenomena with the essential inner core, the life-style of such a difficult child. We come to understand that the disturbing behavior is related to and grows out of a particular conception, or misconception, of life and that the whole personality is a unity which shows the same direction of movement at whatever point it is observed.

3. THE APPROACH TO THE PARENT[12]

We must always act on the assumption that the parents are not responsible for all the bad qualities the child shows. The parents are after all not skillful pedagogues, and they usually have only tradition to guide them. The parents should never be reproached even when there are just grounds. We can achieve much more when we succeed in establishing a sort of pact, when we persuade the parents to change their attitude and work with us according to our methods. It is of no avail to point out to them the faults in their past treatment. What we must do is to try to make them adopt a new procedure.

We must first of all win the parents. If the parents come to us to consult us, they do this out of a certain feeling of imperfection. They subject themselves to our critique from their sense of responsibility. Before doing anything else we must lift this burden from them. I tell them always: "I can see that you are on the right track," even when I am convinced of the contrary, for if I want to be of use, I must know how to choose the adequate method. It is always advisable to use such qualifying phrases as "perhaps" or "I think that the following might prove effective." I have seen in the autobiography of Benjamin Franklin that he proceeded similarly: he dispensed with all dogmatic statements.

I have found that one does well not to question the mother too much on details. It is very important to appraise the essential point of the case, but it is also important not to confront the mother directly with what one has understood. One must keep this to oneself and only make allusions to it, occasionally. Eventually we can give the parents some ideas, but it is impossible to modify an intrenched system with a few words.

COMMENT   *How the account of the mother sheds light on the case is illustrated in the following example given by Rayner: "The mother, if talking freely of her past and present methods, will usually let us see why the child is persisting in his tactics. For instance, she will show how zealous she is in reminding the forgetful child, in reassuring or comforting the fearful one, in punishing or warning the naughty one. She may state emphatically that Mary and John are not like Tom—'if only he were like them,'—and we know how often Tom must have heard this; but the mother will maintain that her treatment must be right because it succeeded with the other two" (89, p. 24).*

4. THE APPROACH TO THE CHILD[13]

We psychologists are in a relatively favorable position. The teacher and the mother live with the child the rest of the day. They carry the heaviest burden. We can gain the confidence of the children, and we show them that one must not take the difficulties tragically, but that it is more important to be courageous. A counselor has means by which he can encourage a child in half an hour, a child who feels himself standing close to an abyss. Our position is advantageous for another reason; we are dealing with children who have been criticized. Suddenly they arrive in a new atmosphere where they can see that they are not considered hopeless cases.

It is not enough to be a friend of mankind, a benevolent counselor. Such educators simply make life agreeable for the children; they praise them all the time believing that they will arrive at results through the charm of their personalities. It is only through modesty that one can gain access to the human soul. It is an art to win a person, to awaken in him certain sentiments, to get him to listen and to understand what one explains to him, an art which is indispensable in dealing with children. If the child has understood, that is the first step.

The life-style of every individual can be altered only by the individual's own recognition of his faults and errors. If we have to do with the formation of a mistaken life-style, and if we are in a position to understand the error involved, then, perhaps we may be in a position to reveal evidence enough to convince the child that at a certain point he has made a misstep which must necessarily prove injurious to him if he continues in the mistaken direction. We should not say that the individual must pay for his mistake, but rather that he must inevitably experience the consequences of his error.

Sometimes I find it necessary to put his problem clearly before the child himself, not to humiliate him but to make him understand why he is lazy or cowardly or behind in his work, as a shop teacher might show a boy how to repair a machine by pointing out the maladjustment that keeps it from working properly. I have never known a child who could not understand his difficulties when they were set before him. If I find a child who fails to follow me as I trace the roots of his mistakes, I can always be sure that I have blundered either in interpreting his situation or in describing it to him. Every normal [that is, not feeble-minded] child is capable of fathoming the springs of his own action and reaching a true understanding of his own life.

[I shall try to illustrate our approach with the case of an eleven-year-old girl, who on the mornings of schooldays is so nervous that the whole house suffers. She enjoys complete domination over her family, yet does not understand this fact in its context.] If she could be made to realize the truth, if we could show her that the extreme overrating of the everyday problems of school is nothing but bragging and constructing an alibi for possible failure to excel at school, we should be taking an important step in the right direction. We may have to go further, and show her what type of person brags. No one will try to impress other people unless he believes that his actual accomplishments give insufficient testimony of his personal importance. It is evidence that he is too much dependent on the opinion of others.

Our attitude toward the child's behavior might be expressed in some such words as these: "If my opinion is correct, you are quite right in acting as you do—perhaps you should even do more. Everything you do goes to prove that you are a very bright girl who has found the right means of impressing her environment." After going this far, I would have to make my point clear by reference to other occurrences in her life and to her recollections; I might perhaps be able to show her that her position as an only child gave rise to those tendencies which later ripened into positive faults. And I would say: "This is nothing out of the ordinary; these things often happen to spoiled only children, or to children trained in getting things from others and in being the center of attention." Now she will know what she formerly did not realize.

And this new knowledge will, in itself, influence her train of thought. She will find herself making a continual comparison between the old way and the new, and thinking them over. Her actions will be at plain variance with her developing social feeling, and she will begin to curb and control them. In all probability the following developments will occur: During the first days subsequent to this advice, after every demonstration before her family, she will think to herself: "Dr. Adler would say that I did that just to show off." This will continue for a while. If not, I can find some way to help her along. And then the time will come when, in the very midst of the tumult, she will remember how her conduct would appear to me; and this self-consciousness alone will effect a great improvement. And finally she will wake up in the morning with the realization: "Now I'm about to stir up a commotion in the family." And being aware of it, she can then avoid it.

This is the simplest course of treatment. But other ways are possible. I myself prefer a quite different method. After making quite certain that I could risk such a procedure in the case at hand, I would say: "School is the most important thing in the world, and if I were you I would make even a greater fuss about it." By this *reductio ad absurdum* I would spoil her pleasure in her tactics. "You have to be continually kicking up a fuss in order to stress your accomplishments and your own importance. It stands to reason that it would be too hard for you to attract attention by any useful means. And what a wonderful alibi!" There are a hundred different techniques that can serve, as Kaus puts it, to "smirch a clean conscience." For instance, I might say to the girl under consideration: "Write in capital letters over your bed: 'Every morning I must torment my family as much as possible.' Thus in the future you have to do consciously, and with a bad conscience, what you formerly did unaware but with a clean conscience." None of my patients has ever followed advice such as this.

D. Individual Psychology in the School

COMMENT *Adler's broad understanding of psychiatry as a social task led him early in his career to become interested in prophylaxis. He reasoned that adult maladjustment could be reduced most effectively if the early mistaken outlook of the child could be corrected. While it would not be possible to reach each child through his parents, this could be accomplished through the teachers in the schools. Thus Adler embarked upon "teaching the teachers." In the following we are presenting his thoughts as expressed in lectures to teachers on the principles of (1) preventing and correcting early mistakes in the individual school child, and (2) creating a classroom atmosphere which would be conducive to the development of the all-important social interest.*

1. THE INDIVIDUAL CHILD IN SCHOOL[14]

The school is placed between the family and life in society. It has the opportunity of correcting the mistaken styles of life formed under family upbringing, and the responsibility of preparing the child's adjustment to social life so that he will play his individual role harmoniously in the orchestral pattern of society.

By society I understand an unattainable ideal which we can only surmise, since it is beyond all human powers. The main factor [in education] is the practice of the art so to move the child that he, too, will strive for the ideal of a community. The person who naturally should have fulfilled this task is the mother, and we see the outcome of her shortcomings. The mother has two functions: (1) to win the child, to attract his interest, and to stand before his eyes as a fellow man; (2) to direct the interest of this child towards others. The teacher must replace the mother and make corrections where she has made a mistake.

The pampered child and the child with organ inferiorities always want to "exclude" the difficulties of life because by their increased inferiority feeling they are robbed of the strength to cope with them. In school, however, we may control the difficulties, and gradually put these children in a position to solve problems. Thus the school becomes a place where we really educate, and not merely give instruction.

An educator's most important task, one might almost say his holy duty, is to see to it that no child is discouraged at school, and that a child who enters school already discouraged regains his self-confidence through his school and his teacher. This goes hand-in-hand with the vocation of the educator, for education is possible only with children who look hopefully and joyfully upon the future.

Valuable as it is to establish friendly relations with discouraged children through a sympathetic attitude, this is not enough. The friendly relation must be used to stimulate them to continue their improvement. This can be done only by making them more independent, that is, by bringing them through various devices to the point where they necessarily acquire faith in their own mental and physical powers. They simply must be convinced that what they have not yet achieved can readily be attained by industry, perseverance, practice, and courage. One must put tasks in their way which they can accomplish, and from the accomplishment of which they can gain faith in themselves.

The educator's task is much easier when he starts with a single encouraging accomplishment and uses it to make the child believe he can be just as successful in other things. It is enticing the child, as it were, from one fruitful pasture to another.

The theory of heredity must never be emphasized in education or in the theory and practice of psychology. Except in cases of subnormal children and congenital idiots it is proper to assume that everyone can do everything necessary. This is not, of course, to deny the differences of inherited material, but what is important is always the use which is made of it. Right education is the method of developing the individual, with all his inherited abilities and disabilities. By courage and training, disabilities may be so compensated that they even become great abilities.

According to Individual Psychology, "Everybody can accomplish everything," and it is a sign of an inferiority complex when a boy or girl despairs of following this maxim and feels unable to accomplish his goal on the useful side of life.

If we constantly tell a child that he is bad or stupid, he will become convinced in a short time that we are right and will not have sufficient courage thereafter to tackle any task presented to him. He does not understand that the environment originally destroyed his self-confidence and that he is subconsciously arranging his life to prove this fallacious judgment correct.

It is an interesting fact that children know who is the best in spelling, in drawing, in athletics. They can rate each other quite well. The great danger is that they may minimize themselves. They believe, "Now I can never catch up." This is not true; they can catch up. But the mistake in their judgment must be pointed out to them, if it is not to become an *idée fixe* throughout life. A child who has such an idea will stay where he is. It is important that changes in relative position do take place once in a while. Children should know of this, and be brought to understand its application in their own case.

There is a type of child who is especially discouraged in arithmetic where he has had a poor start and was unable to follow. Such children lack an adequate basis and this causes a good part of their discouragement. They conclude: "I am not gifted in arithmetic." Of all subjects, arithmetic requires most independence. Especially pampered children are far removed from this manner of independent thinking, unless they have had some special training.

I myself have known this difficulty, for I was considered completely incapable at arithmetic. If my father had followed the advice which he was given and had taken me out of school to make me learn a trade, I would perhaps have become a very good locksmith, but I would have continued living in the conviction that there are people who are gifted in arithmetic and others who are not. Having found myself in this predicament I can now say, in full knowledge of the case, that I do not believe in this any longer.

I found myself one day, to my own astonishment, able to complete a problem which had stumped my teacher. The success changed my whole attitude towards mathematics. Now I began to enjoy it and use every opportunity for increasing my ability. In consequence I became one of the best mathematicians in my school.

Punishment is regarded by the child as confirmation of his feeling that he does not belong in school. He will want to avoid school, and look for means of escape, not means of meeting the difficulty.

He may assume some peculiarity which, while not drawing praise from the teacher, may attract the teacher's attention or arouse the admiration of the other children.

Bad intentions on the part of the child are never the beginning, but always the result of a discouragement. We have no occasion to get angry at these bad intentions. They are a last stand of the child to make himself prominent on the bad, the useless side of life, to make himself disagreeably noticed. One should never fight with children, one should only study them, reflect over them, and discover the mistakes in the structure of their style of life.

2. THE CLASSROOM AS A COMMUNITY[15]

As the family should be a unit, with each member an equal part of the whole, so, too, should the class. When they are trained in this way, children are really interested in one another, and enjoy cooperation. I have seen many "difficult" children whose attitude was entirely changed through the interest and cooperation of their fellow children. One child I may mention especially. He came from a home where he felt that everyone was hostile to him, and he expected that everyone would be hostile to him at school. His work at school had been poor, and when his parents heard of it, they punished him at home. At last he found a teacher who understood the circumstances and explained to the other children how this boy believed that everyone was his enemy. The teacher enlisted their help in convincing the boy that they were his friends; and the whole conduct and progress of the boy improved beyond belief.

When a problem arises in the class the teacher can propose that the children talk the matter out. The teacher, of course, would direct the discussion, but the children would have full opportunity for expression. They might analyze the causes of a problem such as laziness and reach some conclusion. The lazy child, who does not know that he is meant, will, nevertheless, learn a great deal from the discussion.

If the class is a unit, the successes of one member are an advantage to the others. Where there are brilliant children in a class, the progress of the whole class can be accelerated and heightened through them, and it is unfair to the other members to deprive them of such a stimulus. I should rather recommend that an unusually bright pupil should be given other activities and interests, painting for example, in addition to the ordinary classwork. His successes in these activities would also widen the interests of the other children and encourage them to go forward.

In public schools it is very difficult [for the teacher to give the slow child individual attention], and I know the objection may be raised that the other children will believe that this one is preferred to them. My answer to this is that a feeling must be developed which will enable the entire class to help the teacher deal with the child. It will help the slow child if the other pupils cooperate in helping him.

Children who lack psychological preparation should not be put into the backward classes. A better way to take care of such children would be to have tutors for them. Besides tutors, there should be clubs, where children could go and get extra tutoring. There they could do their homework, play games, and read books. In this way they could get a training in courage instead of a training in discouragement which is what they derive from classes for backward children. Such clubs, when combined with a greater abundance of playgrounds than we now have, would keep the children completely off the streets and away from bad influences.

A teacher should know all his pupils intimately to establish social interest and cooperation. It would be a great help if children had the same teacher for several years. He could more easily find out and remedy mistakes in a child's style of life; and it would be easier, also, to create a cooperative social unit out of the class.

One frequent suggestion for increasing the unity and cooperation of a class is to make the children self-governing. But in such attempts we must go carefully, under the guidance of a teacher, and assure ourselves that the children are rightly prepared. Otherwise they will look on their self-government as a kind of game. They may be much stricter and severer than a teacher would be; or they may use their meetings to gain a personal advantage, air quarrels, score off one another, or achieve a position of superiority.

COMMENT *By presenting thoughts such as these to educators Adler inspired establishment of a public school in Vienna officially designated as "Individual Psychology Experimental School."*

The leading figures in the experimental school were Ferdinand Birnbaum, Oskar Spiel, and Franz Scharmer. According to Birnbaum (12) the new school was to facilitate education for social living. To this end he endeavored to organize the classroom procedure around the following concepts suggested by E. Otto. The experience community is the outcome of the effort of the teacher to transform the class from a mere aggregate into a cohesive group, which is facilitated by play, excursions, and other group activities. The administration community is a form of self-government. The discussion community is concerned with "life-problems of the individual pupil which may be brought close to a happy solution in group discussion. We have here essentially the same mental processes which make for part of the success of public child-guidance clinics. The child learns to regard his failures not as a private matter, but through and with the eyes of others as a public matter. Thus we succeed in many cases in helping the child to discard the spectacles of his customary 'biased apperception' and to take up an objective position" (12, p. 120). In the mutual-aid community children who have difficulties with their school work or otherwise are tutored or assisted by those in a position to do so. "Children who have recently overcome a certain form of problem behavior help schoolmates who are not yet free of the same difficulty" (11, p. 114). Actual instruction takes the form of the work community which in the days of the experimental school was the generally adopted practice for all Viennese schools. Here the teacher is not the center of the educational process but rather the organizer and leader of group and individual work.

The role of the teacher with regard to the individual child is described in a book by Spiel (98) which presents the applications of Individual Psychology in the Experimental School. The teacher's seven functions are: he must observe and interpret the child's behavior and all forms of expression; he must seek contact with the child; he must unburden him in case of misbehavior by showing understanding rather than moral indignation; he must try to give insight to the child and finally re-educate him. The teacher's over-all function is that of a stage-director or producer who must carefully arrange situations so that they become educationally valuable (99).

An account of the history and functioning of both the guidance clinics and the school is given by Madelaine Ganz (47). The Experimental School operated from 1931 until 1934, when like the clinics it was closed for political reasons. Since the war the work of the original Experimental School has been resumed under the direction of Spiel in one elementary and two secondary demonstration schools of the City of Vienna.

With Adler's emphasis on social interest and social relations it is not surprising that when his ideas received practical implementation in the school this took a form very much like that of sociometric methods (81), group dynamics (70), and student-centered teaching (90, pp. 384-428). This is a further corroboration of the affinity of these trends to Adler's Individual Psychology.

E. Individual Pyschology Interview Guides

1. FOR USE WITH CHILDREN[16]

COMMENT An "Individual Psychology questionnaire, for the understanding and treatment of problem children, formulated with explanatory comments by the International Society for Individual

Psychology" is contained with slight variations in several of Adler's publications (1929a, pp. 110–114; 1930a, pp. 251–258; 1933a, pp. 200–203; 1933b, pp. 299–304). He recommends it as an informal aid, not to be adhered to rigidly, in assessing a child's style of life, in learning what "influences were at work when the child was forming it," and in seeing how this style of life manifests itself in coping with the demands of life. At the same time it may serve, as Adler suggested, as a review and test of the reader's understanding of the principles of Individual Psychology.

Disorders

1. Since when has there been cause for complaint? In what sort of situation, objective and psychological, was the child when the disorder was first noticed?

The following are significant: change of environment, beginning of school, change of school, change of teacher, birth of a sibling, failure in school, new friendships, diseases of the child or the parents, divorce, remarriage, or death of the parents.

2. Was the child conspicuous in some way already at an earlier age? Was this through mental or physical weakness, cowardliness, carelessness, reserve, clumsiness, jealousy, dependence on others when eating, dressing, washing, or going to bed? Was the child afraid of being alone or of darkness? Does he understand his sexual role, the primary, secondary, or tertiary sexual characteristics? How does he regard the opposite sex? How far has he been enlightened on his sexual role? Is he a stepchild, illegitimate, foster child, or orphan? How did his foster parents treat him? Is there still a contact? Did he learn to walk and talk at the right time? Without difficulty? Was the teething normal? Were there striking difficulties in learning to write, draw, do arithmetic, sing, or swim? Did he attach himself very particularly to a single person? To either his father, his mother, a grandparent or nurse?

One should notice any hostile attitude toward life, causes for the awakening of inferiority feelings, tendencies to exclude difficulties and persons, and traits of egotism, sensitivity, impatience, heightened affects, activity, greediness, and caution.

3. Did the child give much trouble? What and whom does he fear the most? Did he cry out at night? Did he wet the bed? Is he domineering? Towards weaker children or towards stronger children as well? Did he show a strong desire to lie in the bed of one of the parents? Was he intelligent? Was he much teased and laughed at? Is he vain about his ap-

pearance in regard to his hair, clothes, shoes? Does he pick his nose or bite his nails? Is he greedy when eating? Has he stolen? Has he difficulties with his bowel movements?

These questions aim to clarify whether the child strives for pre-eminence with greater or lesser activity, and furthermore, whether defiance has prevented the adaptation of his drives to the culture.

Social Relationships

4. Did he make friends easily? Or was he quarrelsome, and did he torment persons and animals? Does he attach himself to younger or older boys or girls? Does he like to be the leader or is he inclined to isolate himself? Does he collect things? Is he stingy or greedy for money?

These questions concern the child's ability to make contact, and the degree of his discouragement.

5. How is he now in all these respects? How does he behave in school? Does he like to go? Does he come late? Is he excited before school and does he get into a rush? Does he lose his books, or school bag? Is he excited about homework and examinations? Does he forget or does he refuse to do his school work? Does he waste time? Is he lazy or indolent? Does he concentrate little, or not at all? Does he disturb the class? How does he regard the teacher? Is he critical, arrogant, indifferent? Does he ask others to help him with his lessons, or does he wait until help is offered? Is he ambitious in gymnastics and sports? Does he consider himself entirely or partially untalented? Is he a great reader? What sort of literature does he prefer? Does he do poorly in all subjects?

These questions reveal the preparation of the child for school, the result of the going-to-school "experiment," and his attitude towards difficulties.

6. Correct information about home conditions, diseases in the family, alcoholism, criminal tendencies, neuroses, debility, lues, epilepsy, the standard of living, deaths in the family, and the age of the child when they occurred. Is he an orphan? Who dominates the family? Is the upbringing strict, nagging, or pampering? Are the children made afraid of life? How is the supervision? Are there step-parents?

Through these questions one sees the child in his family position and can appraise what impressions were conveyed to him.

7. What is the child's position in the sibling sequence? Is he the oldest, the youngest, the only child, the only boy, the only girl? Are there rivalry, much crying, malicious laughter, blind depreciation tendencies towards others?

This is significant for the character of the child and his attitude towards people in general.

Interests

8. What thoughts has the child had on the choice of occupation? What occupation have his family members? How is the marriage of his parents? What does he think about marriage?

These questions allow conclusions regarding the courage and confidence of the child for the future.

9. What are his favorite games, stories, characters in history and fiction? Does he like to spoil other children's games? Does he get lost in fantasy? Is he a cool-headed thinker and does he reject fantasy?

These questions give hints regarding the models of superiority the child may have.

Recollections and Dreams

10. What are the child's earliest recollections? What are his impressive or recurring dreams? Falling, flying, powerlessness, missing the train, racing, being a prisoner, anxiety dreams?

In these experiences one often finds an inclination toward isolation, voices warning toward caution, impulses of ambition, tendency to passivity, preferences for certain persons.

Discouraged Behavior

11. In what respect is the child discouraged? Does he feel neglected? Does he respond to attention and praise? Has he superstitious ideas? Does he avoid difficulties? Does he try his hand at various things only to give them up again? Is he uncertain about his future? Does he believe in the injurious effects of heredity? Was he systematically discouraged by his environment? Is his outlook on life pessimistic?

These questions yield important viewpoints for the fact that the child has lost his self-confidence and seeks his way in an erring direction.

12. Are there further bad habits? Does the child make faces? Does he act stupid, childish, or funny?

These are not very courageous attempts to attract attention.

Organ Inferiorities

13. Has the child speech disabilities? Is he ugly, awkward, club-footed, knock-kneed, or bow-legged? Did he have rickets? Is he poorly developed? Is he abnormally stout, tall, or small? Has he eye or ear defects? Is he mentally retarded? Is he left-handed? Does he snore at night? Is he remarkably handsome?

These questions refer to life-difficulties which the child usually over-rates. Thus he may arrive at a permanent mood of discouragement. One finds a similar faulty development also in very handsome children. They come to believe that they should be given everything without effort and thus they miss the proper preparation for life.

Inferiority [Symptom] Complex

14. Does the child speak openly of his inability, his "lack of talent" for school? For work? Or for life? Does he have thoughts of suicide? Is there any connection in point of time between his defeats and his disorders (waywardness, gang formation)? Does he overrate outward success? Is he submissive, bigoted, rebellious?

These questions refer to forms of expressions of extensive discouragement. They often occur after attempts to get ahead have come to grief, not only on account of their inherent inappropriateness, but also on account of insufficient understanding on the part of the environment. The symptoms are substitute satisfactions in a "secondary theater of operations."

Positive Assets

15. Name the things in which the child is successful.

These are important hints, for it is possible that the interests, inclinations and preparations of the child point to a different direction from that which he has taken so far.

2. FOR USE WITH ADULTS[17]

In case of adult failures I have found the following interview schedule to be valuable. By adhering to it the experienced therapist will gain an extensive insight into the style of life of the individual already within about half an hour. My own inquiries take the following sequence, although they do not always adhere to it. Those who are familiar with medical questioning will not fail to notice the similarity between this and our sequence. For the Individual Psychologist, thanks to the system by which he works, the answers will yield many a glimpse that would otherwise have remained unnoticed.

1. What are your complaints?
2. What was your situation when you first noticed your symptoms?
3. What is your situation now?
4. What is your occupation?

5. Describe your parents as to their character, and their health. If not alive, what illness caused their death? What was their relation to yourself?

6. How many brothers and sisters have you? What is your position in the birth order? What is their attitude toward you? How do they get along in life? Do they also have any illness?

7. Who was your father's or your mother's favorite? What kind of upbringing did you have?

8. Inquire for signs of pampering in childhood (timidity, shyness, difficulties in forming friendships, disorderliness).

9. What illnesses did you have in childhood and what was your attitude to them?

10. What are your earliest childhood recollections?

11. What do you fear, or what did you fear the most?

12. What is your attitude toward the opposite sex? What was it in childhood and later years?

13. What occupation would have interested you the most, and if you did not adopt it, why not?

14. Is the patient ambitious, sensitive, inclined to outbursts of temper, pedantic, domineering, shy, or impatient?

15. What sort of persons are around you at present? Are they impatient, bad-tempered, or affectionate?

16. How do you sleep?

17. What dreams do you have? (Of falling, flying, recurrent dreams, prophetic, about examinations, missing a train.)

18. What illnesses are there in your family background?

FOOTNOTES TO CHAPTER SIXTEEN

1. 1: "Erziehungsberatungsstellen" (1922b), p. 119; 2: *Menschenkenntnis* (1927a), p. 54; 3: "Wo soll der Kampf gegen die Verwahrlosung einsetzen?" (1921), p. 118; 4 and 5: *Der Sinn des Lebens* (1933a), pp. 85–87 and 86–87.

2. 1 and 2: *The Education of Children* (1930a), pp. 27–29 and 96–97; 3: *Individualpsychologie in der Schule* (1929a), p. 20.

3. 1: *Die Technik der Individualpsychologie. Tl. 2.* (1930d), p. 53; 2 and 3: *What Life Should Mean to You* (1931a), pp. 193 and 37–38; 4 and 5: *Sinn des Lebens* (1933a), pp. 146 and 30; 6: "Über individualpsychologische Erziehung" (1918e), p. 239; 7: *Heilen und Bilden* (1922a), p. 19.

4. 1: *What Life Should Mean to You* (1931a), pp. 127–129.

5. 1, 2, 3: *Education of Children* (1930a), pp. 73–74, 67–68, and 73.

6. 1, 2, 3: *Education of Children* (1930a), pp. 39, 40, and 104–105.

7. 1: *Education of Children* (1930a), pp. 142–144.

8. 1 and 3: *Education of Children* (1930a), pp. 64–66 and 67; 2: *Technik der Individualpsychologie* (1930d), p. 118.

9. 1, 2, 3: *Technik der Individualpsychologie* (1930d), pp. 37, 37, and 157.

10. 1 and 2: "A doctor remakes education" (1927f), pp. 490–491 and 493–494.

11. 1, 2, 3: "A school girl's exaggeration of her own importance" (1929g), pp. 3–4, 3, and 3.

12. 1: *Education of Children* (1930a), p. 241; 2 and 3: *Technik der Individualpsychologie* (1930d), pp. 193–194 and 194.

13. 1 and 2: *Technik der Individualpsychologie* (1930d), pp. 194 and 195; 3, 5 to 8: "School girl's exaggeration" (1929g), pp. 6, 11, 11, 11, and 11–12; 4: "A doctor remakes education" (1927f), pp. 492–493.

14. 1, 4, 5, 6, 9, 10, 14, 15: *Education of Children* (1930a), pp. 52, 84, 81 and 73, 53, 126, 174–175, 56, and 54; 2 and 16: *Individualpsychologie in der Schule* (1929a), pp. 6 and 30; 3 and 8: *Science of Living* (1929c), pp. 184 and 227; 7: *Problems of Neurosis* (1929b), p. 4; 11 and 12: *Technik der Individualpsychologie* (1930d), pp. 31 and 139; 13: *What Life Should Mean to You* (1931a), p. 170.

15. 1, 3, 6, 7: *What Life Should Mean to You* (1931a), pp. 163–164, 171–172, 171, and 164; 2 and 5: *Education of Children* (1930a), pp. 189 and 182–183; 4: *The Pattern of Life* (1930b), p. 77.

16. *Sinn des Lebens* (1933a), pp. 200–203.

17. *Sinn des Lebens* (1933a), pp. 204–205.

CHAPTER SEVENTEEN

CRIME AND RELATED DISORDERS

A. The Criminal Personality

1. LACK OF SOCIAL INTEREST[1]

What we understand by crime is an intentional injury of others for one's own advantage. Obviously, then, the problem concerns human beings in whom social interest is not sufficiently developed.

We find the same kind of failure exhibited in criminals as in problem children, neurotics, psychotics, suicides, drunkards, and sexual perverts. Every one of them fails in social interest. Even here, however, there is no sharp distinction between them and other people. No one can be held up as an example of perfect cooperation or perfect social feeling. The failures of criminals are only a severer degree of common failures.

Before I go any further I wish to exclude the idea that criminals are insane. There are psychotics who commit crimes, but their crimes are of quite a different kind. Likewise we must exclude the feeble-minded criminal, who is really only a tool. The true criminals are those who plan the crime. They paint glowing pictures of the prospects, they excite the fancy or ambitions of feeble-minded individuals; then they hide themselves and leave their victims to execute the crime. The same thing holds, of course, when younger people are made use of by old and experienced criminals.

A criminal can cooperate only to a certain degree. When this degree is exhausted, he turns to crime. The exhaustion occurs when a problem is too difficult for him. All problems in our lives are social problems; and these can be solved only if we are interested in others.

We make three broad divisions in the problems of life. First let us take the problems of relationship to other men. Criminals [as we have seen] can sometimes have friends, but only among their own kind. They can form gangs and even show loyalty to one another. But they cannot make friends with society at large, with ordinary people. Criminals treat themselves as a body of exiles and do not understand how to feel at home with their fellow men.

The second group of problems is connected with occupation. A useful occupation implies an interest in other people and a contribution to their welfare; but this is exactly what we miss in the criminal personality. The great majority of criminals are untrained and unskilled workers. If you trace back their history you will find that at school and even before school there was a block here, a stoppage of interest.

The third group includes all the problems of love. A good and fruitful love life calls equally for interest in the other person and for cooperation. It is revealing to observe that half the criminals who are sent to reformatories are suffering from venereal diseases. This would tend to show that they wanted an easy way out for the problems of love. They regard the partner in love merely as a piece of property, and very often they think that love can be bought. It is something they ought to possess, not a partnership in life.

2. THE VESTIGE OF SOCIAL INTEREST[2]

To commit a crime, the criminal has to goad himself to it. This is a bright spot since it may be taken as evidence that even the criminal has some social interest. The trouble is that he has not enough of it. For the purpose of committing his crime he must overcome, both mentally and emotionally, whatever amount of social interest he possesses. There is a wonderful illustration of this in Dostoievsky's Raskolnikov. Raskolnikov lies in his bed for two months considering whether or not he dare commit a murder. He tries to kill his social feeling by picturing to himself how much good he could do with the money of his victim. At the end he exclaims, "Am I Napoleon or am I a louse?" Now he is prepared; he behaves like Napoleon and murders the old woman. What has happened? He has selected a comparison, a kind of metaphor. This has no connection with reality, since he is, of course, neither Napoleon nor a louse. But he sets up these alternatives because he does not want to give up the crime which is his goal.

The criminal always looks for excuses and justifications, for extenuating circumstances, and for reasons that "force" him to be a criminal. It is not easy to pierce through the wall of social feeling; but if he is to commit a crime he must find a way—perhaps through brooding over his wrongs, perhaps through intoxication—to get rid of this hindrance.

3. DEGREE OF ACTIVITY[3]

The criminal differs from other failures in one point: he retains a certain amount of activity, which he throws on the useless side of life. And to a certain extent he can cooperate there with those whom he sees as like himself, with his own type, with other criminals. Here he differs from the neurotic, the suicide, or the drunkard.

Lack of social interest, already in the child, will assume a variety of colors depending upon whether he takes an active or passive attitude toward life. Even in a passive way he can expect everything from others; but if he shows more activity he will take from others for himself whatever he wants that is not given to him voluntarily. Right here is the beginning of delinquency, the psychological structure of a child who is a potential delinquent.

4. THE PRIVATE WORLD OF THE CRIMINAL[4]

If I am right in my observations, criminals look and speak and listen in a different way from other people. They have a private logic, a private intelligence. We can observe this in the way they explain their crimes. A criminal will say, "I saw a man who had nice trousers, and I hadn't; so I had to kill him." Now if we grant him that his desires are all important, and that there is no call for him to make a living in a useful way, his conclusion is intelligent enough; but it is not common sense. We can understand, then, how criminals, if they see attractive things and want to obtain them in an easy way, conclude that they must take them from this hostile world, in which they are not at all interested. They are suffering from a wrong outlook upon the world, a wrong estimate of their own importance and the importance of other people. [See also pp. 150–151.]

Like all ambitious persons they prepare an alibi whenever threatened with a defeat that might injure their prestige. "Prestige diplomacy" is characteristic of ambitious people. We are not surprised that at St.

Helena, Napoleon said, "If I had only gone to Spain first and then to Russia, the whole world would now be at my feet." These alibis are both a comfort and a challenge to be cleverer next time. Thus the criminal preserves his feeling of worth and his psychological balance. For him his failure was due to a trifle only.

Crime is a coward's imitation of heroism. Criminals think they are courageous; but we should not be fooled into thinking the same. All criminals are actually cowards. They are evading problems they do not feel strong enough to solve. We can see their cowardice in the way in which they face life, as well as in the crimes they commit. They guard themselves by darkness and isolation; they surprise somebody and draw their weapons before he can defend himself. They like to believe that they are heroes; but this is their mistaken schema of apperception, a failure of common sense. We know that they are cowards, and if they were sure we knew it, it would be a big shock to them. It swells their vanity and pride to think of themselves as overcoming the police; and often they think, "I can never be found out."

In all this we can see the criminal's inferiority complex. He is running away from the tasks of life in association. He feels himself incapable of normal success. His training away from cooperation has genuinely added to his difficulties. He hides his feeling of inadequacy by developing a cheap superiority complex.

5. A CASE[5]

Now let us turn to a case and see whether we can discover these points of Individual Psychology theory, in spite of the fact that the description was not written for this purpose. The case I shall give is from 500 *Criminal Careers* by Sheldon and Eleanor T. Glueck; the case of "Hard-boiled John." This boy explains the genesis of his criminal career: "I never thought I would let myself go. Up to fifteen or sixteen I was about like other kids. I liked athletics and took part in them. I read books from the library, kept good hours, and all that. My parents took me out of school and put me to work and took all of my wages except fifty cents each week."

Here he is making an accusation. If we questioned him about his relation to his parents, and if we could see his whole family situation, we could find out what he really experienced. At present we must regard it only as an affirmation that his parents were not cooperative.

"I worked about a year, then I began going with a girl and she liked a good time."

We find this often in the careers of criminals; they attach themselves to a girl who wants a good time. Recall what we mentioned before: this is a problem and tests the degree of cooperation. He goes with a girl who wants a good time, and he has only fifty cents a week. We should not call this a true solution for the problem of love. There are other girls, for example. He is not on the right track. In these circumstances I should say, "If she wants a good time she is not the girl for me." There are different estimates of what is important in life.

"You can't give a girl a good time these days, even in N——, on fifty cents a week. The old man wouldn't give me any more. I was sore and had it on my mind: how could I make more money?"

Common sense would say, "Perhaps you could look around and earn more"; but he wants it easy, and if he wishes to have a girl it is for his own pleasure and nothing more.

"One day along came a fellow I got acquainted with."

When a stranger comes along, it is another test for him. A boy with the right ability for cooperation could not be seduced. This boy is on a path which makes it possible for him to be seduced.

"He was a 'right guy' (that is, a good thief; an intelligent, capable fellow who knows the business, and will 'divvy up with you and not do you dirt'). We put through a lot of jobs in N—— and got away with it, and I have been at it ever since."

We hear that the parents own their own home. The father is foreman in a factory, and the family is only just able to make ends meet. This boy is one of three children; and up to the time of his misconduct no member of the family had been known to be delinquent.

He admits having first had heterosexual experience at the age of fifteen. I am sure some people would say that he is oversexed. But this boy has no interest in other people and only wants pleasure. Anybody can oversex himself. There is no difficulty in it. He is searching for appreciation in this respect: he wants to be a sexual hero.

At sixteen he was arrested with a companion for breaking and entering and larceny. Other points of interest follow and confirm what we have said. He wants to be a conqueror in appearances, to attract the attention of girls, to win them by paying for them. He wears a wide-brimmed hat, red bandanna handkerchief, and a belt with a revolver in it. He assumes the name of a Western outlaw. He is a vain boy: he wants to appear a hero and has no other way. He admits having done whatever he was accused of, "and a lot more." He has no scruples about property rights.

"I do not think that life is worth living. For humanity in general I have nothing but the utmost contempt."

All these conscious thoughts are really unconscious, that is, he does not understand them; he does not know what they mean in their coherence. He feels that life is a burden, but he does not understand why he is discouraged.

"I have learned not to trust people. They say thieves won't do each other, but they will. I was with a fellow once, treated him white; and he did me dirt."

"If I had all the money I wanted, I would be just as honest as anybody. That is, if I had enough so I could do what I wanted to without working. I never liked work. I hate it and never will work."

We can translate this last point as follows: "I am compelled to repress my wishes and therefore I am a criminal. It is repression which is responsible for my career." It is a point deserving much thought.

"I have never committed a crime for the sake of doing the crime. Of course there is a certain 'kick' in driving up to a place in an automobile, putting through your job, and making your get-away."

He believes it is heroism and does not see it is cowardice.

"When I was caught before at one time I had fourteen thousand dollars' worth of jewellery, but I didn't know any better than to go and see my girl, and cashed in only enough to pay my expenses to go to her, and they caught me."

These people pay their girls and so gain an easy victory. But they think of it as a real triumph.

"They have schools here in the prison, and I am going to get all the education I can get—not to reform myself, but to make myself more dangerous to society."

This is the expression of a very bitter attitude toward mankind. He does not want mankind. He says:

"If I had a son I would wring his neck. Do you think I would ever be guilty of bringing a human being into the world?"

B. Development of the Criminal Personality

1. INTERACTION OF SUBJECTIVE AND OBJECTIVE FACTORS[6]

If you trace back the life of a criminal, you will almost always find that the trouble began in his early family experiences.

But it was not the environment itself that counted; it was rather that the child misunderstood his position, and there was no one by his side to explain it to him. There is no compulsion either in environment or in heredity. Children of the same family and the same environment can develop in different ways. Sometimes a criminal springs from a family of irreproachable record. Sometimes children of good character and behavior are found in a family of very bad record with frequent experiences of prisons and reformatories.

Heredity and environment contribute something to a child's development; but we are not so much concerned with what a child brings into the world, or with the experiences he encounters, as with the way he utilizes them.

With the commonly inadequate development of social interest the inclination to crime is more prevalent than the actual commission of crime. The latter requires, in addition, an external "cause." This is found in the difficult situation which is never missing from any crime. The criminal sees in the commission of his crime the only possible relief from the burden of his difficult situation, his only possibility of success. The same situation, however, will appear quite insignificant to the non-criminal. It is like a test of the criminal's social interest. For instance, a man who has no money and wants to take a girl out may become a burglar.

The main features of the criminal's personality have already been decided by the time he is four or five years old. By that time he has already made those mistakes in his estimate of himself and of the world which we see displayed in his criminal career. From then on it is easy for such a child to deceive himself and intoxicate himself with the feeling that he is neglected. He looks for evidence to prove that his reproach is true. His behavior becomes worse; he is treated with more severity; he finds a confirmation for his belief that he is thwarted and put in a back seat. Because he feels deprived, he begins to steal; he is found out and punished and now he has still more evidence that he is not loved and that other people are his enemies. He begins to play truant and hides himself away where he cannot be discovered. In these places he finds other boys who have had the same experience and have taken the same road. They understand him; they flatter him, play on his ambitions, and give him the hope of making his mark on the useless side of life. It is in this way that thousands of children join criminal gangs; and if in later life we treat them in the same fashion, they will find only new evidence that we are their enemies and only criminals are their friends.

Later on, the criminal turns everything which he experiences into a justification for his attitude; and if his experiences do not quite fit into his scheme, he broods on them and licks them into shape until they are more amenable. If a man has the attitude, "Other people misuse me and humiliate me," he will find plenty of evidence to confirm him. He will be looking for such evidence, and evidence to the contrary will not be noticed.

It happens, too, that criminals improve in later life; a burglar, after he has reached the age of thirty, may settle down and become a good citizen. If crime were an inborn defect, or if it were unalterably built in by the environment, this fact would be quite beyond understanding. From our own point of view, however, it can be understood very well: Perhaps the individual is in a more favorable situation, in that there are fewer demands on him or he has already gained what he wanted. Thus the mistakes in his style of life are no longer brought to the surface. Or perhaps, he is growing older and fatter, less suited for a criminal career; his joints are stiff and he cannot climb so well; burglary has become too hard for him.

2. SIGNIFICANT OBJECTIVE FACTORS[7]

It is easy to see that in unhappy or broken marriages the cooperative spirit is not being properly developed. The child's first tie is with his mother, and the mother, perhaps, did not wish to widen the child's social interest to include the father and other children or grown-ups. Or, again, the child may have felt himself to be the boss of the family; when he is three or four years old, another child comes along and the first one feels that he has suffered a reverse, has been ousted from his position. It is also always difficult for the other children if one child in the family is especially prominent or gifted. Such a child gains most attention and the others feel discouraged and thwarted. We can often see the unhappy development of children who have been outshone in this way, and have not been shown how they themselves could use their own capabilities. Amongst them we may find criminals, neurotics, or suicides.

Among criminals there is a large proportion of orphans and of illegitimate children; no one was present who could win their affection and transfer it to their fellow beings. Unwanted children, especially if they know and feel that nobody wanted them, often take to criminal practices.

The feeling of inferiority can be centered around an organ inferiority. But even when I first wrote about organ inferiorities, I recognized that it is not the organism which is to blame, but our methods of education. A child burdened with imperfect organs is only interested in himself alone if nobody is at his side to develop his interest in others.

Among criminals we also often find ugly persons, a fact which has been used as evidence for the importance of heredity. But think how it must feel to be an ugly child! He is at a great disadvantage. Perhaps he is the child of a race mixture which meets with social prejudice. If such a child is ugly, his whole life is overburdened; he does not possess what we all like so much, the charm and freshness of childhood. But all these children, if they were treated in the right way, would develop social interest.

We sometimes find among criminals unusually handsome boys and men. While some would consider the ugly individuals as victims of bad hereditary traits, including physical stigmata such as deformed hands or cleft palate, what would they say about these handsome criminals? In reality they, too, have grown up in a situation where it was difficult to develop social interest; they were pampered children.

There are two types of criminals. The first does not know that there is social interest in the world, having never experienced it. He has a hostile attitude toward other people; his look is hostile and he regards everybody as an enemy; he has never been able to find appreciation. The other type is the pampered child; he was taught to consider himself important through the mere fact of his existence, without making any creative effort to deserve the good opinion of his fellows. Such children, therefore, lose the ability to struggle; they want always to have notice taken of them and are always expecting something. If they do not find an easy way to satisfaction, they blame the environment for it.

Poverty, also, offers opportunities for a mistaken interpretation of life. A child from a poor home may meet social prejudice. Later he comes across rich people who lead an easy life. He feels they have no more right to indulgence than he has. No useful goal ever came from envy; a child in these circumstances can easily misunderstand and think that the way to superiority is to get money without working for it.

It is not economic difficulty that forces him into crime. Truly enough, if times are hard and people are more burdened, crimes increase. Statistics show that sometimes the number of crimes increases in accordance with a rise in the price of wheat. This is no sign, however, that the economic situation causes the crime. It is much more a sign that many people are limited in their behavior, including their capacity for cooperation; when these limits are reached they can no longer contribute.

When a country is prosperous, criminal tendencies appear which were not present at other times. For instance, when times were comparatively good for almost everyone in the United States, when there was no crisis, the increase of crime was laid to prohibition, or to the fact that people became rich easily.

c. Treatment and Preventive Measures

1. TREATING THE CRIMINAL[8]

A criminal will interpret punishment only as a sign that society is against him, as he always thought. Punishment does not deter him. Even the electric chair can act as a challenge. A criminal who is condemned to be electrocuted will often spend his time considering how he might have avoided detection: "If I only had not left my spectacles behind!" Many criminals are not very fond of their lives; some of them at certain moments of their lives are very near suicide.

From the psychologist's standpoint, all harsh treatment in prison is a challenge, a trial of strength. In the same way, when criminals continually hear, "We must put an end to this crime wave," they take it as a challenge. They feel that society is daring them and continue all the more stubbornly. In the education of problem children, too, it is one of the worst errors to challenge them: "We'll see who is stronger! We'll see who can hold out longest!"

They see their contact with society as a sort of continuous warfare, in which they are trying to gain the victory; if we take it in the same way ourselves, we are only playing into their hands.

What shall we do? With the criminal, as with the neurotic, we can do absolutely nothing, unless we succeed in winning him for cooperation. I cannot stress this point too strongly. Everything is secured if we can win the interest of the criminal for human welfare, for other human beings; if we can train him for cooperation and set him on the way towards solving the problems of life by cooperative means. If we fail to do this, we can do nothing. The task is not simple. We cannot win him by making things easy for him, any more than by making them hard for him. We cannot win him by pointing out that he is wrong and arguing with him. His mind is made up. He has been seeing the world in this way for years. If we are to change him we must find the roots of his pattern. We must discover where his failures first began and the circumstances which provoked them. It is his original mistakes which we must understand and correct. We must look for the first development of his attitude.

The criminal's mistaken picture of the world can be traced in his earliest childhood recollections. One hears, for example, things like the following: "I was helping with the wash, when I saw a piece of money on the table; so I took it. This was when I was six years old." Or again: "My mother was careless about leaving money lying about, so each week I took some of it." Such lack of social interest bound up with activity will be found again and again in the early recollections of delinquents; and that in these early recollections the pampered style of life, combined with great activity, is clearly expressed, I hold to be one of the most significant findings of Individual Psychology.

The criminal has chosen the wrong means; we must show him where he has chosen them and why, and we must train him in the courage to be interested in others and to cooperate. If we understand that crime is not an isolated thing in itself but the symptom of an attitude to life, and if we can see how this attitude arises, then, instead of having an insoluble problem before us, we can set to work with the confidence that we can accomplish a change.

While I do not believe it would be possible to give every criminal an individual treatment, we could contribute much by a group therapy. [See p. 348.]

2. CRIME PREVENTION[9]

I am convinced that we could change every single criminal. But consider what a work it would be to take every single criminal and treat him so that we changed his style of life. If we cannot alter every criminal, we can do something to relieve those people who are not strong enough to cope with their burdens. With regard to unemployment, for example, and the lack of occupational training and skill, we should make it possible that everyone who wants to work can secure a job. We should also train children better for their future occupation, so that they can face life better and with a greater sphere of activity. Such training can be given also in our prisons. To some extent steps have already been taken in this direction, and perhaps all we need do here is to increase our efforts.

We can make teachers the instruments of social progress by training them to correct mistakes made in the family, i.e., to develop the social interest of the children and spread it towards others. This is an entirely natural development of the school. Because the family is not able to bring up the children for all the tasks of later life, mankind has established schools as the prolonged arm of the family.

We should avoid in our social life everything which can act as a challenge to the criminal or to poor and destitute people. If there are great extremes of poverty and luxury, those who are badly off become irritated and are challenged too much. We should therefore diminish ostentation. It would be much better if we were more silent, did not mention the names of criminals nor give them so much publicity. It would be very helpful if we increased our efforts to discover those who were responsible for crimes. As far as I can see, at least forty per cent of criminals, and perhaps far more, escape detection. This fact is always at the back of the mistaken view of a criminal; almost every criminal has experienced occasions when he committed crimes and was not found out.

Finally, if it were fully recognized everywhere that crime is cowardice and not courage, I believe that the greatest self-justification would be taken away from criminals, and no child would choose to train himself for crime.

D. Drug Addiction and Alcoholism[10]

As a rule less activity will be found among drug addicts. Environment, temptation, acquaintance with drugs like morphia and cocaine either through illness or the medical profession, provide opportunities for becoming a drug addict. These will, however, become effective only in situations where the person concerned is confronted by a problem which seems insoluble. As in suicide, a veiled attack on others who will have the sorrow or care is seldom lacking. In alcoholism a special component element of taste plays a part, as I have shown, just as total abstinence is also made essentially easier by the want of a liking for alcohol. Very frequently the beginning of addiction shows an acute feeling of inferiority marked by shyness, a liking for isolation, oversensitivity, impatience, irritability, and by neurotic symptoms like anxiety, depression, and sexual insufficiency. Or the craving may start with a superiority complex in the form of boastfulness, a malicious criminal tendency, a longing for power. Excessive smoking, too, and the craving for strong, black coffee characterize the mood of discouragement and indecision. By a trick, the oppressive feeling of inferiority is temporarily removed or, as in criminal deeds, it may even be transformed into increased activity. The immediate effects of the drug often give the victim a feeling of being unburdened. In the cases of drug addiction all failures will be attributed to the unconquerable vice, whether the failure be in social relations, in work, or in love.

In all cases of addiction we are dealing with people who are seeking alleviation in a certain situation. In a comparative way of speaking one might say that morphinism and alcoholism are the daydreams of the adult. Such persons have built up their original character in a situation of great pampering, in which they were dependent upon others. Usually this involved exploiting the mother. Used to the presence of one person, every situation without that person appears unacceptable. Such pampered individuals are the easiest to tempt.

E. Sexual Perversions

1. GENERAL CONSIDERATIONS[11]

The common factors in sexual perversion (homosexuality, sadism, masochism, masturbation, fetishism) can be summarized as follows: (1) Every perversion is the expression of an increased psychological distance from the opposite sex. (2) The perversion indicates a more or less deep-seated revolt against the normal sexual role, and is at the same time a purposeful, although unconscious, device to enhance a lowered self-esteem. (3) Inclinations toward perversion in men are compensatory tendencies to alleviate a feeling of inferiority in the face of the overrated power of women. And likewise, perversions in women are attempts to compensate for the feeling of female inferiority in the face of the assumedly stronger male. (4) The tendency to depreciate the normally-to-be-expected partner is never absent, and consequently animosity and the struggle against him are essential in the attitude of the pervert. (5) Perversion emerges regularly from a personality which generally shows traits of excessive oversensitivity, ambition, and defiance. Egocentric impulses, distrust, and the desire to dominate are prevalent; the inclination to "join in the game" is weak in both men and women. Consequently we also find a strong limitation of social interest.

The perverted individual keeps at a distance from the problem of love, or moves toward it only slowly. Here we also find the exclusion tendency, which is seen most clearly in homosexuality. This exclusion is not merely an accident; it is a matter of self-training. There can be no sexual perversion without preparation.

Only those who have noted this training will understand that sexual perversion is an artificial product. Each person has formed it for himself; he has been directed to it by the psychological constitution he has himself created, although he may have been misled into it by his inherited physical constitution which makes the deviation easier for him.

2. HOMOSEXUALITY[12]

There is no physiopathological basis (such as femininity or endocrine variations) which would obligate an individual to seek stimulation or satisfaction from the same sex. The belief in compelling causes of homosexuality, in its innate character, in its unalterability, may easily be unmasked as a scientific superstition.

An argument against the hereditary view of homosexuality is the frequent occurrence of noncompulsive homosexuality, that is, casual homosexual experiences, in childhood, in boarding schools, on long journeys as in the case of sailors, or in the life of soldiers and of prisoners. Many reliable sources consider noncompulsive homosexuality almost a normal manifestation in the life of every individual. Understanding of homosexuality thus is to be gained not from the homosexual act itself but only from a grasp of the whole personality. When we disregard his insufficiency in the sexual relationship, we still find that the homosexual does not live like someone who feels himself adequate to life.

The driving and fixating factor is the biased homosexual perspective, a safeguard against the fear of the partner. Homosexuality is the miscarried attempt at compensation of persons with a distinct inferiority feeling, and corresponds in its disturbed social activity to the patient's attitude toward the problem of society. It is a revolt against the demands of social life, and aims at a fictitious, subjectively founded triumph. Aside from the sexual manifestations, the homosexual, female as well as male, aims at a fictitious feeling of superiority through the use of a trick, a vice, or a gesture of revolt. This revolt originates in a belligerent, inimical position of the child in the family. Oppositely, the rejection of homosexuality is spontaneously founded in social interest, and waxes and wanes in accordance with the strength of the social connectedness. We must oppose the designation of homosexuality as a crime. The homosexual has been led astray by a generally human weakness in thinking. His argumentation is supported by much scientific superstition, and he should not be punished for acts of inner necessity arising from a situation which until now has been misjudged by science as well as himself. Here as in other kinds of suffering there should be compulsory therapy.

Lesbian love may be the result of the masculine protest, one of the many forms of which is the passion to play the part of a man. In this case female homosexuality is to be understood as a superiority complex based on an inferiority complex, "only a girl."

3. SADISM AND MASOCHISM[13]

Sadists like masochists (like all perverts) are discouraged individuals. The former seek at least a semblance of power or of an unconscious supermanliness in a situation of uncontested superiority. The masochist overemphasizes his weakness. But even in this weakest manifestation—which occasionally, as in flagellation and thoughts of penance, seeks a ridiculous justification—the compensatory line which strives upward is never absent. The sadist is the "triumphant vanquished," the masochist the beaten victor.

The goal of superiority is especially evident in the sadistic type, by which I mean the type whose will to dominate is connected with sexual irritation. Regarding masochism, it was a notable advance in the understanding of the psychological structure of perversion when we could prove that the symptoms of masochistic cases also are governed by a personal goal of superiority. The masochistic attitude signifies: "I am not governed by your power of attraction; it is you who must do what I would have you do."

How little these forms of expression are based on causality or innate drive abnormalities is shown by the frequent fluid transitions from sadism into masochism, or from homosexuality into masochism or sadism. In every person we find traits of defiance and obedience, of dominance and submission, which serve the striving for significance. Thus the coexistence of sadism and masochism in the flight of the pervert from the problem of love is to be explained.

The purpose of most masochistic subjects is to escape love and marriage, because they do not feel strong enough to risk a defeat. They will regard avoidance of defeat, even through ignominious escape, exactly as if it were a goal of superiority. By means of the masochistic tendencies they are able to exclude all the really eligible members of the other sex. A man whom I cured of homosexuality went so far as to have a masochistic relation with a prostitute. Through homosexuality he excluded *all* women, and in his periods of masochism he excluded all worth-while women.

4. OTHER PERVERSIONS[14]

Former explanations of *fetishism* usually stopped at the point where the social significance of this perversion begins. There we find that by displacing the sexual accent to the fetish the sexual partner becomes depreciated; no longer the person, but often a completely incidental detail receives sexual rank and dignity. In fetishism the struggle of the pervert for superiority over the opposite sex brings him to a stronger dependency on incidentals and to less dependency on his partner, thus ending with an amelioration of his feelings of fear and weakness toward the other sex. A connection of fetishism with all other perversions, neuroses, and criminal inclinations can easily be understood from this point of view.

The same observations can be made in *exhibitionism*, the passive form of which is found in *voyeurism*, a still stronger expression of discouragement. In exhibitionism the fight against the norms of society is always present. The inclination to frighten and harm children by exposing oneself and to disparage others by exposing them assigns to this perversion a place close to sadism.

In *masturbation*, whether physical or mental, a certain consistency is always apparent; it is the sexual attitude which is appropriate to the isolated individual. Correctly interpreted, it is the wish to exclude sexual partnership. The patient will always regard a partner as the author of his or her humiliation.

The sexual function, like all other functions, begins without social interest. Eating, excreting, looking, hearing, talking, are in the beginning only controlled by the needs of the child's body. The ordinary educative and cultural influences assist the child's creative powers to bring about an accord between his functions and the demands of social life. The degree of social interest gained by the child will decide the extent to which this accord will be attained. Social interest is equally valuable in regard to the sexual function which in the beginning of life is a function for one person and is clearly expressed in masturbation. A lack of conditions favorable to the growth of this sexual function into a social function, that is, a task for two persons of different sexes, obstructs its right evolutionary development for love and procreation and for the preservation of mankind. All forms of perversions and deficiencies are varieties of masturbation, representing the first phase of the sexual function. Proof of this can be found in the style of life of all perverts and in the manner in which they relate themselves to outside problems.

FOOTNOTES TO CHAPTER SEVENTEEN

1. 1: "The prevention of delinquency" (1935d), p. 4; 2 to 7: *What Life Should Mean to You* (1931a), pp. 197, 199–200, 201, 201–202, 202, and 203.
2. 1: "Prevention of delinquency" (1935d), p. 8; 2: *What Life Should Mean to You* (1931a), pp. 230–231.
3. 1: *What Life Should Mean to You* (1931a), p. 230; 2: "Prevention of delinquency" (1935d), pp. 5–6.
4. 1, 3, 4: *What Life Should Mean to You* (1931a), pp. 203–204, 204–205, and 232; 2: "Prevention of delinquency" (1935d), pp. 7–8.
5. *What Life Should Mean to You* (1931a), pp. 209–213.
6. 1, 2, 3, 5, 6, 7: *What Life Should Mean to You* (1931a), pp. 206, 206 and 198–199, 220, 218–222, 218, and 199; 4: "Prevention of delinquency" (1935d), pp. 6–7.
7. 1 to 8: *What Life Should Mean to You* (1931a), pp. 205–206, 208, 207, 208, 208–209, 209, 207, and 201; 9: "Prevention of delinquency" (1935d), p. 3.
8. 1 to 4, 6, 7: *What Life Should Mean to You* (1931a), pp. 219–220, 213–214, 220, 217–218, 228 and 229, and 234; 5: "Prevention of delinquency" (1935d), p. 9.
9. 1 to 4: *What Life Should Mean to You* (1931a), pp. 233–234, 237, 234 and 235, and 228.
10. 1: *Social Interest* (1933b), pp. 140–141; 2: "Rauschgift" (1931c), pp. 1–19.
11. 1: *Das Problem der Homosexualität*, (1930c), pp. 5–6; 2 and 3: *Social Interest* (1933b), pp. 190 and 191, and 197–198.
12. 1 and 3: *Homosexualität* (1930c), pp. 65 and 66; 2: "Über die Homosexualität" (1918b), pp. 128–129 and 131; 4: *Der Sinn des Lebens* (1933a), p. 42.
13. 1 and 3: *Homosexualität* (1930c), pp. 71–74 and 70; 2 and 4: *Problems of Neurosis* (1929b), pp. 130 and 131.
14. 1 and 2: *Homosexualität* (1930c), pp. 75 and 76; 3: *Problems of Neurosis* (1929b), p. 131; 4: *Social Interest* (1933b), pp. 200–201.

CHAPTER EIGHTEEN

GENERAL LIFE PROBLEMS

COMMENT "For the sake of clarity" Adler divided all the problems of life into three parts: "problems of behavior toward others, problems of occupation, and problems of love" (1935a, p. 6). The first category, the problems of social relations, is, of course, the superordinated one and has been the subject matter throughout this book, so that it need not be treated further.

The present chapter deals firstly with Adler's thoughts and suggestions regarding occupation, which are concerned mostly with occupational interest and its guidance. The problems of love and marriage, a favorite topic of Adler's many popular lectures, will be dealt with next. Finally we shall present Adler's views on the two critical developmental stages beyond childhood, namely, adolescence and old age.

A. Occupation

1. EARLY SIGNS OF INTEREST[1]

Both marriage and occupation demand power of independent action and readiness to accept the division of labor. These qualities cannot exist without a certain degree of social interest and adaptation, and it is often at the time when the choice of an occupation becomes necessary that the lack of social adjustment appears.

There are some people who could choose any occupation and never be satisfied. What they wish is not an occupation but an easy guarantee of superiority. They do not wish to meet the problems of life, since they feel that it is unfair of life to offer them problems at all. These, again, are the pampered children who wish to be supported by others.

Through the way in which the child thinks, behaves, and characteristically perceives, his interest becomes specialized for his future occupation. The degree of interest, however, is increased or decreased depending on his sense of the attainability of his goal of superiority. In the course of his development, the child will concretize his goal in various unattainable forms, which he must be able to abandon without any fundamental discouragement. The closer his social contact remains, the more common-sense conceptions of superiority will he develop. A child's idea of superiority is, of course, very often influenced by the desire to surpass the father in his occupation. Thus, if his father is a public-school teacher, a boy may want to become a professor. As a rule we find that the more often the child changes his choice of occupation, the more he understands reality. The child paints a new picture of his future action from time to time; but always determined by the same prototype motive.

The choice of the occupation is foreshadowed by some dominant interest. The development of this interest into the concrete realization of work is often a lengthy process of self-training in which we can see the same idea adapting itself successively to various material possibilities. To play at sewing with needle and thread need not reveal a future tailor, it may just as well be the first step towards the career of a surgeon. A great interest in playing with toy soldiers may be a preparation for military life, but it may also be the prelude to success as the director of a department store. Wherever we find an ability it is the result of an interest in which the child has trained himself, stimulated by the totality of his circumstances. So clearly does this appear that we are justified in believing that anyone could accomplish anything, given the right training and the correct method. [See pp. 206 and 343.]

2. GUIDING THE CHILD'S INTEREST[2]

A child's development is much simpler if he knows from childhood on which occupation he would like to take up in later life. If we ask children what they would like to be, most of them will give an answer. When they say that they want to be airplane pilots or engine drivers they do not know why they are choosing this occupation. It is our task to recognize their underlying motives, to see the way they are striving, what is pushing them forward, where they have placed their goal of superiority, and how they feel they can make it concrete. The answer they give shows us only one kind of occupation which seems to them to represent superiority; but from this occupation we can see also other opportunities for helping them to reach their goal.

It is an advantage to ask children early what their occupation is going to be; and I often put this question in schools so that the children are led to consider the point and cannot forget the problem or wish to hide their answer. I ask them also why they have selected this occupation and am often told very revealing details. In a child's choice of occupation we can observe his whole style of life. He is showing us the main direction of his striving and what he values most in life.

In vocational guidance early recollections should be considered very important. For example, when a child mentions impressions of someone talking to him, of the sound of the wind or of a bell ringing, we know that he is an acoustic type and can guess that he might be suited for some profession connected with music. In other recollections we can see impressions of movement. These are individuals who demand more activity; perhaps they would be interested in occupations which require outdoor work or travel.

We must let the child place his own value on an occupation since we ourselves have no means of saying which occupation is higher and which is lower. If he really does his work and occupies himself in a contribution to others, he is on the same level of usefulness as anyone else. His only task is to train himself, try to support himself, and set his interest in the framework of the division of labor.

If "to make money" is the child's only goal and no social interest is bound up with it, there is no possible reason why he should not make money by robbing and swindling other people. If, in a less extreme attitude, only a small degree of social interest is combined with the goal, his activities will still not be of much advantage to his fellows, although he may make plenty of money. Even a mistaken way may sometimes seem to be successful in one point. If, on the other hand, an individual goes through life with the right attitude, we cannot promise that he will meet immediate success. But we can promise that he will keep his courage and will not lose his self-esteem.

B. Love and Marriage

1. THE SOCIAL NATURE OF MARRIAGE[3]

If I were asked to say what love and marriage mean, I should give the following definition, incomplete as it may be: "Love, with its fulfillment, marriage, is the most intimate devotion towards a partner of the other sex, expressed in physical attraction, comradeship, and the decision to have children. It can easily be shown that love and marriage are one side of cooperation in general, not a cooperation for the welfare of two persons only, but a cooperation also for the welfare of mankind."

Our first finding in the problem of love is that it is a task for two individuals. For many people this is bound to be a new task. To some degree we have been trained to work alone; to some degree, to work in a group. But we have generally had little experience of working two by two. This new condition, therefore, raises a difficulty; but it is easier to solve if these two people have been interested in their fellows, for then they can learn more easily to be interested in each other. We may say that for a full solution of this cooperation of two, each partner must be more interested in the other than in himself. This is the only basis on which love and marriage can be successful.

If each partner is to be more interested in the other partner than in himself, there must be equality. If there is to be so intimate a devotion, neither partner can feel subdued nor overshadowed. Equality is only possible if both partners have this attitude. It should be the effort of each to ease and enrich the life of the other. In this way each will be safe; each will feel that he is worthwhile and that he is needed. The fundamental guarantee of marriage, the meaning of marital happiness, is the feeling that you are worthwhile, that you cannot be replaced, that your partner needs you, that you are acting well, and that you are a fellow man and a true friend.

Cooperation demands a decision for eternity; and we regard only those unions as real examples of love and as real marriages in which a fixed and unalterable decision has been taken. This includes the decision to have children, to educate them, to train them in cooperation, and to make out of them, as far as we can, fellow men, equal and responsible members of the human race. A good marriage is the best means we have for bringing up the future generation of mankind; and marriage should always have this in view. It is impossible to have the real intimate devotion of love if we limit our responsibility to five years, or regard the marriage as a trial period. If we contemplate such an escape, we do not collect all our powers for the task. We cannot love and be limited.

2. SEX IN MARRIAGE[4]

At the end of all my lectures I have to reply to questions about love and marriage, and my questioners often appear to have been misled by some psychological reading into believing that the sexual impulse is the central motive to which every other activity is related. I have never seen the reason for placing this unnatural emphasis upon one single function of life. I admit, of course, its great, although very variable, importance. But to detect transposed sexual elements in a variety of manifestations is practically not very useful, even if possible.

Love is not a purely natural task, as some psychologists believe. Sex is a drive or instinct; but the question of love and marriage is not quite simply how we are to satisfy this drive. Wherever we look, we find that our drives and instincts become developed, cultivated, and refined.

Many men, and especially many women, through mistakes in their development, have trained themselves to dislike and reject their sexual role. They have hindered their natural functions and are physically not capable, without treatment, of accomplishing a successful marriage. This is what I have called the masculine protest which is very much provoked by the overvaluation of men in our present culture. Both men and women will overstress the importance of being manly, and will try to avoid being put to the test. We can suspect this attitude in all cases of frigidity in women and impotence in men. [See pp. 312–313.]

The feelings belonging to sex always appear when an individual desires to approach his sexual goal. By concentration, he tends to exclude conflicting tasks and incompatible interests; and thus he evokes the appropriate feelings and functions. The lack of these feelings and functions—as in impotence, premature ejaculation, perversion, and frigidity—is established by refusing to exclude inappropriate tasks and interests.

If the partners are really interested in each other, there will never be the difficulty of sexual attraction coming to an end. This stop implies always a lack of interest; it tells us that the individual no longer feels equal, friendly, and cooperative towards the partner, no longer wishes to enrich his life. People may think, sometimes, that the interest continues but the attraction has ceased. This is never true. Sometimes the mouth lies or the head does not understand; but the functions of the body always speak the truth. If the functions are deficient, it follows that there is no true agreement between these two people. They have lost interest in each other. One of them, at least, no longer wishes to solve the task of love and marriage but is looking for an evasion and escape.

We know that there is the possibility of a break in the relation, but this is easiest to avoid if we regard marriage and love as a social task. We shall then try every means to solve the problem. It is important to realize that love by itself does not settle everything, and that it is better to rely upon work, interest, and cooperation to solve the problems of marriage. There is nothing at all miraculous in this whole relationship. The attitude of every individual towards marriage is one of the expressions of his style of life: we can understand it if we understand the whole individual, not otherwise.

I believe that the intimate devotion of love and marriage is best secured if there have not been sexual relations before marriage. I have found that secretly most men do not really like it if the partner is able to give herself before marriage. Sometimes they regard it as a sign of easy virtue and are shocked by it. Moreover, in the present state of our culture, if there are intimate relations before marriage the burden is heavier for the girl.

The question of birth control causes a good deal of agitation today. Humanity has no doubt become less rigorous in its demand for unlimited offspring, and many facts in our growing culture have helped to assign to love, in addition to its original task of serving procreation, and almost independent of it, a new role, a higher level, an increase in happiness which certainly also contributes to the welfare of humanity. This developmental advance cannot be checked by laws and regulations once it has been gained. The question of deciding the number of children had best be left entirely to the woman. In the case of artificial interference with pregnancy both mother and child would probably be best safeguarded if, in addition to medical considerations, a qualified psychological consultant were called in.

3. EARLY PREPARATION FOR MARRIAGE[5]

Certainly love in all its thousand variations is a feeling of belongingness and hence is characterized by its content as a social feeling. Therefore, that man and that woman will be best prepared for love, marriage, and parenthood who surpass all others in being fellow men.

When children give early evidence of their interest in the other sex and choose for themselves the partners whom they like, we should never interpret it as a mistake, or a nuisance, or a precocious sex influence. Still less should we deride it or make a joke of it. Instead we should rather agree with the child that love is a marvelous task, a task for which he should be prepared, a task on behalf of the whole of mankind. Thus we can implant an ideal in the child's mind, and later in life such children will be able to meet each other as well-prepared comrades and as friends in an intimate devotion. It is revealing to observe that children are spontaneous and whole-hearted adherents of monogamy; and this often in spite of the fact that the marriages of their parents are not always harmonious and happy.

We are always better prepared if the marriage of our parents has been harmonious. Children gain their earliest impression of marriage from the life of their parents; and it is not astonishing that the greatest number of failures in life are among the children of broken marriages and unhappy family life. If the parents are not able themselves to cooperate, it will be impossible for them to teach cooperation to their children. We can often best consider the fitness of an individual for marriage by learning whether he was trained in the right kind of family life and by observing his attitude towards his parents, sisters and brothers. We must, however, be careful on this point because a man is not determined by his environment but by his estimate of it. Very unhappy experiences in his parents' home may only stimulate him to do better in his own family life. He may be striving to prepare himself well for marriage. We must never judge or exclude a human being because he has an unfortunate family life behind him.

The worst preparation is when an individual is always looking for his own interest. If he has been trained in this way, he will be thinking all the while what pleasure or excitement he can get out of life. He will always be demanding freedom and reliefs, never considering how he can ease and enrich the life of his partner.

A child who has been pampered at home often feels neglected in marriage. He may develop into a great tyrant in marriage. It is interesting to observe what happens when two pampered children marry each other. Each of them is claiming interest and attention and neither can be satisfied. The next step is to look for an escape; one partner begins a flirtation with someone else in the hope of gaining more attention.

One of the ways in which social interest can be trained is through friendship. Training in friendship is a preparation for marriage. Games might be useful if they were regarded as a training in cooperation; but in children's games we find too often competition and the desire to excel. It is very useful to establish situations in which two children work together, study together, and learn together. Dancing is a type of activity in which two people have to accomplish a common task, and I think it is good for children to be trained in dancing. I do not exactly mean the dancing we have today, where we have more of a show than of a common task. If, however, we had simple and easy dances for children, it would be a great help for their development.

The right preparation for marriage includes also the right preparation for work.

In our own cultural conditions, and only in these conditions, it is generally expected that the man should be the first to express attraction and make the first approach. Therefore, it is necessary to train boys in the masculine attitude, that is, to take the initiative, not to hesitate or look for an escape. Of course, girls and women are also engaged in wooing, they also take the initiative; but in our prevailing cultural conditions, they feel obliged to be more reserved. Their wooing is expressed in their whole gait and person, in the way they dress, the way they look, speak, and listen. A man's approach, therefore, may be called simpler and shallower, a woman's deeper and more complicated.

The child gains his impressions of what is congenial and attractive in the other sex from the members of the other sex in his immediate surroundings; these impressions are the beginnings of physical attraction. Sometimes he is influenced also by creations of art. Thus everybody is drawn by an ideal of beauty and in later life has no longer a free choice in the broadest sense but only along the lines of his training. Sometimes if a boy experiences difficulties with his mother, and a girl with her father, as happens often if the cooperation in marriage is not firm, they look for an antithetic type.

4. MISTAKEN EXPECTATIONS[6]

When people look upon love and marriage as a solution for a personal problem, this is really making these into a mere patent medicine. We cannot look on love and marriage as a remedy for a criminal career, drunkenness, or neurosis. A neurotic needs to have the right treatment before he enters love and marriage, or else he is bound to run into new dangers and misfortunes.

In other ways, also, marriage is entered into with inappropriate aims. Some people marry for economic security; they marry because they pity someone; or they marry to secure a servant. I have even known cases where people have married to increase their difficulties. A young man, perhaps, is in difficulties about his examinations or his future career. He feels that he may very easily fail, and if he fails he wishes to be able to excuse himself. He takes on the additional task of marriage, therefore, in order to have an alibi.

It is also a great mistake if a marriage is contracted out of fear and not out of courage. We can understand by courage one side of cooperation, and if men and women choose their partners out of fear it is a sign that they do not wish for a real cooperation. This also holds good when they choose partners who are drunkards or very far below them in social status or in education. They are afraid of love and marriage and wish to establish a situation in which their partner will look up to them.

Some people are incapable of falling in love with one person; they must fall in love with two at the same time. They thus feel free; they can escape from one to the other, and never undertake the full responsibilities of love. Both means neither. There are other people who invent a romantic, ideal, or unattainable love; they can thus luxuriate in their feelings without the necessity of approaching a partner in reality. A high ideal of love can also be used to exclude all possibilities, because no one will be found who can live up to it.

5. CRITERIA FOR MARITAL CHOICE[7]

Every individual has his characteristic approach in wooing. In this we can see whether he is confident and cooperative; or is interested only in his own person, suffers from stage fright, and tortures himself with the question, "What sort of a show am I making? What do they think of me?" We cannot judge a man's fitness for marriage entirely by his courtship, for there he has a direct goal before him, and in other ways he may be indecisive. Nevertheless we can gather from it sure indications of his personality.

There are a thousand signs by which one can understand whether or not a person is prepared for marriage. Thus one should not trust a person in love who comes late for an appointment without an adequate excuse; such action shows a hesitating attitude, a sign of lack of preparation for the problems of life. Another sign of lack of preparation is if one member of a couple always wants to educate or criticize the other. To be very sensitive is also a bad sign, since it indicates an inferiority complex. The person who has no friends and does not mix well in society is not well prepared for marital life. Delay in choosing an occupation is also not a good sign. A pessimistic person is ill-fitted, doubtless because pessimism betrays a lack of courage to face situations. If, as we have seen, someone looks for an ideal marriage partner and never finds him, we may be sure that such a person is suffering from a hesitating attitude and does not want to go on at all. Yet despite this list of undesirable persons it should not be so difficult to choose the right one, or rather one along the right lines, since we cannot expect to find the ideal person.

For the right choice of a partner, in addition to physical and intellectual suitability and attraction, the following qualities, which indicate a sufficient degree of social interest, ought principally to be taken into consideration: (1) capacity for retaining friendship; (2) an ability to be interested in his work; (3) more interest in the partner than in self.

There is an old German method for finding out whether a couple is prepared for marriage. It is the custom in rural districts to give the couple a double-handled saw, each person to hold one end, and then have them saw the trunk of a tree while all the relatives stand around and watch. Now sawing a tree is a task for two persons. Each one has to be interested in what the other is doing and harmonize his strokes with his. This method is thus considered a good test of fitness for marriage.

c. Adolescence

1. THE PROBLEM OF ADOLESCENCE[8]

There are whole libraries of books on adolescence, and almost all of them deal with the subject as if it were a dangerous crisis at which the whole character of an individual could change. There are many dangers in adolescence, but it is not true that it can change character. It provides the growing child with new situations and new tests. He feels that he is nearing the front of life. Mistakes in his style of life may reveal themselves which were hitherto unobserved.

For almost every child, adolescence means one thing above all else: he must prove that he is no longer a child. If we might, perhaps, persuade him that he can take this for granted, a great deal of tension would be drawn from the situation. But if he feels he must prove it, naturally enough he will overstress his point. Very many of the expressions of adolescence are the outcome of the desire to show independence, equality with adults, and manhood or womanhood. The direction of these expressions will depend on the meaning which the child has attributed to being "grown-up." If it has meant to be free from control, the child will fight against restrictions. Many children at this time begin to smoke, to swear, and to stay out late at night. Some of them reveal an unexpected opposition to their parents; and their parents are puzzled to know how such an obedient child could suddenly grow so disobedient. It is not really a change of attitude. The apparently obedient child was always in opposition to his parents; but when he had more freedom and strength, he felt able to declare his enmity.

For the most part a child is given more freedom and independence during his adolescence. If the parents try to continue their supervision, however, the child will make still stronger efforts to avoid control. We are then provided with the typical picture of "adolescent negativism."

All the dangers of adolescence come from a lack of proper training and equipment for the three problems of life. If the children are afraid of the future, it is natural enough that they should try to meet it by the methods which call for least effort. The more such a child is ordered about, exhorted, and criticized, the stronger becomes his impression that he is standing before an abyss. Unless we can encourage him, every effort to help him will be a mistake and damage him still further.

Although a few children at this time wish to remain children, by far the great majority will make some sort of attempt to behave in an adult fashion. If they are not really courageous, they offer a sort of caricature of the adult; they imitate the gestures of men, like to spend money freely, begin flirtations and have love affairs. In more difficult cases, where a boy does not see his way to meet the problems of life yet keeps a certain degree of activity, he begins to embark on a criminal career. This is especially likely if he has already committed delinquencies without being found out and thinks that he can be clever enough to avoid detection again.

If the degree of activity is smaller, the easy way of escape is neurosis. [As we have seen] neurotic symptoms appear when an individual is confronted by social problems which he is not prepared to meet in a social way. The difficulty provides a great tension. During adolescence the physical condition is especially responsive to such tensions, and all the organs may become irritated and the whole nervous system affected. An individual in such a case begins to regard himself, privately and before others, as free from responsibility because of his suffering; and the structure of a neurosis is complete.

A great number of failures in adolescence come from the pampered children; the approach of adult responsibilities is an especial strain to the children who have been accustomed to have everything done for them by their parents. At this time we find apparent reversals of progress. Children of whom most was expected may begin to fail in their studies and their work; and children who had previously seemed less gifted may begin to overtake them and to reveal unsuspected abilities. It is no contradiction to their previous history. Perhaps a child who was very promising now begins to feel afraid of disappointing the expectations with which he has been burdened. So long as he was helped and appreciated, he could go forward; but when the time comes to make independent efforts, his courage fails, and he retreats. Others are stimulated by their new freedom. They see the road towards the fulfillment of their ambitions clear before them. They are full of new ideas and new projects. Their creative life is intensified, and their interest in all the aspects of our human process becomes more vivid and eager. These are the children who have kept their courage, and to whom independence means, not difficulty and the risk of defeat, but wider opportunity to make achievements and contributions.

Children who have previously felt slighted and neglected now, perhaps, when they are more widely connected with their fellows, conceive the hope that they can find appreciation. It is dangerous enough for a boy if he is only looking for praise; but girls have often less self-confidence and see in the appreciation of others the only way of proving their worth. Such girls easily fall a prey to men who understand how to flatter them. I have often found that girls who felt unappreciated at home began to have sex relations, not merely to prove that they are grown-up, but because they hoped, by this means, to achieve at last a position in which they are appreciated and the center of attention.

2. SEX BEHAVIOR[9]

Both girls and boys often overvalue and exaggerate sexual relations in their adolescence. They wish to prove that they are grown-up and go too far. If a girl, for example, is fighting with her mother and always believes that she is being suppressed, she will frequently, as a protest, have sexual relations with any man she meets.

Many girls reveal what I have called the masculine protest. This can express itself in many varieties of behavior. Sometimes we see only a dislike and avoidance of men. Sometimes we find a dislike of the feminine role expressed more actively in adolescence. Girls will behave more boyishly than before. They will wish to imitate boys and will find it easier to imitate them in their vices, in smoking, drinking, swearing, joining gangs, and displaying their sexual freedom. Often they explain that boys would not be interested in them if they behaved in any other way.

Where the dislike of the feminine role is still further developed, we find the appearance of homosexuality or other perversions and of prostitution. From their early life all prostitutes have had the firm conviction that nobody likes them. They believe that they were born for a lower role and that they can never win the real affection or interest of any man. We can understand how in these circumstances they are inclined to throw themselves away, to depreciate their sexual role, and to regard it only as a means for making money. This dislike of the feminine role does not arise during adolescence. We can always find that the girl, from her first childhood, had disliked being a girl; but in her childhood she had not had the same need or opportunity for expressing her dislike.

Not only girls, but boys as well, may suffer from a "masculine protest"; all children who overvalue the importance of being masculine see masculinity as an ideal and are dubious whether they are strong enough to achieve it.

Boys who are not sure that they can acquit themselves well in their sexual role often, during adolescence, tend to imitate girls, to become effeminate and to take on the vices of girls who have been pampered, show themselves coquettish, pose, and cultivate a temperament.

3. SEX EDUCATION[10]

I should never encourage parents to explain the physical relations of sex too early in life or to explain more than their children wish to learn. In my own experience children who were introduced to the facts of adult relations in early life, at four, five or six years of age, and children who had precocious experiences, are always more scared of love in later life. Bodily attraction suggests to them also the idea of danger. If a child is more grown-up when he has his first explanations and experiences, he is not nearly so frightened. There is so much less opportunity for him to make mistakes in understanding the relations.

The key to helpfulness is never to lie to a child, never to evade his questions, to understand what is behind his questions, to explain only as much as he wishes to learn and only as much as we are sure he can understand. Officious and intrusive information can cause great harm. In this problem of life, as in all others, it is better for a child to be independent and learn what he wants to know by his own efforts. If there is trust between himself and his parents he can suffer no injury. He will always ask what he needs to know. There is a common superstition that children can be misled by the explanations of their comrades. I have never seen a child, otherwise healthy, who suffered harm in this way. Children do not swallow everything that their schoolmates tell them; for the most part they are very critical, and, if they are not certain that what they have been told is true, they will ask their parents or their brothers and sisters. I must confess, too, that I have often found children more delicate and tactful in these affairs than their elders.

At the age of two a child should be told that he is a boy or a girl. It should also be explained to him that his sex can never be changed, and that boys grow up to be men and girls, to be women. If this is done, then a lack of sex knowledge is not so dangerous.

The real problem of sex education is not the explanation of the physiology of sexual relationships, but the proper preparation of the whole attitude towards love and marriage. This is closely related to the question of social adjustment. If a person is not socially adjusted he will make a joke out of the question of sex and look at things entirely from the point of view of self-indulgence.

Children should not be stimulated by too much kissing and embracing; this is cruel to the child, especially in the adolescent period. Nor should children be stimulated mentally on the subject of sex. It happens very often that a child will discover some frivolous pictures in the father's library. We hear constantly of such cases in the psychological clinics. Children should not be able to lay hands on books which deal with sexual matters on a level above their age; nor should they see moving pictures in which the sex theme is exploited.

During puberty children are easily attracted to pornographic books. The increased sexual drive and the longing for experience turn their thoughts in this direction. The means to combat such harmful influences are: preparation of children for their role as fellow men, clarification of their sexual role at an early age, and friendly relations with their parents.

D. Old Age[11]

Not much is done for old people in our culture. They have much leisure and do not know what to do with it; young people do not understand them and shrink away from them; they often experience disappointments. Many persons seem to be changed when they are older, and this is mainly due to the fact that they feel futile and useless. They try to prove their worth and value again in the same way as adolescents do. They interfere and want to show in many different ways that they are not old and will not be overlooked, or else they become disappointed and depressed.

From this it follows that the period of aging results in a strong feeling of inferiority. Especially will all those suffer in whom we find the neurotic disposition. In most instances of breakdown there is a history of previous neurotic manifestations. The breakdown itself may be brought on by old age, the climacteric in women, signs of impotence in men, feelings of intellectual insufficiency, the dissolution of the family, the marriage of a son or daughter, financial losses, or being relieved of offices and honors. The real position of aging people in our society is severely threatened because the value of work is almost decisive for the evaluation of the personality. Old age with its losses thus acts like other disparagements of the self-esteem.

Furthermore, aging people are too much criticized for their ways, their desires, their clothes, and their work efficiency. A neurotically disposed individual will easily sense this criticism as a barrier and will shrink back even where possibilities for satisfaction still exist. He will force himself into submission, will want to annihilate his feelings and wishes without coping with them. These will then flare up more intensely when a renunciation without compensation is enforced. Thus it happens that the actively hostile character-traits become more prominent; that envy, jealousy, avarice, the craving to dominate, and sadistic tendencies of all sorts become accentuated and never satisfied.

Regularly the complaint of aging neurotics runs: "I am slighted; I have gotten too little out of life; I shall never achieve anything again." And then they develop the guiding line: "Act as if you still would have to achieve significance." Continuously they pay attention to the unreached and unreachable. When this is carried into the erotic field, as it often is, sex becomes the symbol of the unreachable goal. But one must avoid the mistake of taking this sexual fiction, which we might call a manner of speech or sexual jargon, for a genuine sensation.

Another such fiction is the climacteric. The climacteric of the woman becomes effective psychologically, irrespective of the metabolic events, by increasing the inferiority feeling; simultaneous metabolic disorders may merely modify or intensify the neurotic aspect making themselves felt specifically through an increase in insecurity. Likewise, the neurosis of the "masculine climacteric" is only indirectly influenced by the atrophy of the genitals, but can become increased through the aggravating abstraction: "I am no longer a man, I am a woman."

Very frequently one finds rapid physical deterioration and psychological shock as the expression of the fear of complete annihilation. Women are especially often affected by the superstition of the dangers of the climacteric. Those suffer in particular who have seen a woman's value not in the ability to cooperate but in youth and beauty. They often take up a hostile defensive attitude as though against an injustice done them, and fall into low spirits which may develop into depression.

The fear of growing old and the fear of death will not terrify the person who is certain of his immortality in the form of his children and in the consciousness of his contribution to the ever-growing culture.

When people grow old they should have room to expand and more occupations and interests. But just the reverse happens in our society; we give old people no opportunity for continued self-expression. Thus they feel put back, relegated to a corner so to speak. This is a pity because they could accomplish much more and would be infinitely happier if they had more of an opportunity for working and striving. Owing to our mistaken social customs we put old people on the shelf often while they are still full of activity. One should never advise such a man at the age of sixty, seventy, or even eighty to retire, since it is much easier to continue in one's occupation than to change one's whole scheme of life.

FOOTNOTES TO CHAPTER EIGHTEEN

1. 1, 3, 4: *Problems of Neurosis* (1929b), pp. 148, 148–149, and 147–148; 2: *What Life Should Mean to You* (1931a), p. 244.

2. 1 to 5: *What Life Should Mean to You* (1931a), pp. 243, 244, 245, 244, and 249.

3. 1 to 4: *What Life Should Mean to You* (1931a), pp. 263, 266–267, 267, and 273.

4. 1: *Problems of Neurosis* (1929b), p. 46; 2 to 7: *What Life Should Mean to You* (1931a), pp. 265, 276, 31–32, 279, 280–281, and 276–277; 8: *Der Sinn des Lebens* (1933a), pp. 40–41.

5. 1: "Verzärtelte Kinder" (1930g); 2 to 9: *What Life Should Mean to You* (1931a), pp. 269, 271–272, 272, 275, 277–278, 278, 278–279, and 270–271.

6. 1 to 4: *What Life Should Mean to You* (1931a), pp. 284, 284–285, 277, and 275–276.

7. 1: *What Life Should Mean to You* (1931a), p. 278; 2 and 4: *Science of Living* (1929c), pp. 245–246 and 247; 3: *Social Interest* (1933b), p. 63.

8. 1 to 8: *What Life Should Mean to You* (1931a), pp. 182, 182–183, 183, 185, 185, 186, 187–188, and 188.

9. 1 to 5: *What Life Should Mean to You* (1931a), pp. 190–191, 191–192, 192, 192, and 193.

10. 1 and 2: *What Life Should Mean to You* (1931a), pp. 269–270 and 270; 3 to 6: *The Education of Children* (1930a), pp. 221, 223, 225, and 108–109.

11. 1: "Failures of personalities" (1941), p. 8; 2 to 5: *Über den nervösen Charakter* (1912a), 4th ed., pp. 80, 80, 81, and 82; 6: *Sinn des Lebens* (1933a), pp. 43–44; 7: *Education of Children* (1930a), p. 202.

CHAPTER NINETEEN

PROBLEMS OF SOCIAL PSYCHOLOGY

COMMENT   All of Adler's Individual Psychology was a social psychology, in that it emphasized not only values and the social nature of man, but also the practical, that is, social application of psychological theory. The reader will have become amply aware of this. Adler's social concern actually antedated his psychology; he showed from his student days a lively interest in the social problems of the day and "was linked to the cause of social betterment" (15, p. 46). This undoubtedly influenced his psychology. Adler himself stated: "A psychological system has an inseparable connection with the life-philosophy of its formulator" (1935c, p. 4).

Adler's writings on social psychology specifically are few. Some of them reflect his practical interest, as when at the end of the first World War he expressed himself in pamphlet form and in general journals on political problems of the day. In these papers influences of his early political conviction as a Social Democrat can be noted. Soon, after, however, he separated himself from any political movement (15, p. 48). Adler saw Individual Psychology as "the heir to all great movements whose aim is the welfare of mankind" (p. 463).

A. The Dynamics of Group Psychology

COMMENT   Adler's views of the dynamics of group psychology are, as the reader will expect, an application of his theory of human dynamics to problems of this particular field. He sought to explain the phenomena of group behavior on the basis of striving for superiority, social interest, and the subjects' interpretations of their situation.

Very similar dynamics are today recognized in social psychology by the field theorists. We have in mind particularly the work by Krech and Crutchfield, which in many ways comes close to being the equivalent of an extension of Adlerian theory into social psychology. To quote: "All groups serve to meet the dominance needs of some of their members and the belongingness needs of most of their members. . . . These common needs . . . are served by all groups . . . whatever the nature of their unique functions" (63, p. 383). And: "People direct their actions in terms of their own beliefs and attitudes" (63, p. 173).

1. THE GROUP MIND[1]

It is generally agreed that there is such a phenomenon as group psychology, and generally the same subject matter is understood by this term. But we are hard put to it when we attempt to say how the group mind comes into being, or to explain its value and significance for the progress of mankind and to point out the constructive forces residing in it. Usually it is Le Bon to whom reference is made whenever the topic of the group mind is brought up. Yet, despite his valuable contributions he has not advanced beyond the conclusions that the group mind is greater than the sum of individual wills and temperaments, and that a group movement may pursue both good and evil undertakings.

The group mind is the conflux of individual yearnings and aspirations. Thus group psychology must certainly be considered from the same point of view as the psychology of the individual. The particular way in which each person appears important in his own eyes determines his decisions on, and attitudes toward, all problems of his life. It also determines his attitude toward group behavior and group ideas. Here we can clearly observe the relation of the individual to the group, and the influence exerted by group opinions upon the individual.

The group mind expresses the merits and deficiencies of the individual minds which prevail at the time. The individual minds are combined, not according to their particular individual qualities, but according to their general bearing on and attitude toward the stream of human evolution. The attitude may run either with this stream or against it.

The group mind is the similarity in the styles of life of the more active members in each generation. This is true of all social behavior, of art as well as politics and philosophy. The less active members will either be overwhelmed or will run with the crowd until another group absorbs them.

2. THE STRIVING FOR SUPERIORITY[2]

In group psychology we must first of all reckon with a striving to overcome a minus-situation. Taking this for granted we arrive at the well-authenticated view that, in the group as in the individual, the urge to surmount obstacles may produce an endless number of reversals and failures and mistakenly directed attempts.

Even the failing social movements, with their thousands of human sacrifices, were able to get under way and to gain momentum for a limited time, only by giving to the individual and the group a promise, though an illusory one, of an enhanced sense of importance. Such movements seemed to rescue the individuals from their feelings of inferiority and give them a new sense of importance by condemning others to insignificance. Thus we observe in the group mind the same desolate spectacle as in the individual when he goes astray because his powers of cooperation have not been sufficiently developed in childhood. In such a case he invariably strives for a sense of personal importance apart from the general welfare; he deceives himself, and gladly permits himself to be deceived by empty phrases and allegories, abandoning common sense and striking out on the path of a "private intelligence."

Individual Psychology has most clearly explained this interaction of power tendencies in individuals and groups. The demand for power arises from the childhood feeling of weakness and the effort to make this feeling more bearable. While the thinking, feeling, and volition of present-day man is determined primarily by his striving for personal superiority, even where he believes himself to be serving higher ideals, this is counteracted by the experience of the overpowering necessity of social efforts. Individual Psychology has also shown that thirst for dominance, ambition, and striving for power over others, together with the multitude of concomitant traits, are not innate or unalterable. To the extent that science in general, short-sighted and too easily inclined to create justification for the status quo, declares, as does popular psychology, that these traits are innate and unalterable characteristics of human nature, it actually protects these traits and prevents their reduction through social interest.

3. SOCIAL INTEREST[3]

The second basic principle permeating all human evolution, according to Individual Psychology, is social interest which is inherent in every human society. The degree to which social interest is developed in a person gives the measure, not only of his desires, but even more of his actions. The same holds good for groups. History judges human actions according to the degree of social interest which is expressed in them. Without exception those deeds and events are regarded as great and valuable which are saturated with social interest, thus promoting the welfare of the whole. Lack of social interest, always due to an increased inferiority feeling, drives the individual into neurosis or crime, and groups and nations toward the abyss of self-extermination.

Individual Psychology maintains that the power of social interest lies at the basis of all social products, such as language and reason or "common sense." Whether social interest will be a potent or an insignificant force depends on whether it has been cultivated or has remained undeveloped.

All social movements, be they party, national, or class movements, should be judged only in accordance with their ability to further interest in our fellow men. There are many ways to help in increasing cooperation; perhaps there are better and worse ways, but, if the goal of cooperation is granted, it is useless to attack one method because it may not be the best.

In the great and small religious movements; in the great achievements of philosophy, science, art, and political wisdom; as in the individual men and women who strive to penetrate to the truth, or seek to refine and dignify the thought, emotion, sight, and hearing of mankind, consciously or unconsciously, there is expressed the most exalted ideal purpose: "Love thy neighbor." One guiding thought embraces and unites them all, the desire to create their worth and find their sense of importance in their contributions to the welfare of others. Only such people, as individuals or as groups, possess the impulse to new and better works and finer thought, for they alone feel themselves firmly established in the vast process of evolution.

4. THE LEADER[4]

If the life tendencies of an individual coincide completely or almost completely with the direction of a social movement, if the yearning of the group is represented in him, if he can lend his voice and his arm to the dumb and obscure striving of his people or his group, he is a chosen leader of men. All great achievements of humanity originate in the social genius of individuals. The questions of an age reach out for an answer, and find it in a man. In him mankind's struggle for salvation is re-enacted, only with a greater clarity and intensity than in other men. The very essence of his being is this struggle, and therefore he cannot fit himself into the inherited forms of life. They cramp him, and he tries to burst them. In order to adjust himself to existence, he has to reorganize it. But he can succeed only if his endeavor coincides with a social current and serves to promote and to elevate the group. The power of the individual leader, of the "great man," is limited by the preparation of the group, by their capacity to fall in line with him.

What are the personal requirements of such leadership? A strongly developed social interest is the first of all. An optimistic outlook and sufficient self-confidence are just as necessary. The leader must be endowed with the capacity for quick action; he must not be a dreamer or an onlooker; he must have ease in making contact with people; and he must possess tact so as not to frustrate the assent of others. His preparation and training must be above the average. He must, in a word, be a real human being who possesses courage and skills. In him becomes realized what other men dream about.

B. Social Hostility

COMMENT   Isolation, prejudice and other forms of social hostility are frequently found as expressions of the lack of social interest. They are inadequate ways of raising the self-esteem. Such forms will be resorted to particularly when increased inferiority feelings are present. Consequently individuals who as a group are exposed to particularly unfavorable circumstances are most prone to express hostile traits of all sorts, because they are most likely to develop increased inferiority feelings. These matters will be presented in the first three sections of this part.

The next section expresses Adler's conviction of the responsibility of the psychologist to work against social conditions which tend to increase inferiority feelings. The last section contains suggestions to the victims of social hostility to strengthen them against aggression by giving them a better understanding of the dynamics of the aggressor.

1. ISOLATION AND HOSTILITY[5]

In our present-day culture, people are still easily misled to isolate themselves, and to separate themselves into nations, creeds, and classes. In all manners of isolation the familiar traits of ambition and vanity take the particular form of contrasting oneself with the others and of proving, by withdrawing from them, that one is different. The most that can be achieved in this way is an imaginary glory. The seemingly innocuous attitude of the individual who isolates himself is but one form of hostility. Withdrawal may also be a group trait. Everyone knows entire families who seal themselves hermetically against others. Closer observation always shows the hostility of such families and their belief that they are better and nobler beings than the others. The isolation tendency may pass into classes, religions, races, and nations. It is sometimes an illuminating experience to walk through a strange town and see how certain social strata set themselves off from others on their promenades and even in the structure of their houses.

Isolation usually results in further conflict, which after a while resolves itself into nothing, or in an obsolete, emasculated tradition. It is always a part of such hostility that the class or people who isolate themselves consider themselves particularly distinguished and spiritually chosen, and think only ill of their neighbors. The possibility and the danger of an increase in hostility lies in the fact that one usually hears only those spokesmen who try to fan and increase the hostility of others out of their own hostile mood and in their own interest. They strive from their own insecurity towards superiority and independence at the expense of others.

The isolation tendency offers certain individuals the opportunity to exploit latent antagonisms and to set one group against another in order to command and to satisfy their own personal vanity.

2. PREJUDICE AND HOSTILITY[6]

Those who have travelled have found that people everywhere are approximately the same in that they are always inclined to find something by which to degrade others. Everyone seeks a means which permits him to elevate himself at little cost. The Frenchman considers the German inferior, whereas the German, in turn, considers himself as belonging to a chosen nation; the Chinaman disdains the Japanese. One sees this also between the bourgeois and proletarian. Until mankind consents to take a step forward in its degree of civilization, these hostile trends [prejudices] must be considered not as specific manifestations, but as the expression of a general and erroneous human attitude.

What I have said concerning the hatreds and jealousies between nations and groups also holds good of the bitter struggle between the sexes, a struggle that is poisoning love and marriage and is ever born anew out of the inferior valuation of woman. The idealized picture of overestimated masculinity imposes both on the boy and the grown-up man the obligation of appearing, if not being, superior to woman. This causes him to distrust himself, to exaggerate his demands on life and his expectations from it, and increases his sense of insecurity. On the other hand, a girl feels that she is valued less than a boy, and this may stimulate her either to exaggerated efforts to make up for her inadequacy and to fight real or apparent depreciation on all sides, or else may cause her to resign herself to her supposed inferiority.

The original subjugation of women came with the invention of war and the consequent rise in the importance attached to physical strength and endurance; the inequality of women is greater in warlike countries. But the higher development of technology, of science, and undoubtedly of love as well, has unceasingly encouraged the rise of women and promoted their participation in public life. The conflict resulting from the attempt to subjugate women has played great havoc both in private and social life. Among the most bloody and contemptible efforts to force women back into a subordinate position, the three hundred years of witch-burnings occupy a prominent place.

3. SOCIOLOGICAL FACTORS FACILITATING HOSTILITY[7]

Difficulties in earning a livelihood, bad working conditions, inadequate educational and cultural facilities, a joyless existence, and continuous irritation, all these factors increase the feeling of inferiority, produce oversensitivity, and drive the individual to seek "solutions." To an individual in this state of mind any outside interference appears as a threat to his security and rouses him to active or passive self-defense. Motives of hatred appear most clearly in the economic disturbances of our time. The class struggle is carried on by groups made up of individuals whose quest for an inwardly and outwardly balanced mode of life is thwarted. Such mass movements, in turn producing further disturbing motives in the individuals, proceed with a firm and resolute step toward destructive aims. Destruction means to the masses a release from situations felt intolerable and thus appears to them as a preliminary condition of improvement.

In the group mind are reflected the positive or negative impressions of social life which the individuals have received in childhood. The degree to which their social interest has been cultivated and intensified, or stunted and limited, determines the direction which a group will take. In the group the style of life of the individual members is manifested, either as actively opposing, or as tolerating and submitting to injustice.

Apparently it is the total circumstances, the total relationships of life and of the environment, which send out their waves into the nursery. The child is confronted with the difficulties his father finds in earning a living; he notes the hostility of life even when he does not speak of it. Just consider the forceful impression a child receives whose parents live in a poor home and in a straitened social situation, compared to that of a child in whom the feeling of the hostility of life does not become so clear. These two types are so different that one can tell them apart by their mode of speech, by their glance. The second type will make friends with the world more easily, because he does not know about its difficulties or overcomes them more easily. He will take an entirely different stand in life, full of self-confidence and courage, and will show this even in his bodily bearing.

I have investigated what children in poor neighborhoods feared the most, and found that in most cases it was whipping. Such children grew up in fear of a strong father, foster father, or mother and carry this feeling of fear into adulthood. The average proletarian indeed gives the impression of being less friendly towards the world than the bourgeois who is more courageous. The children from better neighborhoods usually gave school work as their greatest fear. Thus they do not fear persons or their own immediate environment, but stand in the middle of life, where there are tasks and work which they fear.

4. THE SOCIAL RESPONSIBILITY OF THE PSYCHOLOGIST[8]

The honest psychologist cannot shut his eyes to social conditions which prevent the child from becoming a part of the community and from feeling at home in the world, and which allow him to grow up as though he lived in enemy country. Thus the psychologist must work against nationalism when it is so poorly understood that it harms mankind as a whole; against wars of conquest, revenge, and prestige; against unemployment which plunges peoples into hopelessness; and against all other obstacles which interfere with the spreading of social interest in the family, the school, and society at large.

We should be concerned to create and foster those environmental influences which make it difficult for a child to get a mistaken notion of the meaning of life and to form a faulty style of life. Since social movements spring from, and are borne by, the style of life that predominates in one or two generations, the student of group psychology must necessarily make himself familiar with the facts about the development of styles of life. Once the style of life has been formed, it can be corrected only when the individual fully realizes the error he committed in the use he has made of his environment as well as his heredity.

When a social movement has gone astray, this recognition of a basic mistake is equally necessary. An erring social movement can be modified or allayed only when the group has been brought to the realization that a genuine feeling of significance cannot be achieved by a false means; or, in other words, that a release from a feeling of insignificance must be effected in a more useful, productive, friendly way. Hence, anyone who hopes to put a stop to misdirected social movements must be able to prove cogently that the feeling of insignificance of the group can be securely relieved only by some other and better means, one which is more in tune with the spirit and the idea of the community of mankind.

5. EXPLAINING THE AGGRESSOR TO THE VICTIM[9]

When I have had occasion to talk with individuals of oppressed races, as with Jews and Negroes, I have called their attention to the very great tendency to oppress one's neighbor. Is there any human being who has not felt the jealousy and envy of others against him? Why should one be obliged to take seriously the criticisms and vexations of which one can become the object in matters of nationality, religion, or even hair color?

We know that children with red hair are exposed to teasing from which they then suffer. This is one of many ancient superstitions which represent gross errors.

One must explain to such children that there is a whole series of injustices in mankind, that people often find a means of oppressing others, and that this always takes the same form. If one people wants to depreciate another, if one family considers itself superior to another, then they stress particular traits to use as a point of attack. But this takes place only if the object of the attack lends himself to it. The red-haired boy must understand that he is not there to serve as a target for the others in letting them irritate him. It is the same all through life; if someone shows irritation, the attack persists. The red-haired boy must consider the attack on account of his hair as a sign of stupidity on the part of the one who launches it.

c. On the Psychology of Political Coercion and War

COMMENT *The selections in this section were, with one exception, written by Adler in 1918–1919, immediately after World War I during which he had served as a physician in the Austrian army. The first three sections are from an article in which he attempted to clarify the fundamental difference between socialism and Russian communism, the last two from a pamphlet published for the purpose of showing the untenability of the concept of the collective guilt of a people. This material then was written partly for a political purpose, in accordance with Adler's conception of the social responsibility of the psychologist.*

1. THE ABUSE OF SOCIAL INTEREST[10]

The common people seem always to have been on the track to social interest, and every intellectual and every religious uprising has been directed against the striving for power; the logic of the communal life of man has always asserted itself. But all this has always ended again in the thirst for dominance. All social legislation of the past, the teachings of Christ, and the tablets of Moses have fallen, again and again, into the hands of power-craving social classes and groups. These abused the most sacred concepts, resorting to the refined tricks of forgery, in order to channel the always-emerging manifestations and creations of social interest into the paths of power tendencies. Thus social interest was rendered ineffective for the common weal.

The better socially adjusted individual or group is at a disadvantage in the social struggle. Their feeling of being in the right lets them sleep quietly. The unsocial or antisocial individual or group is always more restless and alert in planning attacks. The lazy, slow-moving, and undecided people, wishing only to live like a worm in an apple, are an easy prey to the more active antisocial group.

The present stage of our culture and insight still permits the power principle to prevail. However, it can be adhered to no longer openly but only through the exploitation of social interest. An unveiled and direct attack of violence is unpopular and would no longer be safe. Thus when violence is to be committed this is frequently done by appealing to justice, custom, freedom, the welfare of the oppressed, and in the name of culture.

The truths and necessities gathered from the coercion of the communal life of man are distorted by those who cultivate the power principle and whose deepest intention is always: "Through truth to falsehood!" It is in this way that the disastrous exploitation of social interest by the striving for power comes about. Social interest is transformed from an end into a means and is pressed into the service of nationalism and imperialism. Only in socialism does social interest, in the form of the demand for unfettered human relations, remain as an end, as the ultimate goal. All the ingenious socialistic utopists as well as all great reformers of mankind have always intuitively placed mutual aid above the struggle for power.

2. COERCION[11]

The most important characteristic of Bolshevism is the enforcement of socialism by violence. Many people think of this as a matter of course. But granted that the simplest way to create everything that is good and promising would be by means of force, where in the life of man or in the history of mankind has such an attempt ever succeeded? The struggle for power has a psychological aspect, the description of which appears to us today as an urgent duty. Even where the welfare of the subjugated is obviously intended, the use of even moderate power stimulates opposition everywhere, as far as we can see. Human nature generally answers external coercion with a countercoercion. It seeks its satisfaction not in rewards for obedience and docility, but aims to prove that its own means of power are the stronger.

The results of the application of power are apt to be disappointing to both parties. No blessing comes of the use of power. In power politics the man in power wins followers who are actually his opponents and who are only attracted by the intoxication of power. And he finds opponents among those who might be his followers if they had not automatically become oppositional. Those who are excluded from power lie in wait for the revolt and are receptive to any argument.

3. THE FUTURE OF BOLSHEVISM[12]

The rule of Bolshevism is based on the possession of power. Thus its fate is sealed. While this party and its friends seek ultimate goals which are the same as ours, the intoxication of power has seduced them. Now the terrible mechanism is automatically released in the unprepared minds of men whereby attacks are answered with counterattacks, without regard for the goal of society, only because the mutual will to power is threatened. Cheap reasons are given to justify action and reaction. Fair becomes foul, foul becomes fair! The Bolshevists must reply by reinforcing their power positions. There can be no reduction in violence, but only further increases, as is always the case when power has the decisive word. If there is any means to call a halt, it can only be the remembrance of the miracle of social interest which we must perform and which will never succeed through the use of power. For us the way and the tactics are determined by our highest goal: the cultivation and strengthening of social interest.

4. MOTIVES FOR WAR AND COLLECTIVE GUILT[13]

Among the draftees [in the Austrian army during World War I] there was the most vehement rejection of war service, as the draft officers and physicians quite correctly assumed, and as they could also readily observe. There were no differences in the refutation of the war; at most, people's methods differed.

But what about the volunteers? The majority of them, enlisted men as well as officers, aimed right from the start at a certain favorable position as the lesser of two evils. There was in addition, of course, a smaller group of adventurers who in their ignorance had counted on a very short and gay war and had volunteered for the front. But the larger number chose this as a way to escape the unpleasantnesses of their home, their job, and other urgent problems. There were some among them who lived in discord with their parents, and went to the front as a way of committing suicide; there were husbands who acted in anger over a ruined life, and so forth. There were also high-minded individuals as, for example, a man who was to receive home leave after he had recovered from a wound. He refused his furlough pass with the words: "This is not the time for such nonsense. I am certainly not interested in the war; we all had our fill of it long ago. But I cannot leave my friends and comrades alone at the front."

Now one wants to burden the people with the guilt of the war. If one has lived among this people one will acquit them of any war guilt. They were immature, had no guiding lines and no leader. They were pushed and driven to slaughter. No one told them the truth; their writers and journalists were under the spell and in the pay of the military. It is not the people who should be asked to do servitude and penance; but those who thought up this degradation, materialized it, and participated in it with forethought should be held responsible for it. Let us rather ask forgiveness of the people and let us consult how the harm done them can be made good.

5. THE INTERIORIZATION OF EXTERNAL DEMANDS[14]

Most of those who volunteered for the war service and most of those who retained their enthusiasm and composure were but the victims of a false pride. To judge them by the cheers, the bragging, the gay songs, or the urge to excel, which could frequently be seen in the beginning of the war, would show a poor understanding of human nature. Herded together, with blinkers on, this is how we all received the merciless call to die. There was no way out, no protection from the bullet or the court-martial. And so the people acted in a way that would at least make their situation more bearable; they made a virtue out of necessity. From the chaos with which they were faced, they picked up the call to war of the general staff, and whereas in the beginning they still answered it against their will, staggering in the direction in which they had been ordered, suddenly it seemed to them as if they themselves had uttered the call. From then on they felt easier; they had found the desired escape. Now they were no longer whipped dogs exposed against their will to the rain of bullets, but heroes and defenders of the Fatherland and of their own honor. After all, they themselves had uttered the call to war, and thus they went into the holy battle as defenders of the right in the intoxication of their regained self-esteem. Thus, in the attempt to find themselves again at any price, they were freed by a psychological device from the feeling of deepest humiliation and degradation, and evaded the realization that actually they were but the sorry victims of the power urges of others. They dreamed of self-willed and self-sought deeds of heroism.

Those who swallowed the god of the general staff and now spoke through him made this change not because of sympathy or belligerent urges. It was when the individual had lost all sense of direction, when he saw himself in deepest disgrace, deprived of all freedom and human rights, that he reached in despair for the slogan of the overpowering suppressor. Then he could act as if he himself had proclaimed the war. Now at least he had some support and was rid of his feelings of disgrace and lowliness.

COMMENT *Here Adler describes the psychological device that was described before him by his colleague Furtmüller (see p. 147). The device, which could be called interiorization of the external demands, however, remained unnamed. In the particular form shown above, it has gained prominence in the psychological literature in recent years under the psychoanalytic term "identification with the aggressor."*

Two years after the appearance of the above paper by Adler, Freud, in 1921, in Group Psychology and the Analysis of the Ego (39), wrote about a mechanism of making foreign demands one's own and traced it to an original identification with the father. Anna Freud expanded the concept of identification to include identification with the aggressor, which she discussed in detail as one of the ego defense mechanisms (32, pp. 117–131). She thus described and named a process which Adler had indicated, although only briefly, above.

D. The Psychology of Religion

COMMENT   *Adler made repeated references in his various writings to religion and the concept of God. The occasion for a more comprehensive presentation of this topic was a discussion, in the form of a small book, held jointly with Ernst Jahn, a Protestant minister. The topic of the discussion was guidance and psychotherapy from the religious and Individual-Psychological points of view. The main difference, relevant here, which, according to Jahn, emerged from the discussion was that for Adler God is an idea, whereas for the minister God is reality (1933c, p. 94).*

1. THE CONCRETIZATION OF PERFECTION[15]

The contemplation of a deity is a concretization of the idea of perfection, greatness and superiority, which has been obvious in man's thinking and feeling since time immemorial. The desire to be in God, to follow His call, to be one with Him, are goals of a striving, not a drive or an instinct. From this striving there follow the appropriate attitudes, thoughts, and feelings. God can be recognized and manifest only within a thought process which moves toward the quality of height and greatness, and only within feelings which experience greatness as redemption from oppressing tensions and inferiority feelings. The idea of God and the immense significance of this idea for mankind can be understood and appreciated from the point of view of Individual Psychology as follows. It is the concretization and interpretation of the human recognition of greatness and perfection, and the dedication of the individual as well as of society to a goal which rests in the future and which enhances in the present the driving force toward greatness by strengthening the appropriate feelings and emotions.

Each individual forms an image of the functioning and shape of the supreme being which differs from that of the next man by nuances of a thousand-fold variation. No wonder that the scale of concretizations ranges all the way from personification to its opposite.

Now that man no longer sees himself as the center of world events, he is satisfied with a more meager concretization of the image of God and is inclined to conceive it as causally acting forces of nature. Individual Psychology, however, because of its essential views, would have to regard such an unpremised mechanistic position as an illusion, inasmuch as it is without goal and direction. In this the mechanistic position is like drive psychology which is cut from the same cloth. While the materialistic view lacks the goal, which after all is the essence of life, the religious view, far ahead in this respect, on the other hand lacks the causal foundation, for God cannot be proven scientifically; He is a gift of faith.

Individual Psychology would have to proceed differently [from both the mechanistic and the religious view.] It would consider unessential the question whether man is the center of the world. Its intention would be to make him the center. In this way mankind attains a task and a goal which, although unattainable, points the way and the direction. Man has always taken this path, for, with his bodily and psychological disposition, he must strive continuously towards self-preservation and ascendency. In this manner he found God whose function it is to point the way. God, as man's goal, is the harmonic complementation for the groping and erring movements on the path of life. The striving to gain strength from the divine goal always flows from man's insecurity and constant inferiority feeling. The fact that the form of the ideal varies is not essential. Whether the highest effective goal is called God or Socialism or, as we call it, the pure idea of social interest, it always reflects the same ruling, completion-promising, grace-giving goal of overcoming.

2. THE SANCTIFICATION OF HUMAN RELATIONS[16]

In man's strongest endeavor to create an image of omnipotence should we not expect to find that which has always been and will be man's hourly concern? This concern is for the preservation and the ascendency of mankind as a whole as well as for the individual members. It has taken an unthinkably long time and it has required a large number of tentative attempts for us to recognize a satisfactory image, to experience the revelation of a supreme being who would lead one to the hope and belief of security for the species and for the individual. It certainly was a nonverbal, nonconceptual insight of religious fervor in which the sacred uniting of man with the goal-setting God first took place, as it still takes place today in every religious soul.

The strong possibilities of a concretization of a goal of perfection, and the irresistible attraction to it are firmly anchored in human nature. So, too, are the possibilities of a psychological union with others. The sanctification of these possibilities strengthened them and their development by setting the thinking and feeling apparatus into continuous movement. Included in this progressive strengthening were the ties between mother and child, of marriage, and of the family, all to the advantage of the care of the young. At the same time life and the love of one's neighbor were sanctified. Probably the strongest and most significant step towards the preservation and perfection of man was taken when he accomplished his unification with God as the redemption from all evil.

Should, or could, man have waited until he recognized through scientific illumination the necessity for brotherly love and the common weal, for the proper relationship of mother and child, the social lawfulness in the cooperation of the sexes, and the interest in the labor of one's fellow man? Such an intellectual clarification, which leads to the most profound recognition of interconnectedness, which closes all doors to error, and proves that virtue is teachable, has as yet not become realized by many. Religious faith is alive and will continue to live until it is replaced by this most profound insight and the religious feeling which stems from it. It will not be enough for man to taste of this insight; he will have to devour and digest it completely.

The primal energy which was so effective in establishing regulative religious goals was none other than that of social feeling. This was meant to bind human beings more closely to one another. It must be regarded as the heritage of evolution, as the result of the upward struggle in the evolutionary urge.

The worship, too, of a fetish, of a lizard, of a phallus as a fetish in a prehistoric tribe does not seem to be scientifically justifiable. Still we should not overlook the fact that this primitive conception of the universe has furthered communal life, the social feeling of humanity, since every one who was under the spell of the same religious fervor was regarded as a brother, as taboo, and was accorded the protection of the large tribe.

The fact that an increasingly large portion of mankind resists religion does not arise from the essential nature of religion. This resistance rather originates from the contradictions which have resulted between the action of the power apparatus of the religions and their essential nature, and probably also from the not infrequent abuses of religion.

3. INDIVIDUAL PSYCHOLOGY, RELIGION, AND OTHER SOCIAL MOVEMENTS[17]

Individual Psychology has recognized the amount of social interest which dwells in each human being, and traces it as an inviolable part of human nature to innate dispositions which await development. Society, as Individual Psychology refers to it, is an ideal, always unattainable, but always beckoning and direction-giving. This society, the power of the logic of man's living together, blesses those who follow it and punishes the unwilling and erring. The growing influence of this ideal community in the life of peoples creates institutions to act continuously as a goal, to strengthen the weak, to support the falling, and to heal the erring, taking the bodily and psychological well-being of all into account as an incontestable factor. Even here, however, abuses occur readily among adherents of Individual Psychology as well as others. Movements which, independently of us, have made society the goal of their striving, are responsible for showing that the good of all is assured by their conduct, not only by their words and feelings. I would acknowledge as valuable any movement which guarantees the welfare of all as its final goal.

Since Individual Psychology is not interested in the verbal expression of feelings, but only in the intensity of the movement by which they are expressed, it will evaluate the members of various religions not by the way they represent their feelings, but by the movement of the whole individual follower, i.e., by their fruits. That these fruits must be recognized sub specie aeternitatis may be said parenthetically. Individual Psychology does not deny that the religions with their powers, their church institutions, their influence on school and education, have a strong advantage. It will be satisfied in the practical application of its science to protect and further the sacred good of brotherly love where the religions have lost their influence.

I regard it as no mean commendation when it is emphasized that Individual Psychology has rediscovered many a lost position of Christian guidance. I have always endeavored to show that Individual Psychology is the heir to all great movements whose aim is the welfare of mankind. Although its scientific foundation obligates it to a certain intransigence, it is eager to receive stimulation from all fields of knowledge and experience and to return the stimulation. In this sense it has always been a liaison work. It is connected with all great movements through the common urge which guides the development of every science and technology, the urge toward a higher development of mankind and the welfare of all.

FOOTNOTES TO CHAPTER NINETEEN

1. 1 to 4: "Mass psychology" (1934c), pp. 111, 117 and 116, 114, and 120.
2. 1 and 2: "Mass psychology" (1934c), pp. 117 and 118; 3: "Bolschewismus und Seelenkunde" (1918a), pp. 598–600.
3. 1: "Salvaging mankind by psychology" (1925), p. 333; 2 and 4: "Mass psychology" (1934c), pp. 111–112 and 118–119; 3: *What Life Should Mean to You* (1931a), p. 254.
4. 1 and 2: "Salvaging mankind" (1925), p. 334.
5. 1, 2, 3: *Menschenkenntnis* (1927a), pp. 187, 188, and 188.
6. 1: *Die Technik der Individualpsychologie. Tl. 2.* (1930d), p. 139; 2: "Salvaging mankind" (1925), p. 335; 3: "Mass psychology" (1934c), p. 117.
7. 1: "Salvaging mankind" (1925), p. 333; 2: "Mass psychology" (1934c), p. 120; 3 and 4: "Verwahrloste Kinder" (1920), pp. 251 and 251–252.
8. 1: "Die Formen der seelischen Aktivität" (1933f), pp. 1–5; 2 and 3: "Mass psychology" (1934c), p. 119.
9. 1, 2, 3: *Technik der Individualpsychologie* (1930d), pp. 138–139, 131, and 138.
10. 1, 3, 4: "Bolschewismus" (1918a), pp. 597, 599, and 598; 2: "Psychiatric aspects regarding individual and social disorganization" (1937a), p. 778.
11. 1 and 2: "Bolschewismus" (1918a), pp. 598–599 and 599.
12. 1: "Bolschewismus" (1918a), p. 600.
13. 1, 2, 3: *Die andere Seite* (1919), pp. 9, 12, and 12.
14. 1 and 2: *Die andere Seite* (1919), pp. 13–14 and 14–15.
15. 1 to 4: "Religion und Individualpsychologie" (1933c), pp. 58–59, 60, 60, and 60–61.
16. 1, 2, 3, 6: "Religion und Individualpsychologie" (1933c), pp. 62, 62, 62, and 62–63; 4 and 5: *Social Interest* (1933b), pp. 273 and 272.
17. 1, 2, 3: "Religion und Individualpsychologie" (1933c), pp. 63, 66, and 92.

ADLER BIBLIOGRAPHY

This is not a complete bibliography of Adler. Only items to which reference is made in the text or the chapter footnotes are listed here. But it may be said that all his major writings are included.

If an English translation is known, it is listed after the German title. When the English translation has been used, it is enclosed in parentheses and the references refer to it. When the translation has not been used, it is enclosed in brackets.

References are listed by the earliest known date for the presentation of the material. Where our source is of a later date and the first presentation was in print, we list the item "as reprinted in" the source used; where the first presentation was not in print, we list the item "in" the source used.

1904. Der Arzt als Erzieher. In *Heilen und Bilden*, 1914a, pp. 1–10.

1907a. *Studie über Minderwertigkeit von Organen*. Berlin, Vienna: Urban & Schwarzenberg. (*Study of Organ Inferiority and Its Psychical Compensation; a Contribution to Clinical Medicine*. New York:Nervous & Mental Diseases Publishing Company, 1917.)

1907b. Die Theorie der Organminderwertigkeit und ihre Bedeutung für Philosophie und Psychologie. In *Heilen und Bilden*, 1914a, pp. 11–22.

1908a. Der Aggressionstrieb im Leben und in der Neurose. *Fortschritte der Medizin*, **26**, 577–584. As reprinted in *Heilen und Bilden*, 1914a, pp. 23–32.

1908b. Das Zärtlichkeitsbedürfnis des Kindes. In *Heilen und Bilden*, 1914a, pp. 50–53.

1908c. Zwei Träume einer Prostituierten. Z. *Sexualwissensch.*, **1**, 103–106.

1909. Über neurotische Disposition; zugleich ein Beitrag zur Ätiologie und zur Frage der Neurosenwahl. In E. Bleuler, and S. Freud, Eds. *Jahrbuch f. psychoanal. & psycho-pathol. Forschung*, Bd. I. Leipzig:Deuticke. As reprinted in *Heilen und Bilden*, 1914a, pp. 54–73.

1910a. Der psychische Hermaphroditismus im Leben und in der Neurose. *Fortschritte der Medizin*, **28**, 486–493. As reprinted in *Heilen und Bilden*, 1914a, pp. 74–83.

1910b. Trotz und Gehorsam. *Monatshefte für Pädagogik und Schulpolitik*, Heft 9. As reprinted in *Heilen und Bilden*, 1914a, pp. 84–93.

1910c. Über männliche Einstellung bei weiblichen Neurotikern. *Zentbl. Psychoanal.*, **1**, 174–178. As reprinted in *Praxis und Theorie*, 1924, pp. 77–81, with additional material to p. 100. [The masculine attitude in female neurotics. In *Practice and Theory*, 1927b, pp. 109–143.]

1911a. Die Rolle der Sexualität in der Neurose. In *Heilen und Bilden*, 1914a, pp. 94–103.

1911b. "Verdrängung" und "männlicher Protest"; ihre Rolle und Bedeutung für die neurotische Dynamik. In *Heilen und Bilden*, 1914a, pp. 103–114.

1911c. Beitrag zum Verständnis des Widerstands in der Behandlung. *Zentbl. Psychoanal.*, **1**, 214–219. As reprinted in *Praxis und Theorie*, 1924, pp. 101–107. [The concept of resistance during treatment. In *Practice and Theory*, 1927b, pp. 144–154.]

1911d. Erklärung. *Zentbl. Psychoanal.*, **1**, 433.

1912a. *Über den nervosen Charakter; Grundzüge einer vergleichenden Individual-Psychologie und Psychotherapie*. Wiesbaden:Bergmann. 4th ed., Munich:Bergmann, 1928. [*The Neurotic Constitution*. New York: Dodd, Mead & Co., 1926.]

1912b. Zur Erziehung der Eltern. In *Heilen und Bilden*, 1914a, pp. 113–129.

1912c. Organdialekt. In *Heilen und Bilden*, 1914a, pp. 130–139.

1912d. Zur Theorie der Halluzination. In *Praxis und Theorie*, 1924, pp. 36–41. [Contributions to the theory of hallucination. In *Practice and Theory*, 1927b, pp. 51–58.]

1913a. Aus den individualpsychologischen Ergebnissen bezüglich Schlafstörungen. *Fortschritte der Medizin*, **31**, Heft 34. As reprinted in *Praxis und Theorie*, 1924, pp. 121–128. [Individual-psychological conclusions on sleep disturbances. In *Practice and Theory*, 1927b, pp. 172–183.]

1913b. Der nervöse Charakter. In *Heilen und Bilden*, 1914a, pp. 140–150.

1913c. Individualpsychologische Behandlung der Neurosen. In D. Sarason, Ed.: *Jahreskurse für arztliche Fortbildung*. Munich:Lehmann, pp. 39–51. As reprinted in *Praxis und Theorie*, 1924, pp. 22–35. [Individual-psychological treatment of neuroses. In *Practice and Theory*, 1927b, pp. 32–50.]

1913d. Individualpsychologische Bemerkungen zu Alfred Bergers "Hofrat Eysenhardt." *Z. psychol. Medizin & Psychotherapie*, **5**, 77–89. As reprinted in *Praxis und Theorie*, 1924, pp. 197–207. [Individual-psychological remarks on Alfred Berger's Hofrat Eysenhardt. In *Practice and Theory*, 1927b, pp. 263–279.] Quoted material only in *Praxis und Theorie*, 2nd ed., 1924, p. 197.

1913e. Zur Rolle des Unbewussten in der Neurose. *Zentbl. Psychoanal.*, **3**, 169–174. As reprinted in *Praxis und Theorie*, 1924, pp. 162–167. [On the role of the unconscious in neurosis. In *Practice and Theory*, 1927b, pp. 227–234.]

1913f. Traum und Traumdeutung. *Zentbl. Psychoanal.*, **3**, 574–583. As reprinted in *Praxis und Theorie*, 1924, pp. 153–161. [Dreams and dream-interpretation. In *Practice and Theory*, 1927b, pp. 214–226.]

1914a. With Carl Furtmüller, Eds.: *Heilen und Bilden; ärztlich-pädagogische Arbeiten des Vereins für Individualpsychologie*. Munich:Reinhardt.

1914b. Das Problem der "Distanz"; über einen Grundcharakter der Neurose und Psychose. *Int. Z. Indiv. Psychol.*, **1**, 8–16. As reprinted in *Praxis und Theorie*, 1924, pp. 71–76. [The problem of distance; a basic feature of neurosis and psychosis. In *Practice and Theory*, 1927b, pp. 100–108.]

1914c. Lebenslüge und Verantwortlichkeit in der Neurose und Psychose; ein Beitrag zur Melancholiefrage. *Int. Z. Indiv. Psychol.*, **1**, 44–53. As reprinted in *Praxis und Theorie*, 1924, pp. 177–184. [Life-lie and responsibility in neurosis and psychosis; a contribution to melancholia. In *Practice and Theory*, 1927b, pp. 235–245.]

1914d. Nervose Schlaflosigkeit. *Int. Z. Indiv. Psychol.*, **1**, 65–72. As reprinted in *Praxis und Theorie*, 1924, pp. 115–120. [Nervous insomnia. In *Practice and Theory*, 1927b, pp. 163–171.]

1914e. Melancholie und Paranoia; individualpsychologische Ergebnisse aus den Untersuchungen der Psychosen. In *Praxis und Theorie*, 1924, pp. 185–196. [Melancholia and paranoia; Individual-psychological results obtained from a study of psychoses. In *Practice and Theory*, 1927b, pp. 246–262.]

1914f. Die Individualpsychologie, ihre Voraussetzungen und Ergebnisse. *Scientia*, **16**, 74–87. As reprinted in *Praxis und Theorie*, 1924, pp. 1–10. [Individual psychology, its assumptions and its results. In *Practice and Theory*, 1927b, pp. 1–15.]

1914g. Zur Kinderpsychologie und Neurosenforschung. *Wien. klin. Wschr.*, **27**, 511–516. As reprinted in *Praxis und Theorie*, 1924, pp. 42–54. [The study of child psychology and neurosis. In *Practice and Theory*, 1927b, pp. 59–77.]

1918a. Bolschewismus und Seelenkunde. *Int. Rundschau* (Zurich), **4**, 597–600.

1918b. Über die Homosexualität. In *Praxis und Theorie*, 1924, pp. 129–139. [Homosexuality. In *Practice and Theory*, 1927b, pp. 184–196.]

1918c. Die Zwangsneurose. In *Praxis und Theorie*, 1924, pp. 140–147. [Compulsion neurosis. In *Practice and Theory*, 1927b, pp. 197–207.]

1918d. Dostojewski. In *Praxis und Theorie*, 1924, pp. 208–215. [Dostoievsky. In *Practice and Theory*, 1927b, pp. 280–290.]

1918e. Über individualpsychologische Erziehung. In *Praxis und Theorie*, 1924, pp. 234–240. [Individual-psychological education. In *Practice and Theory*, 1927b, pp. 317–326.]

1919. *Die andere Seite; eine massenpsychologische Studie über die Schuld des Volkes*. Vienna:Leopold Heidrich G. m. b. H.

1920. Verwahrloste Kinder. In *Praxis und Theorie*, 1924, pp. 250–257. [Demoralized children. In *Practice and Theory*, 1927b, 339–350.]

1921. Wo soll der Kampf gegen die Verwahrlosung einsetzen? *Soziale Praxis* (Vienna). As reprinted in *Heilen und Bilden*, 1922a, pp. 116–118.

1922a. With Carl Furtmüller and Erwin Wexberg, Eds.: *Heilen und Bilden: Grundlagen der Erziehungskunst für Ärzte und Pädagogen*, 2nd ed. Munich:Bergmann.

1922b. Erziehungsberatungsstellen. In *Heilen und Bilden*, 1922a, pp. 119–121.

1923a. Fortschritte der Individualpsychologie. *Int. Z. Indiv. Psychol.*, 2, No. 1, 1–7; No. 3, 10–12. (Progress in Individual Psychology. *Brit. J. Med. Psychol.*, 4, 22–31, 1924.)

1923b. Die Tragfähigkeit der menschlichen Seele. *Int. Z. Indiv. Psychol.*, 2, No. 2, p. 42.

1923c. Psychische Kausalität. *Int. Z. Indiv. Psychol.*, 2, No. 6, p. 38.

1924. *Praxis und Theorie der Individualpsychologie; Vorträge zur Einführung in die Psychotherapie für Ärzte, Psychologen und Lehrer*, 2nd ed. (1st ed., 1920) Munich:Bergmann. [*Practice and Theory of Individual Psychology*. New York: Harcourt, Brace & Co., 1927.]

1925. Salvaging mankind by psychology. *The New York Times*, Sept. 20, IX, p. 12. As reprinted in *Int. Z. Indiv. Psychol.*, 3, 332–335, 1924–1925.

1926a. Geleitwort. *Individuum und Gemeinschaft*. Munich:Bergmann, No. 1, ix–xi.

1926b. Individualpsychologie. In Emil Saupe, Ed. *Einführung in die neuere Psychologie* (4th and 5th eds., 1931), Osterwieck-Harz:A. W. Zickfeldt, pp. 399–407.

1927a. *Menschenkenntnis*. Leipzig:Hirzel. 5th ed., Zurich:Rascher, 1947. [*Understanding Human Nature*. New York:Greenberg, Publisher, Inc., 1927.]

1927b. *The Practice and Theory of Individual Psychology*. New York:Harcourt, Brace & Co.

1927c. Zusammenhänge zwischen Neurose und Witz. *Int. Z. Indiv. Psychol.*, 5, 94–96.

1927d. Individualpsychologie und Wissenschaft. *Int. Z. Indiv. Psychol.*, 5, 401–409.

1927e. Individual Psychology. *J. abnorm. soc. Psychol.*, 22, 116–122.

1927f. A doctor remakes education. *Survey*, 58, 490–495.

1928. Kurze Bemerkungen über Vernunft, Intelligenz und Schwachsinn. *Int. Z. Indiv. Psychol.*, 6, 267–272.

1929a. *Individualpsychologie in der Schule; Vorlesungen für Lehrer und Erzieher*. Leipzig:Hirzel.

1929b. *Problems of Neurosis; a Book of Case-Histories*. London:Kegan Paul, Trench, Truebner & Co.

1929c. *The Science of Living*. New York:Greenberg, Publisher, Inc.

1929d. *Problems of Neurosis*, 1929b, Chap. 7. Reprinted with minor changes as: Position in family constellation influences life style. *Int. J. Indiv. Psychol.*, 3, 211–227, 1937.

1929e. *Problems of Neurosis*, 1929b, Chap. 8. Reprinted with minor changes as: Significance of early recollections. *Int. J. Indiv. Psychol.*, 3, 283–287, 1937.

1929f. Die Individualpsychologie in der Neurosenlehre. *Int. Z. Indiv. Psychol.*, 7, 81–88.

1929g. Übertreibung der eigenen Wichtigkeit. *Int. Z. Indiv. Psychol.*, 7, 245–252. Also ɪn *Die Technik der Individualpsychologie*. Tl. 2. 1930d, Chap. 1. (A sch ɔl girl's exaggeration of her own importance. *Int. J. Indiv. Psychol.*, 3, 3–12, 1937.)

1930a. *The Education of Children.* New York:Greenberg, Publisher, Inc.

1930b. *The Pattern of Life.* New York:Rinehart & Company, Inc.

1930c. *Das Problem der Homosexualitat; erotisches Training und erotischer Rückzug.* Leipzig:Hɪrzel.

1930d. *Die Technik der Individualpsychologie. Tl. 2. Die Seele der schwererziehbaren Schulkinder.* Munich:Bergmann. (*La psychologie de l'enfant difficile; technique de la Psychologie Individuelle comparée.* Paris:Payot, 1952.) Note: Page references in the text are to the French edition, the original edɪtion not having been available.

1930e. Nochmals—Dɪc Einheɪt der Neurosen. *Int. Z. Indiv. Psychol.*, 8, 201–216.

1930f. Individual Psychology. In Murchison, Carl, Ed. *Psychologies of 1930.* Worcester, Mass.:Clark University Prcss, pp. 395–405.

1930g. Verzärtelte Kinder; Einleitung zum 5. Internat. Kongress für Individualpsychologie, Berlin, Sept. Unpublished manuscript of ten pages in the possession of Emery I. Gondor.

1931a. *What Life Should Mean to You.* Boston:Little, Brown & Company.

1931b. Der nervose Charakter. *Beɪhefte Z. angew. Psychol.*, No. 59, 1–14.

1931c. Rauschgift. *Fortschritte Medizin*, 49, 535–540, 571–575. As reprinted in *Int. Z. Indɪv. Psychol.*, 10, 1–19, 1932.

1931d. The case of Mrs. A.; the dɪagnosis of a life-style. *Indiv. Psychol. Pamphlets*, No. 1, 15–46.

1931e. Zwangsneurose. *Int. Z. Indiv. Psychol.*, 9, 1–16. (Compulsion neurosis. *Int. J. Indiv. Psychol.*, 2, No. 4, 3–22, 1936.)

1931f. Trick und Neurose. *Int. Z. Indiv. Psychol.*, 9, 417–423. (Trick and neurosis. *Int. J. Indiv. Psychol.*, 2, No. 2, 3–10, 1936.)

1932a. Personlichkeit als geschlossene Eɪnheit. *Int. Z. Indiv. Psychol.*, 10, 81–89.

1932b. Der Aufbau der Neurose. *Int. Z. Indiv. Psychol.*, 10, 321–328. (The structure of neurosis. *Int. J. Indiv. Psychol.*, 1, No. 2, 3–12, 1935.)

1933a. *Der Sinn des Lebens.* Vienna, Leipzig:Rolf Passer. [*Social Interest; a Challenge to Mankind*, 1933b.]

1933b. *Social Interest; a Challenge to Mankind.* London:Faber & Faber, Ltd., 1938. Translated from *Der Sinn des Lebens*, 1933a.

1933c. Relɪgion und Individualpsychologɪe. In Ernst Jahn and Alfred Adler: *Religion und Individualpsychologɪe; eine prinzipielle Auseinandersetzung uber Menschenführung.* Vienna, Leɪpzig:Rolf Passer, pp. 58–92.

1933d. Review of *The Wisdom of the Body* by Walter B. Cannon. (New York:W. W. Norton & Company, Inc., 1932.) *Int. Z. Indɪv. Psychol.*, 11, 154.

1933e. Über den Ursprung des Strebens nach Überlegenheit und des Gemein-schaftsgefühles. *Int. Z. Indiv. Psychol.*, 11, 257–263.

1933f. Die Formen der seelischen Aktivität; ein Beitrag zur individualpsy-chologischen Charakterkunde. *Ned. Tijdschr. Psychol.*, 1, 229–235. As reprinted in *Int. Z. Indiv. Psychol.*, 12, 1–5, 1934.

1933g. Vor- und Nachteile des Minderwertigkeitsgefühls. *Päd. Warte*, 40, 15–19.

1934a. Lecture to the Medical Society of Individual Psychology, London. *Indiv. Psychol. Pamphlets*, No. 13, 11–24.

1934b. Körperliche Auswirkungen seelischer Störungen. *Int. Z. Indiv. Psy-chol.*, 12, 65–71. (Physical manifestations of psychic disturbances. *Indiv. Psychol. Bull.*, 4, 3–8, 1944.)

1934c. Zur Massenpsychologie. *Int. Z. Indiv. Psychol.*, 12, 133–141. (Mass psychology. *Int. J. Indiv. Psychol.*, 3, 111–120, 1937.)

1935a. The fundamental views of Individual Psychology. *Int. J. Indiv. Psy-chol.*, 1, No. 1, 5–8.

1935b. Der Komplexzwang als Teil der Persönlichkeit und der Neurose. *Int. Z. Indiv. Psychol.*, 13, 1–6.

1935c. Vorbeugung der Neurose. *Int. Z. Indiv. Psychol.*, 13, 133–141. (Pre-vention of neurosis. *Int. J. Indiv. Psychol.*, 1, No. 4, 3–12, 1935.)

1935d. Die Vorbeugung der Delinquenz. *Int. Z. Indiv. Psychol.*, 13, 197–206. (The prevention of delinquency. *Int. J. Indiv. Psychol.*, 1, No. 3, 3–13, 1935.)

1936a. On the interpretation of dreams. *Int. J. Indiv. Psychol.*, 2, No. 1, 3–16.

1936b. Das Todesproblem in der Neurose. *Int. Z. Indiv. Psychol.*, 14, 1–6.

1936c. Die Symptomwahl des Kindes. *Int. Z. Indiv. Psychol.*, 14, 65–80. (How the child selects his symptoms. *Indiv. Psychol. Bull.*, 5, 67–78, 1946.) Also cited are a few unpublished pages from the manuscript of this paper.

1936d. Neurotisches Weltbild. *Int. Z. Indiv. Psychol.*, 14, 129–137. (The neurotic's picture of the world. *Int. J. Indiv. Psychol.*, 2, No. 3, 3–13, 1936.)

1937a. Psychiatric aspects regarding individual and social disorganization. *Amer. J. Sociol.*, 42, 773–780.

1937b. Selbstmord. *Int. Z. Indiv. Psychol.*, 15, 49–52.

1939. [Autobiographical notes.] In Bottome, Phyllis. *Alfred Adler; a Biogra-phy.* New York: G. P. Putnam's Sons, pp. 9–12.

1941. Failures of personalities. *Indiv. Psychol. Bull.* (*News*), 1, Nos. 8–9, 2–8.

1944. Sleeplessness. *Indiv. Psychol. Bull.*, 3, 60–64.

GENERAL BIBLIOGRAPHY

1. Adler, Alexandra. *Guiding Human Misfits; a Practical Application of Individual Psychology*. New York:Philosophical Library, Inc., 1948.
2. Alexander, Franz, Thomas M. French, *et al. Psychoanalytic Therapy; Principles and Application*. New York:The Ronald Press Company, 1946.
3. Allport, Gordon W. *The Nature of Personality; Selected Papers*. Cambridge, Mass.:Addison-Wesley Press, Inc., 1950.
4. Allport, Gordon W. *Personality; a Psychological Interpretation*. New York:Henry Holt & Company, Inc., 1937.
5. Allport, Gordon W. Prejudice: a problem in psychological and social causation. *J. Social Issues*, Suppl. Series, No. 4, 4–26, 1950.
6. Allport, Gordon W. The psychological nature of personality. *The Personalist*, 34, 347–357, 1953.
7. Anderson, John E. Personality organization in children. *Amer. Psychologist*, 3, 409–416, 1948.
8. Ansbacher, H. L. Causality and indeterminism according to Alfred Adler, and some current American personality theories. *Indiv. Psychol. Bull.*, 9, 96–107, 1951.
9. Ansbacher, H. L. "Neo-Freudian" or "Neo-Adlerian"? Report on a survey conducted among members of the American Psychoanalytic Association. *Amer. Psychologist*, 8, 165–166, 1953.
10. Asch, Solomon. *Social Psychology*. New York:Prentice-Hall, Inc., 1952.
11. Birnbaum, Ferdinand. Die Anwendung der Individualpsychologie in der Schule. *Int. Z. Indiv. Psychol.*, 9, 171–182, 1931. (Applying Individual Psychology in school. *Int. J. Indiv. Psychol.*, 1, No. 3, 109–119, 1935.)
12. Birnbaum, Ferdinand. Die individualpsycholigische Versuchsschule in Wien. *Int. Z. Indiv. Psychol.*, 10, 176–183, 1932. (The Individual-psychological experimental school in Vienna. *Int. J. Indiv. Psychol.*, 1, No. 2, 118–124, 1935.)
13. Boring, E. G. The nature of psychology. In E. G. Boring, H. S. Langfeld, and H. P. Weld, Eds.: *Foundations of Psychology*. New York:John Wiley & Sons, Inc., pp. 1–18, 1948.
14. Bosshard, Heinrich M. Review of "Socio-psychiatric research; its implications for the schizophrenia problem and for mental health" by H. S. Sullivan. (*Amer. J. Psychiatry*, 10, 977–991, 1931.) *Int. Z. Indiv. Psychol.*, 9, 411, 1931.

15. Bottome, Phyllis. *Alfred Adler; a Biography.* New York:G. P. Putnam's Sons, 1939.
16. Bottome, Phyllis. *Private Worlds.* Boston:Houghton Mifflin Co., 1934.
17. Brachfeld, Oliver. *Inferiority Feelings; in the Individual and the Group.* New York:Grune & Stratton Inc., 1951.
18. Brown, John F. Freud and the scientific method. *Philosophy of Science,* **1,** 323–337, 1934.
19. Bruck, Antonio. Adlerian philosophy. *Indiv. Psychol. Bull.,* **6,** 80–87, 1947.
20. Bruner, Jerome S. Personality dynamics and the process of perceiving. In Robert R. Blake, and Glenn V. Ramsey, Eds., *Perception; an Approach to Personality.* New York:The Ronald Press Co., pp. 121–147, 1951.
21. Brunswik, Egon. The conceptual framework of psychology. *International Encyclopedia of Unified Science,* **1,** No. 10, 1952.
22. Bühler, Karl. *Die geistige Entwicklung des Kindes.* 4th edition. Jena: Gustav Fischer, 1924.
23. Cattell, Raymond B. Principles of design in "projective" or misperception tests of personality. In H. H. Anderson and G. L. Anderson, Eds.: *An Introduction to Projective Techniques,* NewYork:Prentice-Hall, Inc., pp. 55–98, 1951.
24. Colby, Kenneth Mark. On the disagreement between Freud and Adler. *Amer. Imago,* **8,** 229–238, 1951.
25. Colm, Hanna. Healing as participation; comments on Paul Tillich's existential philosophy. *Psychiatry,* **16,** 99–111, 1953.
26. Dollard, John and N. E. Miller. *Personality and Psychotherapy: An Analysis in Terms of Learning, Thinking, and Culture.* New York:McGraw-Hill Book Company, Inc., 1950.
27. Dreikurs, Rudolf. The immediate purpose of children's misbehavior, its recognition and correction. *Int. Z. Indiv. Psychol.,* **19,** 70–87, 1950.
28. Dreikurs, Rudolf. The socio-psychological dynamics of physical disability; a review of the Adlerian concept. *J. Social Issues,* **4,** No. 4, 39–54, 1948.
29. Fletcher, J. M. Homeostasis as an explanatory principle in psychology. *Psychol. Rev.,* **49,** 80–87, 1942.
30. Fletcher, J. M. The wisdom of the mind. *Sigma Xi Quarterly,* **26,** 6–16, 1938.
31. Freschl, Robert. Von Janet zur Individualpsychologie. *Zentbl. Psychoanal.,* **4,** 152–164, 1914.
32. Freud, Anna. *The Ego and the Mechanisms of Defence,* 3rd impression. London:Hogarth Press, 1948.
33. Freud, Sigmund. *The Basic Writings of Sigmund Freud.* New York: Modern Library, Inc., 1938. (As originally published in *Three Contributions to the Theory of Sex* (Mon. #7), Nervous and Mental Disease Monographs, New York.)
34. Freud, Sigmund. *Beyond the Pleasure Principle* (1920). New York: Liveright Publishing Corp., 1950.

35. Freud, Sigmund. *Civilization and its Discontents* (1929), London:The Hogarth Press, Ltd., 1946.

36. Freud, Sigmund. *Collected Papers*, Volumes I–V. London:The Hogarth Press, Ltd., 1924–1950.

37. Freud, Sigmund. *The Ego and the Id.* (1923). London:The Hogarth Press, Ltd., 1949.

38. Freud, Sigmund. *A General Introduction to Psychoanalysis* (1917). New York:Garden City Publishing Company, 1943.

39. Freud, Sigmund. *Group Psychology and the Analysis of the Ego* (1921). New York:Liveright Publishing Corporation, 1949.

40. Freud, Sigmund. *Inhibitions, Symptoms and Anxiety.* London:Hogarth Press, Ltd., 1936.

41. Freud, Sigmund. *New Introductory Lectures on Psychoanalysis* (1933). New York: W. W. Norton & Company, Inc., 1933.

42. Freud, Sigmund. *An Outline of Psychoanalysis.* (1940), New York: W. W. Norton & Company, Inc., 1949.

43. Fromm, Erich. *Escape from Freedom.* New York:Farrar and Rinehart, Inc., 1941.

44. Furtmüller, Carl. Alfred Adler. (Unpublished manuscript.)

45. Furtmüller, Carl. Geleitwort. In Adler, Alfred and Furtmüller, Carl, Eds. *Heilen und Bilden.* Munich:Reinhardt, pp. iii-viii, 1914.

46. Furtmüller, Carl. Psychoanalyse und Ethik. *Schriften d. Vereins fur freie psychoanal. Forsch.* Munich:Reinhardt, No. 1, 1912.

47. Ganz, Madelaine. *La Psychologie d'Alfred Adler et le Developpement de l'Enfant.* Geneva, 1935. (*The Psychology of Alfred Adler and the Development of the Child.* London:Routledge & Kegan Paul, Ltd., 1953.)

48. Goldstein, Kurt. *The Organism; a Holistic Approach to Biology Derived from Pathological Data in Man.* New York:American Book Company, 1939.

49. Heidbreder, Edna F. The normal inferiority complex. *J. abnorm. soc. Psychol.*, **22**, 243–258, 1927.

50. Hinrichsen, Otto. Unser Verstehen der seelischen Zusammenhänge in der Neurose und Freud's und Adler's Theorien. *Zentbl. Psychoanal.*, **3**, 369–393, 1913.

51. Hitschmann, Edward. The history of the aggression-impulse. *Samiksa*, (Calcutta, India), **1**, 137–141, 1947. Also in *Yearbook of Psychoanalysis*. New York:International Universities Press, Inc., V. 4, 1948.

52. Holub, Martha. Gespräche mit Eltern und Kindern. *Int. Z. Indiv. Psychol.*, **8**, 441–458, 1930. (Conversations with parents and children. *Int. J. Indiv. Psychol.*, **1**, No. 2, 96–112, 1935.)

53. Horney, Karen. *The Neurotic Personality of Our Time.* New York: W. W. Norton & Company, Inc., 1937.

54. Horney, Karen. *Our Inner Conflicts.* New York:W. W. Norton & Company, Inc., 1945.

55. Hull, Clark L. Modern behaviorism and psychoanalysis. *Trans. N. Y. Acad. Sci.*, **1**, Ser. II, 78–82, 1939.

56. Irwin, Francis W. Motivation. In Harry Helson, Ed.: *Theoretical Foundations in Psychology*. New York:D. Van Nostrand Company, Inc., pp. 200–253, 1951.

57. James, Walter T. Karen Horney and Erich Fromm in relation to Alfred Adler. *Indiv. Psychol. Bull.*, **6**, 105–116, 1947.

58. James, William. *Pragmatism: A New Name for Some Old Ways of Thinking*. New York:Longmans, Green & Co., 1907.

59. Jaspers, Karl. *Allgemeine Psychopathologie*, 4th ed. (1st ed., 1913) Berlin and Heidelberg:Springer Verlag, 1946. English translation: *General Psychopathology*. Chicago, Ill., Chicago University Press, 1963.

60. Koffka, Kurt. *Principles of Gestalt Psychology*. New York:Harcourt, Brace & Co., 1935.

61. Kogan, L. S., and J. McV. Hunt. After comments. *Psychol. Service Center J.*, **2**, 132–138, 1950.

62. Kohler, Wolfgang. *The Place of Value in a World of Facts*. New York: Liveright Publishing Corp., 1938.

63. Krech, David, and R. S. Crutchfield. *Theory and Problems of Social Psychology*. New York:McGraw-Hill Book Company, Inc., 1948.

64. Kries, Johannes v. Über die Natur gewisser mit den psychischen Vorgängen verknüpfter Gehirnzustände. *Z. Psychol.*, **8**, 1–33, 1895.

65. Leeper, R. W. A motivational theory of emotion to replace 'emotion as disorganized response.' *Psychol. Rev.*, **55**, 5–21, 1948.

66. Lewin, Kurt. Action research and minority problems. *J. Social Issues*, **2**, No. 4, 34–46, 1946.

67. Lewin, Kurt. *A Dynamic Theory of Personality; Selected Papers*. New York:McGraw-Hill Book Company, Inc., 1935.

68. Lewin, Kurt. *Principles of Topological Psychology*. New York:McGraw-Hill Book Company, Inc., 1936.

69. Lewin, Kurt. Psychoanalysis and topological psychology. *Bull. Menninger Clin.*, **1**, 202–212, 1937.

70. Lewin, Kurt. The Research Center for Group Dynamics at Massachusetts Institute of Technology. *Sociometry*, **8**, 126–136, 1945.

71. Lewin, Kurt. Time perspective and morale. In G. Watson, Ed.: *Civilian Morale*. Boston: Houghton Mifflin Company, 1942.

72. Lewis, Nolan D. C. Foreword to Adler, Alfred, *Study of Organ Inferiority and Its Psychical Compensation*. New York:Nervous and Mental Disease Publishing Company, 1917. Reprint edition, pp. vii–ix, 1945 (?).

73. Long, Lewis M. K. Alfred Adler and Gordon W. Allport; A comparison on certain topics in personality theory. *Amer. J. Indiv. Psychol.*, **10**, 43–53, 1952–1953.

74. MacKinnon, Donald W., and A. H. Maslow. Personality. In Harry Helson, Ed.: *Theoretical Foundations of Psychology*. New York:D. Van Nostrand Company, Inc., pp. 602–655, 1951.

75. MacLeod, R. B. The place of phenomenological analysis in social psychological theory. In John H. Rohrer, and Muzafer Sherif, Eds.: *Social Psychology at the Crossroads*. New York:Harper & Brothers, pp. 215–241, 1951.

76. Maslow, A. H. Conflict, frustration and threat. *J. abnorm. soc. Psychol.*, **38**, 81–86, 1943.

77. Maslow, A. H. Frustration, threat and deprivation. *Psychol. Rev.*, **48**, 364–366, 1941.

78. Maslow, A. H. *Motivation and Personality*. New York:Harper & Brothers, 1954.

79. Maslow, A. H. Some theoretical consequences of basic need-gratification. *J. Personality*, **16**, 402–416, 1948.

80. Maslow, A. H. A theory of human motivation. *Psychol. Rev.*, **50**, 370–396, 1943.

81. Moreno, J. L. *Group Therapy*. New York:Beacon House, Inc., 1945.

82. Murphy, Gardner. *Historical Introduction to Modern Psychology*. Revised Edition. New York:Harcourt, Brace & Co., 1949.

83. Murphy, Gardner. *An Introduction to Psychology*. New York:Harper & Brothers, 1951.

84. Murphy, Gardner. *Personality; A Biosocial Approach to Origins and Structure*. New York:Harper & Brothers, 1947.

85. Murray, Henry A. *Explorations in Personality*. New York:Oxford University Press, Inc., 1938.

86. Neuer, Alexander. Ist Individualpsychologie als Wissenschaft möglich? *Int. Z. Indiv. Psychol.*, **1**, 3–8, 1914–1916.

87. Neumann, Johannes. Über den Münchener Kurs über Psychotherapie an Kindern und Jugendlichen vom 2.–4. August, 1928. *Int. Z. Indiv. Psychol.*, **6**, 492–495, 1928.

88. Orgler, Hertha. *Alfred Adler, the Man and his Work*. London:The C. W. Daniel Co., Ltd., 1939.

89. Rayner, Doris. Individual Psychology and the children's clinic. *Indiv. Psychol. Pamphlets*, No. 7, 20–28, 1933.

90. Rogers, C. R. *Client-centered Therapy; its Current Practice, Implications, and Theory*. Boston:Houghton Mifflin Company, 1951.

91. Sachs, Hanns. *Freud; Master and Friend*. Cambridge, Massachusetts: Harvard University Press, 1946.

92. Schmidt, Heinrich. *Philosophisches Wörterbuch*. 9th ed. Leipzig: Alfred Kröner, 1934.

93. Seelbach, Hans. Verstehende Psychologie und Individualpsychologie; ein Vergleich der psychologischen Richtungen von Dilthey, Jaspers und Spranger mit der Individualpsychologie Alfred Adler's. *Int. Z. Indiv. Psychol.*, **10**, 262–288, 368–391, 452–472, 1932.

94. Seidler, Regine, and Ladislaus Zilah. The Vienna Child Guidance Clinics. In Alfred Adler, and associates. *Guiding the Child on the Principles of Individual Psychology*. New York:Greenberg, Publisher, Inc., pp. 9–27, 1930.

95. Simpson, George Gaylord. *The Meaning of Evolution*. New Haven:Yale University Press, 1949. Reprint edition New York:Mentor Books, 1951.

96. Syngg, Donald, and A. W. Combs. *Individual Behavior; a New Frame of Reference for Psychology*. New York:Harper & Brothers, 1949.

97. Sperber, Manes. *Alfred Adler; der Mensch und seine Lehre.* Munich: Bergmann, 1926.

98. Spiel, Oskar. *Am Schaltbrett der Erziehung.* Vienna:Verlag für Jugend und Volk, 1947.

99. Spiel, Oskar. Technology of mental hygiene in school. *Indiv. Psychol. Bull.,* **9,** 4–8, 1951.

100. Spranger, Edward. *Types of Men.* Halle:Niemeyer, 1928.

101. Stekel, Wilhelm. *The Autobiography of Wilhelm Stekel.* New York: Liveright Publishing Corp., 1950.

102. Stern, William. *General Psychology from the Personalistic Standpoint.* New York:The Macmillan Company, 1938.

103. Stern, William. Personalistische Psychologie. In Saupe, Emil, Ed. *Einfuhrung in die neuere Psychologie.* Osterwieck-Harz: A. W. Zickfeldt, 1926; pp. 187–197, 4th and 5th ed. 1931.

104. Sullivan, Harry Stack. Socio-psychiatric research; its implications for the schizophrenia problem and for mental hygiene. *Am. J. Psychiatry,* **10,** 977–991, 1931.

105. Sward, Keith, Review of *Our Inner Conflicts* by Karen Horney. (New York: W. W. Norton & Company, Inc., 1945). *J. abnorm. soc. Psychol.,* **41,** 496–499, 1946.

106. Sward, Keith. Review of *Psychoanalytic Therapy; Principles and Applications* by Franz Alexander, Thomas M. French, *et al.* (New York: Ronald Press, 1946.) *Science,* Dec. 12, 1947. 600–601.

107. Symonds, Percival M. *The Ego and the Self.* New York:Appleton-Century-Crofts, Inc., 1951.

108. Thilly, Frank and Ledger Wood. *A History of Philosophy.* New York: Henry Holt & Company, Inc., 1951.

109. Thompson, Clara. "Penis envy" in women. *Psychiatry,* **6,** 123–125, 1943.

110. Thompson, Clara. *Psychoanalysis; Evolution and Development.* New York:Hermitage House, Inc., 1950.

111. Vaihinger, Hans. *The Philosophy of 'As If'; a System of the Theoretical, Practical and Religious Fictions of Mankind.* New York:Harcourt, Brace & Company, 1925.

112. Way, Lewis. *Adler's Place in Psychology.* New York:The Macmillan Co., 1950.

113. Wechsler, David. Cognitive, conative, and non-intellective intelligence. *Amer. Psychologist,* **5,** 78–83, 1950.

114. Wechsler, David. *The Measurement of Adult Intelligence.* 3rd ed. Baltimore:The Williams & Wilkins Co., 1944.

115. Wertheimer, Max. *Uber Gestalttheorie; ein Vortrag.* Erlangen: Verlag der Philosophischen Akademie, 1925. (Gestalt theory. *Social Research,* **11,** 78–99, 1944.)

116. Wertheimer, Max. *Productive Thinking.* New York:Harper & Brothers, 1945.

117. Windelband, Wilhelm. *Geschichte und Naturwissenschaft*. 3rd ed. unchanged. Strassburg:J. H. Ed. Heitz, 1904.

118. Wittels, Fritz. The neo-Adlerians. *Amer. J. Sociol.*, 45, 433–445, 1939.

119. Wittels, Fritz. *Sigmund Freud; his Personality, his Teachings, and his School*. London:Allen & Unwin, Ltd.; New York:Dodd, Mead & Co., 1924.

120. Woodworth, R. S. *Experimental Psychology*. New York:Henry Holt & Co., Inc., 1938.

121. Woodworth, R. S. Reënforcement of perception. *Amer. J. Psychol.*, 40, 119–124, 1947.

INDEX

Note: Page references for material by Adler, including quotations from Adler in the comments, are in roman type. Page references for material by the editors and by Colby, Furtmüller and Vaihinger are in italics.